READINGS IN

MEASUREMENT AND EVALUATION IN EDUCATION AND PSYCHOLOGY

WILLIAM A. MEHRENS
Michigan State University

HOLT, RINEHART AND WINSTON
New York   Chicago   San Francisco   Atlanta
Dallas   Montreal   Toronto   London   Sydney

Library of Congress Cataloging in Publication Data
Main entry under title:

Readings in measurement and evaluation in education
    and psychology.

    Includes bibliographies and index.
    1. Educational tests and measurements.   2. Men-
tal tests.   I. Mehrens, William A.
LB3051.R355   371.2'6   75-23067
ISBN 0-03-089680-0

6 7 8 9   090   9 8 7 6 5 4 3 2 1

PREFACE

This book of readings is intended to be useful as a supplementary text in introductory courses in measurement and evaluation in education and/or psychology. Two questions deserve immediate answers: (1) why should an instructor use any supplementary book of readings, and (2) why should another book of readings be published?

Supplementary texts are not required by all or probably even a majority of professors. This may be because they feel outside reading is unimportant or because they feel it is preferable for students to go to the library and read the articles directly from the journals. I believe that reading more material than is presented in a basic textbook is useful. Measurement and evaluation is a broad and dynamic topic. Few, if any, textbook authors are expert enough to write clearly, concisely, and accurately in all areas. Students can profit from reading articles which cover topics in greater detail than presented in traditional texts. Buying a book of readings is far more convenient and probably less expensive than making trips to the library. Finally, the need to expose a student to a library seems patronizing.

But why another book of readings? Are there not plenty to choose from? As a matter of fact, I believe several good ones are available. But the editors of those books have somewhat different opinions as to the "best" set of readings and I don't entirely agree with any of them. This collection of articles offers a different sampling, one that hopefully will appeal to the idiosyncratic opinions of some of my colleagues as the one most useful in helping to achieve their particular purposes.

The readings in this text are organized into six major units: (I) The roles of measurement and evaluation, (II) Basic principles of measurement, (III) Constructing, administering, and analyzing tests, (IV) Standardized evaluation procedures, (V) Reporting and using test results, and (VI) Trends and issues in evaluation (Unit VI is the longest of the six units). These are the major topics covered in most measurement texts. A textbook reference chart on page viii relates the chapters in several popular measurement texts to the six units of this book. Noticeably, most texts follow a similar topical outline.

To assist the users of this book, each unit and each article is preceded by an introduction and each unit concludes with a list of selected references for further study.

The selection of the articles in this book was based on the following criteria: relevance, authority, readability, and recency. Only a very few articles require any statistical sophistication. Those were included because they excellently cover very important topics that cannot be adequately treated in a simple fashion.

The major contributions of an edited book are due to the original authors of the articles. I deeply appreciate both the authors and publishers for granting permission to reproduce these articles. I also would like to thank Professor Robert C. Craig and several anonymous reviewers for their helpful suggestions concerning the selection and organization of the articles. Finally I wish to thank Dick Owen and other members of the Holt staff for their fine editorial assistance.

September 1975

William A. Mehrens
East Lansing, Michigan

CONTENTS

Preface   iii

Textbook Reference Chart   viii

Unit I
THE ROLE OF MEASUREMENT AND EVALUATION   1

THE ROLE OF MEASUREMENT IN EDUCATION: SERVANT,
SOULMATE, STOOLPIGEON, STATESMAN, SCAPEGOAT, ALL OF
THE ABOVE AND/OR NONE OF THE ABOVE
Richard E. Schutz   2
FUNCTIONAL TYPES OF STUDENT EVALUATION
Peter W. Airasian and George F. Madaus   9
THE MENACE OF TESTING RECONSIDERED   Henry S. Dyer   26

Unit II
BASIC PRINCIPLES OF MEASUREMENT   33

RELIABILITY AND CONFIDENCE   Alexander G. Wesman   35
ASSUMPTIONS UNDERLYING THE USE OF CONTENT VALIDITY
Roger T. Lennon   45

THE RELATIONSHIP OF VALIDITY COEFFICIENTS TO THE
PRACTICAL EFFECTIVENESS OF TESTS IN SELECTION:
DISCUSSION AND TABLES   H. C. Taylor and J. T. Russell   55
METHODS OF EXPRESSING TEST SCORES
Harold G. Seashore   65

Unit III

CONSTRUCTING, ADMINISTERING, AND ANALYZING TESTS   71

MEASUREMENT AND THE TEACHER   Robert L. Ebel   73
BEYOND BEHAVIORAL OBJECTIVES   Albert R. Wight   80
ON THE RELIABILITY OF RATINGS OF ESSAY EXAMINATIONS
William Coffman   93
TEST PERFORMANCE AND THE USE OF OPTIONAL QUESTIONS
Joseph DuCette and Stephen Wolk   104
CLASSROOM TESTING PROCEDURES, TEST ANXIETY AND
ACHIEVEMENT   Ronald N. Marso   112
USING ITEM ANALYSIS TO IMPROVE TESTS
Allan Lange, Irvin J. Lehmann, and William A. Mehrens   120

Unit IV

STANDARDIZED EVALUATION PROCEDURES   125

THE STORY BEHIND THE MENTAL MEASUREMENTS
YEARBOOKS   Oscar K. Buros   127
LOST: OUR INTELLIGENCE? WHY?   Quinn McNemar   137
INTELLIGENCE HAS THREE FACETS   J. P. Guilford   157
SOME PRINCIPLES OF INTEREST MEASUREMENT
Frederic Kuder   168
THE DISTINCTION BETWEEN SEX RESTRICTIVENESS AND SEX
BIAS IN INTEREST INVENTORIES
Dale J. Prediger and Gary R. Hanson   187
SOME RECENT TRENDS IN PERSONALITY ASSESSMENT
Lewis R. Goldberg   197

Unit V
REPORTING AND USING RESULTS   218

THE POSITIVE FUNCTION OF GRADES   Robert A. Feldmesser   220
A,B,C GRADES? DON'T KNOCK IT!   William E. McMahon   230
PROPOSED PRINCIPLES FOR THE MANAGEMENT OF
SCHOOL RECORDS   Russell Sage Foundation   233
FAMILY EDUCATIONAL RIGHTS AND PRIVACY ACT OF 1974
Section 438 of Public Law 93-380   238
RELEASING TEST SCORES: URGENT OR UNTHINKABLE
Gene R. Hawes   241
USE STANDARDIZED TESTS IN EVALUATING TEACHERS?
Robert L. Ebel   263
A MODEL FOR INCREASING THE MEANING OF STANDARDIZED
TEST SCORES   Richard C. Cox and Barbara G. Sterrett   265

Unit VI
TRENDS AND ISSUES IN EVALUATION   268

THE SOCIAL CONSEQUENCES OF EDUCATIONAL TESTING
Robert L. Ebel   270
ISSUES AND PROCEDURES IN THE DEVELOPMENT OF
CRITERION REFERENCED TESTS   Stephen P. Klein and
Jacqueline Kosecoff   276
THE CONFESSIONS OF A FRUSTRATED EVALUATOR
Joseph S. Renzulli   294
THE RHETORIC AND THE REALITIES OF ACCOUNTABILITY
Allan C. Ornstein and Harriet Talmage   303
ACCOUNTABILITY IN EDUCATION AND ASSOCIATED
MEASUREMENT PROBLEMS   J. Wayne Wrightstone,
Thomas P. Hogan, and Muriel M. Abbott   318
COMMON FALLACIES ABOUT HEREDITY, ENVIRONMENT,
AND HUMAN BEHAVIOR   Anne Anastasi   345
THE NEW DEFINITIONS OF TEST FAIRNESS IN SELECTION:
DEVELOPMENTS AND IMPLICATIONS   Ronald L. Flaugher   359

Name Index   369

Subject Index   373

Textbook Reference Chart Relating Chapters of Basic Measurement Textbooks to Units of This Book

Authors of Texts	Unit I	Unit II	Unit III	Unit IV	Unit V	Unit VI
1. Ahmann & Glock	1	8, 9, 10	2, 3, 4, 5, 6, 7	11, 12, 13	15, 16	
2. Aiken	1	3	2	4, 5, 6, 7, 8, 9		10
3. Anastasi	1, 2	3, 4, 5, 6	7	8, 9, 10, 11, 12, 13, 14, 15, 16, 17, 18, 19, 20	22	21
4. Brown	1, 2	3, 4, 5, 6, 7		9, 10, 11, 12	8	13
5. Chase	1, 2	3, 4	5, 6	7, 8, 9, 10, 11	12, 13	
6. Cronbach	1, 2	4, 5, 6	3, 17	7, 8, 9, 10, 11, 12, 13, 14, 15, 16, 18, 19		
7. Ebel	1, 2	11, 15, 16, 19	3, 4, 5, 6, 7, 8, 9, 10, 13, 14	18, 20, 21	12, 17	
8. Green	1, 2	3, 4	9, 10, 11, 12, 13	5, 6, 7, 8	14, 15	16
9. Gronlund	1	4, 5, 15	2, 3, 6, 7, 8, 9, 10, 11	12, 13, 14	17, 18	
10. Horrocks & Schoonover	1, 2, 3	4	21	5, 6, 7, 8, 9, 10, 11, 12, 13, 14, 15, 16, 17, 18, 19, 20	22, 23, 24	
11. Karmel	1	4, 5	3, 13, 14, 15	6, 7, 8, 9, 10, 11, 12	16, 17	2
12. Lien	1, 2	3, 7, 8	5, 6	4	9, 10	
13. Mehrens & Lehmann	1	4, 5, 6	2, 7, 8, 9, 10, 11, 12	13, 14, 15, 16	17	3, 18, 19

	Unit I	Unit II	Unit III	Unit IV	Unit V	Unit VI
14. Noll & Scannell	1, 2	3, 4	6, 7, 8	5, 9, 10, 11, 12, 13, 14, 15	16	
15. Nunnally	1	2, 3	5, 6	8, 9, 10, 11, 12, 13, 14, 15, 16	7, 17	
16. Payne	1	9, 10, 11, 12	2, 3, 4, 5, 6, 7, 8, 13, 16	14, 15	17	18
17. Sax	1	6, 7, 8	3, 4, 5, 9	10, 11, 12, 13, 14, 15, 16	17, 18	2
18. Smith & Adams	1, 2	3, 4, 12, 18	5, 6, 7, 8, 9, 10, 11	14, 15, 16, 17	13	
19. Stanley & Hopkins	1, 7	2, 3, 4, 5	8, 9, 10, 11, 12	14, 15, 16	13, 17	6
20. Ten Brink	1, 3, 4, 5	2	10, 11, 12, 13	14	6, 7, 8, 9	
21. Thorndike & Hagen	1, 2	5, 6, 7	3, 4	8, 9, 10, 11, 12, 13, 14, 15	16, 17, 18, 19,	
22. Wick	1	8, 9, 10	2, 3, 4, 5	7, 11	6, 12	

1. Ahmann, J. Stanley, and Glock, Marvin D. *Evaluating Pupil Growth: Principles of Tests and Measurements* (4th Edition). Boston: Allyn and Bacon, 1971.

2. Aiken, Lewis R., Jr. *Psychological and Educational Testing.* Boston: Allyn and Bacon, 1971.

3. Anastasi, Anne. *Psychological Testing* (3rd Edition). New York: Macmillan, 1968.

4. Brown, Frederick G. *Principles of Educational and Psychological Testing.* Hinsdale, Ill.: Dryden, 1970.

5. Chase, Clinton I. *Measurement for Educational Evaluation.* Reading, Mass.: Addison-Wesley, 1974.

6. Cronbach, Lee J. *Essentials of Psychological Testing* (3rd Edition). New York: Harper & Row, 1970.

7. Ebel, Robert L. *Essentials of Educational Measurement.* Englewood Cliffs, N.J.: Prentice-Hall, 1972.

8. Green, John A. *Introduction to Measurement and Evaluation.* New York: Dodd, Mead, 1970.

9. Gronlund, Norman E. *Measurement and Evaluation in Teaching* (2nd Edition). New York: Macmillan, 1971.

10. Horrocks, John E., and Schoonover, Thelma I. *Measurement for Teachers.* Columbus, Ohio: Merrill, 1968.

11. Karmel, Louis J. *Measurement and Evaluation in the Schools.* Toronto: Macmillan, 1970.

12. Lien, Arnold J. *Measurement and Evaluation of Learning* (2nd Edition). Dubuque, Iowa: William C. Brown, 1971.

13. Mehrens, William A., and Lehmann, Irvin J. *Measurement and Evaluation in Education and Psychology.* New York: Holt, Rinehart and Winston, 1973.

14. Noll, Victor N., and Scannell, Dale P. *Introduction to Educational Measurement* (3rd Edition). Boston: Houghton Mifflin, 1972.

15. Nunnally, Jum C. *Educational Measurement and Evaluation* (2nd Edition). New York: McGraw-Hill, 1972.

16. Payne, David A. *The Assessment of Learning: Cognitive and Affective.* Lexington, Mass.: Heath, 1974.

17. Sax, Gilbert. *Principles of Educational Measurement and Evaluation.* Belmont, Calif.: Wadsworth, 1974.

18. Smith, Fred M., and Adams, Sam. *Educational Measurement for the Classroom Teacher* (2nd Edition). New York: Harper & Row, 1972.

19. Stanley, Julian C., and Hopkins, Kenneth D. *Educational and Psychological Measurement and Evaluation* (5th Edition). Englewood Cliffs, N.J.: Prentice-Hall, 1972.

20. Ten Brink, Terry D. *Evaluation: A Practical Guide for Teachers.* New York: McGraw-Hill, 1974.

21. Thorndike, Robert L., and Hagen, Elizabeth. *Measurement and Evaluation in Psychology and Education* (3rd Edition). New York: Wiley, 1969.

22. Wick, John W. *Educational Measurement.* Columbus, Ohio: Merrill, 1973.

THE ROLE OF MEASUREMENT
AND EVALUATION

unit

I

The basic role of educational measurement and evaluation is to assist educators in making sound decisions. In terms of the decisions that educators must make or assist others in making, can this advisory role be delineated further? Schutz has written an entertaining and thought-provoking article on whether the role of measurement in education is that of servant, soulmate, stoolpigeon, statesman, scapegoat—all of these, or none of them. Next, Airasian and Madaus discuss the multiplicity of purposes evaluation can have in the *classroom* context. They consider four types of evaluation compared across nine different dimensions.

Not everyone thinks the use of measurement and evaluation is honorable. In fact some people feel that testing is a menace. In 1961 Dyer, a widely-known test specialist, published a paper entitled, "Is Testing a Menace to Education?" His answer was a tentative, "Yes, but. . . ." He suggested that "testing is a menace to education primarily because tests are misunderstood and test results are misused by too many educators." That paper received wide circulation. Less well known but equally deserving of attention is his follow-up article reproduced in this unit. Other articles related to the "menace" of testing can be found in Units V and VI.

In this article Schutz analyzes various possible roles of
measurement in education. While reading it you might consider
the following questions:

1. Will the accountability movement increase the stoolpigeon role
   of measurement?
2. Could accountability programs be implemented in such a way
   as to enhance the statesman role?
3. Has the emphasis on program evaluation in education increased
   the soulmate role?
4. How can educators combat the inappropriate scapegoat role
   some people wish measurement to play?

When reading the articles on accountability, evaluation, and
test fairness in Unit VI you might wish to reconsider these
questions.

The Role of Measurement in Education: Servant, Soulmate, Stoolpigeon, Statesman, Scapegoat, All of the Above, and/or None of the Above

RICHARD E. SCHUTZ

As the test-wise amongst us quickly figured out, my title is a conventional
multiple-choice test item. While I know some of you have studied for the test,
we will not be able to take it this morning. I am as disappointed as you are.
The answer sheets were all ordered and proctors had been arranged. I had
hoped that we could draw on the unexcelled resources of the audience to
score, analyze, and report the results back to you during the meeting. All the
psychometric mechanics were in good shape, and I was looking forward to
this innovative psychometric demonstration.

Then it occurred to me that this was a tough test to key. I initially had
construct validity hopes for the item as a minimal intelligence test. But with
no agreement in sight on the key, this appeared an unlikely possibility. Then
for a while, I toyed with the test as a disguised personality inventory. But the
pitfalls of paper-pencil personality instruments are too well known to make
this a profitable pursuit. Reluctantly, I concluded that it would be best to

From *Journal of Educational Measurement*, Fall 1971, *8*, No. 3: 141–146. Reprinted with
permission of author and publisher.

use the available time differently. While the psychometric exercise would have been fun, it would have been a trivial response to the occasion. I still may try to peddle it as a performance contract. If you know any superintendents who would be interested, you are welcome to all of the accountable profit.

It does seem to me that the current role of measurement in education is somewhat analogous to my experience with this multiple-choice item. That is, our psychometric problems are well in hand; they have been well in hand now for several decades, plus or minus a few. Meanwhile, the problems of education are accelerating at a rapidly advancing rate. This suggests that the present focus of educational measurement might better address systematic rather than psychometric considerations. Lest you prematurely conclude that I've joined those who are calling for a measurement moratorium with much less emphasis on testing, I'll anticipate my conclusion that education is currently suffering from a dearth rather than a deluge of measurement. The worthy objectives of present education critics will best be realized by greater rather than less measurement in education.

The nature and direction of possible roles of measurement in education are structured by the options included in the title for the presentation. Let's analyze the options. Had I been asked prior to the early 1960s to clarify the role of measurement in education, I would have unhesitatingly chosen the servant metaphor. This is what I learned as a student and what appears to me to continue to be the current party line. (Its traditional popularity in the measurement community motivated my listing it in the first place decoy position.) In the simple idealized categorical framework which characterized the educational world in which I grew up, the goals and objectives of education were established by educational philosophers. These were translated into teachable form by curriculum specialists. A combination of learning theory and teaching method was the basis for instruction. Measurement subserviently followed, occasionally predicting and selecting, but by and large assessing outcomes reported as normative comparisons among small finite or gross infinite populations of individuals. This perspective of neat categories and simple relationships was outgrown in the '60s; it is anachronistic in the '70s. While one can look back to the days when measurement was the servant of education, it is dangerous to extend the metaphor into the future.

Consider option two. A soulmate is a metaphor above and beyond a servant. In educational measurement this quantum metaphorical leap was made in Scriven's distinction between formative and summative measurement. In formative evaluation, measurement is viewed as an active synergistic partner contributing to, as it draws upon, the resources of other elements of education in a series of feedback loops. This perspective contrasts sharply with the linearly compartmentalized separation of instruction and measurement, which had previously been the prevailing alternative view.

While the conceptual distinction between formative and summative has been acquired by the measurement community, it has yet to be exploited fully. Procedures to operationalize the formative aspects of formative evaluation are almost as elusive as those pertaining to the soul aspects of soulmate. But important inroads are being made. Documentation of these efforts is just beginning to hit the literature. By and large, the chief activity in formative evaluation has occurred in those Educational Laboratories such as the Southwest Regional Laboratory, (SWRL), and Research and Development Centers, such as Pittsburgh and Wisconsin, which have been conducting broad scale systematic instructional development. The results of these efforts include a sequenced combination of instruction and measurement components. The soulmate role of measurement in education will inevitably become increasingly prevalent in the '70s. But good soulmates right now are still scarce. I shall offer a few hints on search techniques later. Meanwhile, try option three.

It is ironic that measurement currently finds itself frequently cast as an educational stoolpigeon, an inherently unpopular and degrading role. Fortunately, it is also a role that is inherently shortlived, and the consequent change is generally for the better. At the moment, however, it is painfully obvious that measurement results are commonly being used to underscore alleged educational deficiencies. For example, measurement results have made it clear that the well intentioned efforts to effect instant educational improvement through desire, however strong, and increased expenditures, however large, are wishful and wasteful. More generally, the wider publicity of the results of state and local standardized testing programs is more frequently adding to the woes of the already harassed and overburdened school administrator rather than ameliorating his problems. It is discouraging to find such basic reporting devices as grade scores and percentile ranks twisted and distorted to support totally unwarranted interpretations of status descriptions of pupil performance, to say nothing of the preposterous inferences concerning status determinants.

In all honesty, however, the fault is not totally outside the measurement community. We have ourselves been slow to discard reporting procedures that are technically suspect and popularly subject to misinterpretation. I could cite several specific examples, but one should suffice. When a change in the statewide California reading tests from one series to another results in a mean difference of 20–30 percentile on equally reputable tests, there is cause for professional as well as public concern. As it happened, the concern in both the professional and public camps was largely misplaced and diffused. The psychometric questions raised were technical and trivial. The politicization of the results was purely partisan and independent of the data. Since the direction of the difference was up rather than down, the school people have tended to use the results to gain further breathing time. However, above the technical bickering and the political axe grinding, the inescapable message is that many youngsters in the California schools read so poorly that they are seriously handicapped in all school activities which involve reading. Consequently, the children are almost certain to experience failure in a large share of instrucion. While it might be argued that more direct and reasonable ways to identify the deficiency other than the testing program could have been used, the fact remains that the statewide testing program is currently the chief mechanism performing this role. It is encouraging to find that the stoolpigeon role appears to be leading to direct and indirect reforms both in testing practice and in instruction which will render this onerous measurement role obsolete.

As for option four, a number of indicators suggest that the statesman role of measurement in education will expand in the future. The National Assessment of Educational Progress is a significant and sophisticated development of the '60s which will have profound positive consequences in the '70s and in subsequent decades. This program represents a major advance and contribution of the educational measurement community and should continue to receive the direct and indirect personal support of each of us. Other signs of measurement influence on educational matters of national import can be seen in the Head Start and Sesame Street evaluations. From a technical psychometric perspective, both the Head Start and Sesame Street studies are infested with deficiencies. And as with the California reading test program, the results have been used to forward political and economic interests. But again, the mainline measurement message has come through and has enhanced the credibility and utility of measurement as a decision making aid in educational matters of state. Preliminary planning of the National Institute of Education is emphasizing a prominent position for measurement, reflecting the confidence and interest of the federal government in the future potential of our field.

Consider option five, the scapegoat role. In contrast to the factors supporting the growth of measurement is the increasing clamor to make measurement the scapegoat for alleged broader educational and social ills. The interests of a minority of self-styled humanists, dissidents, and ethnic militants appear to be forwarded by taking loud and extreme positions against all forms of measurement. In this situation, measurement is regarded as a tool of the establishment. Since the establishment is by definition bad, so is measurement, and must be demolished along with the establishment. To entertain the expectation that this argument can be assailed by superior logic or other reason-based strategies is foolish; to accede to the unreasonable demands out of sympathy or other emotions is equally foolish. This is not, however, to suggest that such criticism should be either dismissed or discounted. The critics are serious and dedicated. Our responses should recognize and at least match these characteristics. In some areas agreement can be reached and common effort mounted to correct the abuse. In other areas differences can be clarified to a point where either further effort can be directed toward a common resolution or agreement reached that a plurality of options is possible and desirable. While the possibility of a scapegoat role for measurement in education is present, there is neither justification nor need for the measurement community to create conditions that increase this probability.

As any test construction specialist worth his salt knows, the options "all of the above" and "none of the above" detract from the quality of an item by introducing additional ambiguity. Rather than further increasing ambiguity in the time remaining, I should like to try to expand our perspective a bit.

It seems clear to me that the measurement perspective reflected in our tests and our practices is much more constrained than it could or should be at the present time. The popular way to expand has been to sharpen our psychometric technical scalpels and to carve more differentiated abstract traits. Thus, we can produce measures of nearly every rubric under the sun. But the Guilford and Cattell super-batteries are testimony to the diminishing practical utility of further expansionist efforts along these dimensions. This is in no way to disparage our current test products as reflected in an embellished Buros-based collection. These should be exploited for all they are worth.

However, neither need we conclude that we have exhausted the ore in the measurement mine. As an example, I'd like to consider what occurs if we limit ourselves simply to the area of achievement testing in instruction and introduce two new dimensions: time in the form of increased frequency of testing and recipients in terms of the relevant audiences receiving the test results. Table 1 summarizes the framework.

The framework is at a vice presidential (or associate superintendent) level of detail. In some sectors of the framework, activity has not proceeded

TABLE 1   Instructional Testing Domains

Timing	Primary Report Recipient	Area
Intra-Lesson	Learner	Self-Directed Testing
End-of-Lesson	Tutor	Learning Mastery Testing
End-of-Unit	Teacher	Instructional Management Testing
End-of-Program		
Program Specific	Parent	Summative Testing
Program Comparative	Curriculum Specialist	Program Fair Testing
Program Independent	Administrator	Standardized Testing
Program Irrelevant	Theorist	Transfer-of-Training Testing

much further than this slogan level. In most sectors, however, work is actively underway in several places across the country, including SWRL. It will take a decade of the best R&D effort we are able to mount nationally to bring the slogans to operational options. My purpose here is not to describe what needs to be done but only to illustrate the new domains which are opened in building systemetrically on a sound psychometric base.

The first column of Table 1 introduces the terms lesson, unit, and program. For rule of thumb in the present "subject matter by grade" conceptual framework of instruction, lessons typically recur daily, units every three to six weeks, and programs every semester or academic year. Both the measurement and instructional implications differ depending upon the interval. For the most part, educational measurement specialists have abrogated their role in lesson and unit testing, leaving this to the teacher or the textbook author. The increasing availability of the computer and automated peripheral devices, together with the increasing sophistication of programmatic instructional development technology, makes these promising new areas for measurement applications. At the present time the best examples of self-directed testing are being conducted under the slogan "computer-assisted instruction." Although this is a hot research area, it is far away from cost-feasible widespread use —probably ten years.

Learning mastery testing research is similarly flying the computer banner as "computer-assisted testing." The instructional software here is now further advanced than the equipment hardware. (The problem is not with the computer per se but with peripheral input-output equipment. It is an interesting switch to admonish equipment manufacturers that they are lagging behind educational requirements.) If the required resources can be coordinated, learning mastery testing should be a practically feasible option within five years.

Instructional management testing could be equated with the measurement component of computer managed instruction. CMI is now feasible, but ironically, it is only feasible in a manual rather than a computerized form. The economics of resources in education are currently such that designated human resources can perform the essential CMI tasks at less cost than can a computer. Within the next five years manual CMI systems will inevitably come into widespread use, and equipment may well be developed to make automation feasible.

Consider for a moment the middle column of the table. The measurement community has given little attention to tailoring the reports of measurement results to specific audiences. I have listed here in ascending order the persons involved in direct instructional contact. The same measurement data may be of interest to every role in the middle column. But the differential characteristics of each role suggest differences in the consequences, aggregation, and format of the results derived from the measure. Customizing the results for each group is both challenging intellectually and useful practically.

Move now to the end-of-program testing. This has been the bread-and-butter of educational measurement. I bear no strong brief for the specific categorizations listed here. My main purpose is to demonstrate that we have tended to squeeze more into and out of standardized achievement tests than is reasonable considering the disparate contingencies and audiences involved. One reason for listing the parent as the prime report recipient for program specific test results is that such measurement is the only testing where it makes sense to test every pupil. The other domains can be much more efficiently done on a pupil sampling basis, which introduces important cost and effort economies.

The psychometric technology related to summative testing and program fair testing is available but not widely reported. The more generic rubric is criterion-referenced testing and the technology is again scattered in staff reports emanating from the Wisconsin and Pittsburgh R&D Centers, American Institutes for Research, Educational Testing Service, and SWRL.

Norm-referenced standardized achievement tests are so well known to us that we frequently consider them *the* instructional tests. The table would also recognize criterion-referenced standardized tests, with the batteries produced by the National Assessment of Educational Progress a quality example to begin filling the category.

The last row of the table is a bit tongue-in-cheek, but I do feel that many journal articles produced in the past could be justified in no other way. I wouldn't want to rule out such activity, but it should not interfere with progress in other instructional testing domains. No single domain among those enumerated here is inherently better than another; each has a respectable function which should be recognized and nurtured.

After 70 years of solid scientific and technological building, the measurement field is in sound position to contribute significantly to the education profession and to the societal and personal objectives to which the profession is devoted. But this contribution will require expanded effort by the educational measurement community. In the battle of bumper stickers which is being hotly contested on the California freeways, we see signs of "America: Love it or leave it," opposed by "America: Change it or lose it." As frequently happens, it appears that both God and reason are partly on the side of each ideological camp. For measurement in education as well as for America in the world, more productive possibilities are created by the position, "Love it and change it." To further develop a given state-of-affairs is always much more difficult than to destroy it, but the prospects for positive human enhancement have never been brighter. Expanded activity in measurement offers considerable potential for enhancing the state-of-affairs in education in particular and in our nation in general. We've only just begun.

This article, like the preceding one by Schutz, discusses several purposes of measurement and evaluation. The four types of evaluation discussed are placement, formative, diagnostic, and summative. Historically many educators overemphasized summative evaluation and underemphasized the others. The balance has changed considerably in recent years. But it is important to emphasize the authors' point that the four types interact "to provide the classroom teacher with a data base from which to make different types of judgments about student learning."

Try to relate the various types and dimensions of evaluation discussed in this article to the roles discussed by Schutz.

Functional Types of Student Evaluation

PETER W. AIRASIAN
GEORGE F. MADAUS

Authors' abstract   Although recent emphasis in the evaluation literature has concentrated upon curriculum evaluation, student evaluation remains a pervasive and crucial feature of all teaching. This article defines four types of student evaluation: *placement, formative, diagnostic,* and *summative.* These types are contrasted across nine dimensions: function, time, characteristics of evidence, evidence-gathering techniques, sampling, scoring and reporting, standards, reliability, and validity. Examples of and interactions between the four types across the nine dimensions are cited. This article indicates the multiplicity of evaluative roles and techniques applicable to evaluating students. It is argued that we must conceive of evaluation as involving a much broader role than simply grading student achievement at the end of instruction. Three of the four evaluation types described are consciously intended to enhance student learning prior to the making of grading judgments.

From the mid-'30's until the early '60's, primarily as a result of the writings of Tyler (1934, 1950), the emphasis in evaluation has been concentrated on teachers and their unique instructional objectives. Two factors have been instrumental in shifting the focus in the evaluation literature away from the classroom teacher. The first was the advent, during the late '50's and early '60's, of large-scale curriculum development projects, especially in the physi-

From *Measurement and Evaluation in Guidance,* Jan. 1972, *4,* No. 4: 221–233. Copyright 1972 American Personnel and Guidance Association. Reprinted with permission of author and publisher.

cal sciences. The appearance of these projects generated concern about the role of evaluation in course development and improvement (Cronbach, 1963; Grobman, 1968; Scriven, 1967; Stake, 1967).

The second factor, while harder to pinpoint in time, is no less a reality. It is the growing recognition that the busy teacher, responsible for varied work of large and varied classes, seldom has the time to carry out individually the operations called for in the Tyler rationale (Bloom, Hastings, & Madaus, 1971; Eisner, 1967; Jackson, 1968; Madaus, 1969).

Despite this shift in perspective, student evaluation of some kind is a pervasive and crucial feature of all instruction. Some evaluation is spontaneous, unsystematic, and informal, for the most part based on such cues as momentary facial expressions, shifts in posture, tone of voice, etc. (Jackson, 1968). On the other hand, some student evaluation is based on more systematic and quantitative data, derived principally from paper-and-pencil tests. The purpose of this article is to define four types of student evaluation (placement, formative, diagnostic, and summative) by comparing these evaluation types across nine dimensions (function, time, characteristics of evidence, evidence-gathering techniques, sampling, scoring and reporting, standards, reliability, and validity). Interactions are also described.

Table 1 (pp. 12–15) contrasts the four types of evaluation across the nine dimensions to be discussed. The remainder of this article treats each dimension separately, referring the reader to the appropriate row of the table.

COMPARISON OF THE FOUR EVALUATION TYPES

Function of Evaluation

The first distinction between the four types of evaluation resides in the teacher's purpose for determining, valuing, describing, or classifying aspects of student behavior. At different instructional junctures teachers need to judge student progress. While the intent of evaluation at each juncture is to judge students, the purposes and consequences of the judgments can vary widely. The first row of Table 1 contrasts the different purposes of placement, formative, diagnostic, and summative evaluation. Each type described is, in the true sense of the word, an evaluation. However, evaluation performed for different purposes engenders varied procedures.

As the name implies, *placement evaluation* is used to place a student. In many individualized instructional programs, as well as in more traditional instructional arrangements, the concept of correct student placement is central. For example, some schools refuse to permit a student who fails French I to enroll in French II. Other schools use a more sophisticated form of placement by specifying a series of skills, which students must have mastered prior to admittance to particular courses. However, the concept of placement can be defined more broadly than these examples indicate. Thus, based on prior achievement or the presence of certain cognitive and affective characteristics, a student can be placed (a) at the most appropriate point in an instructional sequence, (b) in a particular instructional method, or (c) with an appropriate teacher.

The following analogy illustrates the concept of placing a student at the optimum point in an instructional sequence. Picture each of the necessary prerequisite skills, as well as anticipated objectives of a course, as units on a number line. Absence of prerequisite skills is analogous to the negative numbers, while the presence of these skills, but the absence of student mastery of any of the anticipated course objectives, is analogous to the zero point. The objectives of the course are analogous to the positive numbers along the line. A primary purpose of placement evaluation is to locate a student on this "instructional number line." In many schools, if not in most, students are in fact "placed" at our imaginary zero point without regard to their prerequisite skills or their prior mastery of certain course objectives.

Matching a student with an instructional method or with a particular teacher is still in its infancy. However, as research on the efficacy of such placement becomes more abundant, it may be possible to place students either with the most appropriate teacher (Thelen, 1967) or in the optimal instructional mode (Bracht, 1969). Strategies of Mastery Learning (Block, 1971) that call for different instructional modes for different learners and the widespread availability of the green, yellow, and blue versions of Biological Sciences Curriculum Study (BSCS) Biology represent steps in the direction of this form of student placement.

Formative evaluation is intended to provide both student and teacher with information about progress toward mastery of the general course objectives. It is not used to grade students, but instead provides information that directs subsequent teaching or study. While formal procedures for formative evaluation have been developed (Airasian, 1968, 1971), teachers who administer nongraded "spot" quizzes or who use various observational cues to assess the progress of instruction are carrying out a type of formative evaluation in the sense that they are gauging the ongoing success of instruction. Such information is used less to grade students than to make instruction responsive to identified student weaknesses and strengths.

Summative evaluation is used to certify or grade students at the completion of relatively large blocks of instruction—e.g., units, terms, or semesters. Summative evaluations produce the marks typically averaged into student grades. The result of a summative examination is in the most real sense "final" and is likely to follow the student throughout his academic career. It is this use of evaluation that is currently under attack by students and educational critics.

TABLE 1   Comparison of Four Types of Classroom Evaluation

	Placement	Formative	Diagnostic	Summative
Function of Evaluation	to place students by a. determining the degree to which prerequisite entry behaviors or skills are present or absent b. determining entering mastery of the course objectives c. matching students to alternative teachers or instructional modes according to characteristics known or thought to optimize achievement	Formative evaluation is contributory. Its functions are a. to provide on-going feedback to the teacher for the purposes of 1. choosing or modifying subsequent learning experiences 2. prescribing remediation of group or individual deficiencies b. to provide on-going feedback to the student for the purpose of directing advanced or remedial study	to recognize psychological, physical, or environmental symptoms manifested by students with extraordinary or recurrent learning and/or classroom problems	to grade, certify, or attest to student learning or teacher effectiveness
Time of Evidence Gathering	prior to entry into an instructional unit	several times prior to the completion of instruction on a predefined segment (unit chapter, etc.) of a course	While a teacher should always be sensitive to the manifestation of symptoms known to be related to learning difficulties he should be particularly attentive to students when classroom or learning difficulties cannot be explained in terms of cognitive or instructional variables.	at the conclusion of a unit, course, or year's instruction

TABLE 1 (cont.)

	Placement	Formative	Diagnostic	Summative
Behavioral Characteristics of Evidence Gathered	dependent on the functions stated above: typically cognitive or psycho-motor when the function is to determine whether or not prerequisite entry behaviors are present or to determine the student's prior mastery of course objectives; may also be affective when the purpose is to match students to alternative teachers or instructional modes.	cognitive or psychomotor	physical (vision, auditory perception, dominance and laterality, general health, etc.); psychological (intelligence, emotional maladjustment, social maladjustment, etc.); environmental (nutritional, parent-child relationships, peer influences, etc.).	depends on course objectives; higher or lower level cognitive behaviors, affective and/or psychomotor
Evidence Gathering Techniques	depend on type of placement sought, but could include: a. commercial tests (Intelligence, achievement, diagnostic, etc.) b. teacher-made instruments (formative, summative, specially designed pre-tests, observation, interviews, checklists, video-tapes, etc.)	a series of teacher-made achievement measures; supply, essay, or selection tests, interviews, video-tapes, checklists, etc.	primarily observational although for certain symptoms general screening techniques to confirm hypotheses may be available to the classroom teacher (e.g. vision). Generally, upon noting symptoms, the teacher forwards his observations to proper agencies, e.g. guidance counselor, nurse, school psychologist, etc.	primarily internally or externally constructed achievement tests

TABLE 1 (cont.)

	Placement	Formative	Diagnostic	Summative
Sampling Considerations for Evidence Gathering	depend on the functions specified above; evidence must be gathered on a. each prerequisite entry behavior b. a representative sample of course objectives c. those behaviors related to a construct(s) which in turn are known or thought to be related to different types of teachers or to alternative modes of instruction	a. where the objectives of an instructional segment are interrelated (cognitively or sequentially within cognitive levels) the sample should include all objectives in the segment. b. where the objectives of a predefined instructional segment are not interrelated, the determination may depend on such considerations as the use of an objective in subsequent learning; the extent to which an objective integrates or reinforces prior learning, etc.	Sampling in the psychometric sense is not applicable. An ad hoc observational process designed to construct and confirm hypotheses about suspected causes of disorders.	weighted sample of course objectives; weighting may be in terms of teaching emphasis, purpose of evaluation, time spent, transferability of objectives, perceived importance in society, etc.
Scoring and Reporting	patterns, profiles, subscores, etc. for all functions except placing students out of a course (where total score may be utilized)	patterns of item responses, abilities mastered or not mastered, etc. All reporting must be free of any intimation of a mark, grade, or certification.	an anecdotal report containing specific behavioral instances forwarded to the appropriate referral agency.	sum of total number of correct responses, either by objective or on total exam; reported as letter or number grade, standard score, percentile, etc.

TABLE 1 (cont.)

	Placement	Formative	Diagnostic	Summative
Standards Against Which Scores Are Compared	predetermined norm or criterion referenced standards	criterion referenced standards	compare manifested behavior against specified abnormal behaviors	almost exclusively norm referenced
Reliability	dependent on the trait measured, and the consequences of the judgments	stability and/or consistency of item response patterns	recurrence of behavioral symptoms	internal consistency
Validity	primarily content validity but also construct validity (where students are matched with teachers or instructional strategies)	primarily content validity but also construct validity (where hierarchies of objectives are involved)	face validity	content validity

Peter W. Airasian
George F. Madaus
Boston College
Chestnut Hill, Mass.
1970

The final type of evaluation, *diagnostic evaluation*, is used to identify students whose learning or classroom behavior is being adversely affected by factors external to instructional practices. We define the domain of diagnostic evaluation to encompass physical, environmental, emotional, or psychological factors generated outside the classroom. Thus, many Headstart programs did not result in improved learning until someone realized that students who did not have an adequate breakfast prior to the start of school were more prone to concentrate on food than on their instruction. Similarly, recognition that a particular student has sight or hearing difficulties that inhibit his learning is diagnostic evaluation. Teachers must be able to recognize factors that are in a sense extra-classroom but that adversely affect a child's classroom performance.

It must be stated explicitly at this juncture that any system of student evaluation incorporating two or more of the types we propose should not operate as a set of independent subsystems. The four evaluation types, then, interact to provide the classroom teacher with a data base from which to make different types of judgments about student learning. The primary distinction we are striving to make relates to the purpose of performing an evaluation. The remaining categories in Table 1 overlap and interact to a large extent.

Time of Evidence-Gathering

It is clear from the different purposes of the four evaluation types that evidence for each type is gathered at different times. Any complete student evaluation system provides for continual evidence-gathering of one form or another. The second row of Table 1 contrasts the time points at which evidence is gathered for placement, formative, summative, and diagnostic evaluation.

Since the aim of placement is to facilitate learning by identifying the student's optimum starting point or by providing him with the most reinforcing environment (in terms of teacher and materials), placement considerations occur prior to the start of instruction. In many circumstances, however, students may be "replaced" (in the sense of placing them again or differently) if the original placement proves to be less than ideal. Usually, evidence from formative evaluations provides the basis for replacing students. Occasionally, however, identification and remediation of a physical deficit identified during diagnostic evaluation may call for "replacing" a student.

Formative evaluation takes place as instruction unfolds. Summative evaluation, because of its grading or certifying function, takes place at the conclusion of an instructional unit. Like formative evaluation, diagnostic evaluation is a continual act that admits to no definite time constraints. The teacher should always be sensitive to the manifestation of behavioral symptoms assumed to be related to extra-classroom causes of learning difficulties. The four types of evaluation emphasize that teachers ought to be continually gathering evidence about student learning.

Behavioral Characteristics of Evidence Gathered

One problem that must be faced by any evaluation system is the definition of the behavioral domains to which evaluation with different purposes must attend. Row 3 of Table 1 contrasts the four evaluation types across the behavioral characteristics of evidence gathered.

When we place students in an instructional sequence, assess the ongoing progress of instruction, or grade student achievement, we evaluate vis-à-vis the anticipated outcomes or objectives of our course. It is only natural, then, that formative, summative, and two types of placement evaluation (determining attainment of prerequisite skills or prior mastery of course objectives), gather evidence from similar behavioral domains. Since the majority of objectives defined and fostered in our schools are cognitive or psychomotor, these are the behavioral characteristics evaluated. The objectives of instruction form a focal point around which evidence-gathering considerations for placement, formative, and summative evaluation overlap.

Under certain conditions, placement and summative evaluation may also be directed toward the gathering of affective data. Placement evaluation should involve gathering of affective data if its purpose is to match student characteristics with either a certain type of teacher or with a certain mode of instruction, since the basis for matching will likely have more to do with personality and style than with intellective capacity. Some schools permit teachers to select their next year's class on the basis of the consonance between the teacher's instructional style and expectations and the student's perceived learning style and motivation. The aim is to define and match teachers and students on noncognitive factors so as to produce a harmonious, unfrustrating, and efficient learning environment.

There are two occasions when summative evaluation should also involve gathering affective data. The first is when the course objectives include affective outcomes. The second is when it is deemed important to gather evidence about the unintended outcomes that always occur as a by-product of instruction. Evaluative evidence about student performance should not be limited to data about course objectives. When a particular set of objectives is chosen, a tradeoff is involved in the sense that certain other desirable objectives may have to be neglected or deemphasized. It is important to know the cost of such tradeoffs, especially in terms of student attitudes.

If summative affective data are gathered, a strong case can be made against grading individual students on the basis of the data. Given the moral considerations involved in grading students' interests, attitudes, or values, the authors feel that the proper focus is the degree to which the class as a whole manifests particular affects. Data should be gathered to preserve anonymity and to permit inferences to be made that will not harm the individual.

No reference to affective evidence is made under formative evaluation. The reason is that nothing is as yet known about either the methodology required by or the consequences resulting from such a practice. The guidelines for summative evaluation of affective behavior, however, would likely hold as well for formative evaluation. That is, the data should be gathered anonymously and used to make judgments about group rather than individual affects.

While the characteristics of the evidence gathered in placement, formative, and summative evaluation are all related more or less directly to the objectives of a course, diagnostic evaluation seeks different types of data. The behavioral characteristics of the evidence gathered during diagnostic evaluation do not fall in the usual categories of cognitive, affective, or psychomotor, but rather are classified as physical, psychological, or environmental. Diagnostic evaluation seeks to go beyond identifying objectives that students have not learned. It strives to provide hypotheses related to extra-classroom factors that explain *why* students have not learned. Physical or biological factors may include problems of vision, speech, or general health. Psychological factors involve emotional or social maladjustment. Environmental factors include such things as dietary problems or a disrupted or disadvantaged home life.

Evidence-Gathering Techniques

In the fourth row the techniques used to gather evidence for each of the four types of evaluation are compared. To place a student at the appropriate instructional starting point or out of a course entirely, and to evaluate student learning formatively or summatively, achievement data are needed. For each evaluative purpose, we need to determine what and how much students have learned. The use made of such information would vary according to the purpose of the evaluation.

Although commercially available intelligence, achievement, and readiness tests can provide useful data, particularly for placement and summative decisions, locally constructed achievement tests are probably more valuable. The use of standardized tests presents the very real danger that course objectives will be altered to coincide with the skills required to perform well on the standardized test. Since student achievement is evaluated relative to the objectives of a course, and since courses vary from locale to locale, standardized instruments are unlikely to provide specific enough information for decision-making. They are designed to sample objectives that cut across curricula and geographical regions and, consequently, are not the most parsimonious means of gathering placement, formative, or summative data. Achievement measures constructed at the local level and directed toward the course objectives will provide more salient evidence.

Useful achievement measures need not be conceived of solely as paper-and-pencil tests. A great deal of useful data about students' skills and behaviors can be acquired by such techniques as observation, checklists, interviews, videotape recordings, and the like. There are many school subjects such as shop, art, physical education, and speech, where major emphasis in evaluation is on what a student does rather than what he knows. Observational-type evaluative procedures are more relevant evidence-gathering techniques for these courses than are paper-and-pencil instruments. In general, too little attention has been paid to the use of teacher observation and intuition as an appropriate evidence-gathering technique for evaluation. This is especially true of formative, placement, and diagnostic evaluation, where the consequences of incorrect judgments do not leave irreparable scars on students.

In diagnostic evaluation, many schools periodically employ general visual and auditory screening techniques to identify students with sight or hearing difficulty. The primary evidence-gathering technique utilized in diagnostic evaluation, however, is that of sensitive teacher observation. Elementary school teachers are usually in a better position than secondary teachers to carry out diagnostic evaluation, since most elementary schools are organized with a single teacher teaching a given class. Prolonged student contact makes it easier to identify symptoms indicative of physical, psychological, or environmental causes of learning disorders. Such observation, to be sure, presupposes teacher familiarity with symptoms related to these extra-classroom causes. Once a teacher observes the symptoms, the correct procedure generally is to refer the student to the nurse, social worker, or other individual within the school system who is best prepared to provide assistance.

Sampling Considerations for Evidence-Gathering

Although the two types of placement evaluation as well as formative and summative evaluation are primarily concerned with gathering cognitive or psychomotor achievement data, the differences in purposes and timing call for different approaches to determining the characteristics of the sample of items to be used in evidence-gathering.

If entry into a course is determined by the extent to which a student has mastered a series of prerequisite skills, the instrument used in placement evaluation must include items evaluating each skill. Suppose that entry into Algebra I is dependent on prior mastery of ability to add signed numbers, to multiply and divide fractions, and to translate word problems into equations.

Each of these abilities is prerequisite to being able to function at even a minimal level of competency in Algebra I. It is not sufficient for a placement instrument to gather data about only one or two of these abilities, since success in algebra is predicated on all. Similarly, in formative evaluation, where the attempt is to identify unmastered course objectives early enough to permit remediation prior to grading, each objective must be tested in order to obtain usable feedback.

To elaborate, consider the objectives sampled in a formative versus a summative evaluation. An algebra course may have as one of its ultimate objectives "to solve unfamiliar word problems by means of simultaneous equations." Items that evaluate this general course aim are appropriate for summative evaluation. We expect various topics covered in the course to contribute to the student's ability to achieve the objective. At the end of the term or semester we would want to know, for purposes of grading, whether a student had mastered the objective. Mastery of this general objective, however, implies that the student has mastered a series of more specific objectives—for example, "to solve simultaneous equations," "to translate word problems into equations," and so on (Airasian, 1971). If grading is the aim of evaluation, data about performance on the more general objectives are sufficient; but if evaluation is intended to identify learning weaknesses prior to grading, evidence about the student's ability to perform each of the more specific behaviors implied by the general objective should be obtained. Formative evaluation cannot help the student to direct his study if items testing each relevant skill are not included. Formative evaluation must be capable of telling the student to "learn to solve simultaneous equations" or "learn to state word problems in terms of equations" rather than the more general, and less useful, "work harder," "study more," etc., type of evaluation.

Evaluation instruments built along formative and summative lines can be useful for placing students at a particular point in instruction or out of a course entirely. Some courses, primarily at the college level, permit students who can pass the final examination to place out of the course. The reasoning is that if a student can pass the summative examination on the first day of class, his time will be more beneficially spent in some other course. Formative evaluation instruments that test the more specific skills required by the general course objectives are useful for determining that point in the course continuum where a student should be placed. In general, one could administer formative tests until a student evidenced nonmastery of a skill important for learning later skills. He would be placed at that point in the course where the unmastered skill was taught.

Since observations are gathered in an ad hoc manner in diagnostic evaluation, sampling in the usual sense of the word is not meaningful. It may be that the tell-tale symptoms of extra-classroom difficulties do not regularly manifest themselves. Further, to wait for additional occurrences may retard remedial action. The best approach for a teacher who suspects extra-classroom causes to be at the root of learning disorders is to talk to the appropriate referral agency (nurse, social worker, etc.) about his observations and hypotheses. The expert could then either see the child or direct the teacher to look for additional behavioral symptoms.

Scoring and Reporting

Row 6 of Table 1 distinguishes the scoring and reporting procedures employed by the four evaluations. The concern in this category is how to array and record most meaningfully the scores obtained from the varied evidence-gathering techniques.

In placement evaluation—except when a student places out of a course —evidence should be reported in terms of profiles, patterns, or subscores on the objectives or characteristics in question, so that student mastery of each prerequisite skill or course objective can be viewed. Since placement is concerned with the extent to which a student possesses particular skills, abilities, or characteristics vis-à-vis those needed for effective functioning in a course, scoring and reporting techniques that sum disparate pieces of data do not provide the specificity necessary for accurate placement, except when students are placed out of a course based on their performance on a summative examination.

Since the results of formative evaluation are used to direct teachers' and students' activities while instruction is in progress, feedback must be highly specific. Consequently, scoring and reporting should be based on response patterns on items testing skills taught in relatively short instructional blocks. In formative evaluation, as in placement evaluation, a total score hides more than it reveals.

Diagnostic evaluation is based on teacher observation. Clearly, it is difficult, if not impossible, to quantify such observations. As a result, the concept of a score per se is not applicable. The most appropriate form for diagnostic data is a written, anecdotal report that summarizes the teacher's observations.

Standards Against Which Scores Are Compared

Scores by themselves are often meaningless. A set of standards against which to compare scores is needed for proper interpretation. Row 7 of Table 1 shows that the different types of evaluation employ different standards in keeping with varying functions or purposes.

Standards are of two types—norm-referenced and criterion-referenced. In the former type, performance is judged relative to some larger group, usually the class as a whole. In the latter type, performance is judged relative to some absolute definition of mastery or adequacy. When we use summative evaluations to grade students we usually employ norm-referenced standards. That is, whether a student receives an A or a B is determined by how he performs in comparison with other students in the class. At one time or another all of us have had the experience of scoring 85 out of 100 on a test but receiving a C grade because most other students achieved higher than 90 on the test. "Grading on a curve" is another way of indicating norm-referenced standards.

Most placement, formative, and diagnostic evaluation data are judged in terms of criterion-referenced standards. Criteria of satisfactory performance are established prior to the evaluation and the evaluation results are compared with these criteria. For example, one might decide that placement in a particular course is dependent on mastery of each of eight prerequisite skills, or of any six of the eight. Placement with a particular teacher might depend on finding any four characteristics of the student that are similar to the teacher's characteristics. Or, the criterion for advancement to a succeeding topic in a course might be set at 90 percent mastery on the formative evaluation instrument testing mastery of the prior topic. Finally, one might decide that if a student manifests at least three symptoms consonant with a particular environmental, physical, or psychological difficulty, he will be referred for treatment. In each of these instances, the decisions made about an individual student depend only on his performance relative to the defined criterion. The performance of other students in the class is irrelevant when criterion-referenced standards are used. Placement, formative, and diagnostic evaluation represent situations when we are less interested in comparing a student with his peers than in studying him against independent criteria deemed indicative of acceptable learning or functioning.

Reliability

The reliability considerations for the evidence gathered under each evaluation approach are shown in Row 8. Rather than dwell on particular types of reliability amenable to the different types of evaluation, we shall consider those characteristics of the evidence gathered that must be shown to be reliable. Traditional approaches to the question of reliability stress the need for consistent, accurate data if judgments made on the basis of the data are to be valuable. While we subscribe to such a point of view, we see differences in the stringency with which it can be applied. Basically, the consequences of the judgments should determine, to a great extent, the degree of reliability required.

In placement evaluation, in which the intent is to place a student at his proper instructional starting point after which there is little latitude to "replace" him, the consequence of the decision is great. Thus, a high reliability is required of the instruments used to gather placement data. When placement decisions can be readily modified and systematic "replacing" is possible, the reliability considerations can be less stringent.

In formative evaluation, item response patterns must be demonstrated to be reliable, i.e., consistent, if instructional decisions are to be made with any degree of confidence. The reliability sought in diagnostic evaluation involves the recurrence of observed behavioral symptoms. The realm of diagnostic evaluation being what it is, however, particular observed symptoms can either disappear or become more pronounced over time. Therefore, our use of the term *recurrence* does not necessarily connote stability over time.

As is often the case in placing students, formative decisions can usually be rectified with relative ease. In diagnostic evaluation there is usually less harm in making an incorrect referral than in failing to refer at all. Thus, reliability constraints are less important in these types of evaluation. Summative decisions, however, are generally final. The results often follow a student throughout his academic career. Further, summative decisions made at particular points in a student's schooling are likely to serve the function of systematically reducing future options. A student who fails ninth grade algebra is unlikely, given present school organization and selection practices, to be admitted to college as a mathematics major. Because of the gravity of decisions made on the basis of summative evaluations, such evaluations should provide highly reliable, consistent data.

Validity

The final comparison, validity, is detailed in Row 9. Since placement, formative, and summative evaluation are tied closely to the objectives of a course, the principal consideration in determining the validity of their evidence-gathering techniques is content validity—that is, whether the technique appropriately evaluates the objectives of instruction.

Less central, yet important, is the construct validity of placement and formative instruments. Matching students either to teachers or to particular instructional modes involves a construct or constructs hypothesized to be related to optimum placement. We might, for example, start out with the hunch that authoritarian teachers are best for authoritarian students. Determining whether our initial hunch is in fact borne out is a problem of construct validity. Similarly, the construct validity of a formative instrument that purports to measure a hierarchy of skills leading to a more general objective can be tested by determining whether students who fail an item testing a particular objective fail all succeeding items testing more complex objectives. These validity considerations are more in the realm of research concerns than in the realm of classroom concerns.

To discuss validity in diagnostic evaluation we have resurrected the term "face validity," not because the term itself is important, but rather because it is familiar to most evaluators and because it briefly describes the characteristic of the validity involved. The symptoms observed by the teacher are valid if they appear to be symptoms of psychological, physical, or environmental causes of learning disability. Teachers are not trained psychologists, social workers, or nurses. Their primary function, in this context, is to recognize symptoms. It is the trained specialist, to whom the teacher refers particular cases, who must determine whether the teacher's observations are valid.

SUMMARY

We have attempted here to indicate the multiplicity of purposes evaluation can have in the classroom context, and to view evaluation as a system that collects a variety of data, at different times, to facilitate different types of judgments. In the explication of the four types across the nine dimensions it should have become apparent to the reader that the notion of an evaluative system is an appropriate one, since many of the considerations inherent in one type of evaluation are applicable in carrying out other types. The four types proposed overlap and interact to some extent on all dimensions with the exception of purpose.

To reiterate, our intent is not to suggest that the individual teacher be responsible for the development and implementation of such a complete evaluation system; however, neither is it our intent to suggest that the individual teacher disregard a formal system of evaluation in favor of the more spontaneous and informal evaluation practices that have been operative for so long. What is needed is a careful consideration of how the four types of evaluation can be made available to the individual teacher. In addition, we must conceive of evaluation as involving a much broader role than simply grading student achievement at the end of instruction. The interaction between various parts of the evaluation system proposed here are consciously designed and intended to enhance student learning so that in the future less emphasis need be placed on making fine, often meaningless, distinctions between individuals on the basis of final classroom achievement.

REFERENCES

Airasian, P. W. Formative evaluation instruments. *Irish Journal of Education,* 1968, *2,* 127–135.
Airasian, P. W. The role of evaluation in mastery learning. In J. Block (Ed.),

Mastery learning: Theory and practice. New York: Holt, Rinehart & Winston, 1971. Pp. 77–88.

Block, J. H. (Ed.) *Mastery learning: Theory and practice.* New York: Holt, Rinehart & Winston, 1971.

Bloom, B. S., Hastings, J. T., & Madaus, G. F. *Handbook on formative and summative evaluation of student learning.* New York: McGraw-Hill, 1971.

Bracht, G. H. The relationship of treatment tasks, personological variables, and dependent variables to aptitude-treatment-interaction. Unpublished doctoral dissertation, University of Colorado, 1969.

Cronbach, L. J. Course improvement through evaluation. *Teachers College Record,* 1963, *64,* 672–683.

Eisner, E. W. Educational objectives help or hindrance? *The School Review,* 1967, *75,* 250–260.

Grobman, H. (Ed.) *Evaluation activities of curriculum projects.* American Educational Research Association Monograph Series on Curriculum Evaluation, No. 2. Chicago: Rand McNally, 1968.

Jackson, P. W. *Life in Classrooms.* New York: Holt, Rinehart & Winston, 1968.

Madaus, G. F. The cooperative development of evaluation systems for individualized instruction. Keynote address to the annual Southeast Invitational Conference on Measurement in Education, University of Tennessee, Knoxville, Tennessee, October 3, 1969. (mimeo)

Scriven, M. The methodology of evaluation. In R. Stake (Ed.), *Perspectives of curriculum evaluation.* American Educational Research Association Monograph Series on Curriculum Evaluation, No. 1. Chicago: Rand McNally, 1967. Pp. 39–83.

Stake, R. E. The countenance of educational evaluation. *Teachers College Record,* 1967, *68,* 523–540.

Thelen, H. Matching teachers and pupils. *National Education Association Journal,* 1967, *56,* 18–20.

Tyler, R. W. *Constructing achievement tests.* Columbus: Ohio State Press, 1934.

Tyler, R. W. *Basic principles of curriculum and instruction: Syllabus for education 305.* Chicago: University of Chicago Press, 1950.

This paper is a follow-up to an article written by the same author three years earlier. In that article, Dyer suggested that testing was a menace because tests were misunderstood and test results misused. In this paper Dyer expands on the difference between his optimistic view of testing and the pessimistic view of its detractors. Note his suggestions on how to respond to the negative tones of the detractors. Note also the distinctions Dyer makes between the label IQ, which both he and the critics fault, and intelligence tests, which he considers useful.

Dyer correctly points out that test scores are not the *cause* of individual differences or of the educational problems such differences generate. To attack testing as the cause of these problems is another example of the scapegoat role Schutz mentioned in the first article of this unit.

Although Dyer does not use the words placement, formative, diagnostic, and summative as discussed in the previous article, be aware of his examples of functions that would fall in those categories.

The Menace of Testing Reconsidered

HENRY S. DYER

Back in 1961 a number of state education journals carried an obscure article with the title, "Is Testing a Menace to Education?" Its author was himself a tester, and he surprised some of his colleagues by answering his own question in the affirmative.

Following this episode there appeared a rash of highly critical books and articles on the same subject by writers *outside* the testing profession. Three books stand out as especially devastating: *The Tyranny of Testing* by Banesh Hoffmann (1962); *The Brain Watchers* by Martin Gross (1962); and *They Shall Not Pass* by Hillel Black (1963).

The juxtaposition of publication dates makes it almost seem as though that original obscure article on the testing menace had triggered the subsequent barrage. But this is highly unlikely, for most of the big guns were in the making before the article appeared. Furthermore, although its title had some initial shock value, its tone was mild and its thesis in favor of more and better testing.

From Henry S. Dyer, "The Menace of Testing Reconsidered," *Educational Horizons* (Fall 1964) Vol. XLIII, No. 1, pp. 3–8. Reprinted with the permission of the author and publisher.

It took the position that testing was a menace to education, not because the tests were faulty, but because too many educators seemed to misconceive the basic principles of educational and psychological measurement and were therefore apt to misinterpret or overinterpret test scores. It described nine misconceptions that were thought to be the most troublesome. The author hoped that by calling the attention of educators to these matters there might be some reduction in the misuse of tests and some increase in the educational benefits that can undoubtedly accrue from their wise and imaginative use in the classroom, the guidance office, the college admission office, and anywhere else where educational decisions are made. In other words, he was not against testing; he was very much in favor of it. He still is, I know. I wrote the article.

The principal difference between my view of testing and that of its detractors is that my view is optimistic and theirs is pessimistic. I truly believe that testing in one form or another is absolutely indispensable to effective education and that it is therefore incumbent upon all teachers, professors, guidance counselors, supervisors, principals, superintendents, admissions officers, deans, and even college presidents to make it their business to understand the principles, the pitfalls, and the possibilities of educational measurement. They should know in the marrow of their bones that without proper measurement properly applied, all education is a rudderless ship adrift on uncharted waters and going nowhere.

Granted that there have been some educational crimes committed through the misuse of tests, nevertheless the educational crimes committed because of the failure to use any tests at all have been, I suspect, far more destructive of the welfare of students and the good of society. Tests are a menace to education only in the sense that automobiles are a menace to physical well-being. If you use them wrong, you get into trouble. If you use them right, you open up all sorts of new possibilities for the betterment of mankind.

The detractors of testing tend to think otherwise. The most favorable attitude among them rarely gets beyond the grudging admission that tests may be a necessary evil, that the most they do is to serve as baling wire to hold together the chaotic enterprise we miscall an educational system, and that as soon as we can bring order and right thinking into the management of learning, testing will become an unmourned relic of the past. This is the *most* favorable attitude. The least favorable is something else again. It boils down to the proposition that all standardized tests are works of the devil which have been perpetrated upon defenseless school children by test makers in a nefarious conspiracy to inhibit learning and impair human development.

Such reactions have a somewhat negative tone. What should we do about them? There are several things we might do. We might spend a lot of time picking apart the arguments and trying to set the record straight. This is probably a waste of time that would be better spent improving tests and training people how to use them intelligently. Or we might examine the arguments dispassionately to see whether they touch any vulnerable spots in the testing enterprise which we may have overlooked and ought to do something about. This could be worthwhile, for it is not unlikely that a critic looking in from the ouside may see weaknesses that the professional who is looking out from the inside fails to see. In other words, to the extent that the outside critics are rational—and occasionally they are—we should take them seriously.

But I think perhaps the most profitable approach to the writings that are critical of testing would be to analyze their irrationalities in some detail to see whether we can find out what is eating the authors. I remember long ago getting into a controversy with a professor of the classics who was very much heated up about what he thought to be the inadequacy of the College Board test in Latin. His arguments were not making much sense and his own colleagues in the classics were not agreeing with him. What was wrong? Ultimately the facts came out: his own child had got a low score in Latin.

I am not suggesting that all the critics of testing may have been similarly bitten. What I am suggesting is that the worries that lie behind their verbal thrusts may well reflect similar worries in significant segments of the school-age population. Most of the critics come out of the humanist tradition. They perceive testing as an impersonal process that fails to take account of the individuality of the student. No doubt some students, maybe many students, share this attitude. If this is so, then the menace of testing is not a menace to the quality of instruction or the quality of guidance or the quality of college selection or placement. It is, rather, a menace that resides to a greater or less extent in the perceptions of certain of the individuals tested. Testing for them is perceived as a threat to their self-esteem.

I have no idea how widespread this anxiety about testing is nor how deeply it troubles those who are afflicted by it. But I think we should be concerned to find out how widespread and deepseated it is, for, to the extent it exists, it poses a tough problem not only for specialists in educational measurement but for educators generally. On the one hand, as I have already indicated, good measurement is essential to good education in all its aspects. It is essential to sound instruction as a means of identifying the pupil's needs and providing feedback on how the needs are being met. It is essential to guidance as a means of helping the pupil evaluate himself and his possibilities. It is essential to the administration of school systems as a means of locating soft spots in the curriculum and suggesting what should be done to strengthen them. It is essential to college admissions as a method of assessment that cuts across the enormous diversity of educational experience out of which the candidates come.

On the other hand, if testing is such a threat to the self-esteem of some of the youngsters we are trying to educate that they reject it or put false values upon it, how are we to get on with the job of helping such people make the most of themselves? I suspect that this dilemma is more illusory than real, but on the off-chance that it isn't, let's look into it a little further.

It cannot be emphasized too often that human judgment is always at the center of the process of measurement, whether it be educational measurement or any other kind of measurement. The minimum requirement of educational measurement is that the judgment must involve comparison, that is, the comparison of one student's response to a test situation with the responses of other students to the same test situation. One must be able to say that Student A's response is better, or more clearly correct, or more insightful, say, than Student B's response. In the case of an essay test and most other types of free response tests, the comparative judgment is made by presumably competent examiners *after* the students have been exposed to the test situation. In the case of a multiple-choice test, the comparative judgment is ordinarily made by competent examiners *before* the students are exposed to the test situation. There is the explicit judgment that a given option in each question is to be regarded as the best response, and there is the implicit judgment that if Student A chooses more of such options than Student B, then A is the better performer.

In connection with standardized tests, we have developed a formidable apparatus of scales and norms to facilitate the comparison of one individual with any number of other individuals. The scales and norms are a device for translating the basic human judgments involved in the make-up of the test into a system of numbers that enables one to apply these judgments universally. Thus, for instance, we can say that on this standardized test of listening comprehension in French, Mary Jones's performance exceeds that of 25 per cent or 50 per cent or 95 per cent of all 12th grade girls who have had four years of audio-lingual instruction. In making this kind of comparative judgment, we have to bear in mind that all judgments, whether derived from a testing situation or from some other source, are fallible. We have to take into account the strong possibility that on a second trial with the same test, or a parallel form of it, the student's position in the group with which he or she is being compared will change, simply because of the accidents of sampling. But this does not alter the fact that the measurement of Mary's or William's performance *always* involves a comparative judgment. The student is judged to be above or below somebody else with respect to some category of behavior that is thought to be educationally important.

This conception of educational measurement as a more or less refined form of comparative judgment would not, I suspect, fit altogether comfortably into the conceptual scheme of a radical empiricist. He might say that in the case of multiple-choice questions, for instance, the selection of options to be keyed "right" should not depend on the judgment of the test maker; it should depend, rather, on purely empirical data of the kind which shows that students who pick a given answer tend to do significantly better in school or college than those who pick other answers. This is a pleasing way of approaching the matter because it appears to get the test maker off the hook. But in point of fact it only postpones the issue. Somebody somewhere is making the comparative judgments that constitute the success criterion which is used to select the items and the options that "work." These somebodies are commonly teachers who express their comparative judgments in the form of grades. Thus, no matter how earnestly one may try to conceive of the measurement process as purely objective and empirical, one finally has to face the fact that human judgments of human behavior make up the ultimate raw material from which all educational and psychological measurements derive. And these judgments are always comparative judgments.

Now it is proverbial that compraisons are odious—especially among human beings and more especially for those who come out on the short end. It can be tough on Johnny to find himself consistently among the bottom ten per cent on a reading test or a test of college aptitude or a test in science. It can be tough not just because of the opportunities it appears to cut off, but also because of the grim realization that so many others are out ahead in the race for personal recognition. In short, it can be tough because it hurts his self-esteem. No doubt some youngsters are a good deal more sensitive to the odium of comparison than others. And no doubt the more sensitive ones may react in a variety of ways; some may simply withdraw from the struggle; some may dig in harder to try to improve themselves; and some may compensate by seeking other forms of recognition—for instance, by becoming a star athlete or by burning down the school building.

The social and emotional problems that are likely to be implicit in the comparison of one student's performance with that of his fellows are not easy problems, nor do they have simple solutions. Certainly it is no solution to abolish all forms of testing as some of our critics suggest. To follow this advice would be to sweep the fundamental problem under the rug and pretend it had gone away. Individual differences in the behavior of human beings exist whether we measure them or not. They are there. They are all-pervasive. They are inescapable. And they account for the rich diversity of accomplishment as well as the tension and frustration, the hope and despair that characterize any human society. Test scores are not the cause of individual differences or of the educational problems such differences generate; they are merely more or less accurate representations of some of the differences. To attack testing as such, therefore, is to attack that which symbolizes and highlights many of the educational problems needing our attention. It is to attack the methods by which we discover the problems. It is the type of attack that fails to come to grips with the problems themselves. It is a form of blind symbol smashing.

Symbol smashing of the right sort can be useful if one does not get into a confusion between the symbol and that which is symbolized. We all know that there are certain symbols which tend to become embedded in the culture and which are false stereotypes leading people away from the kinds of perceptions that enable them to cope effectively with experience. Such symbols can do with a bit of smashing. In the field of psychological measurement, for instance, the IQ is the sort of false symbol that we would be better off without. It is a dubious normative score wrapped up in a ratio which is justified on the basis of two impossible assumptions about the genetic determination of human behavior and the equivalence of human experience. It has generated all sorts of futile controversy about the determinants of mental growth. It has fouled up any number of experiments in the teaching-learning process. It has misled teachers and guidance counselors into untenable decisions about students. And it has been used to support the iniquitous and meaningless proposition that Negroes are genetically inferior to whites.

The critics are on solid ground when they find fault with the IQ as such; they are dead wrong, however, when they attribute to the intelligence test the same sort of deficiencies they find in the IQ. Any test, including any intelligence test, is a collection of tasks that serves as a tool for comparing the performance of one individual with that of others. It is never a perfect tool, but its imperfections are not of the same character as those to be found in the symbol we call the IQ, or any other false symbol. The test carries within it no necessary assumptions about the nature or genesis of human ability. It is merely a device for ordering individuals in accordance with the way they respond to a situation the test presents here and now. An achievement test serves the same purpose. The essential meaning of a test score resides in the tasks that make up the test and in the relationships that exist between the quality of performance on these tasks in this situation and the quality of performance on other tasks in other situations. It is only as we expand this network of relationships that we shall eventually come to understand more fully how children learn and develop and thus be better able to help each one of them along the road to maturity.

Which is to say we need more and better testing, not less, if we are to cope imaginatively with the extraordinary problems in education that lie ahead of us. If the critics of testing can help clear away some of the cobwebs of superstition that get in the way of good testing, more power to them, but if they foster a new superstition that testing is a symbol of all that is bad in the treatment of the young, then it is they, not testing, who are a menace to education.

What are the implications of all this for the classroom teacher? As I conceive of it, educational measurement is or ought to be central in her work. Every teacher at one time or another is a maker of tests, a giver of tests, and an interpreter of test scores, and the quality of her teaching depends to a very considerable extent on the wisdom she brings to her testing.

If, as I have suggested, educational measurement is in essence an exercise in comparative judgment, then any teacher who knows what she is about must be continuously engaged in the measurement process. Measurement is not something outside and apart from instruction; it is intimately involved in every phase of it, for it is the means by which the teacher keeps in touch with the minds of her pupils and thereby is enabled to shape the classroom situation so that learning goes forward in useful directions. How does Johnny's work in fractions today compare with what he was doing with them yesterday? What proportion of the class is getting the central message in this Shakespearean sonnet? Questions like these are questions in measurement and unless a teacher is constantly asking and answering them for herself, her teaching will be blind and only randomly related to what her class learns.

I have spoken of how testing might be a threat to a pupil's self-esteem. It seems to be that the most natural way of mitigating the threat is to get pupils accustomed to the idea that testing is an ordinary part of the strategy of teaching and learning, that comparisons need not be so terribly odious if the purpose is to bring about self-understanding and growth. No one is in a better position than the classroom teacher to lead the pupil into this way of perceiving the matter. But she must begin with herself.

Paul Buck, the former Provost of Harvard, writing in a collection of essays on *Examining in Harvard College* sums it up thus: "Examinations," he says, "are the pulse of the learning process. They may be used to measure not only the quantity of learning but also the quality of teaching."

Any teacher who presumes to have a firm hand on the "pulse of the learning process" had better look to her measurements.

RECOMMENDED READING FOR UNIT I

Dyer, Henry S. "Is Testing a Menace to Education?" *New York State Education,* October 1961, 49: 16–19.

Lennon, Roger T. "Testing: Bond or Barrier between Pupil and Teacher." *Education,* September 1954 (also as *Test Service Notebook 82,* Harcourt Brace Jovanovich).

Merwin, Jack C. "Educational Measurement of What Characteristic of Whom (or What) by Whom and Why." *Journal of Educational Measurement,* 1973, 10, 1: 1–6.

Turnbull, William W. "Relevance in Testing." *Science,* June 1968, 160, 28: 1424–1429.

BASIC PRINCIPLES
OF MEASUREMENT

unit

II

There are certain qualities that every measurement device should possess. Two of the most important technical concepts are reliability and validity. In addition, a test should provide scores that can be interpreted easily and accurately. The five articles in this unit relate to these topics.

Reliability is typically defined as the degree of consistency between two measures of the same thing. There are several different ways of estimating this degree of consistency, and various factors which will affect these estimates. The article by Wesman discusses these aspects of reliability as well as questioning how high a reliability coefficient should be.

Validity is frequently defined as the degree to which a test is capable of achieving certain aims. But this definition is oversimplified. The latest *Standards For Educational and Psychological Tests* (1974) describes three kinds of validity: content validity, criterion-related validity, and construct validity. (The Lennon article mentions four kinds; predictive and concurrent validity are subsets of criterion-related validity.) Content validity, primarily important in achievement testing, is related to how adequately the content of the test samples the domain about which inferences are to be made. Lennon defines and explains content validity more fully, discusses when one should use it, and comments on three basic assumptions underlying the use of content validity.

Criterion-related validity pertains to the empirical technique of studying the relationship between predictor, or test, scores and some independent external measure, or criterion. There are many ways of expressing the degree of the existing relationship. The correlation coefficient or some mathematical function of it is the most common expression. The Taylor and Russell article is a classical paper showing the relationship of validity coefficients to the practical effectiveness of tests in selection. Careful reading of the Taylor-Russell article should do much to alleviate the confusion that often exists in this area.

Construct validity is the degree to which the test scores can be accounted for by certain explanatory constructs in a psychological theory. No articles on construct validity are presented in this unit. Careful study of the topic is more important for advanced study; interested readers should check such classics as Cronbach and Meehl (1955), Bechtoldt (1959), and Campbell and Fiske (1959).

To know a person's observed or raw score on a measuring instrument gives us some information about his performance. But ordinarily that score can be made more meaningful by converting it to a type of score that presents normative or relative information. Seashore has written the most popular article on norm-referenced methods of expressing test scores. The figure in his article shows the relationships among the types of scores if the original set of scores is normally distributed. Careful study of this figure should help readers understand the relationships among various norm-referenced expressions.

For any measuring instrument to be useful, it must be reliable. In this article, Wesman describes two purposes of reliability coefficients: to estimate the precision of the measuring instrument and to estimate the consistency of the examinees' performances. Which estimate would be more useful for judging the potential usefulness of a test in long range prediction?

Other questions for your consideration after reading the articles are:

1. Why does a test need to be more reliable for individual decision making than group decision making?
2. If a test has a reliability coefficient of .88 based on a sample of fourth, fifth, and sixth graders can we make any statements about what the reliability coefficient would be based on only sixth graders?
3. Why are internal consistency estimates of reliability inappropriate for speeded tests?

Reliability and Confidence

ALEXANDER G. WESMAN

The chief purpose of testing is to permit us to arrive at judgments concerning the people being tested. If those judgments are to have any real merit, they must be based on dependable scores—which, in turn, must be earned on dependable tests. If our measuring instrument is unreliable, any judgments based on it are necessarily of doubtful worth. No one would consider relying on a thermometer which gave readings varying from 96° to 104° for persons known to have normal temperatures. Nor would any of us place confidence in measurements of length based on an elastic ruler. While few tests are capable of yielding scores which are as dependable as careful measurements of length obtained by use of a well-marked (and rigid!) ruler, we seek in tests some satisfactory amount of dependability—of "rely-ability."

It is a statistical and logical fact that no test can be valid unless it is reliable; knowing the reliability of a test in a particular situation, we know the limits beyond which validity in that situation cannot rise. Knowing reliability, we know also how large a band of error surrounds a test score—how precisely or loosely that score can be interpreted. In view of the importance of the concept of reliability, it is unfortunate that so many inadequacies in the reporting and use of reliability coefficients are to be found in the literature. This article is intended to clarify some aspects of this very fundamental characteristic of tests.

From *Test Service Bulletin*, No. 44, May 1952. Reprinted with permission of the publisher, The Psychological Corporation.

Reliability coefficients are designed to provide estimates of the consistency or precision of measurements. When used with psychological tests, the coefficients may serve one or both of two purposes: (1) to estimate the precision of the test itself as a measuring instrument, or (2) to estimate the consistency of the examinees' performances on the test. The second kind of reliability obviously embraces the first. We can have unreliable behavior by the examinee on a relatively reliable test, but we cannot have reliable performance on an unreliable instrument. A student or applicant suffering a severe headache may give an uncharacteristic performance on a well-built test; the test may be reliable, but the subject's performance is not typical of him. If, however, the test items are ambiguous, the directions are unclear, or the pictures are so poorly reproduced as to be unintelligible—if, in short, the test materials are themselves inadequate—the subject is prevented from performing reliably, however propitious his mental and physical condition.

This two-fold purpose of reliability coefficients is reflected in the several methods which have been developed for estimating reliability. Methods which provide estimates based on a single sitting offer evidence as to the precision of the test itself; these include internal consistency estimates, such as those obtained by use of the split-half and Kuder-Richardson techniques when the test is given only once, as well as estimates based on immediate retesting, whether with the same form or an equivalent one. When a time interval of one or more days is introduced, so that day-to-day variability in the person taking the test is allowed to have an effect, we have evidence concerning the stability of the trait and of the examinee as well as of the test. It is important to recognize whether a reliability coefficient describes only the test, or whether it describes the stability of the examinee's performance as well.

HOW HIGH SHOULD
A RELIABILITY COEFFICIENT BE?

We should naturally like to have as much consistency in our measuring instruments as the physicist and the chemist achieve. However, the complexities of human personality and other practical considerations often place limits on the accuracy with which we measure and we accept reliability coefficients of different sizes depending on various purposes and situations. Perhaps the most important of these considerations is the gravity of the decision to be made on the basis of the test score. The psychologist who has to recommend whether or not a person is to be committed to an institution is obligated to seek the most reliable instruments he can obtain. The counselor inquiring as to whether a student is likely to do better in one curriculum or another may settle for a slightly less reliable instrument, but his demands should still be high. A survey of parents' attitudes towards school practices needs only moderate reliability, since only the *average* or group figures need to be highly dependable and not the specific responses of individual parents. Test constructors experimenting with ideas for tests may accept rather low reliability in the early stages of experimentation—those tests which show promise can then be built up into more reliable instruments before publication.

It is much like the question of how confident we wish to be about decisions in other areas of living. The industrial organization about to hire a top executive (whose decisions may seriously affect the entire business) will usually spend large sums of time and money to obtain reliable evidence concerning a candidate's qualifications for the job. The same firm will devote far less time or money to the hiring of a clerk or office boy, whose errors are of lesser consequence. In buying a house, we want to have as much confidence in our decision as we can reasonably get. In buying a package of razor blades, slim evidence is sufficient since we lose little if we have to throw away the entire package or replace it sooner than expected. The principle is simply stated: the more important the decision to be reached, the greater is our need for confidence in the precision of the test and the higher is the required reliability coefficient.

TWO FACTORS AFFECTING THE INTERPRETATION OF RELIABILITY COEFFICIENTS

Actually, there is no such thing as *the* reliability coefficient for a test. Like validity, reliability is specific to the group on which it is estimated. The reliability coefficient will be higher in one situation than in another according to circumstances which may or may not reflect real differences in the precision of measurement. Among these factors are the range of ability in the group and the interval of time between testings.

Range of Talent

If a reliability estimate is based on a group which has a small spread in the ability measured by the test, the coefficient will be relatively low. If the group is one which has a wide range in that particular talent, the coefficient will be higher. That is, the reliability coefficient will vary with the range of talent in the group, even though the accuracy of measurement is unchanged. The following example may illustrate how this comes about. For simplicity, we have used small numbers of cases; ordinarily, far larger groups would be required to ensure a coefficient in which we could have confidence.

In Table 1 are shown the raw scores and rankings of twenty students on two forms of an arithmetic test. Looking at the two sets of rankings, we

TABLE 1   Raw Scores and Ranks of Students on Two Forms of an Arithmetic Test

Student	Form X		Form Y	
	Score	Rank	Score	Rank
A	90	1	88	2
B	87	2	89	1
C	83	3	76	5
D	78	4	77	4
E	72	5	80	3
F	70	6	65	7
G	68	7	64	8
H	65	8	67	6
I	60	9	53	10
J	54	10	57	9
K	51	11	49	11
L	47	12	45	14
M	46	13	48	12
N	43	14	47	13
O	39	15	44	15
P	38	16	42	16
Q	32	17	39	17
R	30	18	34	20
S	29	19	37	18
T	25	20	36	19

see that changes in rank from one form to the other are minor; the ranks shift a little, but not importantly. A coefficient computed from these data would be fairly high.

Now, however, let us examine only the rankings of the five top students. Though for these five students the shifts in rank are the same as before, the importance of the shifts is greatly emphasized. Whereas in the larger group student C's change in rank from third to fifth represented only a ten per cent shift (two places out of twenty), his shift of two places in rank in the smaller top group is a forty per cent change (two places out of five). When the entire twenty represent the group on which we estimate the reliability of the arithmetic test, going from third on form X to fifth on form Y still leaves the student as one of the best in this population. If, on the other hand, reliability is being estimated only on the group consisting of the top five students, going from third to fifth means dropping from the middle to the bottom of this population—a radical change. A coefficient, if computed for just these five cases, would be quite low.

Note that it is not the small number of cases which brings about the lower coefficient. It is the narrower range of talent which is responsible. A coefficient based on five cases as widespread as the twenty (e.g., pupils A, E, J, and T, who rank first, fifth, tenth, fifteenth, and twentieth respectively on form X), would be at least as large as the coefficient based on all twenty students.

This example shows why the reliability coefficient may vary even though the test questions and the stability of the students' performances are unchanged. A test may discriminate with satisfactory precision among students with wide ranges of talent but not discriminate equally well in a narrow range of talent. A yardstick is unsatisfactory if we must differentiate objects varying in length from 35.994 to 36.008 inches. Reliability coefficients reflect this fact, which holds regardless of the kind of reliability coefficient computed. It should be obvious, then, that *no reliability coefficient can be properly interpreted without information as to the spread of ability in the group on which it is based.* A reliability coefficient of .65 based on a narrow range of talent is fully as good as a coefficient of .90 based on a group with twice that spread of scores. Reliability coefficients are very much a function of the range of talent in the group.

Interval between Testings

When two forms of a test are taken at a single sitting, the reliability coefficient computed by correlating the two forms is likely to overestimate somewhat the real accuracy of the test. This is so because factors such as mental set, physical condition of examinees, conditions of test administration, etc.—factors which are irrelevant to the test itself—are likely to operate equally on both forms, thus making each person's pair of scores more similar than they otherwise would be. The same type of overestimate may be expected when reliability is computed by split-half or other internal consistency techniques, which are based on a single test administration. Coefficients such as these describe the accuracy of the test, but exaggerate the practical accuracy of the results by the extent to which the examinees and the testing situation may normally be expected to fluctuate. As indicated above, coefficients based on a single sitting do not describe the stability of the subjects' performances.

When we set out to investigate how stable the test results are likely to be from day to day or week to week, we are likely to underestimate the test's accuracy, though we may succeed in obtaining a realistic estimate of stability of the examinees' performances on the test. The underestimation of the test's accuracy depends on the extent to which changes in the examinees have taken place between testings. The same influences mentioned above—mental set, physical condition of examinees, and the like—which *increase* coefficients based on a single sitting are likely to *decrease* coefficients when testing is done on different days. It is unlikely for example, that the same persons who had headaches the first day will also have headaches on the day of the second testing.

Changes in the persons tested may also be of a kind directly related to the content of the particular test. If a month has elapsed between two administrations of an arithmetic test, different pupils may have learned different amounts of arithmetic during the interval. The second testing should then show greater score increases for those who learned more than for those who learned less. The correlation coefficient under these conditions will reflect the test's accuracy *minus* the effect of differential learning; it will not really be a reliability coefficient.

For most educational and industrial purposes, the reliability coefficient which reflects *stability of performance* over a relatively short time is the more important. Usually, we wish to know whether the student or job applicant would have achieved a similar score if he had been tested on some other day, or whether he might have shown up quite differently. It would be unfortunate and unfair to make important decisions on the basis of test results which might have been quite different had the person been tested the day before or a day later. We want an estimate of reliability which takes into account accidental changes in day-to-day ability of the individual, but which has not been affected by real learning between testings. Such a reliability coefficient would be based on two sittings, separated by one or more days so that day-to-day changes are reflected in the scores, but not separated by so much time that permanent changes, or learning, have occurred.[1] Two forms of a test, administered a day to a week apart, would usually satisfy these conditions. If the same form of a test is used in both sittings, the intervening time should be long enough to minimize the role of memory from the first to the second administrations.

Ideally, then, our reliability coefficient would ordinarily be based on two different but equivalent forms of the test, administered to a group on two separate occasions. However, it is often not feasible to meet these conditions: there may be only one form of the test available, or the group may be available for only one day, or the test may be one which is itself a learning experience. We are then forced to rely on coefficients based on a single administration. Fortunately, when such coefficients are properly used they usually provide close approximations to the estimates which would have been obtained with alternate forms administered at different times.

SOME COMMON MISCONCEPTIONS

Reliability of Speed Tests

Although estimates of reliability based on one administration of the test are often satisfactory, there are some circumstances in which *only* retest methods are proper. Most notable is the case in which we are dealing with an easy test given under speed conditions. If the test is composed of items which almost anyone can answer correctly given enough time but which most people tested cannot finish in the time allowed, the test is largely a measure of speed. Many clerical and simple arithmetic tests used with adults are examples of speed tests. Internal consistency methods, whether they are of the Kuder-Richardson or of the split-half type, provide false and often grossly exaggerated estimates of the reliability of such tests. To demonstrate this problem, two forms of a simple but speed-laden clerical test were given to a group. For *each* form the odd-even (split-half) reliability coefficient was found to be over .99. However, when scores on Form A were correlated with scores on Form B, the coefficient was .88. This latter value is a more accurate estimate of the reliability of the test.[2] Many equally dramatic illustrations of how spurious an inappropriate coefficient can be may be found readily, even in manuals for professionally made tests.

If a test is somewhat dependent on speed, but the items range in difficulty from easy to hard, internal consistency estimates will not be as seriously misleading as when the test items are simple and the test is highly speeded. As the importance of speed diminishes, these estimates will be less different from the coefficients which would be obtained by retest methods. It is difficult to guess how far wrong an inappropriate coefficient for a speeded test is. *Whenever there is evidence that speed is important in test performance, the safest course is to insist on an estimate of reliability based on test-and-retest*, if necessary with the same but preferably with an alternate form of the test.

Part vs. Total Reliability

Some of the tests we use are composed of several parts which are individually scored and the part scores are then added to yield a total score. Often, reliability is reported only for the total score, with no information given as to the reliability of the scores on the individual parts. This may lead to seriously mistaken assumptions regarding the reliability of the part scores—and, thus, of the confidence we may place in judgments based on the part scores. The longer a test is, other things being equal, the more reliable it is; the shorter the test, the lower is its reliability likely to be. A part score based on only a portion of the items in a test can hardly be expected to be as reliable as the total score; if we treat the part score as though it has the reliability of the total score, we misplace our confidence—sometimes quite seriously.

As an example, we may look at the Wechsler Intelligence Scale for Children, one of the most important instruments of its kind. Five subtests are combined to yield a total Verbal Score for this test. The reliability coefficient for the Verbal Score, based on 200 representative ten-year-olds, is .96 —high enough to warrant considerable confidence in the accuracy of measurement for these youngsters. For the same population, however, a single subtest (General Comprehension) yields a reliability coefficient of only .73—a far less impressive figure. If we allow ourselves to act as though the total test reliability coefficient of .96 represents the consistency of measurement we can expect from the Comprehension subtest, we are likely to encounter unpleasant surprises on future retests. More importantly, any clinical judgments which ignore the relatively poor reliability of the part score are dangerous. Test users should consider it a basic rule that *if evidence of adequate reliability for part scores is missing, the part scores should not be used.*

Reliability for What Group?

This question may be considered as a special case under the principles discussed above with respect to range of talent. It is worth special consideration because it is so often ignored. Even the best documented of test manuals present only limited numbers of reliability coefficients; in too many manuals a single coefficient is all that is made available. On what group should a reliability coefficient be based?

When we interpret an individual's test score, the most meaningful reliability coefficient is one based on the group with which the individual is competing. Stated otherwise, the most appropriate group is that in which the counselor, clinician or employment manager is trying to make decisions as to the relative ability of the individuals on the trait being measured. Any one person is, of course, a member of many groups. An applicant for a job may also be classified as a high school or college graduate, an experienced or inexperienced salesman or bookkeeper, a local or out-of-state person, a member of one political party or another, below or above age thirty, etc. A high school student is a boy or girl; a member of an academic, trade or commercial school group; a member of an English class, a geometry class, or a woodworking or cooking class; a freshman or a junior; a future engineer or nurse or garage mechanic. Obviously, it would be impossible for a test manual to offer reliability for *all* the groups of which any one individual is a member.

The appropriate group is represented by the individual's present competition. If we are testing applicants for clerical work, the most meaningful reliability coefficient is one based on applicants for clerical work. Coefficients based on employed clerical workers are somewhat less useful, those based on high school graduates are still less useful; as we go on to *more general* groups —e.g., all high school students or all adults—the coefficients become less and less meaningful. Similarly, as we go to *less relevant* groups (even though they may be quite specific) the reliability coefficients are also less relevant and less meaningful. The reliability of a test calculated on the basis of mechanical apprentices, college sophomores, or junior executives reveals little of importance when we are concerned with clerical applicants. What we need to know is how well the test discriminates among applicants for clerical work. If we can define the population with even greater specificity and relevance—e.g., female applicants for filing jobs—so much the better. *The closer the resemblance between the group on which the reliability coefficient is based and the group of individuals about whose relative ability we need to decide, the more meaningful is that coefficient of reliability.*

Test Reliability vs. Scorer Reliability

Some tests are not entirely objective as to scoring method; the scorer is required to make a judgment as to the correctness or quality of the response. This is frequently true in individually-administered tests (Wechsler or Binet for example), projective techniques in personality measurement (Rorschach, Sentence Completion, etc.) and many other tests in which the subject is asked to supply the answer, rather than to select one of several stated choices. For tests such as these, it is important to know the extent of agreement between the persons who score them. Test manuals usually report the amount of agreement by means of a coefficient of correlation between scores assigned to a set of test papers by two or more independent scorers.

Such a correlation coefficient yields important information—it tells us how objectively the test can be scored. It even contributes some evidence of reliability, since objectivity of scoring is a factor which makes for test reliability. Such a coefficient should not, however, be considered a reliability coefficient for the test; it is only an estimate of *scoring* reliability—a statement of how much confidence we may have that two scorers will arrive at similar scores for a given test paper. Moreover, it is possible for a test to be quite unreliable as a measuring instrument, yet have high scoring objectivity. We should remember that many objective tests—those in which the person selects one of several stated options—are not very reliable, yet the scoring is by definition objective. A short personality inventory may have a retest reliability coefficient of .20; but if it is the usual paper-and-pencil set of questions with a clear scoring key, two scorers should agree perfectly, except for clerical errors, in assigning scores to the test. The coefficient of correlation between their sets of scores might well be 1.00.

In short, information as to scorer agreement is important but not sufficient. The crucial question—How precisely is the test measuring the individual?—is not answered by scorer agreement; a real reliability coefficient is required.

A PRACTICAL CHECK-LIST

When reading a test manual, the test user would do well to apply a mental check-list to the reliability section, raising at least the following questions for each reliability coefficient:

1. What does the coefficient measure?

    a. Precision of the test—coefficient based on single sitting?

    b. Stability of examinees' test performances—coefficient based on test-and-retest with a few days intervening?

2. Is it more than a reliability coefficient? . . . does it also measure constancy of the trait? . . . is the coefficient based on test-and-retest with enough intervening time for learning or similar changes to have occurred?

3. Do scores on the test depend largely on how rapidly the examinees can answer the questions? If so, is the reliability coefficient based on a test-and-retest study?

4. Are there part scores intended for consideration separately? If so, is each part score reliable enough to warrant my confidence?

5. Is the group on which this coefficient is based appropriate to my purpose? Does it consist of people similar to those with whom I shall be using the test?

6. Since a reliability coefficient, like any other statistic, requires a reasonable number of cases to be itself dependable, how large is the group on which the coefficient is based?

If, and *only* if, the coefficients can be accepted as meeting the above standards, one may ask:

7. In view of the importance of the judgments I still make, is the correlation coefficient large enough to warrant my use of the test?

A reliability coefficient is a statistic—simply a number which summarizes a relationship. Before it takes on meaning, its reader must understand the logic of the study from which the coefficient was derived, the nature of the coefficient and the forces which affect it. Statistics may reveal or conceal—what they do depends to a very large extent on the logical ability and awareness the reader brings to them. Figures do lie, to those who don't or won't understand them.

NOTES

[1] A coefficient which is based on two testings between which opportunity for learning has occurred is a useful statistic. It may provide evidence of how much individual variation in learning has taken place, or of the stability of the knowledge, skills or aptitudes being measured. It is similar to a reliability coefficient, and is in part a function of the reliability of the two measurements; but such a coefficient should not be interpreted as simply estimating reliability—it requires a more complex interpretation.

[2] Manual for the *Differential Aptitude Tests*, Revised Edition, page 65. The Psychological Corporation, 1952.

Validity is usually considered the single most important characteristic of a test. In this article Lennon discusses one particular type of validity, content validity. After completing the article you should be able to answer the following questions.

1. If I wish to use the results from an arithmetic test to decide whether or not to take algebra am I using the test as a sample or sign?
2. Which of the three assumptions mentioned by Lennon are of questionable validity in personality assessment?
3. If a test has high content validity for Miss Jones' seventh grade math class does it necessarily have high content validity for Miss Smith's class? Why or why not?
4. This article was written prior to the recent emphasis on criterion-referenced tests and no mention is made of the distinction between normative- and criterion-referenced tests. Would a criterion-referenced test need to fulfill any additional assumptions in order to have content validity? If so, what would they be? (You may need to wait until you have read the Klein and Kosecoff article in Unit VI to answer this question.)

Assumptions Underlying the Use of Content Validity

ROGER T. LENNON

The concept of *validity* of educational and psychological tests and diagnostic aids has been the subject of increasingly penetrating and sophisticated analysis, as befits its central position in test theory. While it cannot yet be asserted that our notions of validity are as fully elaborated, or even as generally agreed upon, as might be desired, we have assuredly come a long way from the time when the classic definition of validity as "the extent to which a test measures whatever it purports to measure" could be regarded as adequate.

KINDS OF VALIDITY

A reflection of the present stage of refinement of the validity concept is to be found in the *Technical Recommendations for Psychological Tests*,* produced

From *Educational and Psychological Measurement*, 1956, 16: 294–304. Reprinted with permission of author and publisher.

* References appear on p. 70.

by the APA Committee on Test Standards (American Psychological Association, 1954). This Committee found it useful to distinguish four senses in which the term *validity* may be used, or four aspects of validity, namely, content validity, predictive validity, concurrent validity, and construct validity. Differentiation of the validity concept in this wise stems from a recognition of the various uses made of tests and psychological aids, and of the consequent variations in the kinds of evidence appropriate for judging their probable goodness or usefulness.

CONTENT VALIDITY: A DEFINITION

Our present concern is with the first of the above named aspects of validity, namely, content validity. The term *content validity* is not defined in the text of APA's Technical Recommendations, but the meaning intended may readily be inferred from such statements in the report as these:

> Content validity is evaluated by showing how well the content of the test samples the class of situations or subject matter about which conclusions are to be drawn.

and again

> Content validity is indicated by a description of the universe of items from which selection was made, including a description of the selection process.

The *Technical Recommendations for Achievement Tests* produced by a joint committee of the American Educational Research Association and the National Council on Measurements Used in Education (1955) adopted the APA committee's usage. The AERA report similarly offers no formal definition of the term "content validity," stating merely that "content validity is concerned with the sampling of a specified universe of content."

We propose in this paper to use the term *content validity* in the sense in which we believe it is intended in the APA Test Standards, namely, to denote *the extent to which a subject's responses to the items of a test may be considered to be a representative sample of his responses to a real or hypothetical universe of situations which together constitute the area of concern to the person interpreting the test.*

Although the term *content validity* has only in recent years achieved currency in testing literature, the concept has readily identifiable forebears. Early analyses of validity commonly recognized two meanings of the term, often labeled *empirical* or *statistical*, on the one hand, and *logical*, or, for educational tests, *curricular*, on the other; and content validity is a lineal descendant of this second branch of the family. Like many terms, it does not yet have a universally accepted meaning. Anastasi (1961), for example, seems to equate content validity with *logical validity*, or *validity by definition*, even remarking that content validity has occasionally been used to denote a sub-species of *face validity*. In Cureton's usage (Cureton, 1951) content validity (at least for educational achievement tests) is synonymous with what he terms *curricular relevance* or *curricular validity*; and he is at some pains to distinguish it from what he calls *formal relevance* and *face validity*. Hence the need for specifying the sense in which we use the term.

Let it be noted particularly that in the definition proposed above, content validity is ascribed to the subject's responses rather than to the test questions themselves. This is to underscore the point that appraisal of content validity must take into account not only the *content* of the questions but also the *process* presumably employed by the subject in arriving at his response. Since the test user wishes to make inferences about a behavioral universe, the sample must also be a sample of behaviors; and the behaviors are the exam-inee's modes of response and the responses themselves. Hence content validity inheres in the responses, rather than exclusively in the items themselves. A given item may function as a measure of reasoning or generalization for one examinee, but measure merely recall for another. Zimmerman (1954), in a discussion of the nature of the spatial factors, observes that "A problem which would be solved spatially by one might evoke Visualization for an-other, or might be so simple for still another that he would depend more upon Perceptual Speed." Insofar as the items of a test lend themselves to response via different processes for various examinees, the possibility exists that its content validity differs from one examinee to another, even though the test questions are identical for all subjects.

MEASUREMENT OF CONTENT VALIDITY

In speaking of "the *extent*" to which test matches universe, it is clearly implied that some tests possess this property to a greater extent than others. It is not to be inferred, however, that it is possible to express this degree of agreement in any precise quantitative terms. Indeed, as the Test Standards report makes clear, in most classes of situations measured by tests, quanti-tative evidence of content validity is not obtainable. We have no scale for measuring the representativeness of a sample. Content validity, as the Stand-ards point out, is ordinarily to be established deductively, by defining a universe and sampling systematically within the universe. Approaches such as internal consistency analyses, factorial analyses, and Gulliksen's sugges-tions for appraising *intrinsic validity* are helpful in clarification and definition of the universe, and hence not without merit in evaluating content validity; but they cannot be considered sufficient bases for its appraisal.

JUSTIFICATION FOR USE OF CONTENT VALIDITY

Some may be prompted to inquire why it is ever necessary or desirable to rely on content analysis as the basis for appraisal of validity, rather than on an empirical-quantitative approach involving correlation with criterion measures. The answer lies in the fact that in many testing situations (of which achievement testing forms the largest class) there is not available or readily accessible any dependable criterion variable, against which the "validity" of the test may be measured; and secondly, in the fact that there are certain uses of tests for which correlations with either contemporary or subsequent criteria are not meaningful as indicators of validity. When a test is intended to serve as the basis for determining how well an individual would perform at the present time on some universe of situations, and when circumstances do not permit measurement of the responses to the entire universe, then it is clear that the test user must rely upon correspondence between test sample and universe in deciding what confidence he may have in the inferences made on the basis of the test.

To appreciate more fully the types of tests or of testing situations in which the concept of content validity may appropriately be used, it is helpful to recall Goodenough's distinction between tests as *samples* and tests as *signs* (Goodenough, 1949). In the case of tests considered as samples, the tester is concerned with the type of behavior manifested in the test performance in its own right; the criterion, as Goodenough puts it, is intrinsic, and the question of the goodness of the test is a question of the representativeness and adequacy of the sample—a question, that is, of content validity. In the case of tests regarded as *signs*—aptitude tests, for example—the tester is not concerned with the test behavior as such, but only in its relation to some extrinsic criterion; for such tests, predictive and concurrent validity will ordinarily be of major interest.

The American Psychological Association Standards Committee conceives of content validity as appropriate for ability tests, achievement tests, personality inventories, and interest inventories, though not, of course, to the exclusion of evidence on other types of validity. Not all test theorists share the committee's views on the usefulness of a content validity approach for all these types of tests. Anastasi, for example, takes the position that "the use of content validity in the evaluation of aptitude or personality tests has little to commend it," (Anastasi, 1961) on the grounds that a given test may measure different functions in different groups, so that it is impossible to determine the functions measured by the test from an inspection of the content. In the final analysis, the appropriateness of a content validity approach depends on the types of inferences or interpretations to be made of the test results; or conversely, the soundness of various interpretations depends on the varieties of validity evidence at hand.

ASSUMPTIONS UNDERLYING THE USE
OF CONTENT VALIDITY

Having in mind the definition of content validity offered above, and the types of tests in connection with which we are considering this concept, let us turn to a consideration of certain of the assumptions underlying the notion. Three of these assumptions are singled out here for comment, as follows:

1. The area of concern to the tester can be conceived as a meaningful, definable universe of responses.
2. A sample can be drawn from this universe in some purposive, meaningful fashion.
3. The sample and the sampling process can be defined with sufficient precision to enable the test user to judge how adequately performance on the sample typifies performance on the universe.

Assumption 1.   The Area of Concern to the Tester Can Be Conceived as a Meaningful, Definable Universe of Responses. Test theory has consistently held to the view that a test is a sample of behavior from which inferences may be made to a universe of behaviors. Even in the case of tests functioning as signs, to revert for a moment to Goodenough's term, the test behavior is nevertheless only a sample of the many behaviors which might be chosen to function as signs; and even in the case of tests which in effect duplicate the criterion behavior, the test is still a sample in the sense that it represents the behavior at a particular time, under particular circumstances, whereas the criterion is not so restricted. This sample-universe view is, of course, the heart of the notion of content validity.

In some ways this part of test theory may represent a too-facile analogy with statistical theory. In sampling theory, a *universe* is defined as a set or group of individuals having a common character or characteristic. It is essential that the universe be uniform in some meaningful sense—that it possess internal coherence. A universe should constitute a set or class sufficiently well defined so that it is possible to say of any given element that it either does or does not belong in the universe.

We may well inquire how frequently it happens that we can conceive of or define a "universe," in this sense of the word, for test-development purposes or, perhaps more to the point, how often we do it even when it is possible. In achievement testing, we can, to be sure, readily cite certain situations in which the universe can be identified and rigorously defined. The ability to handle correctly the hundred possible addition facts is the often-used illustration of a domain which can be specified with exactness. More often, however, particularly in fields other than achievement, the area of concern to the tester is vastly more complex, multidimensional, and resistant to precise definition. The test-maker's task is made no easier by the unhappy circumstance that the domain which he is attempting to define may be in many respects *terra incognita.*

Let us consider an ability such as "critical thinking." Is it possible to define a domain of critical thinking—to conceive of an exhaustive listing of all the situations in which there might be behavioral manifestations of an ability that is properly termed critical thinking? Again, is it possible to define a universe consisting of all the responses which might properly be designated manifestations of "introversion," or of "emotional stability," or of "ascendancy?" The very asking of these questions calls to mind the many assumptions, value judgments, problems of definition and other difficulties that stand in the way. These difficulties seemed so formidable to Goodenough as to cause her to conclude that in dealing with behavioral matters, we are, as a rule, unable to set precise boundaries for the forms of behavior to which trait names are applied. In her words, "we cannot say, 'Up to this exact point the universe which we call *intelligence* runs, but no further.'"

The difficulty of defining a universe in the realm of educational achievement is inextricably bound up with the difficulty of defining and specifying objectives. Cureton (1951) has furnished an analysis of an area of educational achievement, indicating that an adequate definition of the "universe" in this case must specify at least the following dimensions:

a. the acts or operations of which it is composed
b. the materials acted upon
c. the situations in which the acts or operations properly take place
d. the results or products of these acts or operations
e. the particular aspects of *a* through *d* which are relevant to the purposes at hand

Similar analyses of the universe (or domain or criterion behavior) with which we are concerned in the case of personality or interest inventories, or attitude questionnaires, reveal the complicated, often multidimensional character of these universes. Pursuit of this topic leads quickly into the realm of construct validity, and the types of issues so well set forth in the Cronbach-Meehl analysis of this latter concept (Cronbach & Meehl, 1955).

More often than not we find it desirable to sample from some universe other than the universe in which we are genuinely concerned, either because the universe of concern is unavailable or because in some other respects it is unsuitable as the source of test exercises. In the case of personality inventories, for example, we substitute a universe of responses to verbal situations for the universe of behaviors in which we are really interested. Some even seek to escape the difficulties of defining a universe by asserting that a test is a valid measure of only that hypothetical universe of which its items do constitute a representative sample. This procedure may be logically satisfying, but it still remains to be demonstrated that such a hypothetical universe corresponds to the area or domain in which the test user is genuinely interested.

Assumption 2.   A Sample Can Be Drawn from the Universe in Some Purposive, Meaningful Fashion. Let us assume that, difficult as it may be, we have succeeded in identifying and defining a universe adequately, for practical purposes. How are we to draw a sample from this universe in such a way that we may with confidence generalize from it to the universe? The success with which this is done is the measure of content validity.

Very, very rarely will the test constitute a *random* sample of the universe, In the first place, it is the exceptional test-building situation in which there exists a complete listing of all possible test items—i.e. a catalog of the universe—from which such a sample might be drawn. In the second place, considerations of efficiency of measurement would often argue against a *random* sample as optimum. For example, in constructing a spelling test, there might be agreement on a certain list of words as constituting the universe; but the most reliable test for a given amount of testing time will almost certainly not be made up of a random selection of the words, but of a sample chosen in part on the basis of their respective difficulties.

The goal of sampling for test-making purposes is usually defined as the production of a sample which is "representative"—a goal which is sometimes at odds with other purposes of the test-maker. In achievement testing, for example, items which measure objectives stated in a course of study, but not reflected in the instructional program, are likely to be poor from the standpoint of discrimination; but if they are eliminated on this count, it is at the expense of "representativeness" of the test as a measure of the objectives.

A "representative" sample is one that *re-presents* the universe—that is, one that duplicates or reproduces the essential characteristics of the universe, in their proper proportion and balance. Presumably these essential characteristics and their interrelationships have been specified in the definition of the universe. How now to insure that the test reproduces them? At a superficial level, it is easy to stipulate that the proportionate emphasis given various content sub-areas be similar in the test to what it is in the universe—that the proportion of test questions devoted to each sub-area be in accordance with the sub-area's importance, however this be judged. If we recall, however, the thought advanced earlier, that content validity is a property of the examinee's responses, as well as of the test content, then it is clear that a more fundamental kind of representativeness must be sought. In essence, it would appear that what we are really after is that the variance in the test scores be attributable to the same sources, and in the same proportion, as the variance in the criterion, or universe, behavior. This implies a far more systematic effort than is usually made to specify the sources of variance in the criterion, and their relative importance.

Assumption 3.   The Sample and the Sampling Process Can Be Defined with Sufficient Precision to Enable the User to Judge how Adequately the Sample Performance Typifies Performance on the Universe. The function of all validity information is to permit the test user to estimate with what confidence he may make various kinds of interpretations of the test scores. The APA Test Standards prescribe that the test-maker define the universe which he has undertaken to measure, and the nature of his sample and sampling process, assuming that possession of such information will enable the test user prudently to estimate the dependability of various kinds of inferences. In the absence of such information, the test user is indeed at something of a loss in his efforts to appraise the extent to which he may safely generalize from the test data, except perhaps in the case of tests of certain rather simple functions where the intended universe and the nature of sample are virtually self-evident. Even having such information, however, the test user may not have all the information he needs, for the universe with which he is concerned is likely to differ, in some particulars at least, from the test-maker's universe, which difference may or may not limit the confidence to be reposed in the inferences drawn.

Because the sample which constitutes the test is so far removed from being a random sample, all ordinary notions of sampling errors are quite inappropriate as bases for estimating the confidence that may be reposed in the inferences. Because of the impossibility of expressing content validity in quantitative terms, or of expressing the representativeness of a sample in quantitative terms, the test user, regardless of the quality and completeness of information provided by the test-maker, will almost surely have to be satisfied with rather crude answers to his question, "How confidently can I make this, that, or the other inference from these test data?"

One final word about content validity is in order. Content validity, like all other kinds of validity, is specific to the purpose for which, and the group with which, a test is used. Because the content of a test appears to be something fixed and constant, there is more of a temptation to think of content validity as an invariant property of a test than is true of the criterion-oriented predictive and concurrent validity. A moment's reflection makes clear that the universe with which the test user is concerned will ordinarily not be identical with the universe which the test constructor had in mind. Evidences of content validity for a particular group do not necessarily apply to other groups, for the processes by which one group responds to a set of questions may differ from those by which another group responds to the same questions. Thus, we are forced again to the conclusion that there can be no such thing, in the great majority of cases, as *the* content validity of a test but only a content validity for a particular purpose and a particular group of subjects.

Taylor and Russell point out that in many selection decisions the usefulness of tests with validity coefficients of less than .50 may be considerably greater than one might infer from Kelly's alienation coefficient ($\sqrt{1-r^2}$) or Hull's measure of efficiency $(1 - \sqrt{1-r^2})$.

Some previous study on methods of expressing validity would be helpful in order to fully comprehend this article. Sufficient background can be obtained from the validity section of many basic texts. However, even without the background, readers can understand the main ideas of this article.

Given the present Zeitgeist against the usefulness of tests in selection decisions, this classic article is worth careful study.

The Relationship of Validity Coefficients to the Practical Effectiveness of Tests in Selection: Discussion and Tables

H. C. TAYLOR
J. T. RUSSELL

It has often been pointed out that the magnitude of the correlation coefficient as such is not an adequate representation of the magnitude of the relationship between the two variables which are under consideration. A number of different statistical constants have been proposed by various persons, as giving a more satisfactory representation of the real magnitude of a relationship between two variables. All of these constants are relatively simple functions of the Pearson r.

These include a class of functions of r which bear directly upon an evaluation of the extent to which one variable may be predicted from the other when the correlation coefficient is of a given magnitude. These functions of r include Kelly's alienation coefficient, k, which is $\sqrt{1-r^2}$, and such functions of k as Hull's measure of efficiency, E, which is $1-k$, and Odell's g, which is $k/\sqrt{2}$.

All of these ways of evaluating the correlation coefficient have one fundamental characteristic in common, as might be expected from the fact that they are all closely related to the alienation coefficient. That is, that as

From *Journal of Applied Psychology*, 1939, 23: 565–578. Copyright 1939 by the *American Psychological Association*. Reprinted by permission.

the size of the correlation coefficient increases the extent to which one variable can be predicted from the other increases more and more rapidly. For example, an *r* of .50 is usually considered to be only 13% as good as an *r* of 1.00. It is considered that an *r* of .87 is only half as good as an *r* of 1.00.

The wide-spread acceptance of such measures as the correct way of evaluating correlation coefficients has brought about a considerable pessimism with regard to the validity coefficients which are ordinarily obtainable when tests are tried out in the employment office of a business or industry or in an educational institution. These validity coefficients may range from .20 to .50, although they may occasionally be somewhat higher. It is disconcerting to apply the customary procedures in evaluating these coefficients and discover that the so-called "efficiency" of these tests is only 2% to 13%.

It is the purpose of this paper to point out under the conditions found when tests are used for selection of employees or students, correlation coefficients within the range of .20 to .50 may represent considerably more than 2% to 13% of the effectiveness of an *r* of unity.

Chart 1 illustrates a typical scatter diagram, or normal correlation surface, with test scores represented along the base line and criterion scores along the ordinate. This chart is intended to illustrate the results of a validity check-up of a test in an educational or industrial situation. All persons who are above line SS' (area A + area D) are those who are considered to be satisfactory, while all those below that line (area B + area C) are considered unsatisfactory.

We have divided the persons into those who are below a selected critical test score, represented by the line TT', and those who are above that critical score. The former would obviously be those who would be rejected in terms of their test scores, if the test were used for selective purposes, and the latter those who would be selected if the tests were so used.

The position of line TT', it will be clear, will vary with the employment situation. Under some conditions it might conceivably be necessary to accept practically every applicant who came to the employment office regardless of his qualifications. In such a situation, of course, a test is of no use, no matter what its validity. In other situations, however, it may be possible to select only the most promising tenth, third, or half of those who apply. Line TT', then, represents the *selection ratio*.

It will be noted that as soon as one begins to select persons who are above the critical score, represented by the line TT', one begins to assemble a new employee group which distributes like that portion of the present group which is above line TT', that is, within the area (A + B) on Chart 1. The common assumption is being made, of course, that the applicant group and the present employee group are similarly constituted. Whereas in the original employee group, before using tests for selection, the proportion of

Chart I

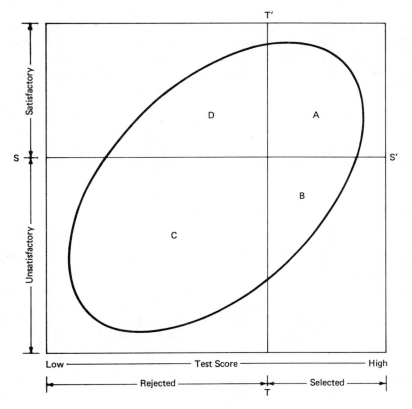

satisfactory employees was represented by $\dfrac{A+D}{A+B+C+D}$; there is now being developed an employee group in which the proportion of satisfactory employees will approach $\dfrac{A}{A+B}$.

It will be clear that if line SS′ and line TT′ are specified, the usefulness of a test may be represented in terms of the ratio, $\dfrac{A}{A+B}$. Furthermore, with line SS′ and line TT′ specified, the usefulness of tests with various validity coefficients can be compared in terms of the respective ratios, $\dfrac{A}{A+B}$, which will be obtained if the tests are used in selection.

Let us now take a typical example. Let us suppose that we consider half of our present employee group to be satisfactory. In other words, area (A+D) is 50% of the total area, and line SS′ is thus placed at the mean or

55

median of the criterion distribtuion. We have, let us say, a test with a validity coefficient of .50 and the employment situation is such that we need to take only the best 30% of those who apply for employment. In other words, line TT' is so set that (A + B) will contain 30% of the total area. Under these circumstances, 74% of those chosen will be successful and only 26% unsuccessful. Now, let us compare that figure with what would be obtained under the same circumstances if the validity coefficient were zero, and if the validity coefficient were unity. If the validity coefficient were zero, we would obviously get the same proportions of unsuccessful and successful employees as if we were not using the test at all. In other words, half of those chosen would be successful. If the coefficient were unity, under these circumstances, *all* of those selected would be successful. That is, the lowest possible validity would result in the selection of employees 50% of whom will be successful, and the best possible validity would result in the selection of employees 100% of whom will be successful. When the validity of the test is .50, the use of the test results in the selection of employees 74% of whom will be successful. The practical usefulness of a test which increases the proportion of successful employees to this extent does not seem to be adequately expressed by the efficiency figure of 13% which is usually associated with a test of that validity. If we can choose the best one out of ten, a validity coefficient of .50 increases the proportion of successful employees to .84.

Chart 2   Predictive Value of D for Various Selection Ratios When 50 Percent of the Employee Group Are Considered to be Successful

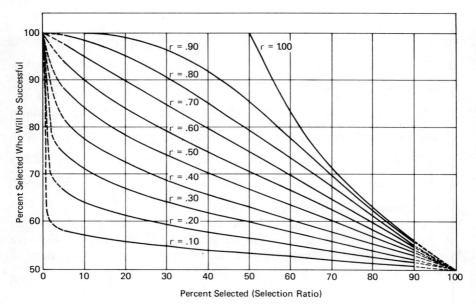

In general, with a given proportion of the present group being considered successful and with a given validity coefficient, the usefulness of the test with that validity increases as one is in a position to accept a smaller and smaller proportion of the candidates for employment.

Chart 2 shows the relationships between r and the selection ratio when one considers 50% of the present employee group to be successful. Selection ratios are plotted along the base line, and the per cents of employees chosen by the test who will be successful are plotted along the ordinate. Under these circumstances it will be clear that a new group cannot possibly be chosen which will contain less than 50% of successful people, even if we use a selection device of no validity at all. Hence, all curves start from 50% on the ordinate.

Note that with regard to this entire family of curves, the smaller the selection ratio, the larger is the percent of persons who will be successful among those selected by means of the test. Note also that in the case of correlations below about .70 these curves are positively accelerated toward the left. That is, under the conditions specified in this chart, the usefulness of a test with a validity less than .70 increases more and more rapidly as the selection ratio becomes smaller.

Not only does the usefulness of tests of such validity increase rapidly as the selection ratio is decreased, but their relative usefulness is still further emphasized if one considers what could be accomplished by a test if the validity coefficient were unity. This is shown in the topmost curve on the chart. Note that the per cent of persons chosen who will be successful increases as one cuts down the selection ratio until that point is reached where one is selecting 50% of the applicant group. At this point all of those selected will be successful and, naturally, no further gains can be made as one cuts the selection ratio further. The usefulness of the small correlations, on the other hand, continues to increase to the left of this point. Note that a validity coefficient of .50 is more useful when one is selecting only 20% of the applicant group than a correlation of unity would be if one were selecting 65% of the applicants.

It is our belief that a useful method of evaluating a validity coefficient in the employment situation is to ask oneself the question: If a given per cent of the present employee group is considered successful and if a given proportion of the applicant group is to be selected, what proportion will be successful in the new group selected by means of the test? How does this compare with the proportion of successful persons who could be chosen under equivalent circumstances with a selective device of no validity, and with a selective device of perfect validity?

We do not wish to imply that these relationships have been entirely unrecognized. The importance of the selection ratio as affecting the real usefulness of a validity coefficient was pointed out, for example, by Hull in a footnote (p. 276) in his book, *Aptitude Testing.*[1] Thurstone discusses the matter at some length in his book, *The Reliability and Validity of Tests,*[2] and the relationships can be worked out from *Computing Diagrams for the Tetrachoric Correlation Coefficient.*[3]

We believe, however, that the emphasis in current literature upon the *k* and *E* methods of interpreting correlation coefficients has led to some unwarranted pessimism on the part of many persons concerning the practical usefulness in an employment situation of validity coefficients in the range of those usually obtained. We believe that it may be of value to point out the very considerable improvement in selection efficiency which may be obtained with small correlation coefficients.

TABLES

Making use of Pearson's "Tables for Finding the Volumes of the Normal Bivariate Surface,"[4] we have prepared a set of tables of the relationships among:

1. *Proportion of Employees Considered Satisfactory*, i.e., the proportion of the group now employed (not chosen by means of the test) who are considered satisfactory according to present standards (Area $\dfrac{A+D}{A+B+C+D}$, Chart 1).
2. *Selection Ratio*, i.e., the proportion of applicants to be selected by means of the test.
3. *r*, the validity of the test.
4. *Proportion Satisfactory among Those Selected*, i.e., the proportion of applicants to be selected by means of the test who are expected to be satisfactory according to present standards $\dfrac{A}{A+B}$, Chart 1).

There are eleven tables, corresponding to eleven values of the *Proportion of Employees Considered Satisfactory*, these values being .05, .10, .20, .30, .40, .50, .60, .70, .80, .90, and .95.

The columns of each table correspond to eleven values of the *Selection Ratio*: .05, .10, .20, .30, .40, .50, .60, .70, .80, .90, and .95.

The rows of each table correspond to values of *r* from .00 to 1.00 by intervals of .05.

The argument of these tables is the *Proportion Satisfactory among Those Selected*.

For example, if .60 or 60% of the present employees are considered satisfactory, and if the best .30 of applicants are to be chosen by means of a test with a validity of .70, then .91, or 91%, of those selected can be expected to be satisfactory. Note that with test validities of zero and unity, the proportions satisfactory among those selected would be .60 and 1.00 respectively.

Tables of the Proportion Who Will be Satisfactory among Those Selected, for Given Values of the Proportion of Present Employees Considered Satisfactory, the Selection Ratio, and *r*.

Proportion of Employees Considered Satisfactory = .05
Selection Ratio

r	.05	.10	.20	.30	.40	.50	.60	.70	.80	.90	.95
.00	.05	.05	.05	.05	.05	.05	.05	.05	.05	.05	.05
.05	.06	.06	.06	.06	.06	.05	.05	.05	.05	.05	.05
.10	.07	.07	.07	.06	.06	.06	.06	.05	.05	.05	.05
.15	.09	.08	.07	.07	.07	.06	.06	.06	.05	.05	.05
.20	.11	.09	.08	.08	.07	.07	.06	.06	.06	.05	.05
.25	.12	.11	.09	.08	.08	.07	.07	.06	.06	.05	.05
.30	.14	.12	.10	.09	.08	.07	.07	.06	.06	.05	.05
.35	.17	.14	.11	.10	.09	.08	.07	.06	.06	.05	.05
.40	.19	.16	.12	.10	.09	.08	.07	.07	.06	.05	.05
.45	.22	.17	.13	.11	.10	.08	.08	.07	.06	.06	.05
.50	.24	.19	.15	.12	.10	.09	.08	.07	.06	.06	.05
.55	.28	.22	.16	.13	.11	.09	.08	.07	.06	.06	.05
.60	.31	.24	.17	.13	.11	.09	.08	.07	.06	.06	.05
.65	.35	.26	.18	.14	.11	.10	.08	.07	.06	.06	.05
.70	.39	.29	.20	.15	.12	.10	.08	.07	.06	.06	.05
.75	.44	.32	.21	.15	.12	.10	.08	.07	.06	.06	.05
.80	.50	.35	.22	.16	.12	.10	.08	.07	.06	.06	.05
.85	.56	.39	.23	.16	.12	.10	.08	.07	.06	.06	.05
.90	.64	.43	.24	.17	.13	.10	.08	.07	.06	.06	.05
.95	.73	.47	.25	.17	.13	.10	.08	.07	.06	.06	.05
1.00	1.00	.50	.25	.17	.13	.10	.08	.07	.06	.06	.05

Proportion of Employees Considered Satisfactory = .10
Selection Ratio

r	.05	.10	.20	.30	.40	.50	.60	.70	.80	.90	.95
.00	.10	.10	.10	.10	.10	.10	.10	.10	.10	.10	.10
.05	.12	.12	.11	.11	.11	.11	.11	.10	.10	.10	.10
.10	.14	.13	.13	.12	.12	.11	.11	.11	.11	.10	.10
.15	.16	.15	.14	.13	.13	.12	.12	.11	.11	.10	.10
.20	.19	.17	.15	.14	.14	.13	.12	.12	.11	.11	.10
.25	.22	.19	.17	.16	.14	.13	.13	.12	.11	.11	.10
.30	.25	.22	.19	.17	.15	.14	.13	.12	.12	.11	.10
.35	.28	.24	.20	.18	.16	.15	.14	.13	.12	.11	.10
.40	.31	.27	.22	.19	.17	.16	.14	.13	.12	.11	.10
.45	.35	.29	.24	.20	.18	.16	.15	.13	.12	.11	.10
.50	.39	.32	.26	.22	.19	.17	.15	.13	.12	.11	.11
.55	.43	.36	.28	.23	.20	.17	.15	.14	.12	.11	.11
.60	.48	.39	.30	.25	.21	.18	.16	.14	.12	.11	.11
.65	.53	.43	.32	.26	.22	.18	.16	.14	.12	.11	.11
.70	.58	.47	.35	.27	.22	.19	.16	.14	.12	.11	.11
.75	.64	.51	.37	.29	.23	.19	.16	.14	.12	.11	.11
.80	.71	.56	.40	.30	.24	.20	.17	.14	.12	.11	.11
.85	.78	.62	.43	.31	.25	.20	.17	.14	.12	.11	.11
.90	.86	.69	.46	.33	.25	.20	.17	.14	.12	.11	.11
.95	.95	.78	.49	.33	.25	.20	.17	.14	.12	.11	.11
1.00	1.00	1.00	.50	.33	.25	.20	.17	.14	.13	.11	.11

59

Proportion of Employees Considered Satisfactory = .20
Selection Ratio

r	.05	.10	.20	.30	.40	.50	.60	.70	.80	.90	.95
.00	.20	.20	.20	.20	.20	.20	.20	.20	.20	.20	.20
.05	.23	.23	.22	.22	.21	.21	.21	.21	.20	.20	.20
.10	.26	.25	.24	.23	.23	.22	.22	.21	.21	.21	.20
.15	.30	.28	.26	.25	.24	.23	.23	.22	.21	.21	.20
.20	.33	.31	.28	.27	.26	.25	.24	.23	.22	.21	.21
.25	.37	.34	.31	.29	.27	.26	.24	.23	.22	.21	.21
.30	.41	.37	.33	.30	.28	.27	.25	.24	.23	.21	.21
.35	.45	.41	.36	.32	.30	.28	.26	.24	.23	.22	.21
.40	.49	.44	.38	.34	.31	.29	.27	.25	.23	.22	.21
.45	.54	.48	.41	.36	.33	.30	.28	.26	.24	.22	.21
.50	.59	.52	.44	.38	.35	.31	.29	.26	.24	.22	.21
.55	.63	.56	.47	.41	.36	.32	.29	.27	.24	.22	.21
.60	.68	.60	.50	.43	.38	.34	.30	.27	.24	.22	.21
.65	.73	.64	.53	.45	.39	.35	.31	.27	.25	.22	.21
.70	.79	.69	.56	.48	.41	.36	.31	.28	.25	.22	.21
.75	.84	.74	.60	.50	.43	.37	.32	.28	.25	.22	.21
.80	.89	.79	.64	.53	.45	.38	.33	.28	.25	.22	.21
.85	.94	.85	.69	.56	.47	.39	.33	.28	.25	.22	.21
.90	.98	.91	.75	.60	.48	.40	.33	.29	.25	.22	.21
.95	1.00	.97	.82	.64	.50	.40	.33	.29	.25	.22	.21
1.00	1.00	1.00	1.00	.67	.50	.40	.33	.29	.25	.22	.21

Proportion of Employees Considered Satisfactory = .30
Selection Ratio

r	.05	.10	.20	.30	.40	.50	.60	.70	.80	.90	.95
.00	.30	.30	.30	.30	.30	.30	.30	.30	.30	.30	.30
.05	.34	.33	.33	.32	.32	.31	.31	.31	.31	.30	.30
.10	.38	.36	.35	.34	.33	.33	.32	.32	.31	.31	.30
.15	.42	.40	.38	.36	.35	.34	.33	.33	.32	.31	.31
.20	.46	.43	.40	.38	.37	.36	.34	.33	.32	.31	.31
.25	.50	.47	.43	.41	.39	.37	.36	.34	.33	.32	.31
.30	.54	.50	.46	.43	.40	.38	.37	.35	.33	.32	.31
.35	.58	.54	.49	.45	.42	.40	.38	.36	.34	.32	.31
.40	.63	.58	.51	.47	.44	.41	.39	.37	.34	.32	.31
.45	.67	.61	.55	.50	.46	.43	.40	.37	.35	.32	.31
.50	.72	.65	.58	.52	.48	.44	.41	.38	.35	.33	.31
.55	.76	.69	.61	.55	.50	.46	.42	.39	.36	.33	.31
.60	.81	.74	.64	.58	.52	.47	.43	.40	.36	.33	.31
.65	.85	.78	.68	.60	.54	.49	.44	.40	.37	.33	.32
.70	.89	.82	.72	.63	.57	.51	.46	.41	.37	.33	.32
.75	.93	.86	.76	.67	.59	.52	.47	.42	.37	.33	.32
.80	.96	.90	.80	.70	.62	.54	.48	.42	.37	.33	.32
.85	.99	.94	.85	.74	.65	.56	.49	.43	.37	.33	.32
.90	1.00	.98	.90	.79	.68	.58	.49	.43	.37	.33	.32
.95	1.00	1.00	.96	.85	.72	.60	.50	.43	.37	.33	.32
1.00	1.00	1.00	1.00	1.00	.75	.60	.50	.43	.38	.33	.32

Proportion of Employees Considered Satisfactory = .40
Selection Ratio

r	.05	.10	.20	.30	.40	.50	.60	.70	.80	.90	.95
.00	.40	.40	.40	.40	.40	.40	.40	.40	.40	.40	.40
.05	.44	.43	.43	.42	.42	.42	.41	.41	.41	.40	.40
.10	.48	.47	.46	.45	.44	.43	.42	.42	.41	.41	.40
.15	.52	.50	.48	.47	.46	.45	.44	.43	.42	.41	.41
.20	.57	.54	.51	.49	.48	.46	.45	.44	.43	.41	.41
.25	.61	.58	.54	.51	.49	.48	.46	.45	.43	.42	.41
.30	.65	.61	.57	.54	.51	.49	.47	.46	.44	.42	.41
.35	.69	.65	.60	.56	.53	.51	.49	.47	.45	.42	.41
.40	.73	.69	.63	.59	.56	.53	.50	.48	.45	.43	.41
.45	.77	.72	.66	.61	.58	.54	.51	.49	.46	.43	.42
.50	.81	.76	.69	.64	.60	.56	.53	.49	.46	.43	.42
.55	.85	.79	.72	.67	.62	.58	.54	.50	.47	.44	.42
.60	.89	.83	.75	.69	.64	.60	.55	.51	.48	.44	.42
.65	.92	.87	.79	.72	.67	.62	.57	.52	.48	.44	.42
.70	.95	.90	.82	.76	.69	.64	.58	.53	.49	.44	.42
.75	.97	.93	.86	.79	.72	.66	.60	.54	.49	.44	.42
.80	.99	.96	.89	.82	.75	.68	.61	.55	.49	.44	.42
.85	1.00	.98	.93	.86	.79	.71	.63	.56	.50	.44	.42
.90	1.00	1.00	.97	.91	.82	.74	.65	.57	.50	.44	.42
.95	1.00	1.00	.99	.96	.87	.77	.66	.57	.50	.44	.42
1.00	1.00	1.00	1.00	1.00	1.00	.80	.67	.57	.50	.44	.42

Proportion of Employees Considered Satisfactory = .50
Selection Ratio

r	.05	.10	.20	.30	.40	.50	.60	.70	.80	.90	.95
.00	.50	.50	.50	.50	.50	.50	.50	.50	.50	.50	.50
.05	.54	.54	.53	.52	.52	.52	.51	.51	.51	.50	.50
.10	.58	.57	.56	.55	.54	.53	.53	.52	.51	.51	.50
.15	.63	.61	.58	.57	.56	.55	.54	.53	.52	.51	.51
.20	.67	.64	.61	.59	.58	.56	.55	.54	.53	.52	.51
.25	.70	.67	.64	.62	.60	.58	.56	.55	.54	.52	.51
.30	.74	.71	.67	.64	.62	.60	.58	.56	.54	.52	.51
.35	.78	.74	.70	.66	.64	.61	.59	.57	.55	.53	.51
.40	.82	.78	.73	.69	.66	.63	.61	.58	.56	.53	.52
.45	.85	.81	.75	.71	.68	.65	.62	.59	.56	.53	.52
.50	.88	.84	.78	.74	.70	.67	.63	.60	.57	.54	.52
.55	.91	.87	.81	.76	.72	.69	.65	.61	.58	.54	.52
.60	.94	.90	.84	.79	.75	.70	.66	.62	.59	.54	.52
.65	.96	.92	.87	.82	.77	.73	.68	.64	.59	.55	.53
.70	.98	.95	.90	.85	.80	.75	.70	.65	.60	.55	.53
.75	.99	.97	.92	.87	.82	.77	.72	.66	.61	.55	.53
.80	1.00	.99	.95	.90	.85	.80	.73	.67	.61	.55	.53
.85	1.00	.99	.97	.94	.88	.82	.76	.69	.62	.55	.53
.90	1.00	1.00	.99	.97	.92	.86	.78	.70	.62	.56	.53
.95	1.00	1.00	1.00	.99	.96	.90	.81	.71	.63	.56	.53
1.00	1.00	1.00	1.00	1.00	1.00	1.00	.83	.71	.63	.56	.53

Proportion of Employees Considered Satisfactory = .60
Selection Ratio

r	.05	.10	.20	.30	.40	.50	.60	.70	.80	.90	.95
.00	.60	.60	.60	.60	.60	.60	.60	.60	.60	.60	.60
.05	.64	.63	.63	.62	.62	.62	.61	.61	.61	.60	.60
.10	.68	.67	.65	.64	.64	.63	.63	.62	.61	.61	.60
.15	.71	.70	.68	.67	.66	.65	.64	.63	.62	.61	.61
.20	.75	.73	.71	.69	.67	.66	.65	.64	.63	.62	.61
.25	.78	.76	.73	.71	.69	.68	.66	.65	.63	.62	.61
.30	.82	.79	.76	.73	.71	.69	.68	.66	.64	.62	.61
.35	.85	.82	.78	.75	.73	.71	.69	.67	.65	.63	.62
.40	.88	.85	.81	.78	.75	.73	.70	.68	.66	.63	.62
.45	.90	.87	.83	.80	.77	.74	.72	.69	.66	.64	.62
.50	.93	.90	.86	.82	.79	.76	.73	.70	.67	.64	.62
.55	.95	.92	.88	.84	.81	.78	.75	.71	.68	.64	.62
.60	.96	.94	.90	.87	.83	.80	.76	.73	.69	.65	.63
.65	.98	.96	.92	.89	.85	.82	.78	.74	.70	.65	.63
.70	.99	.97	.94	.91	.87	.84	.80	.75	.71	.66	.63
.75	.99	.99	.96	.93	.90	.86	.81	.77	.71	.66	.63
.80	1.00	.99	.98	.95	.92	.88	.83	.78	.72	.66	.63
.85	1.00	1.00	.99	.97	.95	.91	.86	.80	.73	.66	.63
.90	1.00	1.00	1.00	.99	.97	.94	.88	.82	.74	.67	.63
.95	1.00	1.00	1.00	1.00	.99	.97	.92	.84	.75	.67	.63
1.00	1.00	1.00	1.00	1.00	1.00	1.00	1.00	.86	.75	.67	.63

Proportion of Employees Considered Satisfactory = .70
Selection Ratio

r	.05	.10	.20	.30	.40	.50	.60	.70	.80	.90	.95
.00	.70	.70	.70	.70	.70	.70	.70	.70	.70	.70	.70
.05	.73	.73	.72	.72	.72	.71	.71	.71	.71	.70	.70
.10	.77	.76	.75	.74	.73	.73	.72	.72	.71	.71	.70
.15	.80	.79	.77	.76	.75	.74	.73	.73	.72	.71	.71
.20	.83	.81	.79	.78	.77	.76	.75	.74	.73	.71	.71
.25	.86	.84	.81	.80	.78	.77	.76	.75	.73	.72	.71
.30	.88	.86	.84	.82	.80	.78	.77	.75	.74	.72	.71
.35	.91	.89	.86	.83	.82	.80	.78	.76	.75	.73	.71
.40	.93	.91	.88	.85	.83	.81	.79	.77	.75	.73	.72
.45	.94	.93	.90	.87	.85	.83	.81	.78	.76	.73	.72
.50	.96	.94	.91	.89	.87	.84	.82	.80	.77	.74	.72
.55	.97	.96	.93	.91	.88	.86	.83	.81	.78	.74	.72
.60	.98	.97	.95	.92	.90	.87	.85	.82	.79	.75	.73
.65	.99	.98	.96	.94	.92	.89	.86	.83	.80	.75	.73
.70	1.00	.99	.97	.96	.93	.91	.88	.84	.80	.76	.73
.75	1.00	1.00	.98	.97	.95	.92	.89	.86	.81	.76	.73
.80	1.00	1.00	.99	.98	.97	.94	.91	.87	.82	.77	.73
.85	1.00	1.00	1.00	.99	.98	.96	.93	.89	.84	.77	.74
.90	1.00	1.00	1.00	1.00	.99	.98	.95	.91	.85	.78	.74
.95	1.00	1.00	1.00	1.00	1.00	.99	.98	.94	.86	.78	.74
1.00	1.00	1.00	1.00	1.00	1.00	1.00	1.00	1.00	.88	.78	.74

Proportion of Employees Considered Satisfactory = .80
Selection Ratio

r	.05	.10	.20	.30	.40	.50	.60	.70	.80	.90	.95
.00	.80	.80	.80	.80	.80	.80	.80	.80	.80	.80	.80
.05	.83	.82	.82	.82	.81	.81	.81	.81	.81	.80	.80
.10	.85	.85	.84	.83	.83	.82	.82	.81	.81	.81	.80
.15	.88	.87	.86	.85	.84	.83	.83	.82	.82	.81	.81
.20	.90	.89	.87	.86	.85	.84	.84	.83	.82	.81	.81
.25	.92	.91	.89	.88	.87	.86	.85	.84	.83	.82	.81
.30	.94	.92	.90	.89	.88	.87	.86	.84	.83	.82	.81
.35	.95	.94	.92	.90	.89	.89	.87	.85	.84	.82	.81
.40	.96	.95	.93	.92	.90	.89	.88	.86	.85	.83	.82
.45	.97	.96	.95	.93	.92	.90	.89	.87	.85	.83	.82
.50	.98	.97	.96	.94	.93	.91	.90	.88	.86	.84	.82
.55	.99	.98	.97	.95	.94	.92	.91	.89	.87	.84	.82
.60	.99	.99	.98	.96	.95	.94	.92	.90	.87	.84	.83
.65	1.00	.99	.98	.97	.96	.95	.93	.91	.88	.85	.83
.70	1.00	1.00	.99	.98	.97	.96	.94	.92	.89	.85	.83
.75	1.00	1.00	1.00	.99	.98	.97	.95	.93	.90	.86	.83
.80	1.00	1.00	1.00	1.00	.99	.98	.96	.94	.91	.87	.84
.85	1.00	1.00	1.00	1.00	1.00	.99	.98	.96	.92	.87	.84
.90	1.00	1.00	1.00	1.00	1.00	1.00	.99	.97	.94	.88	.84
.95	1.00	1.00	1.00	1.00	1.00	1.00	1.00	.99	.96	.89	.84
1.00	1.00	1.00	1.00	1.00	1.00	1.00	1.00	1.00	1.00	.89	.84

Proportion of Employees Considered Satisfactory = .90
Selection Ratio

r	.05	.10	.20	.30	.40	.50	.60	.70	.80	.90	.95
.00	.90	.90	.90	.90	.90	.90	.90	.90	.90	.90	.90
.05	.92	.91	.91	.91	.91	.91	.91	.90	.90	.90	.90
.10	.93	.93	.92	.92	.92	.91	.91	.91	.91	.90	.90
.15	.95	.94	.93	.93	.92	.92	.92	.91	.91	.91	.90
.20	.96	.95	.94	.94	.93	.93	.92	.92	.91	.91	.90
.25	.97	.96	.95	.95	.94	.93	.93	.92	.92	.91	.91
.30	.98	.97	.96	.95	.95	.94	.94	.93	.92	.91	.91
.35	.98	.98	.97	.96	.95	.95	.94	.93	.93	.92	.91
.40	.99	.98	.98	.97	.96	.95	.95	.94	.93	.92	.91
.45	.99	.99	.98	.98	.97	.96	.95	.94	.93	.92	.91
.50	1.00	.99	.99	.98	.97	.97	.96	.95	.94	.92	.92
.55	1.00	1.00	.99	.99	.98	.97	.97	.96	.94	.93	.92
.60	1.00	1.00	.99	.99	.99	.98	.97	.96	.95	.93	.92
.65	1.00	1.00	1.00	.99	.99	.98	.98	.97	.96	.94	.92
.70	1.00	1.00	1.00	1.00	.99	.99	.98	.97	.96	.94	.93
.75	1.00	1.00	1.00	1.00	1.00	.99	.99	.98	.97	.95	.93
.80	1.00	1.00	1.00	1.00	1.00	1.00	.99	.99	.97	.95	.93
.85	1.00	1.00	1.00	1.00	1.00	1.00	1.00	.99	.98	.96	.94
.90	1.00	1.00	1.00	1.00	1.00	1.00	1.00	1.00	.99	.97	.94
.95	1.00	1.00	1.00	1.00	1.00	1.00	1.00	1.00	1.00	.98	.94
1.00	1.00	1.00	1.00	1.00	1.00	1.00	1.00	1.00	1.00	1.00	.95

Proportion of Employees Considered Satisfactory = .95
Selection Ratio

r	.05	.10	.20	.30	.40	.50	.60	.70	.80	.90	.95
.00	.95	.95	.95·	.95	.95	.95	.95	.95	.95	.95	.95
.05	.96	.96	.96	.96	.95	.95	.95	.95	.95	.95	.95
.10	.97	.97	.96	.96	.96	.96	.96	.96	.95	.95	.95
.15	.98	.97	.97	.97	.96	.96	.96	.96	.96	.95	.95
.20	.98	.98	.97	.97	.97	.97	.96	.96	.96	.95	.95
.25	.99	.98	.98	.98	.97	.97	.97	.96	.96	.96	.95
.30	.99	.99	.98	.98	.98	.97	.97	.97	.96	.96	.95
.35	.99	.99	.99	.98	.98	.98	.97	.97	.97	.96	.96
.40	1.00	.99	.99	.99	.98	.98	.98	.97	97	.96	.96
.45	1.00	1.00	.99	.99	.99	.98	.98	.98	.97	.96	.96
.50	1.00	1.00	1.00	.99	.99	.99	.98	.98	.97	.97	.96
.55	1.00	1.00	1.00	1.00	.99	.99	.99	.98	.98	.97	.96
.60	1.00	1.00	1.00	1.00	1.00	.99	99	99	.98	.97	.96
.65	1.00	1.00	1.00	1.00	1.00	1.00	.99	.99	.98	.97	.97
.70	1.00	1.00	1.00	1.00	1.00	1.00	1.00	.99	.99	.98	.97
.75	1.00	1.00	1.00	1.00	1.00	1.00	1.00	.99	.99	.98	.97
.80	1.00	1.00	1.00	1.00	1.00	1.00	1.00	1.00	.99	.98	.97
.85	1.00	1.00	1.00	1.00	1.00	1.00	1.00	1.00	1.00	.99	.98
.90	1.00	1.00	1.00	1.00	1.00	1.00	1.00	1.00	1.00	.99	.98
.95	1.00	1.00	1.00	1.00	1.00	1.00	1.00	1.00	1.00	1.00	.99
1.00	1.00	1.00	1.00	1.00	1.00	1.00	1.00	1.00	1.00	1.00	1.00

NOTES

[1] Clark L. Hull. Aptitude Testing. Yonkers-on-Hudson, N.Y.: World Book Co., 1928.

[2] L. L. Thurstone. The Reliability and Validity of Tests. Ann Arbor, Mich.: Edwards Brothers, Inc., 1931. Pp. 57–61.

[3] L. Chesire, M. Saffir, and L. L. Thurstone. Computing Diagrams for the Tetrachoric Correlation Coefficient. Chicago: The University of Chicago Book Store. 1933.

[4] Karl Pearson. Tables for Statisticians and Biometricians. Part 2. London: Biomertic Laboratory, University College, 1931. Pp. 8–10.

In normative-referenced test interpretation, meaning is added to a person's score by comparing it to the scores of an identifiable norm group. There are various types of derived scores which reveal the relative status of individuals within a group. Seashore discusses some of the more popular derived scores and shows the relationships among them when the scores are normally distributed. After reading the article you should be able to answer the following questions.

1. Joe has a z score of +1.0. What is his percentile? (Assume a a normal distribution.) His T score?
2. Assuming a normal distribution, which one of the following scores represents the highest relative level of achievement? z = 1.5; T = 60; Stanine = 7; Percentile = 84th.
3. If Sue scores at the mean, what is her z score? Her T score? Her stanine score? Her percentile? (Does one need to make any assumptions about the shape of the data distribution to answer these questions?)

Methods of Expressing Test Scores

HAROLD G. SEASHORE

An individual's test score acquires meaning when it can be compared with the scores of well-identified groups of people. Manuals for tests provide tables of norms to make it easy to compare individuals and groups. Several systems for deriving more meaningful "standard scores" from raw scores have been widely adopted. All of them reveal the relative status of individuals within a group.

The fundamental equivalence of the most popular standard score systems is illustrated in the chart on the next page. We hope the chart and the accompanying description will be useful to counselors, personnel officers, clinical diagnosticians and others in helping them to show the uninitiated the essential simplicity of standard score systems, percentile equivalents, and their relation to the ideal normal distribution.

Sooner or later, every textbook discussion of test scores introduces the bell-shaped normal curve. The student of testing soon learns that many of the methods of deriving meaningful scores are anchored to the dimensions and characteristics of this curve. And he learns by observation of actual test

From *Test Service Bulletin*, No. 48, January 1955. Reprinted with permission of publisher, The Psychological Corporation.

score distributions that the ideal mathematical curve is a reasonably good approximation of many practical cases. He learns to use the standardized properties of the ideal curve as a model.

Let us look first at the curve itself. Notice that there are no raw scores printed along the baseline. The graph is generalized; it describes an idealized distribution of scores of any group on any test. We are free to use any numerical scale we like. For any particular set of scores, we can be arbitrary and call the average score zero. In technical terms we "equate" the mean raw score to zero. Similarly we can choose any convenient number, say 1.00, to represent the scale distance of one standard deviation.[1] Thus, if a distribution of scores on a particular test has a mean of 36 and a standard deviation of 4, the zero point on the baseline of our curve would be equivalent to an original score of 36; one unit to the right, $+1\sigma$, would be equivalent to 40, $(36+4)$; and one unit to the left, -1σ, would be equivalent to 32, $(36-4)$.

The total area under the curve represents the total number of scores in the distribution. Vertical lines have been drawn through the score scale (the baseline) at zero and at 1, 2, 3, and 4 sigma units to the right and left. These lines mark off subareas of the total area under the curve. The numbers printed in these subareas are per cents—*percentages of the total number of people.* Thus, 34.13 per cent of all cases in a normal distribution have scores falling between 0 and -1σ. For practical purposes we rarely need to deal with standard deviation units below -3 or above $+3$; the percentage of cases with scores beyond $\pm 3\sigma$ is negligible.

The fact that 68.26 per cent fall between $\pm 1\sigma$ gives rise to the common statement that in a normal distribution roughly two-thirds of all cases lie between plus and minus one sigma. This is a rule of thumb every test user should keep in mind. It is very near to the theoretical value and is a useful approximation.

Below the row of deviations expressed in sigma units is a row of per cents; these show *cumulatively* the percentage of people which is included *to the left* of each of the sigma points. Thus, starting from the left, when we reach the line erected above -2σ, we have included the lowest 2.3 per cent of cases. These percentages have been rounded in the next row.

Note some other relationships: the area between the $\pm 1\sigma$ points includes the scores which lie above the 16th percentile (-1σ) and below the 84th percentile $(+1\sigma)$—two major reference points all test users should know. When we find that an individual has a score 1σ above the mean, we conclude that his score ranks at the 84th percentile in the group of persons on whom the test was normed. (This conclusion is good provided we also add this clause, at least subvocally: *if this particular group reasonably approximates the ideal normal model.*)

The simplest facts to memorize about the normal distribution and the

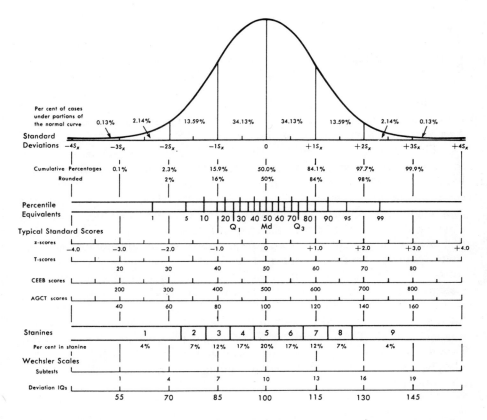

NOTE: This chart cannot be used to equate scores on one test to scores on another test. For example, both 600 on the CEEB and 120 on the AGCT are one standard deviation above their respective means, but they do not represent "equal" standings because the scores were obtained from different groups.

relation of the *percentile* system to deviations from the average in sigma units are seen in the chart. They are

Deviation from the mean	-2σ	-1σ	0	$+1\sigma$	$+2\sigma$
Percentile equivalent	2	16	50	84	98

To avoid cluttering the graph reference lines have not been drawn, but we could mark off ten per cent sections of area under the normal curve by drawing lines vertically from the indicated decile points (10, 20, . . . 80, 90) up through the graph. The reader might do this lightly with a colored pencil.

We can readily see that ten per cent of the area (people) at the middle of the distribution embraces a smaller *distance* on the baseline of the curve than ten per cent of the area (people) at the ends of the range of scores, for the simple reason that the curve is much higher at the middle. A person who is at the 95th percentile is farther away from a person at the 85th percentile in units of *test score* than a person at the 55th percentile is from one at the 45th percentile.

The remainder of the chart, that is the several scoring scales drawn parallel to the baseline, illustrates variations of the *deviation score* principle. As a class these are called *standard scores*.

First, there are the *z-scores*. These are the same *numbers* as shown on the baseline of the graph; the only difference is that the expression, σ, has been omitted. These scores run, in practical terms, from -3.0 to $+3.0$. One can compute them to more decimal places if one wishes, although computing to a single decimal place is usually sufficient. One can compute z-scores by equating the mean to 0.00 and the standard deviation to 1.00 for a distribution of any shape, but the relationships shown in this figure between the z-score equivalents of raw scores and percentile equivalents of raw scores are correct only for normal distributions. The interpretation of standard score systems derives from the idea of using the normal curve as a model.

As can be seen, T-scores are directly related to z-scores. The mean of the raw scores is equated to 50, and the standard deviation of the raw scores is equated to 10. Thus a z-score of $+1.5$ means the same as a T-score of 65. T-scores are usually expressed in whole numbers from about 20 to 80. The T-score plan eliminates negative numbers and thus facilitates many computations.[2]

The College Entrance Examination Board uses a plan in which both decimals and negative numbers are avoided by setting the arbitrary mean at 500 points and the arbitrary sigma at another convenient unit, namely, 100 points. The experienced tester or counselor who hears of a College Board SAT-V score of 550 at once thinks, "Half a sigma (50 points) above average (500 points) on the CEEB basic norms." And when he hears of a score of 725 on SAT-N, he can interpret, "Plus $2\frac{1}{4}\sigma$. Therefore, better than the 98th percentile."

During World War II the Navy used the T-score plan of reporting test status. The Army used still another system with a mean of 100 and a standard deviation of 20 points.

Another derivative of the general standard score system is the *stanine* plan, developed by psychologists in the Air Force during the war. The plan divides the norm population into nine groups, hence, "standard nines." Except for stanine 9, the top, and stanine 1, the bottom, these groups are spaced in half-sigma units. Thus, stanine 5 is defined as including the people who are within $\pm 0.25\sigma$ of the mean. Stanine 6 is the group defined by the half-sigma distance on the baseline between $+0.25\sigma$ and $+0.75\sigma$. Stanines 1 and 9 include all persons who are below -1.75σ and above $+1.75\sigma$, respectively. The result is a distribution in which the mean is 5.0 and the standard deviation is 2.0.

Just below the line showing the demarcation of the nine groups in the stanine system there is a row of percentages which indicates the per cent of the total population in each of the stanines. Thus 7 per cent of the population will be in stanine 2, and 20 per cent in the middle group, stanine 5.

Interpretation of the Wechsler scales (W-B I, W-B II, WISC, and WAIS) depends on a knowledge of standard scores. A subject's raw score *on each of the subtests* in these scales is converted, by appropriate norms tables, to a standard score, based on a mean of 10 and a standard deviation of 3. The sums of standard scores on the Verbal Scale, the Performance Scale, and the Full Scale are then converted into IQ's. These IQs are based on a standard score mean of 100, the conventional number for representing the IQ of the average person in a given age group. The standard deviation of the IQs is set at 15 points. In practical terms, then, roughly two-thirds of the IQs are between 85 and 115, that is, $\pm 1\sigma$.[3] IQs of the type used in the Wechsler scales have come to be known as *deviation IQs*, as contrasted with the IQs developed from scales in which a derived mental age is divided by chronological age.

Users of the Wechsler scales should establish clearly in their minds the relationship of subtest scaled scores and the deviation IQs to the other standard score systems, to the ordinary percentile rank interpretation, and to the deviation units on the baseline of the normal curve. For example, every Wechsler examiner should recognize that an IQ of 130 is a score equivalent to a deviation of $+2\sigma$, and that this IQ score delimits approximately the upper two per cent of the population. If a clinicial wants to evaluate a Wechsler IQ of 85 along with percentile ranks on several other tests given in school, he can mentally convert the IQ of 85 to a percentile rank of about 16, this being the percentile equal to a deviation from the mean of -1σ. Of course he should also consider the appropriateness and comparability of norms.

Efficiency in interpreting test scores in counseling, in clinical diagnosis, and in personnel selection depends, in part, on facility in thinking in terms of the major interrelated plans by which meaningful scores are derived from raw scores. It is hoped that this graphic presentation will be helpful to all who in their daily work must help others understand the information conveyed by numerical test scores.

NOTES

[1] The mathematical symbol for the standard deviation is the lower case Greek letter sigma or σ. These terms are used interchangeably in this article.

[2] T-scores and percentiles both have 50 as the main reference point, an occasional source of confusion to those who do not insist on careful labelling of data and of scores of individuals in their records.

[3] Every once in a while we receive a letter from someone who suggests that the Wechsler scales ought to generate a wider range of IQs. The reply is very simple. If we want a wider range of IQs all we have to do is to choose a *larger arbitrary* standard deviation, say, 20 or 25. Under the present system, $\pm 3\sigma$ gives IQs of 55 to 145, with a few rare cases below and a few rare cases above. If we used 20 as the standard deviation, we would *arbitrarily* increase the $\pm 3\sigma$ range of IQs from 55-145 to 40-160. This *is* a wider range of numbers! But, test users should never forget that adaptations of this kind do not change the responses of the people who took the test, do not change the order of the persons in relation to each other, and do not change the psychological meaning attached to an IQ.

RECOMMENDED READING FOR UNIT II

American Psychological Association. *Standards for Educational & Psychological Tests.* Washington, D.C.: APA, 1974.

Bechtoldt, H. P. "Construct Validity: A Critique," *American Psychologist*, 1959, 14: 619–629.

Campbell, Donald T., and Fiske, Donald W. "Convergent and Discriminant Validation by the Multitrait-Multimethod Matrix," *Psychological Bulletin*, 1959, 56: 81–105.

Cronbach, Lee J. and Meehl, Paul E. "Construct Validity in Psychological Tests," *Psychological Bulletin*, 1955, 52: 281–302.

Dion, Robert. "Norms are Not Goals," *Newsletter of the Elementary School Principals Association of Connecticut*, October 1958.

Doppelt, Jerome E. "How Accurate Is a Test Score?" *Test Service Bulletin No. 50.* New York: The Psychological Corporation.

Ebel, Robert L. "Must All Tests Be Valid?" *American Psychologist*, 1961, 16: 640–647.

REFERENCES*

American Educational Research Association and National Council on Measurements Used in Education. *Technical Recommendations for Achievement Tests.* National Education Association, January 1955.

American Psychological Association. *Technical Recommendations for Psychological Tests and Diagnostic Techniques.* Supplement to *Psychological Bulletin*, 51, No. 2, March 1954.

Anastasi, Anne. *Psychological Testing.* New York: The Macmillan Company, 1954.

Cronbach, Lee J. and Meehl, Paul E. "Construct Validity in Psychological Tests." *Psychological Bulletin*, LII (1955), 281–302.

Cureton, Edward E. Chapter 16, Validity, in *Educational Measurement* (E. F. Lindquist, ed.) Washington, D.C.: American Council on Education, 1951.

Goodenough, Florence L. *Mental Testing.* New York: Rinehart and Company, 1949.

Zimmerman, Wayne S. "Hypotheses Concerning the Nature of the Spatial Factors." *Educational and Psychological Measurement*, XIV (1954).

* For "Assumptions Underlying the Use of Content Validity" by Roger T. Lennon on pp. 45–52.

CONSTRUCTING, ADMINISTERING, AND ANALYZING TESTS

unit
III

Teacher-made tests are the major bases for evaluating students' progress in school. Thus, it is important that the quality of these tests be high. In the first article in this unit, Ebel presents ten principles of educational measurement. As he concludes, "a teacher whose classroom testing reflects an understanding of these principles will do a better than average job of measuring student achievement."

Objectives are obviously useful in education. But the manner in which objectives should be written and communicated has been a topic of debate. In the second article, Wight reviews many of the problems associated with behavioral objectives.

A variety of item formats can be used for a test. A basic difference is between essay and objective questions. Considerable controversy exists among teachers as to which is better. Measurement experts typically do not feel there can be an answer to the general question. Every item format has advantages and limitations. Some item formats are better for some purposes, others for different purposes. Also, the answer is dependent on the time a teacher has to prepare and grade tests, the number of students tested, the physical facilities, and the teacher's skill. It seems to many of us that teachers are more alert to the weaknesses of objective tests than they are to the weaknesses of essay tests. The two most serious weaknesses of essay tests are poor content sampling and low reader reliability. Coffman points out some of the arguments for essay exams and then turns to a discussion of various sources of error in essay examinations. As he states: "Awareness on the part of the teacher of the factors contributing to unreliability . . . is a first step in improving the reliability of the teacher's essay examinations."

Some teachers believe that the problem of poor content sampling in essay tests can be overcome through the use of optional questions. In general, measurement experts are against this procedure. The article by DuCette and Wolk helps to explain why.

Three issues that have received considerable attention in classroom testing are the effects of test anxiety, the value of frequent exams, and the role of feedback on exams. Marso reports on a study that examined these variables. The implications of his findings are that classroom teachers should incorporate frequent, graded tests followed by class discussion in their instructional procedures.

Classroom teachers often bypass quality control checks on their tests. Probable causes are that they do not know how or they think it will be too time consuming. The article by Lange, Lehmann, and Mehrens shows the value of item analyses in improving tests. Revising items based on item analyses proved both to be more useful and efficient than writing new items.

Ebel presents and supports ten principles of educational
measurement classroom teachers should consider. While a few
are controversial most are well accepted by measurement experts.
Principle four is probably the most controversial but numbers three
and five also have been debated. If you disagree with Professor
Ebel what arguments can you advance in support of your position?

Measurement and the Teacher

ROBERT L. EBEL

The principles of measurement of educational achievement presented in this
article are based on the experience and research of a great many people who
have been working to improve classroom testing. The particular principles
discussed here were selected on the basis of their relevance to the questions
and problems which arise most often when tests of educational achievement
are being considered, prepared and used. While some of the principles may
seem open to question, we believe a case can be made in support of each one.

1. *The measurement of educational achievement is essential to effective
education.* Learning is a natural, inevitable result of human living. Some
learning would occur even if no special provision were made for it in
schools, or no special effort were taken to facilitate it. Yet efficient learning
of complex achievements, such as reading, understanding of science, or literary appreciation, requires special motivation, guidance and assistance.
Efforts must be directed toward the attainment of specific goals. Students,
teachers and others involved in the process of education must know to what
degree the goals have been achieved. The measurement of educational achievement can contribute to these activities.

It is occasionally suggested that schools could get along without tests,
or indeed that they might even do a better job if testing were prohibited. It
is seldom if ever suggested, though, that education can be carried on effectively by teachers and students who have no particular goals in view, or who
do not care what or how much is being learned. If tests are outlawed, some
other means of assessing educational achievement would have to be used in
their place.

2. *An educational test is no more or less than a device for facilitating,
extending and refining a teacher's observations of student achievement.* In
spite of the Biblical injunction, most of us find ourselves quite often passing
judgments on our fellow men. Is candidate A more deserving of our vote than
candidate B? Is C a better physician than D? Is employee E entitled to a

raise or a promotion on his merits? Should student F be given a failing mark? Should student L be selected in preference to student M for the leading role in the class play?

Those charged with making such judgments often feel they must do so on the basis of quite inadequate evidence. The characteristics on which the decision should be based may not have been clearly defined. The performances of the various candidates may not have been observed extensively, or under comparable conditions. Instead of recorded data, the judge may have to trust his fallible memory, supplemented with hearsay evidence.

Somewhat similar problems are faced by teachers, as they attempt to assess the achievements of their students. In an effort to solve these problems, tests have been developed. Oral examinations and objective examinations are means for making it easier for the teacher to observe a more extensive sample of student behavior under more carefully controlled conditions.

The price that must be paid for a test's advantages of efficiency and control in the observation of student achievements is some loss in the naturalness of the behavior involved. In tests which attempt to measure the student's typical behavior, especially those aspects of behavior which depend heavily on his interests, attitudes, values or emotional reactions, the artificiality of the test situation may seriously distort the measurement obtained. But this problem is much less serious in tests intended to measure how much the student knows, and what he can do with his knowledge. What is gained in efficiency and precision of measurement usually far outweighs what may be lost due to artificiality of the situation in which the student's behavior is observed.

3. *Every important outcome of education can be measured.* In order for an outcome of education to be important, it must make a difference. The behavior of a person who has more of a particular outcome must be observably different from that of a person who has less. Perhaps one can imagine some result of education which is so deeply personal that it does not ever affect in any way what he says or does, or how he spends his time. But it is difficult to find any grounds for arguing that such a well concealed achievement is important.

If the achievement does make a difference in what a person can do or does do, then it is measurable. For the most elementary type of measurement requires nothing more than the possibility of making a verifiable observation that person or object X has more of some defined characteristic than person or object Y.

To say that any important educational outcome is measurable is not to say that satisfactory methods of measurement now exist. Certainly it is not to say that every important educational outcome can be measured by means of a paper and pencil test. But it is to reject the claim that some important educational outcomes are too complex or too intangible to be measured. Importance and measurability are logically inseparable.

4. *The most important educational achievement is command of useful*

knowledge. If the importance of an educational outcome may be judged on the basis of what teachers and students spend most of their time doing, it is obvious that acquisition of a command of useful knowledge is a highly important outcome. Or if one asks how the other objectives are to be attained—objectives of self-realization, of human relationship, of economic efficiency, of civic responsibility—it is obvious again that command of useful knowledge is the principal means.

How effectively a person can think about a problem depends largely on how effectively he can command the knowledge that is relevant to the problem. Command of knowledge does not guarantee success, or happiness, or righteousness, but it is difficult to think of anything else a school can attempt to develop which is half as likely to lead to these objectives.

If we give students command of knowledge, if we develop their ability to think, we make them intellectually free and independent. This does not assure us that they will work hard to maintain the status quo, that they will adopt all of our beliefs and accept all of our values. Yet it can make them free men and women in the area in which freedom is most important. We should be wary of an educational program which seeks to change or control student behavior on any other basis than rational self-determination, the basis that command of knowledge provides.

5. *Written tests are well suited to measure the student's command of useful knowledge.* All knowledge can be expressed in propositions. Propositions are statements that can be judged to be true or false. Scholars, scientists, research workers—all those concerned with adding to our store of knowledge, spend most of their time formulating and verifying propositions.

Implicit in every true-false or multiple-choice test item is a proposition, or several propositions. Essay tests also require a student to demonstrate his command of knowledge.

Some elements of novelty are essential in any question intended to test a student's command of knowledge. He should not be allowed to respond successfully simply on the basis of rote learning or verbal association. He should not be asked a stereotyped question to which a pat answer probably has been committed to memory.

6. *The classroom teacher should prepare most of the tests used to measure educational achievement in the classroom.* Many published tests are available for classroom use in measuring educational aptitude or achievement in broad areas of knowledge. But there are very few which are specifically appropriate for measuring the achievement of the objectives of a particular unit of work or of a particular period of instruction. Publishers of textbooks sometimes supply booklets of test questions to accompany their texts. These can be useful, although all too often the test questions supplied are of inferior quality—hastily written, unreviewed, untested, and subject to correct response on the basis of rote learning as well as on the basis of understanding.

Even if good ready-made tests were generally available, a case could still be made for teacher-prepared tests; the chief reason being that the process of test development can help the teacher define his objectives. This process can result in tests that are more highly relevant than any external tests are likely to be. It can make the process of measuring educational achievement an integral part of the whole process of instruction, as it should be.

7. *To measure achievement effectively the classroom teacher must be (a) a master of the knowledge or skill to be tested, and (b) a master of the practical arts of testing.* No courses in educational measurement, no books or articles on the improvement of classroom tests, are likely to enable a poor teacher to make good tests. A teacher's command of the knowledge he is trying to teach, his understanding of common misconceptions regarding this content, his ability to invent novel questions and problems, and his ability to express these clearly and concisely; all these are crucial to his success in test construction. It is unfortunately true that some people who have certificates to teach lack one or more of these prerequisites to good teaching and good testing.

However, there are also some tricks of the trade of test construction. A course in educational measurement, or a book or article on classroom testing can teach these things. Such a course may also serve to shake a teacher's faith—constructively and wholesomely—in some of the popular misconceptions about the processes of testing educational achievement. Among these misconceptions are the belief that only essay tests are useful for measuring the development of a student's higher mental processes; that a test score should indicate what proportion a student does know of what he ought to know; that mistakes in scoring are the main sources of error in test scores.

8. *The quality of a classroom test depends on the relevance of the tasks included in it, on the representativeness of its sampling of all aspects of instruction, and on the reliability of the scores it yields.* If a test question presents a problem like those the student may expect to encounter in his later life outside the classroom, and if the course in which his achievement is being tested did in fact try to teach him how to deal with such problems, then the question is relevant. If the test questions involve, in proportion to their importance, all aspects of achievement the course undertakes to develop, it samples representatively. If the scores students receive on a test agree closely with those they would receive on an independent, equivalent test, then the test yields reliable scores.

Relevance, representativeness and reliability are all matters of degree. Procedures and formulas for calculating estimates of test reliability are well developed, and are described in most books on educational measurement. Estimates of representativeness and relevance are more subjective, less quantitative. Yet this does not mean that relevance and representativeness are any less important than reliability. The more a test has of each the better. While it is possible to have an irrelevant and unrepresentative but highly reliable test, it is seldom necessary and never desirable to sacrifice any one of the three for the others.

Either essay or objective test forms can be used to present relevant tasks to the examinees. Ordinarily, the greater the novelty of a test question, that is, the smaller the probability that the student has encountered the same question before, or been taught a pat answer to it, the greater its relevance. Because of the greater number of questions involved, it is sometimes easier to include a representative sample of tasks in an objective than in an essay test. For the same reason, and also because of greater uniformity in scoring, objective tests are likely to yield somewhat more reliable scores than are essay tests.

9. *The more variable the scores from a test designed to have a certain maximum possible score, the higher the expected reliability of those scores.* Reliability is sometimes defined as the proportion of the total variability among the test scores which is not attributable to errors of measurement. The size of the errors of measurement depends on the nature of the test—the kind and the number of items in it. Hence for a particular test, any increase in the total variability of the scores is likely to increase the proportion which is not due to errors of measurement, and hence to increase the reliability of the test.

Figure 1 shows some hypothetical score distributions for three tests. The essay test consists of 10 questions worth 10 points each, scored by a teacher who regards 75 as a passing score on such a test. The true-false test consists of 100 items, each of which is worth one point if correctly answered, with no subtraction for wrong answers. The multiple-choice test also includes 100 items, each of which offers four alternative answer options. It, too, is scored only for the number of correct answers given, with no "correction for guessing."

Note, in the data at the bottom of Figure 1, the differences among the tests in average score (mean), in variability (standard deviation), in effective range and in estimated reliability. While these are hypothetical data, derived from calculations based on certain assumptions, they are probably reasonably representative of the results most teachers achieve in using tests of these types.

It is possible to obtain scores whose reliability is above .90 using 100 multiple-choice items, but it is not easy to do, and classroom teachers seldom do it in the tests they construct. It is also possible to handle 100-point essay tests and 100-item true-false tests so that their reliability will equal that of a 100-item multiple-choice test. But again, it is not easy to do and classroom teachers seldom succeed in doing it.

10. *The reliability of a test can be increased by increasing the number of questions (or independent points to be scored) and by sharpening the*

Figure 1   Hypothetical Score Distributions for Three Tests

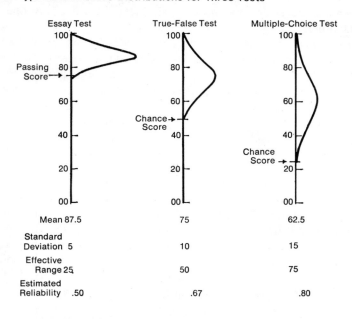

	Essay Test	True-False Test	Multiple-Choice Test
Mean	87.5	75	62.5
Standard Deviation	5	10	15
Effective Range	25	50	75
Estimated Reliability	.50	.67	.80

power of individual questions to discriminate between students of high and low achievement. Figure 2 illustrates the increases of test reliability which can be expected as a result of increasing the number of items (or independent points to be scored) in a test. Doubling the length of a 10-item test whose reliability coefficient is .33 increases the reliability to .50. Doubling again brings it up to .67, and so on. These estimates are based on the Spearman-Brown formula for predicting the reliability of a lengthened test. While the formula requires assumptions which may not be justified in all cases, its predictions are usually quite accurate.

Figure 3 shows how the maximum discriminating power of an item is related to its level of difficulty. These discrimination indices are simply differences between the proportions of correct response from good and poor students. Good students are those whose total test scores fall among the top 27 percent of the students tested. Poor students are those whose scores make up the bottom 27 percent. An item of 50 percent difficulty does not necessarily have (and usually will not have) an index of discrimination of 1.00. Its discriminating power may be zero, or even negative. But items of middle difficulty have higher ceilings on their discriminating power. What is more important, they not only can have, but usually do have, greater discriminating power than very easy or very difficult items. An item that no one answers correctly, or that everyone answers correctly, cannot discriminate at all. Such an item adds nothing to the reliability of a test.

Figure 2   Relation of Test Reliability to Test Length

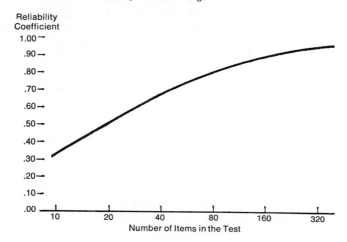

Figure 3   Maximum Discrimination Attainable with Items at Different Levels of Difficulty

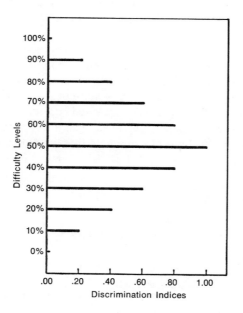

In summary, the 10 principles stated and discussed in this article represent only a sample of the important things classroom teachers need to know about educational measurement. These principles, and the brief discussion of each presented here, may serve to call into question some common practices in classroom testing, or to suggest some ways in which classroom tests might be improved. They are not likely, and are not intended, to say all that needs to be said or do all that needs to be done to improve educational measurement in the classroom. It is our sincere belief, however, that a teacher whose classroom testing reflects an understanding of these principles will do a better than average job of measuring student achievement.

Objectives help an instructor in planning, guide student learning, and provide criteria for evaluating student outcomes. It would be difficult, if not impossible, to teach or measure what students have learned without objectives. Recent statements on objectives have tended to emphasize identifying exactly what student performances or products are the expected outcomes of instruction. These are called behavioral or performance objectives. While these are necessary for the evaluation of instruction, many have debated the necessity and even the wisdom of specifying goals in behavioral terms for purposes of planning an instructional program or communicating to pupils the total goals of the program.

    Wight reviews many problems associated with behavioral objectives. In particular, the problem of confusing the indicator with the objective has been poorly understood by many of the educational technologists. But in spite of the problems, we must infer whether or not we have achieved certain goals or objectives and we can most reasonably make such inferences from observing behavior. Wight therefore suggests that we not discard behavioral objectives, but rather treat the goal and measurement components separately.

Beyond Behavioral Objectives

ALBERT R. WIGHT

It is unlikely that anyone in education will be able to avoid taking a position in respect to behavioral or measurable objectives. With requirements for behavioral objectives being written into accountability legislation, they certainly cannot be ignored. If persons opposing their use (and there are many)

From *Educational Technology*, July 1972, 9–14. Reprinted with permission of the publisher.

are to be heard, they will have to come up with more convincing arguments than those presented in numerous articles over the past few years. If they are to avoid being forced to use behavioral objectives, they may have to show another way to be accountable for educational outcomes.

The problem of accountability is thus central in the controversy over behavioral objectives and provides the behavioral objectivists with their strongest argument. The major purpose of behavioral objectives is to provide clarity of intent in education and precision in the measurement of outcomes. Although some humanistically oriented educators might disagree, it would be difficult to argue that this would not be of benefit to education.

Behavioral objectives, however, have created many problems, and it would appear that there is considerable substance to many of the arguments against their use. The purpose of this article is to examine some of the problems and arguments and to suggest a modified approach to objectives and measurement that hopefully will be acceptable to behaviorists and humanists alike.

A second aspect of the suggested approach involves a more active participation of the student in the entire process of establishing objectives and assessing performance. The argument for more participation would hold whether behavioral objectives are used or not. The use of behavioral objectives certainly does not preclude active participation of students. Objectives developed prior to student involvement should be considered provisional and subject to change with student input, unless it can be specified that certain objectives are required to qualify for a subsequent course, a particular job, etc.

PROBLEMS WITH BEHAVIORAL OBJECTIVES

A number of recent articles have discussed various reasons for the opposition to behavioral objectives (Eisner, 1969; Popham, 1968; Ebel, 1970; Cox, 1971; Miles and Robinson, 1971). A number of these reasons will be explored here.

Triviality

In spite of the arguments of the behavioral objectivists that it should not be so, behavioral objectives too often result in a focus on the trivial and mundane. It is not unusual to find important and meaningful objectives discarded because of the difficulty encountered in attempting to state them as behavioral, measurable outcomes.

It is not only the person inexperienced in writing behavioral objectives who focuses on the trivial. Examine objectives prepared by the experts, and ask yourself how many you would consider personally meaningful and relevant, how many would be intrinsically rewarding, how many have meaning beyond the immediate and usually artificial test situation. If you find most of these unexciting, as you quite likely will, you can expect that students will, too.

Confusing the Indicator with the Objective

The problem of triviality and most other problems with behavioral objectives are a direct result of a means versus ends type of confusion. Behavioral objectivists warn us of the dangers in confusing the strategy, the means of achieving the objective, with the end, the objective itself. What they have failed to recognize is that they have confused the indicator, the means of determining whether the objective has been achieved, with the true objective.

Behavioral objectives contain both a goal component and a measurement component, but the goal component is too often deemphasized to the point that it is virtually non-existent. The behavioral objective becomes in fact a statement of a measurement to be taken sometime prior to the completion of the learning and program, under specified conditions, and with criteria for evaluation. Most so-called behavioral objectives are not really objectives, therefore. They are only indicators (samples of behavior or tests that serve as evidence) that the true objectives have been achieved. Calling them objectives can mislead the teacher and the student into believing that the sample of behavior (the indicator), from which it is inferred that learning has taken place, is the desired end result of the learning activity. We agree with Mager (1968, p. 11) that "learning is for the future," but behavioral objectives can easily result in a focus on the requirements of the present.

Here again, examine most any list of behavioral objectives (particularly those related to higher mental processes or affective outcomes) and ask yourself whether the goal component of the objective statement is really a clear statement of a goal one would want to achieve for the future, or rather a description of an indicator behavior. For example:

> The student is to be able to complete a 100-item, multiple-choice examination on the subject of marine biology. The lower limit of acceptable performance will be 85 items answered correctly within an examination period of 90 minutes [Mager, 1962, p. 56].
>
> Students will exhibit favorable attitudes toward school in general and toward several dimensions of school (teachers, peer relationships, social structure and climate, school subjects) in their responses to the *School Sentiment Index* . . . [Instructional Objectives Exchange, 1970, p. 11].
>
> Given a common disposable object (e.g., paper sack, bottle, cardboard box, plastic container) and the designation of a consumer group (e.g., six- to ten-year-olds, college students, housewives), the student will describe, in

writing, ideas for at least three original marketable products. Each of the three products must be previously unknown to the instructor and class, and be something the target group would be likely to buy, as judged by class vote [Miles and Robinson, 1971].

In the first example (Mager's), the learning objective is almost completely obscured, other than that it has something to do with marine biology. The student's objective here is quite clearly to pass an examination. How does this differ in any way from the traditional classroom where the instructor provides vague goals, if any, and some indication of what will be required to obtain a passing grade?

In the second example (from objectives edited and catalogued by Popham and his associates), it is unlikely that this would be a primary objective of a particular instructional sequence, but rather a hoped-for outcome or by-product of the student's entire educational milieu. It is highly unlikely that a student would see a favorable attitude as his objective, but he very probably would like to experience the conditions toward which he could respond with favorable attitudes. To achieve this "objective" we would not develop an instructional sequence; we would change the system.

We could infer objectives in the third example, but we would have to consult the person who wrote the objective to find out for sure what he was trying to achieve. Hopefully, some time would be spent explaining and clarifying the objective for the students or they might perceive this as a relatively meaningless activity. Even so, it is still likely to be perceived as a test more than as an objective the student would want to achieve, unless he had been involved in defining the objective. It should have more meaning if it were not perceived as a test but as one of a series of activities to afford practice in using one's creative abilities or to develop a catalogue of ideas for possible future use.

Gap between the Indicator and the Goal

Behavioral objectives too often have not resulted in better objectives as much as in better measurement. But the measurement is not always clearly related to a meaningful future goal. With the focus on the indicators, it is easy to lose sight of the true objectives. Providing the student with a comprehensive set of behavioral objectives amounts to explaining in some detail the kinds of examinations he will be given. The indicators help him understand what he must do to satisfy the teacher or meet the requirements of the system, but unless special effort is made to relate the indicator (behavioral objective) to the true objective, performing the prescribed act or demonstrating the behavior may have little meaning for the student.

This gap between the indicator and the objective can only be overcome by special effort to achieve transfer. This effort would not be required, however, if objectives were written that had meaning in the personal life of the student beyond the classroom. Such objectives would have to include something other than a statement of a test performance. Eiss and Harbeck (1969, p. 13) point out another problem:

> In the affective domain, this gap is often very wide, and a given behavior may indicate the attainment of any one of several objectives, depending upon the thinking and motives of the individual exhibiting the behavior. Another difficulty is the operant conditions that we have developed in our students. If they are aware of the behavior desired by the teacher, it will often be produced on demand—the behavior itself will become the goal and not an indication of the attainment of the goal.

Restrictions on Teaching Strategies

When objectives are written in measurement terms, the tendency is to teach (as well as learn) for the test (the indicator), not for the true objective. If the learning activities relate to the objectives, as they should, the use of behavioral objectives can restrict the teacher or learner in the selection of activities or predispose him toward certain activities as opposed to others. This is particularly true with a "properly written objective" where the outcome, the conditions under which the behavior is to be exhibited, and the criteria are clearly prescribed. The learning activity should prepare the student for the task and conditions stated in the behavioral objective, which may thus limit the alternatives available.

Restrictions on Measurement

A program based on behavioral objectives does not provide for measurements other than those prescribed in the objectives. Many opportunities for demonstration of learning or achievement might be presented by the learning activities, however, and these might present better evidence than the measurements specified in the behavioral objectives. Also, a frequent argument is that unstated outcomes are quite likely to be overlooked, unless deliberate effort is made to look for them. Of course, the behavioral objectivist might retort that the use of behavioral objectives does not preclude other measurements for stated outcomes or recognition of unplanned outcomes. The implication when the objective and measurement are combined in one statement, however, is that there should be one measurement for each objective. The tendency is thus toward writing a behavioral objective for each intended outcome, which can and often does result in a book of behavioral objectives, and an obstacle course for the student. With a great many behavioral objectives to assess, little time or energy is left for assessment of unspecified outcomes.

Negative Outcomes

It can be psychologically discouraging to have every objective stated in terms of a task or test to be overcome rather than an aim or direction (something to be acquired or achieved), unless the learner has worked with the teacher in setting these tasks. This focus on a multitude of tasks imposed by the teacher can lower students' aspirations and reduce motivation. The objectives might be attained, but at the expense of exploration, divergent thinking and positive attitudes toward learning.

The need to satisfy the person evaluating the test performance, as opposed to being able to pursue one's own interests and evaluate one's own performance, can and very probably does interfere with the development of self-esteem, self-confidence and sense of control over one's own destiny. A frequent criticism of behavioral objectives suggests that undue emphasis on requirements to meet minimum performance standards can result in an orientation toward doing only what is necessary rather than what is possible, with a possible resulting life style of lower aims and standards.

Control Versus Freedom, or Behaviorists Versus the Humanists

Since behavioral objectives are a product of behaviorism and thus in the pure sense are concerned only with observable behavior, they seldom use measurement that asks the student what he is thinking or feeling. His internal state must be inferred from his behavior. Some behavioral objectivists do not hold this extreme position, of course, but it does dominate the behavioral objectives movement and is stated quite explicitly by many authors. This lack of trust in the student is a major reason for the objections of humanistically oriented educators to the use of behavioral objectives.

In addition to promoting measurement that excludes self-observation and self-report, most guidelines for preparing behavioral objectives imply that someone other than the student should decide what his objectives should be and state the objectives for him. Popham (1968) defended this practice:

> Teachers generally have an idea of how they wish learners to behave, and they promote these goals with more or less efficiency. Society knows what it wants its young to become, perhaps not with the precision that we would desire, but certainly in general. And if the schools were allowing students to "democratically" deviate from societally mandated goals, one can be sure that the institutions would cease to receive society's approbation and support.

This control orientation tends to permeate programs based on behavioral objectives, with a resulting focus on instruction rather than learning, deciding for the student rather than including him in the decisions, and deemphasizing or denying the value of his own inner experience and self-evaluation. Such an approach supports and perpetuates feelings and attitudes that one is not capable of self-evaluation and responsibility but must look to an outside source for direction and control.

AN ALTERNATIVE TO BEHAVIORAL OBJECTIVES

If these potential problems are recognized, they can be reduced to a considerable extent through special effort, particularly if students are involved in defining the objectives. But these problems are less likely to occur and can be overcome more easily if, in addition to student involvement, the goal and measurement components are treated separately and not combined in one statement. This does not mean that we have to give up the gains we have made with behavioral objectives (particularly in respect to measurement), but it should clear up the semantic confusion created when we call an indicator an objective, and should result in both improved objectives and measurement. If we treat the goal statement separately, we can define it and expand it as necessary for clarification, without reducing it to a possibly meaningless and aversive test performance. Treating the measurement component separately allows the selection of any number of indicators and any type of measurement most appropriate to provide the necessary evidence of achievement.

The Goal Statement

Although the principle of separation of goal and measurement components would apply with any type of objective (i.e., program, management, support, etc.), we are concerned here with learning outcomes. We agree with most behavioral objectivists that the goal should be stated in terms of learner performance or achievement. It should also be meaningful to the learner in terms of his interests, aims, ambitions and perceived needs. This means that the initial goal should be stated in general terms that seem worthwhile to the learner. These are usually inner states rather than discrete, observable behaviors. It has proven useful to define goals and objectives in terms of:

1. What the student should (or would like to) be able to do by the end of the learning activity or course;
2. What he needs (or wants) to know, understand or appreciate[1]; and
3. What characteristics (personal or interpersonal) are required to do what he wants effectively; i.e., tact, tolerance, patience, empathy, openness, etc.

Each general goal will have to be further defined and expanded for clarification, but only to the level of specificity that is useful and meaningful. If coping with the sheer magnitude of subobjectives becomes a burden, such objectives are no longer useful.

The general goal can usually be clarified by answering the question: "What does this mean?" or better, "What do I mean by this?" or perhaps still better, "What does this mean to me?" Essentially, the general goal statement names a particular universe of behavior, knowledge, etc. The expansion serves to describe the nature of that universe and to define its parameters. Subobjectives serve to identify and define the various components of the universe.

The subobjectives are very different from behavioral objectives. As opposed to identifying and defining components of the universe, behavioral objectives sample the universe. Thus from the total universe of behaviors, defined by the general goal, sample behaviors (indicators) are identified that hopefully will provide adequate evidence that the total universe of behaviors is available to the learner and will be exhibited when called for. The better the sampling procedure, the more likely this will be so. It is important to bear in mind that these are indicators, not objectives.

An example might help to illustrate. A student or group of students might decide they would like to increase their appreciation of poetry. This, then, would be the general goal, but it would have to be expanded considerably for clarification. The students and teacher together might decide that this means:

a better understanding of content (what the poem is saying);
understanding why men write poetry;
understanding how poetry differs from other forms of writing;
understanding how form relates to content;
understanding why you would choose poetry over another form for expression;
understanding of the structure of poetry;
understanding of the problems of writing poetry;
familiarity with different styles of poetry;
writing some of my own poetry;
finding out what I like and don't like in poetry.

None of these statements involve measurement, but they do define in general terms what the student, at this point in time, means by appreciation of poetry, and they provide him with fairly clear direction. If this is a clear and meaningful goal for him, he will be eager to get on with the learning activity. Each subobjective and its relationship to the goal of appreciation can be defined further at this point or while he is actually engaged in the activity. His understanding of the goal should increase as he pursues each of the subobjectives.

The success one has in overcoming the potential frustration or uncertainty associated with the vagueness of this course of action is highly dependent upon the level of communication between the teacher and the learner. If sufficient agreements are achieved, the problem disappears.

Enroute Objectives

In developing a learning program it is helpful to identify check points or enroute objectives, both as a guide in developing learning strategies and in assessing progress. With the approach suggested here, these also do not include a measurement component but are treated as objectives. Achievement of enroute objectives is treated separately, in statements of what will be used to indicate achievement.

For example, in developing an understanding of the structure of poetry, one might first want to be able to distinguish between rhyme, meter and form before studying these three elements of structure separately. It would be necessary to have some understanding of each of these three areas apart and in combination before the student would be able to analyze the structure of a given poem. A much more detailed series of enroute objectives would be identified as one developed the learning program and sequenced the learning activities. Decisions would then be made regarding the specific indicators that would be used to assess achievement of the objectives.

Measurements

The measurement data provide the indicators (that is, the evidence that the objectives have been achieved), and would often be identical to what is usually called behavioral objectives. The measurement data for a given objective can be developed by asking the following questions:

1. What evidence am I willing to accept that the objective has been achieved? (What will happen? Who will do what? Under what conditions?)
2. How will this evidence (data) be obtained? (When? Where? By whom?)
3. How will the data be evaluated (measurement tools or techniques and criteria of performance)?

The guidelines provided by Mager and others for writing behavioral objectives, measurable objectives, instructional objectives, etc., can provide invaluable assistance in the development of effective measurement procedures, but it is necessary to keep in mind that most of what they call objectives we are treating as indicators.

In developing the measurement procedures, it should be recognized that an important source of assessment data is the self-assessment and verbal report of the student himself, particularly when dealing with internal states, behavior or attitudes that are difficult to observe or measure (such as confidence, interest, comfort, motivation, enjoyment, etc.). There would usually be some observable behavior that would confirm or deny the verbal statement, however, and provisions should be made for collection of data from sources other than the student's verbal report. In most instances it would be appropriate and perhaps even obligatory to confront the student with apparent lack of congruence between the verbal statement and exhibited behavior. This might be important feedback.

Some types of data can, of course, be best obtained from someone other than the student—the way something he does or produces is perceived by others, for example. If these perceptions are related to his learning objectives, this feedback is very important.

Continuing with the goal of increasing appreciation of poetry, one would ask the three questions listed above to assess progress or achievement. For example, familiarity with different styles of poetry might be assessed in many ways; i.e., demonstrated in class discussions, or the student might write poems following given styles. If more precise measurement were necessary, acceptable evidence might take the behavioral objectives form (bear in mind that this is a measurement indicator, not an objective):

> Given ten excerpts from poems representative of the styles of three different periods, the student will correctly match excerpt and period for at least eight of ten examples.

Achieving a better understanding of content might be demonstrated by the student, for example, by:

> Stating in class discussion his interpretation of what a given poet was saying in three different poems. An acceptable interpretation would be determined by the agreement of the teacher, and the majority of the class, or if not agreement, at least a recognition of the plausibility of the interpretation.
>
> Discussing, with the teacher or a small group of his peers, poems that are significant to him because of experiences in his own life that have helped him to interpret them. Accuracy of the interpretation would be determined by the agreement of the teacher or group.

The teacher might have a better understanding of a given poem than any of his students because of his familiarity with the work and life of that particular poet. The life experience each person brings to the poem is different, however, and each person will thus take away something different in terms of self-insight and understanding. If a student's life experience has been very different from that of the teacher, it may be impossible for the teacher to understand what the student has learned. Yet these insights may be important outcomes both in respect to the development of appreciation for poetry and the student's own self-concept. Self-assessment of personal learning should be provided for, therefore, whether communicated to and understood by the teacher or not.

Summary

Separating objectives and measurement offers the following advantages over the use of behavioral objectives:

1. Objectives can be expanded and defined as necessary for clarification, because they are not tied to a particular measurement under restricted conditions.[2]
2. Objectives that have meaning for the future or that are based on student interest will quite probably be more appealing to students than will objectives that in reality are nothing but a test performance (indicator).
3. Measurements (indicators, test performance) are quite likely to be more meaningful and less aversive to students if they are perceived as providing data relative to the achievement of objectives related to their personal interests and life goals.
4. It is easier to see the relationship between the measurement and the objective if the measurement is identified as an indicator of achievement of the objective.
5. Objectives would not restrict the teacher or student in the selection of learning strategies or predispose him toward certain strategies as opposed to others.
6. More flexibility is allowed in measurement and fewer measurements would be required, because one measurement would not be required for each outcome, but more measurements could be taken for particular objectives if more were necessary to provide strategies, as they are with behavioral objectives.
7. Opportunities for measurement can be capitalized on more easily, since both learning strategies and measurement are developed after objectives have been defined. Measurement decisions are not made prior to development of learning strategies, as they are with behavioral objectives.

CONCLUSION

A mistake often made in programs using behavioral objectives (and one that could be repeated with the approach suggested here) is failure to involve the student in establishing objectives, learning programs and assessment procedures. The most effective learning/assessment program is one that the student participates in developing. Modifying Mager (1968, p. vii), the student might use the following guide:

1. Where am I going? (objectives)
2. How do I get there? (learning program)
3. How do I know I am making progress? (assessment against enroute objectives)
4. How do I know when I have arrived? (assessment against outcome objectives)

It is counterproductive to present the student with a comprehensive set of objectives and a complete educational program and assessment plan at the beginning of a course. At this point there is usually a vast gap between the understanding of the student and the teacher. What seems clear, concise and well-organized to the teacher is very often beyond the comprehension of the student. The student cannot be expected to make a sudden leap to the level of understanding achieved through slow, incremental steps by the teacher. The student should not be expected to understand and accept the teacher's objectives for the course or his system of conceptualizing and organizing the course content.

This is not to say that the teacher should not be prepared. He should be well prepared. But no matter how much work has been done, it is better to reconstruct the process and involve the student if his understanding, acceptance and commitment are desired. Considerable skill is required on the part of the teacher in working with the student to develop a set of objectives that are satisfactory and understandable to both. It should be understood that these objectives will be modified and refined as increased understanding is achieved. Allowance should be made for development of new objectives and modification of the curriculum as new discoveries are made and new interests develop.

The ideal would be self-initiated programs based on personal learning objectives. The teacher would then work with the student in the development of a learning program to achieve these objectives. It should be recognized, of course, that the teacher has more experience in the design of programs and usually knows better than the student which activities or strategies have proven more effective than others in achieving given objectives. The student sometimes knows what works best for him, however, and learning to accept the responsibility for his own learning should be a major goal of education (including learning from mistakes and accepting the consequences of undesirable outcomes).

The student should also be involved in the development of assessment plans and procedures, identifying evidence he and the teacher would be willing to accept that given objectives had been achieved. He should then participate in the collection and analysis of the assessment data and in decisions made on the basis of this analysis.

The assessment should allow for serendipity—unanticipated and unplanned outcomes. What did I discover that I did not expect to discover? What new awareness, insight or understanding did I achieve? What new leads does this give me? What new interests have I developed? What have I learned about myself? Herein lies much of the excitement and value of learning.

NOTES

[1] The relationship between 1 and 2 can usually be determined by asking "Why do you want to know (or understand or appreciate)?" This will usually identify what the student wants to be able to do with the knowledge. If the answer is, "Because I find it interesting," however, his objective still should be considered legitimate and worthwhile.

[2] See H. H. McAshan. *Writing Behavioral Objectives: A New Approach.* New York: Harper & Row, 1970, for an attempt to improve the goal component of the behavioral objective statement.

REFERENCES

Cox, C. Benjamin. Behavior as Objective in Education. *Social Education*, May, 1971, 435–449.

Ebel, Robert L. Behavioral Objectives: A Close Look. *Phi Delta Kappan*, November, 1970, *52*: 171–173.

Eisner, Elliott W. Instructional and Expressive Educational Objectives: Their Formulation and Use in Curriculum. *American Educational Research Association Monograph Series on Curriculum Evaluation: No. 3, Instructional Objectives.* Chicago, Rand McNally, 1969, 1–18.

Eiss, Albert F. and Harbeck, Mary Blatt. *Behavioral Objectives in the Affective Domain.* Washington, D.C.: National Science Supervisors Association, 1969.

Instructional Objectives Exchange. *Attitude toward School: Grades K-12.* Los Angeles, California: The Instructional Objectives Exchange, 1970.

MacDonald, James B. and Wolfson, Bernice J. A Case against Behavioral Objectives. *The Elementary School Journal*, December, 1970.

Mager, Robert F. *Preparing Instructional Objectives.* Palo Alto, California: Fearon Publishers, 1962.

Mager, Robert F. *Developing Attitude toward Learning.* Palo Alto, California: Fearon Publishers, 1968.

McAshan, H. H. *Writing Behavioral Objectives: A New Approach.* New York: Harper & Row, 1970.

Miles, David T. and Robinson, Roger E. Behavioral Objectives: An Even Closer Look. *Educational Technology*, June, 1971, 39–44.

Popham, W. James. Probing the Validity of Arguments against Behavioral Goals. Paper presented at AERA annual meeting, Chicago, 1968.

Coffman discusses both the arguments for and weaknesses of essay examinations. If you are an advocate of essay examinations try the rating experiment Coffman describes. The results should help you decide on the fairness of decisions based on your grading of essay examinations.

The articles by Ebel (1971), Palmer (1961), and Hoffmann (1961) referenced at the end of this unit present other views on the issue of item format.

On the Reliability of Ratings of Essay Examinations

WILLIAM E. COFFMAN

For more than half a century, critics have been calling attention to the deficiencies of essay examinations, yet teachers continue to use them. To some extent, the persistence of the essay examination may be only a reflection of the typical tendency of any large enterprise with a long tradition to resist change. On the other hand, the very vigor of essay testing in the face of strong criticism suggests that there may be strong arguments in its favor.

ARGUMENTS FOR ESSAYS

In the first place, a case can be made for the essay examination as a special type of performance test. A major purpose of education is to prepare individuals to interact effectively with other individuals in the realm of ideas. The basic tool of interaction is language, and the educated man is the one who can react appropriately to questions or problems in his field of competence. The scholar performs by speaking and writing. The essay examination constitutes a sample of scholarly performance; hence, it provides a direct measure of educational achievement.

In the second place, the persistence of essay examinations appears to reflect the judgment of teachers that no effective alternatives are available. The typical teacher has grown up with essay examinations; he has encountered a wide variety of them in his own experience as a student, and so far as he can tell, the essay examinations he has prepared seem to have done a satisfactory job. In contrast, when the teacher has tried to prepare objective

From *Research in the Teaching of English*, Spring 1971. Copyright © 1971 by the National Council of Teachers of English. Reprinted by permission of the publisher and the author. This article is taken from a revision that appeared in *Measurement in Education*, Vol. 3, No. 3, March 1972, pp. 1–7.

tests, he has encountered frustration. After a few attempts at building objective tests to measure complex skills and understandings, the typical teacher is likely to return to the familiar essay examination whenever he wishes to do more than measure the student's knowledge of facts.

In the third place, there has been deep concern about the effects of the typical teacher made objective test on students' study habits. Such concern is not without foundation. In many cases, the student obtains his ideas about the things he is expected to learn from the kinds of questions he encounters on examinations; so he governs his study procedures accordingly. Many years ago, Meyer (1934, 1935) reported that the form of the examination expected by students determined the way they went about preparing for the examination. Furthermore, he found that greater achievement on any type of examination followed study in anticipation of an essay examination.

Now there are counter-arguments to each of these. The typical essay examination, with its strict time limits and emotional tensions, is a far cry from the typical setting in which scholarly work proceeds; teachers can, with practice under guidance, learn to prepare good objective tests of important educational objectives; and well-constructed objective tests can provide sound guides to teaching and learning. On the other hand, essay examinations are likely to remain a significant force for a long time to come, particularly in the classroom setting. It therefore seems appropriate to consider ways of minimizing deficiencies in the essay examination when it is used by the individual teacher in measuring outcomes of instruction.

SOURCES OF ERROR

There is extensive evidence that it is difficult to achieve consistency in grading essay examinations. The problem is complex, and appropriate procedures for analyzing it are difficult to design. The accumulated evidence leads, however, to three inescapable conclusions: (1) Different raters tend to assign different grades to the same paper. (2) A single rater tends to assign different grades to the same paper on different occasions. (3) The differences tend to increase as the essay question permits greater freedom of response (Hartog & Rhodes 1936, Vernon & Millican 1954, Findlayson 1951, Pearson 1955, and Noyes 1963).

INTERRATER VARIABILITY

Each of these conclusions is more complex than the simple statement indicates. For example, the grades assigned by different raters may differ as a result of various influences. First, raters may differ in their severity. One may tend to assign relatively high grades while another may tend to assign generally low grades. If some papers are rated by one rater and other papers are rated by another rater, then the level of the mark an examinee receives will depend on which rater happens to rate his paper. Second, raters may differ in the extent to which they distribute grades throughout the score scale. Some tend to distribute scores closely around their average; others will spread scores much more widely. The good student hopes that his paper will be read by the rater who distributes scores widely; the poor student hopes that his paper will be read by the rater who gives few low (or high) scores. Finally, raters differ in the relative values they assign to different papers. A paper judged high by one rater may be judged low by another.

It has sometimes been argued that while the demonstrated differences in ratings assigned by different raters may be relevant to the grading of large-scale essay examinations, they are irrelevant to the grading of classroom tests. Such tests are designed to measure a particular teacher's goals of instruction. The fact that other teachers in other settings might assign different scores to a paper is of no concern. The important point is that the classroom teacher has made his judgment, based on his own goals of instruction and on his own value system.

There is something to be said for this position. The essay examination in the classroom setting is fundamentally different from the essay examination as part of a national testing program. The classroom teacher has direct knowledge of what has been taught and can select questions that require students to apply their knowledge to problems not already dealt with in class. Furthermore, he can instruct the students in how they should deal with questions of particular types. The external examiner, on the other hand, cannot possibly know the details of instruction of the students and has no way of insuring that a question will present the same problem to all examinees. Some of the factors that contribute to error in national testing are not present in classroom testing.

On the other hand, one should not ignore the fact that there remains a problem of scoring reliability. One would hardly defend the right of the teacher to impose an idiosyncratic value system. Ratings that differ too greatly from those of other teachers in the same school will be considered unreliable. Furthermore, ratings will vary from time to time. Whenever a teacher has graded a set of papers, put the papers aside for a period of time, and then graded them a second time, the agreement between the two sets of grades has been less than perfect. The extent to which the ratings will vary from time to time will depend on the individual teacher, the kinds of questions to be graded, and the particular procedure followed in making the ratings. The professional teacher will take steps to find out just how much his own ratings may be expected to vary from time to time.

INTRARATER VARIABILITY

This intrarater variability, like the interrater variability discussed above, consists of three components, one related to the relative standard for different papers, one to the general grading standard, and the third to the variability of the ratings. In other words, if a teacher rates a set of papers twice, without setting up objective controls of some sort, the relative standing of some pupils will shift. In addition, the average rating will be higher one time than the other, and there will be differences in the extent to which the scores are spread out over the range of the ratings.

The extent to which each of these sources of error will be of concern will depend on how the ratings are to be used. If ratings are used only to determine the rank order of pupils, only the first source of error is of concern. If, however, the ratings are treated as direct measures of quality, then all three sources of error become critical. Suppose, for example, that the ratings are made on a percentage basis and that an evaluative scale has been established in advance. Such a situation might be one where the passing grade had been set at 65% and the honor grade at 90%. In such a case, all students would hope that this time the teacher would give generally high rather than low grades. In addition, the poor students would hope that the variability of the scores would be small, that is, that there would be few low (and high) scores; and the good student would wish that the variability would be large, that is, that there would be many high (and low) scores.

The traditional manner of reporting reliability—as a product-moment coefficient of correlation between two sets of ratings—does not adequately assess all of these sources of error in ratings. It takes into account only the fluctuations in relative standing. The formula for computing the coefficient makes an adjustment for any differences in the grading standard or variability between the two sets of ratings. There is, however, a mathematical approach through the analysis-of-variance that provides a way of assessing all three sources of error and of computing different reliability coefficients depending on the way in which the ratings are to be used (Guilford, 1954; Stanley, 1962). It is unlikely, however, that many classroom teachers will have either the technical background to understand this procedure or the computational facility to use it if they did. There is, however, a feasible and meaningful procedure the classroom teacher can use to evaluate his own skill in rating essay examinations.

A RATING EXPERIMENT

The first step in the procedure is to have the pupils identify themselves by number only, so that the ratings won't be influenced improperly by knowledge of which pupil wrote which paper. Next, rate the papers by whatever procedure has been used in the past, but do not record the ratings on the papers. Record them on a separate grading sheet along with the corresponding identification numbers, and then put the papers away in a safe place until there has been time to forget the details of the rating. Use the ratings to make whatever decisions are to be made, that is, determine who made high grades, who made low grades, who failed, or whatever evaluation is usually made, and make a record of these decisions. Several weeks later, repeat the procedure, again assigning ratings and applying the same decision rules. Then count the number of pupils who are placed in a different decision class by the two procedures. What part of the class would be placed in a different group the second time? If the part is small, the reliability is high; if the part is large, the reliability is low.

A good way to summarize such an experiment is illustrated in Table 1. The data are hypothetical, but they are not inconsistent with what is known about variability in ratings from one time to another. The product-moment correlation between the two sets of ratings is .871. Findlayson (1951) reports coefficients ranging .636 to .957 for four raters who re-read two sets of essays. Actually, the reliability for the data in Table 1 based on the analysis-of-variance is .848, somewhat lower than .871 because the second set of scores has a lower average than the first and a greater spread around the average, characteristics that are not reflected in the product-moment correlation.

TABLE 1 Bivariate Frequency Distribution of Hypothetical First and Second Ratings of 25 Papers

Score First Rating	1	2	3	4	5	6	7	8	9	10	11	12	13	14	15	Freq.	Grade
15																	
14																	
13														1		1	
12										1					1	2	A
11								1								1	
10								2		1						3	B
9						1	2		1		1					5	
8						1	3	1								5	
7				1		1										2	C
6						1	1									2	
5		1														1	D
4			1		1											2	
3				1												1	F
2																	
1																	
Frequency	1	1	1	2	3	5	3	3	1	2	1			1	1	25	

The full effect of this difference in reliability depends, however, on how the ratings are to be used. If grades had been assigned on the first set of scores as indicated in the final column of the table, and if grades were then assigned on the basis of the same cutting points for the second set of scores, the table summarizing the two sets of grades would look like Table 2. Twelve of the twenty-five students would be in different grade categories on the two sets. Eight would have received lower grades and four would have received higher grades, reflecting the fact that the second set of ratings is lower on the average. Notice, however, that only one would have received grades that differed by more than one category (the one that received a C on the first rating and an A on the second). The product-moment correlation of these two sets of grades is .767, a figure considerably lower than the .848 obtained with the fifteen-point scale.

The consistency of the two sets of grades would be increased if one were to use different cutting scores for the second set of ratings. If, for example, the cutting scores between A and B were changed from 11–12 to 12–13, that between B and C from 9–10 to 8–9, and that between C and D from 6–7 to 5–6, the summary table would look like Table 3. Here three students would receive lower grades on the second rating and five would receive higher grades. Furthermore, no student's grades on the two sets of

TABLE 2   Bivariate Frequency Distribution of Grades Based on Ratings of Table 1 Assuming No Adjustment in Cutting Scores

First Rating	Second Rating				
	F	D	C	B	A
A				1	2
B			3	1	
C		3	7	1	1
D	1	1	1		
F	2	1			

$r_{12} = .767$

TABLE 3   Bivariate Frequency Distribution of Grades Based on Ratings of Table 1 after Adjusting Cutting Scores

First Rating	Second Rating				
	F	D	C	B	A
A				1	2
B				4	
C		1	9	2	
D	1		2		
F	2	1			

$r_{12} = .869$

ratings would differ by more than one grade category. In other words, by making an adjustment for differences in the averages and in the spread of scores on the two ratings, the percentage of students receiving different ratings would be reduced from 48% (12 out of 25) to 32% (8 out of 25). The product-moment correlation in this case is .869, approximately, the same as that of the original ratings.

This kind of adjustment, however, is after the fact, and takes advantage of any chance factors in the situation. A more systematic way of increasing the reliability of the rating would be to always rate a set of papers twice and add the two sets of ratings together before distributing the grades. Such a procedure, however, would require postponing the reporting of ratings until the second rating could be made. It would scarcely be worth the effort, because there is a much more significant source of error in essay examinations than the error of intraindividual rating variability. That is the error attributable to the sampling of questions.

SAMPLING ERROR

Basic to the concept of sampling reliability is the notion that each sampling unit should be independent and equally likely to be chosen in the sample. In this sense, the basic sampling unit for an essay examination is the question; the size of the sample is determined by the number of different questions in the examination. If the examinee is asked to deal with a number of different aspects of a single topic, the different aspects cannot be considered strictly independent; rather, it is likely that the ability to deal with one aspect of a question is more closely related to the ability to deal with another aspect of the same question than it is with the ability to deal with an aspect of a different question.

There is some evidence that there is an increment in reliability per question if questions are "longer" rather than "shorter" but the increment is not proportional to the time required for longer answers. For example, Godshalk, Swineford, and Coffman (1966) report data indicating that the reliability of a score based on five independent ratings of a twenty-minute essay would be .485 and that a score based on the sum of two such essays would be .655. In contrast, the reliability of a score based on a single forty-minute essay requiring the same amount of testing time as the two twenty-minute essays was only .592 (Godshalk, Swineford, and Coffman, 1966). In general, the greater the number of different questions included in the examination, the higher the reliability of the scores, assuming the same amount of testing time. A major problem facing the teacher who is preparing an essay examination is to effect a satisfactory compromise between the desire to increase the adequacy of the sample by asking many different questions and the desire to ask questions that probe deeply the understanding the student has developed.

It should be recognized that the problem of how large a sample of questions to include is more critical in some situations than in others. If, for example, the test is only one in a series of classroom tests administered as a basis for making tentative decisions about progress to date and next steps to be taken in instruction, then relatively low reliability can be tolerated. Misclassifications at this stage can be corrected on the basis of other tests in the sequence. If, however, the examination is to carry a heavy weight in determining the student's status, as is often the case with a final examination in a course, then it is very important that a sufficiently representative sample of questions be included in the test. Some idea of the relative importance of rating variability and question variability in contributing to the misclassification of students can be developed by preparing two tests considered to be equivalent and then making two ratings of each, say Forms I and II and ratings A and B. Then make four bivariate frequency distributions like the one in Table 1. The distribution for IA and IB and the distribution for IIA and IIB will estimate rating variability. The distributions for IA and IIB and for IIA and IB will estimate score reliability. There will surely be a greater number of discrepancies for the latter two than for the former two.

REDUCING RATING ERROR

Assuming that the problem of sampling questions has been solved, what can the busy teacher do to reduce the error attributable to rating? Four steps seem worthy of consideration: First, use a sufficiently fine scale for recording the ratings. Second, develop clear reference points to anchor the scale. Third, distribute the error randomly rather than systematically. Finally, include multiple rating where feasible. Each of these will be discussed briefly.

1. *Use a Sufficiently Fine Scale.* A comparison of Table 1 and Table 2 illustrates the importance of a sufficiently fine scale. The reliability of the fifteen-point ratings of Table 1 is .848; that of the five-point grade scale is .767. It would be a mistake to combine grades on a number of tests using only a five-point grade scale if the original ratings had been made on a finer scale. On the other hand, too fine a scale may be introducing the appearance of reliability without really achieving any reliable differentiation among the students. Generally, the evidence seems to be that a scale having from seven to fifteen units provides useful information.

2. *Develop Clear Reference Points.* The greater the number of different points on the scale, the more important it is to have clear notions about the characteristics of answers falling at each point. If the examination is concerned with knowledge, one can often define points on the scale by list-

ing the things one would count as evidence. For example, for a question in literature, one might list nine things that could be included in a satisfactory answer and then define the points on a five-point scale in the following manner:

5—Discusses at least four points, describes each accurately, and gives acceptable reasons for each being important; or lists at least seven points.
4—Discusses three points, describes each accurately, and gives acceptable reasons for each being important; or lists at least five.
3—Discusses two points, describes each accurately, and gives acceptable reasons for each being important; or lists at least four.
2—Discusses one point, describes it accurately, and gives an acceptable reason for it being important; or lists at least three.
1—Lists at least two points.

The more clearly the different points on the scale can be defined, the more reliable the rating is likely to be.

If the examination is concerned with the ability to develop a synthesis of several ideas or with other characteristics that are difficult to count, one may anchor the scale by developing model answers. One way of doing this is to write out a top quality answer at the time the examination is prepared and then look through the papers written by the students for a "middle-level" paper, and perhaps for papers illustrating other points on the scale, before beginning the actual rating. Another way of developing an anchor is to let the papers themselves determine the anchor by sorting the papers according to a predetermined distribution that is to be used for every examination for the same class. For example, with a class of twenty-five pupils and a nine-point scale, one might assign the worst paper a one and the best a nine and so on according to the following scheme:

Scale	1	2	3	4	5	6	7	8	9
Number of Papers	1	2	3	4	5	4	3	2	1

Such a system has the advantage that it insures that there will be no shift in either the average score or in the spread of scores regardless of when the papers are rated. It has the disadvantage that one is often forced to assign different ratings to papers that one cannot honestly differentiate. It seems unjust to force the papers into a predetermined distribution, perhaps by flipping a coin. One may consider, however, that the alternative is often to run the risk of creating a greater injustice by the way rating standards may shift from time to time.

3. *Distribute Error Randomly.* One can reduce the probability that errors will be distributed in a biased manner by rating question by question rather than student by student and by giving a number of different tests through the term. Each time a question is to be rated the papers should be arranged in a different order. If such a procedure is adopted it is likely that

a student whose essay was rated too high one time will probably have his paper rated somewhat too low another time so that the sum of his scores over a number of questions (or examinations) will more nearly reflect his actual ability. On the other hand, if all questions on a paper are rated before moving to the next paper, there is the likelihood that whatever errors are being made at the time will be reflected in all of the ratings for a single student. Furthermore, it is likely that systematic error will be introduced in the sense that the impression made by an answer to one question will influence the rating of answers to succeeding questions.

   4. *Include Multiple Ratings.* A teacher can never completely escape the systematic error reflecting his own special biases; he can, however, reduce the effect of variations in his standards from time to time by adopting the procedures outlined above. In addition, he can reduce the effects of personal bias by working cooperatively with other teachers in the rating of essay examinations. One way that this might be accomplished is described by Diederich and Link (1967). In essence, the procedure calls for the development of common examinations to be used throughout a school, each examination to be rated by more than one teacher. In general, two ratings, even if they are made rapidly in order to permit time for a greater number of ratings to be made, will be preferable to a single rating. The sum of the two ratings will be more reliable than a single rating. There is an additional advantage to cooperative grading projects. By making bivariate frequency distributions of the type described in Table 1 using ratings from pairs of teachers, a staff can become aware of the extent to which individuals differ in the three sources of rating error; that is, differences in standards, differences in the tendency to spread scores around the average, and differences in the relative value assigned to different papers. In general, when made aware of discrepancies, teachers tend to move their own ratings in the direction of the average ratings of the group. Over a period of time, the ratings of the staff as a group tend to become more reliable.

SUMMARY

The sources of error in essay examinations are complex. Some error arises because the questions in an examination are only a sample of all the possible questions that might be asked. Some error is the result of differences between raters. Some is due to variability in the judgments of a rater from one time to another. Both interindividual and intraindividual variability can be further broken down into at least three components. The extent to which any of these various sources of error are present depends on how the essay questions are prepared, on how the responses are rated, and on how the scores are used. Awareness on the part of the teacher of the factors contributing to unreliability—an awareness that can be increased by simple experiments—is a first step in improving the reliability of the teacher's essay examinations.

REFERENCES

Diederich, Paul B. and Link, Frances R. Cooperative evaluation in English. *Evaluation as feedback and guide*, edited by Fred T. Wilhelms. Washington, D.C.: Association for Supervision and Curriculum Development, NEA, 1967.

Findlayson, D. S. The reliability of the marking of essays. *British Journal of Educational Psychology*, 1951, 21, 126–134.

Godshalk, F. I., Swineford, Frances and Coffman, W. E. *The measurement of writing ability*. New York: College Entrance Examination Board, 1966.

Guilford, J. P. *Psychometric methods* (Second edition). New York: McGraw-Hill, 1954.

Hartog, P. and Rhodes, E. C. *The marks of examiners*. New York: Macmillan, 1936.

Meyer, G. An experimental study of the old and new types of examination: I. The effect of the examination set on memory. *Journal of Educational Psychology*, 1934, 25, 641–661.

Meyer, G. An experimental study of the old and new types of examination: II. Methods of study. *Journal of Educational Psychology*, 1935, 26, 30–40.

Noyes, E. S. Essay and objective tests in English. *College Board Review*, 1963, No. 49, 7–10.

Pearson, R. The test fails as an entrance examination. *College Board Review*, 1955, No. 25, 2–9.

Stanley, J. C. Analysis-of-variance principles applied to the grading of essay tests. *Journal of Experimental Education*, 1962, 30, 279–283.

Vernon, P. E. and Millican, G. D. A further study of the reliability of English essays. *British Journal of Statistical Psychology*, 1954, 7, 65–74.

Some educators have suggested that the poor content sampling in essay tests could be minimized by providing optional questions. This procedure is not recommended by measurement experts. There are at least three major reasons why optional questions should not be given: "(a) It is difficult to construct questions of equal difficulty; (b) students do not have the ability to select those questions upon which they will be able to do best; and (c) the good student may be penalized because he is challenged by the more difficult and complex questions." (Mehrens and Lehmann, 1973, p. 222)

In this article DuCette and Wolk report the results of an experiment on the efficacy of providing optional questions. Students given optional questions actually achieved lower scores than those students not given options.

Test Performance and the Use of Optional Questions

JOSEPH DuCETTE
STEPHEN WOLK

Authors' abstract   The technique of allowing students optional items on an essay examination was related to test performance. One hundred and eighty-seven graduate students in educational psychology were given either an optional or a non-optional essay examination as a mid-term evaluation. It was found that the Ss given the optional examination achieved significantly poorer scores than those Ss not given options. This result, in conjunction with the established reliability and content validity for the test across experimental conditions, was interpreted as indicative of selective student preparation under the different conditions. The inference was drawn that test format can influence test performance as well as the nature and extent of general classroom achievement.

Every teacher who uses essay questions to evaluate student achievement faces the problem of making sure that his test which supposedly measures a content unit actually contains an adequate sample of that unit. Since an essay test in which all content is covered is usually unfeasible because of time pressures, the typical strategy is to write a test that in total covers as much content as possible, but which then allows the student the option of choosing a certain percentage of the questions asked. Despite the pervasive-

From *The Journal of Experimental Education*, Spring 1972, 40, 3: 21–24. Reprinted with permission of author and publisher.

ness of this technique, however, most testing experts agree that such a procedure is not good testing practice. These warnings concerning the use of options on essay exams usually center on the issues of content validity, reliability, and undesirable study habits and take such forms as: "The use of optional questions would mean that the tests written by different students would represent different sets of goals" (1); or, "When pupils anticipate the use of optional questions they can prepare answers on several topics in advance, commit them to memory, and then select questions where the answers are most appropriate" (2).

Despite such agreement about the inadequacies of giving options in an essay examination, it is clear that most of these criticisms are conceptual rather than empirical. In general, research conducted to delineate the sources of weakness of this common testing format has been less than comprehensive, and, in one instance (5) presents evidence contrary to previously accepted arguments supporting the unreliability of this technique. It becomes apparent, for example, that the effect optional questions have on the content validity of an examination is a function of the discrepancy between the items in assessing different areas of instruction. If an essay examination contains items all of which have a high degree of commonality in sampling content, then any subset of these items will be essentially the same as any other subset. Consequently, giving options in such a case can not have a serious effect on the content validity of the examination. Similarly, such a test would also be far less open to problems concerning inter-item unreliability. In most cases, however, essay examinations are specifically designed so that the items do not sample similar content. Even under these conditions the research concerning optional questions is still not clear.

Wiseman and Wrigley have reported a study that was specifically concerned with the unreliability in assessment when optional questions are used (5). They point out that unreliability of a test can be a function of inter-item variation, inter-scorer variation, and the interaction between these two. While the use of optional questions seems to run the risk of maximizing inter-item variation, and thus unreliability, Wiseman and Wrigley have demonstrated that the source of this variation is not always apparent. Using analysis of covariance, they were able to demonstrate that variation in test scores in an optional essay examination was due predominantly to student differences in specifically required abilities rather than low inter-scorer reliability or intrinsic differences in item difficulty. The authors concluded that:

> The use of essay examinations in which children are allowed to choose one topic out of many seems unlikely, therefore, to introduce any substantial element of error into the marking. Or, to put it in more realistic terms, the reliability would not be likely to rise to any extent if a choice of topic were not permitted. That the abolition of choice might affect reliability and validity adversely still remains a possibility (5:137–138).

It is clear from studies such as this and others (4) that while the conceptual arguments against the use of options in respect to content validity and reliability are often stated, the data supporting these arguments are far from substantial or consistent. Where the data are even more lacking, however, is in relating this testing procedure to student achievement. Edwards and Scannel have noted that this area has been almost totally neglected and remains the one weakest link in the case against the use of options (1). The argument here is that giving options encourages poor preparation on the students' part, resulting in lower test scores and eventually poorer achievement. There are, however, no substantial data to support such an argument at this time. This is an unfortunate lack since of all the issues associated with optional-item tests, that of encouragement of truncated preparation by students is potentially the most disturbing to the ongoing teaching-learning processes in the classroom. Evidence which would support the inference of such preparation would be, of all arguments, the most severe against the employment of such a testing procedure. It is our intention in writing this paper to present such data.

It should be noted that any research designed to support the inference that differences between the test performances of students given options on an examination, as opposed to students not given such options, faces certain inherent problems. In general, these problems are related to the fact that it is difficult to develop a research design which, on the one hand, is valid for the classroom, while on the other maintains a necessary degree of experimental control. As used in this study, giving options on an examination corresponds to an experimental manipulation. As such, the treatment unit should be the individual student. In a practical sense, of course, the treatment unit will always be a class, raising all of the problems inherent in using intact groups. Another problem in this kind of research is that the results will obviously depend on the specific test that is used to measure student achievement. An unreliable test, or an invalid test, or a test which results in an overestimation or an underestimation of student achievement will seriously affect the inferences that can be drawn from the data. In regard to this last point, Meyer has found that students do not always select those options on which their performance could be maximized (3). If the test can allow factors such as this to influence the data, then the case against the use of options will, of necessity, be weakened.

An adequate test of the question being asked in this paper, then, must utilize an experimental design that maintains adequate validity while remaining within the confines of methodological considerations. There would seem to be several necessary steps in such a procedure. First, the examinations (either with options or without) should be given in a real situation where the outcome of the test is important to the student. Second, the test should be scored by the teacher who is ultimately responsible for using the test as an evaluation device. As long as this teacher can demonstrate adequate reliability in his scoring, the necessity of having alternative scorers (which, of course, is completely uncharacteristic of a classroom situation) is alleviated. Finally all of the items on the test should assess a common, clearly circumscribed body of knowledge. This means that every student will be tested on the same body of knowledge but will be allowed to display this knowledge in an individual manner. This would seem to be a sound testing procedure since problems with content validity are minimized while still allowing the student the benefit of any positive morale effect often cited as concommitant with option-giving on an examination. By recognizing and employing such methodological steps in testing, all of which are directly applicable to the classroom, the following research problem is posed; Does the presence of optimal items on an essay examination have an effect on performance in that examination?

METHOD

The results reported in this study were derived from eight classes of educational psychology taught by the senior author over a 2-year period of time. In each of these four semesters the author taught two sections of the same course, each section drawing its students from the same population. In every case the content of the course was the same, an identical textbook was used, and the lectures and classroom demonstrations were as similar as possible under classroom conditions. The data reported here are from the mid-term examination in this course which was identical for all eight classes. Since all of the Ss were evening students at a large metropolitan university, and since there is little interaction between such students from one semester to the next, it was felt that the problem of the questions on the test being known to succeeding classes was a minimal one. To minimize this further, all copies of the test were retained by the instructor after the examination was finished.

The procedure employed in every semester was to randomly assign one class to the option condition and one to the non-option condition. One week prior to the mid-term examination each class was told either that they would be given an essay test on which they could choose certain questions to answer (option condition), or that they would be given a test on which all of the questions had to be answered (non-optional condition). In both cases the classes were given an identical examination. This examination consisted of two groups of three questions which assessed basic knowledge of educational psychology. The items were specifically designed to be equal in difficulty and to have high content commonality. This was determined by a criterion analysis of acceptable answers. In the option condition the students could choose two of the three questions from each section. To equate scores across groups, the lowest score of the three to each section was eliminated for the non-option students. Each question was graded on the basis of 26 points, producing a total of 104 points for the entire exam. For both conditions the students were allowed as much time as they needed to finish the exam. The test was scored item by item without knowledge of the student's name.

RESULTS AND DISCUSSION

Since all of the data reported in this experiment are derived from one test, the nature of this test is of obvious concern. In order to present an accurate picture of this test, several kinds of data will be reported concerning the entire test as well as individual items. Of special interest are the test's reliability, the level of difficulty of each item, and the homogeneity of item content. To ascertain scorer reliability a random sample of the tests was rescored ($N = 50$) by the original scorer in such a way that the original score for each item and the total score were unknown. This resulted in a coefficient of .95 between the original and rescored total. Presented in Table 1 is a summary table containing each item's average difficulty across all subjects in both conditions (Column 1). Column 2 presents the total percentage of the time each question was chosen as an option in the option condition. Column 3 presents the percentage of the time that each item was dropped as one of the lowest scores in the non-option condition.

Tests of significance indicated no differences in level of difficulty between any of the items in the two sections of the exam. There is also no significant difference between the items in relation to the percentage of the time they were chosen by the student in the option condition or dropped in the non-option condition.

Additional data concerning the homogeneity of the items is presented in Table 2. This table presents the intercorrelations of the six items used on the test as well as each item's correlation with the total score.

In summary, these data support four points in relation to the test: 1) the test was reliably scored; 2) the test items were of equal difficulty; 3) there was no distinct pattern of choice in the option condition or rejection in the non-option condition; and 4) the test items were relatively homogeneous in their assessment of content. These data support the idea that the results reported below are due to the experimental manipulation (i.e., the giving of options) rather than to variables within the test itself.

Table 3 represents the means and standard deviation for the option and non-option conditions in the four semesters utilized in this study.

In order to minimize the possible effect of using intact groups, an analysis of variance was computed with groups as one factor. Thus, a 4×2 analysis of variance (semester by test condition) was employed using total

TABLE 1 Mean Point Score, Percentage Choice as an Option, and Percentage Rejection in Scoring for Each Item

Item	Mean score	% Chosen as option	% Rejected in scoring
1	16.56	76	33
2	17.43	58	39
3	16.78	67	28
4	17.69	73	28
5	19.03	64	28
6	18.56	64	39

TABLE 2 Inter-Item and Item by Total Score Correlation Matrix

	Item Numbers					
	2	3	4	5	6	Total
1	.68	.82	.77	.61	.74	.89
2		.74	.68	.41	.57	.88
3			.70	.63	.80	.90
4				.75	.60	.87
5					.34	.79
6						.83

TABLE 3 Means and Standard Deviation of Test Scores by Semester and Test Condition

	Semester				
	1	2	3	4	Total
No Option					
N	23	17	22	34	
Mean	73.17	81.29	77.64	77.74	77.25
S.D.	13.96	13.52	17.93	17.89	16.28
Range	94-48	98-56	101-43	104-43	104-43
Option					
N	21	21	19	30	
Mean	63.57	66.95	66.32	68.20	66.45
S.D.	19.21	23.12	25.50	24.76	23.05
Range	88-31	97-23	101-20	102-17	102-17

scores as the dependent variable. This analysis indicated a significant effect for type of test ($F = 13.92$, df $= 1,179$, $p < .01$) with no significant effect for year and no significant interaction. An F_{max} test was performed on the variances of the treatment conditions. This analysis indicated non-homogeneity of variance across test conditions, a factor which, given the level of significance for this variable, weakens only slightly the inferences that can be drawn from these data.

These data clearly indicate that giving options in the examination used in this study produces poorer test performance. This does not necessarily mean that with another type of test, giving options would not produce the opposite result. As has been mentioned previously, a test whose items are heterogeneous in sample content will probably result in higher test performance for students given options. The ultimate concern of teachers, of course, is not with test performance per se but with the actual achievement that any test supposedly measures. It will be argued in this paper that giving options on an examination not only affects scores but also affects actual achievement.

Previous discussion has established that the test employed in the present study, under the option and non-option conditions, maintained more than a sufficient degree of homogeneity in terms of content analysis. Both the level of difficulty and assessed content areas were relatively homogeneous across items. Since lack of homogeneity has been offered as a determinant of differential performance levels of students when they are given optional questions, the fact that the test used in this experiment did not suffer from these conditions considerably minimized these effects. That such variation in test characteristics was held to a minimum in the present report allows one to infer the potency of another factor, student preparation (and beyond this, general academic achievement), as the primary source of differences in performance.

Educators have argued that the employment of optional questions allows students to study selectively for an examination. Little, if any, evidence has been marshalled to support such a contention. The present data, however, would support the notion of selective or attenuated student preparation in anticipation of an optional essay examination. Specifically, the distributions of scores for the option and non-option conditions indicate a relative negative skewness for the option condition. Thus, there is the presence of more variation in test performance (manifested by non-homogeneity of variance), centered below the mean, for the examination with optional questions. Specifically, there is a noticeably larger frequency of very low scores in the option condition than in the non-option condition. Thus, it appears that in the option condition some students are willing to risk compensating for poor preparation by a strategic choice of items. When such a strategy cannot work, as when the test contains items that are homogeneous in content and reliable, then selective preparation exemplified in the present findings can exert a negative influence on achievement, overriding any positive "morale" effect of partially determining the nature of one's evaluation.

If, indeed, optional questions produce poorer test performance, then such a test format would seem to have highly restricted utility for the classroom. It is instructive that the source of such restriction lies not in any inherent invalidity or unreliability, but rather in the manipulation the teacher unwittingly creates in employing such an assessment technique. Given the wide use of this technique, this would seem to be an important point for teachers to understand.

When one considers that most essay examinations have items much more heterogeneous than those reported in the present study, and probably less reliable, the most likely product that could flow from option-giving on an examination would be a clear distortion of the actual or potential achievement of students. In essence, the guarantee of options on an examination is, for some students, the option of investing less effort, and investing it in a selective manner. Such an outcome could conceivably destroy the coherence of a unit of instruction and seriously weaken the content validity of the examination.

REFERENCES

1. Edwards, A. J.; Scannel, D. P., *Educational Psychology*, International Textbook, Scranton, Pennsylvania, 1968.
2. Gronlund, N. D., *Measurement and Evaluation in Teaching*, Macmillan, New York, 1967.
3. Meyer, G., "The Choice of Questions on Essay Examinations," *The Journal of Educational Psychology*, 30:161–171, 1939.
4. Stalnaker, J. M., "A Study of Optional Questions on Examinations," *School and Society*, 44: 829–832, 1936.
5. Wiseman, S.; Wrigley, J., "Essay-Reliability; The Effect of Choice of Essay-Title," *Educational and Psychological Measurement*, 18:128–138, 1958.

The effects of test anxiety, the value of frequent exams, and the role of feedback on exams are popular topics. Marso reports on a study that examined the effects of these variables on achievement. He uses an inferential statistical procedure called an analysis of covariance. One purpose of an inferential statistics test, or test of significance, is to tell us the probability that observed differences between two or more groups occurred by chance alone. If the probability is small (less than .05), we typically conclude that the differences are not due to chance. The analysis of covariance procedure, as used by Marso, is for the purpose of adjusting for any difference in mental ability among the groups in the analysis. This procedure rules out the possible interpretation that initial differences in mental ability could account for the resultant differences in achievement.

Marso's results suggest that students achieve more from frequent graded tests followed by feedback. Test anxiety does not interact with the various testing procedures. Do you think his findings would hold up for elementary school pupils? What do you think Marso would have found if he had used test anxiety as a dependent rather than an independent variable? Are there methods of providing feedback which could reduce or intensify subsequent test anxiety? Is there any logic to the proposition that frequent testing would reduce test anxiety?

Classroom Testing Procedures, Test Anxiety, and Achievement

RONALD N. MARSO

Author's abstract   Four groups (N = 116) were maintained in a 4-factor analysis of covariance design to determine if more frequent, graded unit examinations followed by test feedback facilitate achievement and allow students with high-measured test anxiety to perform better on final course examinations. The testing procedures studied consisted of the administration of 168 examination items as either three or six unit exams, grading or not grading the unit exams, and providing or not providing class feedback and discussion following the examinations. Analysis of performance on two posttest measures indicated that the subjects achieved more from frequent, graded unit tests followed by feedback; however, variations of these conditions did not appear to influence the performance of the students with high-measured test anxiety.

From *Journal of Experimental Education*, Spring 1970, 38, 3: 54–58. Reprinted with permission of author and publisher.

Evidence indicates an increasing tendency for educators to view classroom testing as an integral part of the teaching-learning process (12). That tests influence learning would seem particularly true of the more frequently administered teacher-devised tests which are closely involved with day-to-day teaching-learning activities in the classroom. Thorndike and Hagan (11:28) stated that: "Testing procedures control the learning process to a greater degree, perhaps, than any other teaching device." The teacher-devised examinations can be used not only to evaluate student progress but also to facilitate student learning; however, few teachers take full advantage of tests as a teaching-aid. Koester (5:208) stated, "Unfortunately tests are too frequently used only to evaluate the scholastic progress of students, and consequently the instructional possibilities are minimized." Regarding testing at the college level Wood (13:2) commented. "Strangely enough, an even more significant lag in the application of basic principles of psychological measurement is evident in our colleges and universities."

If one assumes that tests facilitate learning, then the question arises as to what causes this facilitating effect. Many explanations have been advanced for the facilitating effect of testing upon student achievement, such as knowledge of progress, reduction of anxiety, extrinsic motivation, reinforcement, structuring of the course, guiding student study, and forced practice with the material. None of these explanations however, are well supported by research evidence (6). Some empirical evidence exists which supports more frequent testing, testing with feedback, and grading of tests to facilitate achievement (9,10). Some research has been reported regarding both the inhibiting effect of test anxiety on classroom performance and on testing procedures which reduce this inhibiting effect (7). The purpose of this study was to investigate these testing procedures in a multivariate research design with test anxiety as a classification variable. To clarify further the relationship between testing procedures and achievement, the researcher was attempting to identify some testing procedures which would increase the test performance of students with high-measured test anxiety. Ebel (3), has suggested that frequent similar experiences with tests and avoiding "all the eggs in one basket" situations in grading might allow highly anxious students to perform better.

The procedures were designed to test the following hypotheses: (a) Students exposed to test feedback following unit tests achieve better on a comprehensive final examination. (b) Students taking more frequent unit examinations achieve better on a comprehensive final examination. (c) Students graded for their performance on unit examinations achieve better on a comprehensive final examination. (d) Students with high-measured test anxiety will perform better on a comprehensive final examination after having experienced frequent, graded, unit examinations with feedback.

The sample consisted of 116 students enrolled in four sections of an introductory educational psychology course taught by the author at the University of Nebraska. Students were assigned to sixteen experimental cells in which the following conditions were produced:

(a) *Test Feedback:* Each of the four classes was randomly assigned to one of two test feedback categories, feedback or no-feedback conditions. Following administration of the unit examinations, Ss in the two test feedback classes were presented with the correct response to the test items and were allowed to discuss the items. Thus a form of additional instruction was included in this condition as it typifies existing practices in the classroom. This instruction was counterbalanced in the no-feedback classes by using the time for more regular classroom instruction. Ss in the two no-feedback classes were provided with their letter grade for each unit test, but they were not provided with a discussion of the test items or with knowledge of the appropriateness of their responses to the test items following the administration of the unit examinations.

(b) *Test Frequency:* The four class sections were randomly assigned to two test frequency categories. Ss in two class sections were given six 28-item unit examinations while Ss in the other two class sections were given three 56-item unit examinations during the course. All Ss were exposed to the same 168 test items, only the time presentation of the items was varied. This was done to control item exposure so that this factor did not confound the frequency variable.

(c) *Grading of Unit Tests:* Ss within each of the classes were randomly assigned to two test grading conditions. Ss assigned to an ungraded condition were informed that they were required to take the unit tests but that they would take the tests only for learning purposes as the unit examinations would not be graded. In addition these Ss were informed that they would be graded on the course final examination and the term paper. The fact that all Ss were working for a course grade and were exposed to the test items allowed the researcher to study the effects of grading unit examinations without the potentially confounding effects of differences arising from variations in test item exposure or motivation for course grade. Only two students became displeased with their assigned testing condition; they were given their choice of conditions and excluded from the study.

(d) *Test Anxiety:* Ss within each class were assigned to two levels of test anxiety on the basis of their scores on a measure of test anxiety. Ss who scored above the midpoint for the sample were classified as the high test anxiety students, and Ss who scored below the midpoint for the sample were classified as the low test anxiety students.

As some of the condition assignments were random by class rather than by individual subject, a $2 \times 2 \times 2 \times 2$ analysis of covariance unequal cell-size design was used. The sample assignment procedure resulted in: Ss in the first class section were given six unit tests with feedback; Ss in the second class section were given six unit tests with no feedback; Ss in the third class were given three unit tests with feedback; Ss in the fourth class section were given three unit tests with no feedback; and in addition Ss within the class sections were randomly assigned to either graded or nongraded conditions and were classified as either high or low test anxiety students.

In addition to the testing involved in the experimental conditions, an achievement pretest, two achievement posttests, a measure of mental ability, and a measure of test anxiety were administered to the Ss. The Quick Word Test (QWT) Form Am Level 2 was administered to assess the Ss' mental ability (1). These scores were used as a covariate to adjust for any differences in mental ability among the groups in the statistical analysis. A combination of anxiety scales identified by Carrier and Jewell (2) was used as a measure of test anxiety. These scores were used as a classification variable in the analysis of variance procedures completed on the criterion scores. The pretest achievement measures consisted of fifty-six 4-alternate multiple-choice items selected from an existing departmental examination for the course. Item selection was based upon content validity, cognitive level, and item analysis data derived from two administrations of the exam to two large groups of students who had previously completed the course taught by the author. The pretest scores were used to determine if any difference existed among the groups in prior knowledge of the course materials. Analysis of variance procedures completed on these scores indicated that no difference existed among the groups. This same 56-item examination was readministered at the end of the semester as an unannounced post-test. The second posttest was administered as the regularly scheduled course final examination. It consisted of 125 4-alternate multiple-choice questions which were also selected from an existing departmental examination using the previously mentioned criteria. Regarding the cognitive levels of the items, twenty-nine items were judged to be measuring at the recall level, sixty-seven items at the understanding level, and twenty-nine at the application or higher levels. Of the items, ninety-two had a point biserial correlation of $+.25$ or higher with the total score of the departmental examination. The remaining items had correlations in the lower twenties with the exam total test score or they were rewritten. The Kuder-Richardson lower bound estimates of reliability for the posttests were .77 and .83 respectively.

FINDINGS

The effects of the varied testing procedures were assessed primarily through analysis of covariance procedures completed on the scores obtained from the two posttests and through t-test comparisons between the means on the unit tests. The analysis of covariance of the scores derived from the 56-item unannounced posttest utilizing the QWT scores as a covariate is presented in Table 1. Significant values for the F ratio were obtained for the test frequency factor and for the levels of test anxiety. The F-ratio values for these two factors were 3.98 and 11.62 respectively. Both of these values are significant at the .01 level of confidence. These tests indicate that Ss taking six unit tests scored higher on this posttest than did those students taking three unit tests and that Ss with low tets anxiety scored higher on this posttest than did Ss with high test anxiety. Neither the differences for the other two main effects, although in the predicted directions, nor the interaction effects were significant.

The analysis of covariance of the scores derived from the 125-item announced posttest utilizing the QWT scores as a covariate is presented in Table 2. This analysis yielded significant F-ratio values of 4.83 for the test

TABLE 1   F Tests of ANCOVA Main Effects with QWT Scores as a Covariate and the Unannounced Posttest as the Dependent Variable

Source of Variation	SS	df	MS	F
A Test Feedback	49. 53	1	49. 53	1. 31
B Test Anxiety	440. 54	1	440. 54	11. 62**
C Test Frequency	150. 81	1	150. 81	3. 98**
D Test Motivation	45. 15	1	45. 15	1. 19

All levels of interaction nonsignificant

* $F_{(.05; 1. 99)}$ = 3. 95

** $F_{(.01; 1. 99)}$ = 6. 93

TABLE 2   F Tests of ANCOVA Main Effects with QWT Scores as Covariate and Announced Posttest Scores as the Dependent Variable

Source of Variation	SS	df	MS	F
A Test Feedback	594. 02	1	594. 02	4. 83*
B Test Anxiety	603. 06	1	603. 06	4. 90*
C Test Frequency	118. 62	1	118. 62	. 96
D Test Motivation	72. 65	1	72. 65	. 59

All levels of interaction nonsignificant

* $F_{(.05; 1. 99)}$ = 3. 95

** $F_{(.05; 1. 99)}$ = 6. 93

feedback condition and 4.90 for the test anxiety factor. Both of these values are significant well beyond the .05 level of confidence. These tests indicate that Ss exposed to unit test feedback scored higher on this posttest than did Ss in the no test feedback condition and that Ss classified as having high test anxiety did not perform as well on this criterion measure. The differences appearing for the other two main effects in this analysis, although in the predicted direction, were not significant, and no interaction effects were evi-

TABLE 3   ANCOVA Main Effect Condition Means

Unannounced Posttest	Announced Posttest
$A_1 = 32.4$ $A_2 = 31.1$	$A_1 = 88.3$ $A_2 = 83.7$
$B_1 = 33.9$ $B_2 = 29.7$	$B_1 = 88.5$ $B_2 = 83.6$
$C_1 = 32.9$ $C_2 = 30.6$	$C_1 = 87.0$ $C_2 = 85.0$
$D_1 = 32.4$ $D_2 = 31.1$	$D_1 = 86.8$ $D_2 = 85.2$
A_1 = Feedback	C_1 = Six Unit Tests
A_2 = No Feedback	C_2 = Three Unit Tests
B_1 = Low Anxiety	D_1 = Graded Unit Tests
B_2 = High Anxiety	D_2 = Ungraded Unit Tests

TABLE 4   Means and t Values for Graded and Ungraded Students Taking Six Unit Examinations

Test Number	Graded		Ungraded		
	N	M	N	M	t
1.	33	19.4	32	18.3	1.47
2	31	17.8	33	16.5	1.76*
3	32	18.6	33	16.7	2.60**
4	32	18.3	32	17.6	.77
5	28	18.4	32	16.4	2.49**
6	28	18.6	33	16.3	2.00**

* t $(.05; M_1 \geq M_2) = 1.65$

** t $(.01; M_1 \geq M_2) = 2.33$

TABLE 5   Means and t Values for Graded and Ungraded Students Taking Three Unit Examinations

Test Number	Graded		Ungraded		t
	N	M	N	M	
1	30	37. 3	26	35. 0	1. 47
2	27	38. 2	23	34. 4	2. 09*
3	28	37. 7	23	33. 8	2. 49**

* t $(.05; M_1 \geq M_2) = 1.65$ ** t $(.01; M_1 \geq M_2) = 2.33$

dent. The first order condition means for the analyses completed on the two criterion measures are presented in Table 3.

Although grading of the unit tests resulted in differences only approaching significance on the posttest measures, comparisons of the unit test mean scores for the graded and ungraded groups utilizing t-tests yielded significant differences in favor of the graded group on the second, third, fifth, and sixth tests for Ss taking six unit examinations and on the second and third tests for Ss taking three unit examinations. These results suggest that grading of unit tests does positively influence student achievement even though the gains may be small and possibly temporary in nature. The mean scores on the unit tests and the t-values for the obtained differences are presented in Tables 4 and 5.

SUMMARY AND CONCLUSIONS

College students $(N = 116)$ were assigned to four classroom testing conditions. Ss were given three or six unit examinations, provided with either feedback or no feedback following the unit examinations, and were assigned or not assigned letter grades for their performance on the unit examinations. In addition Ss were classified as having high or low test anxiety. Upon completion of the course an announced and unannounced posttest were administered to the students. A 4-factor analysis of covariance statistical procedure was then completed on the scores derived from the two posttest measures and yielded these findings related to the four basic research hypotheses: (a) Ss exposed to test feedback following unit tests achieved significantly higher on the course final examination. This difference only approached significance on the unannounced posttest. (b) Ss taking six unit tests as compared to three unit tests scored significantly higher on the unannounced posttest measure. The difference only approached significance on the announced final examination. This trend was expected on the basis of past research which indicates that the cramming prior to announced final examinations may reduce the effects of some classroom variables (4,8). (c) Students graded on the unit tests scored significantly greater on the unit tests; however, this difference only approached significance on the posttest measures. (d) Test anxiety did not interact with the testing procedures maintained during this study. On the basis of questionnaire responses, it was found that the highly anxious students did more strongly favor the more frequent unit tests ($X^2 =$ 11.62, significant beyond the .05 level of confidence). However, only slight trends seldom approaching significance were observed regarding interactions between the anxiety factor and the testing procedures. Thus, this study failed to identify testing procedures which allow students with high levels of test anxiety to perform better.

In summation it appears from these data that unit tests and testing procedures do influence student achievement as measured by performance on examinations. In addition these data support previous research and theoretical formulations which suggest that feedback, spacing of learning, motivation, and anxiety are related to student learning in a course of study. The implication for classroom practice seems to be that testing procedures should incorporate frequent, graded, unit tests followed by class discussion. However, the data did not support the contention that the more structured and supposedly less anxiety provoking learning conditions of frequent, graded, unit examinations with feedback would allow students with high measured test anxiety to perform better.

REFERENCES

1. Borgatta, E. F. and Corsini, R. J. *Quick Word Test Manual.* Harcourt, Brace, and World, Inc., Chicago, 1964.
2. Carrier, N. A. and Jewell, D. O. "Efficiency in Measuring the Effect of Anxiety upon Academic Performance," *The Journal of Educational Psychology,* 57: 23–26, 1966.
3. Ebel, R. L. *Measuring Educational Achievement.* Prentice-Hall., Inc., Englewood Cliffs, New Jersey, 1965.
4. Keys, H. "The Influence of Learning and Retention of Weekly as Opposed to Monthly Tests," *Journal of Educational Psychology,* 25: 427–436, 1934.
5. Koester, G. A., "Using Instructor-made Tests for Instructional Purposes," *Educational Research Bulletin,* 36: 207–208, 1957.
6. Lindquist, E. F. (Ed.). *Educational Measurement.* American Council on Education, Washington, D.C., 1951.
7. McKeachie, W. J., Pollie, D., and Speisman, J. "Relieving Anxiety in Classroom Examinations," *Journal of Abnormal and Social Psychology.* 49: 245–249, 1958.

8. Nachman, M. and Opachinsky, S. "The Effects of Different Teaching Methods: A Methodological Study," *Journal of Educational Psychology*, 49: 245–249, 1958.

9. Statler, L. S. and Pophen, I. W. "Quizzes Contribution to Learning," *Journal of Educational Psychology*, 51: 322–325, 1960.

10. Stone, G. R. "The Training Function of Examinations: Retest Performance as a Function of the Amount and Kind of Critique Information," *USAF Personnel Training Research Center Research Report*, No. AFPTRC-TN-55-8, 1955.

11. Thorndike, R. L. and Hagen, E. *Measurement and Evaluation in Psychology and Education*, Third Edition, John Wiley & Sons, New York, 1969.

12. Wingo, M. G. "Methods of Teaching," in C. W. Harris (Ed.), *Encyclopedia of Educational Research, Third Edition*, American Educational Research Association, Macmillan Co., New York, pp. 848–861, 1960.

13. Wood, D. A. *Test Construction*, Charles E. Merrill Books, Inc., Columbus, Ohio, 1961.

Item analysis data help the instructor to judge test quality, revise subsequent tests, increase test construction skills, and provide diagnostic assistance to students and teachers. Yet quality control checks on their tests are often neglected by classroom teachers. Lange, Lehmann, and Mehrens demonstrate the value of item analyses in improving tests. Revising items based on item analyses has proved to be both more beneficial and efficient than writing new items.

Using Item Analysis To Improve Tests

ALLAN LANGE
IRVIN J. LEHMANN
WILLIAM A. MEHRENS

Every major textbook in measurement discusses the improvement of a test through the use of item statistics. Most students taking a course in test construction remember that item analysis can be useful in item selection decisions. Unfortunately, they tend to forget that item analyses can also be useful for item revision. Too frequently a person doing an item analysis of a multiple-choice test fails to go beyond computing the item difficulty and discrimination

From the *Journal of Educational Measurement*, 1967, 4, 2: 65–68. Reprinted with permission of the authors and publisher.

indices. When only this superficial analysis is completed, reasons underlying any item failures can not be discerned and item revision is difficult. It is when the responses to each of the foils have been examined that item revision can be accomplished most effectively.

The purpose of this paper is to study the value of using a complete item analysis in rewriting items that have been shown to lack appropriate discrimination power. The researchers were interested in seeing whether it was more efficient to rewrite "poor" items than to write new items to improve the discrimination power of a test.

METHOD

About 600–700 students take an introductory educational psychology course at Michigan State University each term. For many years, a part of the evaluation procedure has been multiple-choice examinations. The tests are revised each quarter. Past revisions have been conducted primarily by taking previous exam questions that have discriminated well and are still of appropriate content. These were used together with new items written by the instructors. Seldom were individual items rewritten through revision of the foils and even when that was done, no systematic follow-up of these rewritten items was undertaken to determine whether their discriminating powers improved.

An instructor familiar with the course content was asked to review a 60-item test given the previous quarter, and select items that were appropriate in content for the test being prepared. A complete item analysis had been conducted on this test showing the difficulty and discrimination indices, as well as the percent of people in the upper and lower 27% who responded to each alternative.[1] Thirty-two items in this test were found to be still appropriate in content. These 32 items were then examined and 18 were found to be acceptable for use without revision, 14 being in need of revision. These 14 items were revised by an instructor. The major revisions were accomplished by looking at the item analysis data on the foils and revising those foils which were not pulling in the proper direction, that is, those which were not more attractive to the lower group than the upper group. The total time needed for revision was about 1 hour. Examples of the type of revision that was done and the consequences are shown in the following items.

Original Form

Motivation is an internal state. Yet we continually talk as though it were a tangible, measurable quality. As a teacher you would most likely be able to best judge the motivation of a particular student by
 1. giving him an intelligence test.
 2. having his mother in for a parent-teacher conference.

*3. observing his behavior in the classroom and drawing your own conclusions.
4. McClelland's tests of internal motivation.
5. reviewing his past and present academic record.

Item Analysis:

	1	2	3	4	5	OMIT	N = 615
U	0	10	63	5	21	1	DIFF 58
L	2	9	52	11	26	0	DISC 11

Revised Form

Motivation is an internal state. Yet we continually talk as though it were a tangible, measurable quality. As a teacher you would most likely be able to best judge the motivation of a particular student by
1. giving him an interest inventory.
2. having him write an autobiography
*3. observing his behavior in the classroom and drawing your own conclusions.
4. McClelland's tests of internal motivation.
5. reviewing his past and present academic record.

Item Analysis:

	1	2	3	4	5	OMIT	N = 560
U	3	21	53	3	20	0	DIFF 43
L	5	27	32	9	26	0	DISC 21

Of the 14 revised items, 10 considered to have the best chance of showing an improvement were chosen and placed in the new exam along with the 18 good items and 32 new items. Construction of the new items took approximately five times as long per item as the item revisions.

RESULTS

Table 1 shows the item discrimination indices on the 18 items used without revision (control items) and the 10 revised items on both the old and new test. Every one of the 10 *revised* items showed an improvement in discrimination, the lowest increase being 3 and the greatest being 28. Nine of the 18 *control* items improved in discrimination, 8 decreased in discrimination.

Table 2 shows the average discrimination of the control and revised items for both the old and new test as well as the average discrimination of the new items on the new test.[2] The average discrimination of the control items was 2.3 lower in the new test while the average discrimination of the revised items was 10.3 higher. The revised items had a higher average discrimination than the new items written specifically for the exam.

TABLE 1   Item Discrimination

Control Items		Revised Items	
Old Test	New Test	Old Test	New Test
18	21		
29	22	17	24
26	31	17	31
30	9	11	16
30	19	22	25
34	28	16	20
33	36	11	21
27	27	18	46
26	14	23	30
48	43	21	29
27	26	5	22
29	31		
28	29		
32	33		
28	16		
40	41		
24	34		
22	30		

TABLE 2   Average Item Discrimination

	Old Test	New Test
Control Items	29.5	27.2
Revised Items	16.1	26.4
New Items	—	23.6

CONCLUSIONS

The results of this study show that items can be improved, without too much effort, through use of a complete item analysis. The study suggests that revising poor items may be a more economical process for obtaining good items for future tests than by discarding those items and attempting to replace them with new items. In this study it took about 5 times as long to develop a new item as it did to revise an old one, and the discrimination of the new items averaged 2.8 less than the average of the revised items. While some new items must always be written to preserve the validity of a test, there is strong evidence in this study for using the complete item analysis information to revise existing poor items. Far too often, item analysis is used only for item selection. Item revision accomplished through examination of the information concerning the individual distractors can be a valuable, efficient method of improving tests.

NOTES

[1] The discrimination index used was the "D" index. See Findley (1956) and Englehart (1965) for a more thorough discussion.

[2] The average difficulty did not change much between the old and new test for either control or revised items. The items in both the control and revised groups seemed to be slightly easier for those students taking the new test, but the change was very slight indeed.

REFERENCES

Englehart, Max D. A comparison of several item discriminaiton indices. *Journal of Educational Measurement*, 1965, *2*, 69–76.

Findley, W. G. A rationale for evaluation of item discrimination statistics. *Educational and Psychological Measurement*, 1956, *16*, 175–180.

RECOMMENDED READING FOR UNIT III

Berkley, Charles S., and Sproule, Charles F. "Test-anxiety and test-unsophistication: The Effects, the Cures." *Public Personnel Management,* January-February 1973: 55–59.

Coop, Richard H., and White, Kenneth P. "Objectives and Achievement Measurement: The Congruency between Students' and Teachers' Perceptions of Behavioral Objectives." *Educational and Psychological Measurement,* 1972, 32: 355–364.

Ebel, Robert L. "Behavioral Objectives: A Close Look." *Phi Delta Kappan,* November 1970, 52, 3: 171–173.

Ebel, Robert L. "How to Write True-False Test Items." *Educational and Psychological Measurement,* 1971, 31: 417–426.

Foote, Russell, and Belinky, Charles. "It Pays to Switch? Consequences of Changing Answers on Multiple-Choice Examinations." *Psychological Reports,* 1972, 31: 667–673.

Hoffmann, Banesh. "The Tyranny of Multiple-Choice Tests." *Harper's Magazine,* 1961, 222: 37–44.

Mehrens, William A., and Lehmann, Irvin J. *Measurement and Evaluation in Education and Psychology.* New York: Holt, Rinehart and Winston, 1973.

Miles, David T., and Robinson, Roger E. "Behavioral Objectives: An Even Closer Look." *Educational Technology,* June 1971: 39–44.

Murray, C. Kenneth. "The Systematic Observation Movement." *Journal of Research and Development in Education,* Fall 1970, 4: 3–9.

Palmer, Orville. "Sense or Nonsense? The Objective Testing of English Composition." *The English Journal,* 1961, 50: 314–320.

Ramseyer, Gary C., and Cashen, Valjean M. "The Effect of Practice Sessions on the Use of Separate Answer Sheets by First and Second Graders." *Journal of Educational Measurement,* 1971, 8, 3: 177–181.

Wexley, Kenneth N., and Thornton, Carl F. "Effect of Verbal Feedback of Test Results upon Learning." *The Journal of Educational Research,* November 1972, 66, 3: 119–121.

STANDARDIZED EVALUATION PROCEDURES

This unit focuses on standardized evaluation procedures. As demonstrated on the Textbook Reference Chart, the major texts listed devote more chapters to the topics covered in this unit than to any other unit. In spite of this generally extensive coverage "standardized evaluation procedures" covers such a broad array of topics that supplemental reading can be quite valuable.

One of the frustrating aspects of standardized tests is the great quantity of them from which to choose, though many of these are of poor quality. Further, most of the individuals who make test selection decisions are not highly specialized measurement experts trained to judge tests on many different dimensions. Published reviews of tests serve as valuable sources of information for such individuals. The basic references are Buros' *Mental Measurements Yearbooks* (1938, 1941, 1949, 1953, 1959, 1965, 1972) and *Tests in Print* (1974). The latest edition of the *Mental Measurements Yearbook* lists most of the published standardized tests in print at the time the yearbook goes to press. Those tests not reviewed in earlier editions and those previously reviewed that have been revised are described and criticized by educational and psychological authorities.

In the first article in this unit Professor Buros tells us "The Story behind the Mental Measurements Yearbook." It is amazing that one man with the help of his wife could have accomplished so much. The field of measurement and evaluation and every person who needs to select a standardized test, owes much to Buros' efforts and accomplishments.

Intelligence (or aptitude) tests have a long and controversial history. A basic problem is that psychologists do not agree on either the definition or structure of intelligence. Some conceptualize intelligence as a general factor, some as several (six to eight) factors, and others suggest that intelligence is composed of many separate factors. Tests have been developed congruent with these theoretical positions. The controversy exists not only with respect to the theoretical structure of intelligence, but also regarding the practical value of the various types of tests. The McNemar and Guilford articles take different positions on these issues. McNemar advocates that we not lose sight of the value of general intelligence tests. He points to their predictive superiority over multi-factor tests and argues for the construct of general intelligence. Guilford, one of the leading advocates of the multi-factor concept of intelligence, counters McNemar's position. He feels there is sufficient evidence to reject the notion of general intelligence. Articles relating to other issues in aptitude testing, such as test fairness and the genetics-environmental controversy, are found in Unit VI.

The measurement of interests has long been considered useful in assisting people with occupational choice decisions. With the recent impetus of Career Education, measurement of interests, vocational maturity, and occupational information has become more popular. Kuder has long been a leader in the area of interest measurement and his article in this unit presents twelve principles he feels should be followed in developing an interest inventory. Although other leaders in the field are not likely to agree with all twelve of Kuder's principles, most of them would receive general acceptance.

Kuder's principle ten states that it is highly desirable to use the same inventory for both sexes. Within the past few years a flurry of articles has been written regarding the sex bias in interest inventories. The Prediger and Hanson article discusses the distinction between sex restrictiveness and sex bias in interest inventories. Other related articles listed in the references are AMEG Commission (1973), Campbell (1973), and Harmon (1973).

The controversies and difficulties in aptitude and interest assessment pale in significance when compared to personality assessment. Personality assessment is intellectually challenging to psychologists but both psychologists and educators become frustrated in trying to determine practical uses of the assessment results. Goldberg discusses the trends of personality assessment under the headings of "Why Measure That Trait?" "How Measure That Trait?", and "How Use That Measure?". Careful reading of his article will give students a good view of the current state of personality assessment.

The following paper was first presented at a 1968 luncheon
meeting of the Association for Measurement and Evaluation in
Guidance. It discloses some fascinating insights into the many
problems of editing the *Mental Measurements Yearbooks* and the
dedication, courage, and skill of the man who devoted so
much of his professional life to this important task.

The Story behind the Mental Measurements Yearbooks

OSCAR K. BUROS

When I was first asked to give this informal talk on the story behind *The
Mental Measurements Yearbooks*, I was pleased to accept the invitation. I
felt confident that I would have an interesting story to tell. Now I am not
so sure; in fact, I have some doubts. As I dug into the past, skimming over
correspondence and records covering the past 35 years, I was forcefully
reminded of the numerous projects, most of them proclaimed in print, that
we failed to launch. It is with both amusement and sadness that I look back
on the dreams and plans which consumed me in my late 20's and early 30's.
Until I began to prepare this paper, most of these failures had either been
forgotten or were only vaguely remembered.

My presentation is not intended to be a scholarly paper. On the contrary, it will be a light presentation of some of the experiences my wife and
I have had in initiating, preparing, and publishing the MMY's. To my surprise, I have found it difficult to put my thoughts on paper. The MMY's and
our personal lives have been so intertwined, sometimes painfully so, that it
is impossible to disentangle one from the other—it would have been far
easier to present some of my views on testing or statistics. But if you will
bear with me, I shall reminisce and give you a glimpse into some of our
experiences. It will not be the whole story, since to tell all would cause dis-
comfort to some to no purpose. I hope that this informal presentation will
be of interest and that you will accept it with humor and appreciation.

So that you can appreciate better the genesis of *The Mental Measurements Yearbooks,* the first of which was published just 30 years ago, I shall
review some relevant developments in testing in the pre-yearbook period.

Testing specialists had more confidence in the usefulness of standardized tests 50 years ago than they have today. Within 10 years after publication of the first standardized achievement test in 1908, the tests were being

From *Measurement and Evaluation in Guidance*: Vol. 1, No. 2, Summer 1968, pp. 86–95.
Copyright (1968) American Personnel and Guidance Association. Reprinted with
permission.

acclaimed as scientific instruments that would enable a teacher to diagnose and prescribe, to determine teaching efficiency and weaknesses, and to determine precisely a pupil's ability to achieve.

But by the early 20's, more cautious views were beginning to be heard. A few testing specialists began raising questions about reliability, comparability of norms, usefulness of accomplishment quotients, and the like.

In 1925 Giles M. Ruch, a well-known testing specialist in his day, severely criticized test authors and publishers for not providing sufficient data on the construction and validation of their tests. His 1925 article "Minimum Essentials in Reporting Data on Standard Tests" might well be considered the forerunner of the technical recommendations for test manuals prepared by committees of the AERA, APA, and NCME nearly 30 years later.

In 1927 Truman L. Kelley, a distinguished pioneer in testing, made the first attempt to provide test users with assessments of all available standardized tests. His method was a simple one. He and six other testing specialists agreed to rank all known tests in each of about seventy categories. More than 350 tests were ranked for general excellence among competing tests at a given school level. The rankings and additional information on reliability that Kelley compiled were published in his *Interpretation of Educational Measurements*, an important book written primarily for school counselors. Kelley felt very strongly that his test rankings represented an important development in testing. The publishers described the book as "a kind of bureau of standards." Unfortunately, Kelley's pioneer attempt did not prove particularly useful. It probably was presumptuous for these testing specialists to think they could make useful rankings of all existing tests.

In the same year, Stuart Chase and F. J. Schlink published *Your Money's Worth*, a book which led to the establishment of Consumers' Research, Inc., now located in Washington, New Jersey. It was this book and the establishment of Consumers' Research which stimulated me to begin thinking about a test users' research organization.

Very likely, Ruch also was influenced by the founding of Consumers' Research. In 1933 he wrote:

> There is urgent need for a fact-finding organization which will undertake impartial, experimental, and statistical evaluations of tests. . . . This might lead to the listing of satisfactory tests . . . in much the same way that Consumers' Research is attempting to furnish reliable information to the average buyer.

Ruch stated that he had attempted to initiate such a fact-finding organization, but without success.

By this time, I was becoming quite excited about the possibility that I might be instrumental in establishing a bureau of standards in testing. In a paper read in 1935, I said:

This test-the-tests organization should serve as a clearinghouse of information about the tests of all publishers. Studies should continually be in progress to appraise tests from various viewpoints for various purposes. Such an organization would find it relatively easy to weed out the poorest of the tests, and to suggest ways whereby the consumer must modify and supplement standard tests to adequately measure his own objectives. . . . There is a greater immediate need for critical evaluations of existing tests and their uses than for the construction of new tests. If only 10 per cent of the money which foundations have granted to test makers in recent years could have been given to endow a test consumers' research organization, I am sure that the testing movement would be more advanced than it is today.

Over the next 23 years, I made repeated attempts to get financial support for various testing projects. Unfortunately, I have never had what it takes to solicit money from a foundation and my original dream of a test users' research organization never got off the ground.

In 1934 I agreed to prepare an annual review of standardized tests for a well-known journal. The review was to be a critical appraisal of new tests in all fields. Before the tests could be appraised, however, they had to be located. A thorough search resulted in a list of new tests which contained over twice the number I had expected to find. By this time, I realized that it would be presumptuous of me to go ahead with my original plan. Instead, I used materials that I had already assembled to initiate the first in a series of annual test bibliographies entitled *Educational, Psychological, and Personality Tests of 1933*.

It was only after I failed in repeated attempts to secure funds for setting up a fact-finding research organization that I thought of a test-reviewing service. My first plans were to start a test reviewing journal. I finally decided that it would be easier to add a test-reviewing section to the next annual test bibliography. The title, however, was changed to *The Mental Measurements Yearbook*, a name we thought would be equally acceptable to educators, psychologists, and personnel workers in industry.

From the start, the MMY's were planned to meet the needs of all test users. Although I held some unorthodox views on testing, I was determined from the beginning that the MMY's should not be biased in favor of my personal viewpoints, other than my conviction that frankly critical reviews were badly needed. Reviewers representing various viewpoints among psychologists, subject matter specialists, teachers, and test technicians were to be selected. With this as my foremost guiding principle, it became obvious that multiple reviews would be necessary.

During the preparation of *The 1938 Mental Measurements Yearbook*, the president of the American Council on Education learned of my work and asked that I meet with him. As a result of his expressed interest, we made a formal request in January, 1938, for financial assistance to set up a test consumers' research organization at Rutgers University. We did not get the $65,000 requested for a five-year period, but we did receive $350 for extra clerical help and a promise to reconsider the request after publication of the 1938 Yearbook.

The ACE grant made it possible for us to submit—with the names of the reviewers deleted—typescripts of all reviews to publishers prior to sending copy to the printer. We asked publishers to point out factual errors, if any, in the reviews. The response was terrific: telegrams and letters of protest poured in from both authors and publishers. Unlike book publishers, test publishers were not accustomed to critical reviews. Rarely were errors pointed out. In many instances, authors and publishers claimed that they possessed unpublished information that would answer the criticisms of MMY reviewers. Most of the objections were either emotional reactions to criticism or the result of differences in values and standards.

.The author of one of our most widely used tests sent me a telegram which said:

> We strongly protest content of first review and ask that it be withheld until appearance of volume containing full statistical analysis.

(I might add that this volume appeared—four years later.) Specific objections followed in a long letter received the next day. The objections were passed on to our reviewer, who said that the letter contained nothing to cause him to change his evaluation of the test. Nevertheless, he withdrew his review, saying that he had no idea the distinguished author would object so violently. I tried to persuade the reviewer to permit us to publish the review, but he remained firm in his refusal. This and similar experiences made me realize how difficult it is to get honest criticism of the work of men with outstanding reputations.

The tone of some of the more extreme reactions from test authors and publishers is shown by two quotations from their letters. A test author wrote:

> It makes little difference to me how or what you publish about this test. My only comment is that a certain book on *How to Win Friends and Influence People* is undoubtedly less popular with you than its companion volume . . . *How to Lose Friends and Alienate People*. It is really too bad that some one has "burned your toast" too often; why try to take the hide off any publisher, author, or group of publications, where does it get you? My curiosity is a bit aroused, I may even inquire from some of my good friends on the Rutgers faculty what this is all about, but probably I will not take the trouble.

A test publisher wrote:

> I appeal to you in the name of common decency to withhold from publication in your Yearbook or anywhere else the reviews submitted by Reviewers A and B. On the other hand, in the event that you concur thoroughly in the beliefs of Reviewers A and B . . . I assume that you will publish the "re-

views" in your yearbook. In this latter event, I must comfort myself with the thought that we are not the first people who have been maligned and grossly misrepresented in a most unfair and scurrilous manner. Undoubtedly we can stand dirty treatment—although, of course, I don't enjoy it.

Since submission of typescripts of reviews to test publishers revealed very few factual errors and resulted in publication delays, we discontinued the practice.

I hasten to add that following the initial shock caused by reviews in the first Yearbook, test publishers—with rare exceptions—are taking test reviews in their stride. Both authors and publishers have been most restrained in their comments to us.

Within a few days after publication of the 1938 Yearbook, I again made the rounds of foundations, seeking financial assistance. The American Council on Education, which had a sort of option on our proposal, reconsidered our request but again turned us down. Fortunately, federal funds came to our rescue. Since the economy of the country was still sufficiently depressed to make it necessary for the government to provide work relief projects, we managed to get a WPA grant which lasted through the first half of 1940.

For various reasons, my wife and I decided in 1939 that it would be necessary for us to publish and distribute the 1940 Yearbook from our home. The lack of funds forced us to abandon all hope of publishing a volume annually. When WPA assistance suddenly came to a close, my wife enrolled in an intensive one-month course in typing at a local business school. She practiced typing mornings, afternoons, and evenings. I needed her help so badly that she dropped out after three weeks to become my secretary and all-round assistant.

At every step in the planning and manufacture of the Yearbook we were torn between our need to economize and our desire to put out a well-designed book. Many a time my wife and I argued over whether a particular page should be reset, whether an eighth of an inch more space should be inserted between two display heads, whether large and small caps or small caps should be used. Twice my wife spent a full day at the printing plant in Connecticut working with the printers in the composing room to get the effect she wanted.

Professors usually publish their own books only when they cannot get a publisher. This was certainly true of us. Author-published books usually *look* author-published. We are proud that our case was otherwise. The company which supplied the cloth for binding the 1940 Yearbook asked permission to feature our book along with one other in a full-page ad to be run in *Book Binding and Production*. This ad presented a beautiful photograph of the two books with the caption "Books of Distinction" and this text:

These volumes represent a masterful blending of content and cover. Rarely are worthy texts given the careful thought evidenced by the appearance of these books. They possess a quiet dignity which admirably complements their content. These are splendid examples of Terek Cloth to blend with skillful design. Let Terek Cloth help you design your "Book of Distinction."

I was so delighted with the ad that my wife had it framed; for the past 27 years it has decorated my study.

We had neither savings nor property when we decided to become publishers. A $3,500 loan from a brother and smaller loans from others set us up in business. While the 1940 Yearbook was still in press, mailing lists were supplied to our family, who addressed 48,000 penny post cards advertising the book. I had expected to apply my statistical knowledge to study the pulling power of the various mailing lists. The response was so poor, however, that we could tell nothing about the effectiveness of our advertising. Even today, we are unable to estimate the effect of a given ad or review on Yearbook sales.

We first published under the imprint *The Mental Measurements Yearbook*. We later decided that we should have a name more befitting a book publisher. My wife spent several hours leafing through a desk dictionary searching for an interesting name. From a list of a half-dozen possibilities, we finally selected the word *gryphon*, which we thought would have interesting possibilities in typography and later as a colophon. (Gryphon may be spelled in two ways; we selected the spelling used in *Alice's Adventures in Wonderland*.) Since 1941 we have published under the imprint The Gryphon Press.

As book publishers there are no tasks my wife and I have not done. Our first books were delivered in 400-pound crates which were unloaded in our driveway. Because of the tremendous weight, we were forced to open the crates outside and then carry the books to our basement. We learned our lesson. Thereafter, all of our binding orders specified that books must be delivered in cartons not to exceed 60 pounds. Many times, my wife and I have handled one to three tons of books delivered to our home. As we grew older, we reduced the weight limit to 45 pounds.

In the early 1940's, our six-room apartment housed the editorial quarters of *The Mental Measurements Yearbook* as well as the business and shipping departments of The Gryphon Press. Four of the six rooms contained at least one filing cabinet. Books were stacked everywhere; we even placed bookcases in the stairway. Within 48 hours after delivery of the 1940 Yearbook, we had packaged, labelled, and stamped 550 books for mailing. Books were delivered to the post office in a hired truck. Thereafter, we rarely shipped out more than five books a day. We had no car in those early years, so one of us had to take the books to the post office in a taxi and then walk home.

When I look back on the dreams and hopes we had in 1941 for expanding our services to test users, I marvel at the temerity one can have at the age of 35. We attempted to start a quarterly to be called *Mental Measurements Reviews* to supplement the Yearbooks. The project was considered on and off over the next 20 years. We actually started to make sample surveys of school systems to find out what tests were being used and in what quantity. We wanted to supply reviewers with tests and scoring and statistical services to permit them to prepare better reviews. Although these early years were exciting, they were also frustrating—we had the ideas but not the money. Whatever we accomplished, I am sure that it could have been more than doubled had we gotten sufficient backing.

After the war years, I made one last attempt to set up a test users' research organization. This time we sought a half million dollars. For a while it looked as though we might be successful. When that failed, we made no further attempts to get grants. In the meantime, Rutgers University provided sufficient support to permit us to complete the Third and Fourth Yearbooks. The University Press published the Third Yearbook; we have published all succeeding Yearbooks. Income from sales was so low that we were always uncertain whether we would be able to put out another Yearbook. The problem of financing books was a constant worry.

Help came from an unexpected source. Little did I think that the launching of Russia's Sputnik on October 4, 1957, would affect *The Mental Measurements Yearbooks*. We Americans had always thought our educational system the best in the world, but Sputnik forced us to entertain some doubts. In an effort to improve our nation's competitive position, federal money poured into projects designed to discover and develop talent in our schools. It was as much a windfall for us as it was for other publishers. The federal funds provided for counseling and testing caused MMY sales to increase sharply. I am happy to report that, thanks to Sputnik, the MMY's are no longer in the red! It does not follow, however, that the Yearbooks would be self-supporting if published by a commercial publisher with high overhead costs. Since the entire MMY operation is located in our home, our overhead costs are reduced to a minimum.

As we continued to publish the Yearbooks, we were threatened twice with lawsuits for libel. After surveying libel cases involving book reviews, we felt quite safe but were worried about possible delays in getting out the Yearbook. Nevertheless, we decided to play it safe and limit our liability by incorporating. After spending $150 to incorporate, we learned that as editor I was still liable. Furthermore, as a corporation we could not apply publishing losses against my University income for tax purposes. We then disincorporated at a cost of $100 in legal fees. The Internal Revenue Service, wondering what we were up to, conducted an investigation which required us to spend an additional $150 for accounting services. So the threats of lawsuits cost us considerable worry, time, legal and accounting fees—*and* a higher income tax!

It is with mixed feelings that I review our relationships and accomplishments over the past 35 years. We are very pleased, of course, with the reception and recognition the MMY's have received from those who make, sell, or use tests.

We are deeply moved by the tremendous assistance we have received from more than a thousand persons who have reviewed tests for one or more Yearbooks. These busy scholars cannot be praised or thanked too much for their contributions. They have truly made the MMY's a cooperative enterprise. Working with reviewers has been one of my most rewarding experiences, both in what I have learned and in what I have gained in friendships.

Test authors and publishers, with very few exceptions, have been cooperative and helpful. The best of the test publishers are highly professional organizations employing testing specialists who compare with the best, whether judged on competency or professional standards. As you may have noticed, many of the finest reviews in the MMY's are written by employees of test publishers.

The objectives of *The Mental Measurements Yearbooks* have remained essentially unchanged since they were first listed in the 1940 Yearbook. The first three of these objectives are to make readily available:

Comprehensive and up-to-date bibliographies of recent tests published in all English-speaking countries.

Comprehensive and accurate bibliographies of references on the construction, validation, use, and limitations of specific tests.

Frankly critical test reviews, written by persons of outstanding ability representing various viewpoints, which will assist test users to make more discriminating selections of the standard tests which will best meet their needs.

Except for our inability to provide this information annually, we have been reasonably successful in meeting these first three objectives. Our current schedule of a Yearbook every five or six years means, however, that up-to-date information is not available in between Yearbooks. This has been a matter of considerable concern to test users in recent years.

This gap between Yearbooks is being partially filled by test reviews now appearing in the *Journal of Counseling Psychology, Journal of Educational Measurement*, and *Personnel and Guidance Journal*. Our new MEASUREMENT AND EVALUATION IN GUIDANCE, will, I understand, include test reviews as a regular feature.

Another development of considerable importance is the Inter-Association Council on Test Reviewing, recently set up under the chairmanship of Jack C. Merwin. This broad-based committee representing many groups in education and psychology is working on a systematic program to coordinate and supplement present test reviewing outlets.

The first three objectives of the MMY's merely require that information be made available to test users. The remaining objectives require changes in the behaviors of those who make, sell, or use tests—a much more difficult task.

The fourth objective of the MMY is to impel authors and publishers to place fewer but *better* tests on the market and to provide test users with detailed and accurate information on the construction, validation, uses, and limitations of their tests when they are first placed on the market. It is difficult to estimate the effect we have had on publishers. We know that we are having *some* influence; at times, we even think that it has been considerable. The influence the MMY's have had in bringing about improvements in manuals has been supplemented and probably overshadowed by the publication of the Technical Recommendations in 1954. Some publishers do seem to be publishing fewer and better tests, but it is doubtful whether this can be said for the rank and file of test publishers. Test manuals, however, are definitely more informative.

The remaining objectives refer to desired changes in those who buy and use tests. Our major objective is, of course, to help test users select and use tests with discrimination. I have no doubt that we have had considerable success in helping guidance workers, psychologists, and teachers do this. But our success has not been nearly as great as I had anticipated when we began publishing the Yearbooks. It may be that my expectations were too high. Perhaps I should be satisfied knowing that many test users are selecting tests with greater discrimination because of the MMY's. Nevertheless, I am becoming increasingly concerned about those we are not reaching.

A few years back, I made some rather caustic remarks on this subject in *Tests in Print*. I trust that very few of my AMEG fellow-members will feel that I am addressing them personally. Let me quote:

> At present, no matter how poor a test may be, if it is nicely packaged and if it promises to do all sorts of things which no test can do, the test will find many gullible buyers. When we initiated critical test reviewing in *The 1938 Yearbook*, we had no idea how difficult it would be to discourage the use of poorly constructed tests of unknown validity. Even the better informed test users who finally become convinced that a widely used test has no validity after all are likely to rush to use a new instrument which promises far more than any good test can possibly deliver. Counselors, personnel directors, psychologists, and school administrators seem to have an unshakable will to believe the exaggerated claims of test authors and publishers. If these test users were better informed regarding the merits and limitations of their testing instruments, they would probably be less happy and less successful in their work. The test user who has faith—however unjustified—can speak with confidence in interpreting test results and in making recommendations.

The well-informed test user cannot do this: he knows that the best of our tests are still highly fallible instruments which are extremely difficult to interpret with assurance in individual cases. Consequently, he must interpret test results cautiously and with so many reservations that others wonder whether he really knows what he is talking about. Children, parents, teachers, and school administrators are likely to have a greater respect and admiration for a school counselor who interprets test results with confidence even though his interpretations have no scientific justification. The same applies to psychologists and personnel directors. Highly trained psychologists appear to be as gullible as the less well trained school counselors. It pays to know only a little about testing; furthermore, it is much more fun for everyone concerned—the examiner, the examinee, and the examiner's employer.

I hope that all of you will ponder what I have just said before rejecting it as unfounded criticism. It is not enough to give test users the information they need for intelligent action; they must also be induced to use that information and to purchase and use tests accordingly. No matter how much the MMY's and other test-reviewing publications expand the frequency of their services, nothing will be gained unless test users have both the knowledge and the will to use the critical information provided.

I have devoted most of my professional life to making critical information available to all who buy and use tests. Many such persons can and do make intelligent use of the critical information in the MMY's and other sources. Other persons use the MMY's primarily as a bibliography, paying little or no attention to the reviews. Still others probably never consult an MMY or read a journal review. The number in the last two groups, those who lack the knowledge and will to use the critical information available, is much too large. Were this not so, it would be impossible for publishers to market profitably tests either known to be poor or tests for which there is no validity data one way or the other.

If my analysis is correct, it may be that the MMY's and the test-reviewing journals are giving too much emphasis to serving the needs of the converted. More attention must be given to increasing the number of test users with both the ability and the determination to make intelligent use of the relevant information being made available.

Before I close, I would like to say that I consider the formation of AMEG one of the most promising developments in testing in recent years. Guidance workers are in strategic positions to improve school testing practices. Our new journal, *Measurement and Evaluation in Guidance*, will make it possible to extend our influence far beyond our membership. I am confident that AMEG will play an important role in increasing the number of test users with both the knowledge and the will to select and use tests wisely.

REFERENCES

Chase, S., & Schlink, F. J. *Your money's worth: a study in the waste of the consumer's dollar.* New York: Macmillan Co., 1927.

Kelley, T. L. *Interpretation of educational measurements.* Yonkers, N.Y.: World Book Co., 1927.

Ruch, G. M. Minimum essentials in reporting data on standard tests. *Journal of Educational Research,* 1925, *12*, 349–358.

Ruch, G. M. Recent developments in statistical procedures. *Review of Educational Research,* 1933, *3*, 33–40.

Both the concept and testing of intelligence have had a long and controversial history. When intelligence tests were first developed they were thought to measure a general factor. More recently many psychologists have suggested that it is more accurate to think of intelligence as composed of many separate factors resulting in various tests that have been designed to measure those separate factors.

McNemar argues that we should not abandon the concept of general intelligence or the value of general intelligence tests. He points to the general tests' predictive superiority over multi-factor tests in support of his position.

The Guilford article following this one, demonstrates an effective contrast to McNemar's. Recall that Dyer in Unit I was opposed to the label IQ, but in favor of intelligence tests. Do you think Dyer believes in a general intelligence construct or would he be an advocate of the separate factors theory?

Lost: Our Intelligence? Why?[1]

QUINN McNEMAR

The Greeks had a word for it, but the Romans had a word with better survival properties. Regardless of the word, what is now called intelligence has been talked about for at least 2,000 years. And as long as 2,000 years before the advent of attempts to measure intelligence, there seems to have been recognition of the fact that individuals differ in intellectual ability.

From *American Psychologist,* 1964, *19*: 871–882. Copyright (1964) by the *American Psychological Association.* Reprinted by permission.

The earlier attempts at measuring were based on either of two quite distinct conceptions: the Galton-Cattell idea that intellectual ability manifests itself in simple, discrimination functioning, and the Binet notion that cognitive ability reflects itself in more complex functioning. The Binet concept proved to be more fruitful, and by 1925 there was on the market, in addition to various versions of the Binet scale, a flood of group tests of so-called general intelligence.

A few words about definition may be in order. First, it might be claimed that no definition is required because all intelligent people know what intelligence is—it is the thing that the other guy lacks. Second, the fact that tests of general intelligence based on differing definitions tend to intercorrelate about as highly as their respective reliabilities permit indicates that, despite the diversity of definitions, the same function or process is being measured —definitions can be more confusing than enlightening. Third, that confusion might have been anticipated is evident from a recent reexamination of the problem of definition by Miles (1957). This British chappie found himself struggling with the awful fact that the word "definition" itself has 12 definitions. Perhaps the resolution of this problem should be assigned to the newly formed Division of Philosophical Psychology, or maybe the problem should be forgotten since psychologists seem to have lost the concept of general intelligence.

Why has the concept been abandoned? Was it replaced by something else? By something better? Must we admit that the millions who have been tested on general intelligence tests were measured for a nonexistent function? If it is possible that the notion of general intelligence is not lost but merely gone astray, in what corners of what psychological fields should we search for it?

REASONS FOR DISCARDING THE IDEA OF GENERAL INTELLIGENCE

Apparently one reason why concepts are either discarded or modified beyond recognition is that too much is claimed for them. Among the supposed strikes against general intelligence are the following: the earlier false claims about IQ constancy; prediction failures in individual cases; unfounded claims that something innate was being measured by the tests; equally unfounded assertions that nothing but cultural effects were involved; the bugaboo that IQ tests reflect middle-class values; the notion that an IQ standing fosters undesirable expectations regarding school achievement; the idea that IQ differences are incompatible with democracy and lead to educational determinism; and finally, the great stress on general intelligence caused us to ignore other possible abilities.

This last point leads us right into the problem of factor analysis. Spearman died in battle defending his theory of *g*. Under pressure he reluctantly conceded that factors other than *g* might exist, and he frequently said, in effect, I told you so as long ago as 1906. Actually, Spearman was on the run before the invention of modern factor analysis, but it was not until Thurstone's (1938) first major application of his centroid factor method that Spearman's *g* became, seemingly, nonexistent. Thurstone said, "We have not found the general factor of Spearman" and "We cannot report any general common factor in the battery of fifty-six tests [p. vii]." As anticipated by some, Spearman was not prone to admit defeat. He reworked Thurstone's data and a *g* was found, plus some group factors. He charged that Thurstone's rotational process had submerged the general factor.

American factorists found Thurstone convincing. The description of abilities in terms of seven primaries was an attractive package. The so-called primaries were more amenable to specific definition than the old hodgepodge called general intelligence. Despite the fact that Thurstone was able to replicate his findings on samples from two other populations, thus giving credence to his method and results, there were a couple of events that led to some turbulence in his seven-dimension rarified atmosphere. The first of these was a minor study, by one of his own students, based on the intercorrelations of 1916 Stanford-Binet items, in which the *g* refused to be rotated out. But rather than admit that this might be some kind of general intelligence, the author renamed it "maturational level." Incidentally, this illustrates the first cardinal Principle of Psychological Progress: *Give new names to old things.*

The second disturber of the neat little set of primaries, sans a *g*, resulted when Thurstone took the next logical step, that of constructing tests to measure the primaries. It was found that the primaries were themselves intercorrelated whereas it had, at the time, been expected and hoped that they would be independent. The Thurstones (1941, p. 26) readily admitted that a general factor was needed to explain the interrelatedness of the primaries. This eventually led to the idea of oblique axes, which axes were regarded as representing the primaries as first-order factors, whereas the general factor pervading the primaries was dubbed a second-order factor. It began to look as though Spearman was being revisited, except for the little matter of labeling: anything called second-order could not possibly be regarded as of much importance. Furthermore, it could always be said that, in the ability domain, it is less difficult to attribute psychological meaningfulness to first-order than to second-order factors, so why pay much attention to the latter? Thus it was easy for most American factorists to drop the concept of general intelligence and to advocate that tests thereof, despite their proven usefulness over the years, should be replaced by tests of the primaries. Hence the emergence of differential aptitude batteries, about which more later.

Meanwhile, our British cousins did not tag along with the factor methods preferred on this side of the Atlantic. After all, it is possible to use factor methods that permit a sizable general factor, if such exists, to emerge as the very first factor. Being first, it is, presto, the most important, as indeed it is as a factor explaining, for the starting battery as a whole, more variance for more tests than attributable to any American-style primary factor. The methods preferred by the British also yield group factors, apt to bear the same name as the primaries, but of attenuated importance. Apparently the British are skeptical of the multitude of ability factors being "discovered" in America. The structure of intellect that requires 120 factors may very well lead the British, and some of the rest of us, to regard our fractionization and fragmentation of ability, into more and more factors of less and less importance, as indicative of scatterbrainedness. This statement presumes that intellectual abilities are brain centered.

In practically all areas of psychological research the demonstration of trivially small minutia is doomed to failure because of random errors. Not so if your technique is factor analysis, despite its being based on the correlation coefficient—that slipperiest of all statistical measures. By some magic, hypotheses are tested without significance tests. This happy situation permits me to announce a Principle of Psychological Regress: *Use statistical techniques that lack inferential power.* This will not inhibit your power of subjective inference and consequently will progress you right back to the good old days when there was no strangling stat or sticky stix to make your insignificant data insignificant.

It may be a long time before we have an ivory tower, strictly scientific resolution of the issue as to whether a scheme involving primary abilities plus a deemphasized g is preferable to one involving an emphasized g plus group factors. With bigger and better computers we will have bigger, though not necessarily better, factor-analytic studies, but it seems unlikely that such further studies will, in and of themselves, settle the issue under discussion. Until such time as some genius resolves the broader question, so ably discussed by Lee Cronbach in 1957, of the place, if any, of correlational method in a science that aspires to be experimental, we may have to turn to the criterion of social usefulness as a basis for judging whether it is wise to discard general intelligence. Like it or not, much of our heritage in this area is that earlier workers, from Binet on, had as their motivation the solution of social problems, and currently many in the area have a similar motivation.

THE BEARING OF SOCIAL USEFULNESS

In practice, if you believe that the concept of general intelligence has outlived its usefulness, you may choose from among several differential, or multiple, aptitude batteries, which will provide measures of some of the so-called primary mental abilities. If you happen to believe that there is something to general ability, you can find tests to use. The novice looking for these latter tests may have to alert himself to the first Principle of Psychological Progress—the test labels may have changed from "general intelligence" to "general classification" or "scholastic aptitude." If you enjoy riding the fence, you might become a devotee of the practice of the College Board, and others, and measure just two abilities: Verbal and Quantitative.

This is certainly not the place to review the voluminous literature that amply demonstrates the practical utility of tests of general intelligence. Nor is it the place to catalog the misuses of the Stanford-Binet for purposes which Terman never claimed for it, or the misuses of the Wechsler scales for purposes which Wechsler *has* claimed for his scales. Neither the Binet nor the Wechsler provides a factorially pure, unidimensional measure of a *g*. The current Stanford-Binet was in reality constructed too early to benefit from the implication of factor analysis for test purity, whereas the Wechsler scales were based on the impossible premise that 10 or 11 subtests can simultaneously provide diagnostic subscores and a meaningful total score. Of the many group tests that appeared between 1920 and 1945 it can be said that few, if any, provide unidimensional measures of general intelligence. The chief difficulty is that most of them lead to a total score based on a mixture of verbal and mathematical material. Thus, with two main sources of variance, marked qualitative differences can exist for quantitatively similar total scores. The College Board–Educational Testing Service people have justifiably refrained from giving a total score involving verbal plus math, but there are those who question the usefulness of the Board's math score and there are those who criticize the Educational Testing Service for failing to change over to a differential aptitude battery.

Let us next turn to a somewhat more detailed examination of the various so-called multiple aptitude batteries. What and who influenced whom in the development of these batteries is difficult to disentangle. At the risk of oversimplification, it might be said that two prime influences operated.

First, the early factor studies by the Thurstones, by Holzinger, and by Guilford are the progenitors of the Science Research Associates' Primary Mental Abilities (PMA) Test, the Holzinger-Crowder Unifactor Tests, the Guilford-Zimmerman Aptitude Survey, and the Segel-Raskin Multiple Aptitude Tests (MAT).

The second influence, which seems to have emerged from testing experience in the Armed Services during World War II, is the job-element approach, an approach which may or may not differ from the old job-analysis method. For whatever jobs you are dealing with, you study the activities involved in order to decide what aptitudes are called for. Whether or not these aptitudes have been previously isolated by factor analysis is totally irrelevant. It is hoped that some jobs will have aptitudes in common so that the needed number of tests will be less than the number of jobs. The one battery that is built on this approach is the Flanagan Aptitude Classification Tests, a battery that just happens to have the catchy abbreviation, FACT. If we cannot muster any facts in psychology, we can at least have FACT scores!

A cross between testing for factorially defined abilities and job-element derived aptitudes is apparently involved in the General Aptitude Test Battery (GATB) of the United States Employment Service and the Differential Aptitudes Tests (DAT) of the Psychological Corporation, since in both batteries some of the tests seem to have sprung from factor-analysis results and some tests seem to have been thrown in as possible predictors of specific performances.

It is not our purpose to rank order the seven above-mentioned multitest batteries, but a few remarks may be relevant as background for the sequel. Apparently the Employment Service's GATB was made available (but not put on the commercial market) with the idea that there would be a continuing program of validities studies—the accumulation is now impressive. For the DAT of the Psychological Corporation there is an overabundance of data on validity, collected and analyzed prior to marketing the test. Both the Science Research Associates' PMA and FACT were made available without backing for the claimed usefulness of the tests. Belatedly, that is, 6 years after its appearance, some evidence on the predictive validity of FACT has been reported. Validity information for the other three batteries is not entirely lacking, though far from ample. Some will have noted that that fuzzy dodge called factor validity is being ignored here.

Now to get back to our main theme, to what extent have the seven batteries contributed to the demise of general intelligence? In attempting to answer this, one encounters a paradox: Some test authors want to eat their cake and have it too—they attempt to measure factors and g with the same instrument. This is understandable in a couple of instances. Three of the 15 tests of the Employment Service GATB were included to provide a measure of general intelligence, apparently because the authors still saw some merit in a g and were not committed to the factor schemata. Holzinger and Crowder suggest a weighted score for a measure of g, perhaps because of Holzinger's long-time alignment with Spearman. The real teaser is why Thurstone ever sanctioned, if he did, the summing of Science Research Associates' PMA scores to obtain an IQ. One has the uncomfortable feeling that his publishers wished to g garnish the factor cake to make it more palatable in the market place.

Although Segel says nothing in his 1957 article about a general score from the Segel-Raskin MAT, the test publishers say that, in addition to yielding scores for four factors, it also provides a "Scholastic Potential" score. Perhaps Flanagan has not completely broken with tradition since he states that four tests of the FACT battery measure "General College Aptitude"—

a statement made with the same lack of empirical validity as the claim, which should be anxiety producing for those of you who fly a certain airline, that your highly paid pilot shares four of the aptitudes of a plumber!

Apparently, Guilford and Zimmerman and the test people at the Psychological Corporation are willing to stick to the sound principle that a differential test battery cannot provide factor scores that can be summed to obtain a meaningful IQ, or measure of a g.

Parenthetically, it might be said that the California Test of Mental Maturity (CTMM), which, according to the publisher's 1963 catalog, was originally "designed as a group test of intelligence patterned after the individual Stanford-Binet," serves as an illustration of factor icing a g cake. Some multitest batteries and the CTMM have a Madison Avenue advantage: The advertising claims the measurement of not only factors but also g; not only g but also factors. The measurement absurdity is all too apt to go unrecognized by many test users, and hence a sales advantage for the aptitude battery that produces both factor scores and an IQ.

Just how successful have the multitest batteries been? Since by far the most extensive social use of tests has been, and continues to be, in the schools, let us look at the evidence of validity studies therein. As indicated previously, little is known about the predictive usefulness of some of the seven batteries discussed above. The DAT of the Psychological Corporation is the only battery for which adequate predictive (and concurrent) validity data, derived from school sources, are available. It is also the battery that has fared best in the hands of the test reviewers; therefore if we allow the case for differential batteries to rest thereon, we will be looking at the best. So, what is the story?

Recall that the hoped-for advantage of a multitest battery over the old-fashioned general intelligence test was that it would have greater predictive power, a power which could manifest itself in higher validity coefficients for specific subject matter and, perhaps, for overall achievement. It was hoped that such a battery would be truly differential in that particular factors (or subtests) would correlate higher with achievement in some areas than in other areas. Presumably each factor (or subtest) should have unique usefulness. If a battery were truly differential, it would be a boon to school guidance personnel.

Now the manual of the DAT of the Psychological Corporation contains a staggering total of 4,096, yes I counted 'em, validity coefficients. With such a large pool to draw from, one could by gracious selection "show" that the DAT is the answer to the prayer of every counselor, male or female, or by malicious selection one could "prove" that the DAT is far worse than any test ever published. The validity coefficients range all the way down to $-.37$, which is presumably a chance deviation downward from 0, and all the way up to .90, which is likely not a chance deviation downward from unity. But ranges tell us nothing. After a careful perusal of the 4,096 correlations, it seems safe to summarize DAT validities as follows:

1. Verbal Reasoning (analogies to most of you) is the best single predictor; Language Usage, as represented by a sentence test dealing with grammar and word usage, and admittedly more achievement than aptitude, is a close second.
2. Numerical Ability, as measured by a test of simple arithmetic operations, designed to tap arithmetic reasoning without the usual verbal component, is the best predictor of achievement in school mathematics. It does not, however, correlate as well with grades in science as does Verbal Reasoning.
3. Aside from the Numerical Ability test, the only other test that shows differential power as a predictor is the Spelling test—if you cannot spell you may have trouble learning shorthand.
4. The remaining five tests in the battery simply fail to show compelling evidence that they are good in the differential predictive sense. For the Mechanical Reasoning and the Clerical Speed and Accuracy tests this may be understandable in that little of school curricula for Grades 8 through 12 requires such abilities, but one would expect that Abstract Reasoning and Space Relations would fare better than they seem to.

Such data as we have been able to locate for the other six multitest batteries tend to support these findings on the DAT. Aside from tests of numerical ability having differential value for predicting school grades in math, it seems safe to conclude that the worth of the multitest batteries as differential predictors of achievement in school has not been demonstrated. Incidentally, the fact that the Verbal and Numerical tests stand out as the only two useful predictors tends to provide some support for the Educational Testing Service–College Board practice of providing scores for just these two abilities.

And now we come to a very disturbing aspect of the situation. Those who have constructed and marketed multiple aptitude batteries, and advocated that they be used instead of tests of general intelligence, seem never to have bothered to demonstrate whether or not multitest batteries provide better predictions than the old-fashioned scale of general intelligence. Be it noted that we are not discussing experimental editions of tests. Some may say that insofar as a test publisher provides validity data for a new battery it is not necessary to show that the validities are, for the given school condition, better than those of other tests. With this one can agree, but only in case no claims are made, explicitly or implicitly, regarding superior merits for the new battery.

It is far from clear that tests of general intelligence have been outmoded by the multitest batteries as the more useful predictors of school achievement. Indeed, one can use the vast accumulation of data on the validity of the Psychological Corporation's DAT to show that better predictions are possible via old-fashioned general intelligence tests. Consider the fact that a combination of the tests Verbal Reasoning (analogies) and Numerical Ability would be, in terms of content, very similar to many group tests of general intelligence. Consider also that an equally weighted combination of these two tests correlates in the mid-.80s with the Otis S-A, Higher Form. Then, when you turn to a careful study of the empirical validities, as reported in the DAT manual, you will not be surprised at the outcome of the application of a little arithmetic, which leads to the definite conclusion that a simple unweighted combination of the Verbal Reasoning and Numerical Ability tests predicts as well as or, in most instances, better than any subtest taken singly, or in the differential sense.

The manual for the DAT contains the following statement (Bennett, Seashore, & Wesman, 1952):

> Apparently the *Verbal Reasoning* and *Numerical Ability* tests can serve most purposes for which a general mental ability test is usually given in addition to providing differential clues useful to the counselor. Hence, the use of the so-called intelligence test is apparently unnecessary where the *Differential Aptitude Tests* are already being used [p. 71].

Anyone who disagrees with this quotation could, with better justification, say that an intelligence test can serve nearly all, if not all, the purposes for which a multiple aptitude battery is given in the schools because the former, in general, is a better predictor and because, as we saw earlier, the differential clues are too fragmentary to be of use to the counselor. And there is a bonus: one classroom period of testing, compared to six periods. A second bonus: much less costly. A third bonus: fewer scores to confuse the already confused minds of most school counselors.

Thus, we come to the conclusion that general intelligence has not been lost in the trend to test more and more abilities; it was merely misplaced by a misplaced emphasis on a hope that a lot of us, including the speaker, once entertained, a hope that in turn was based on a misplaced faith in factor analysis: *the* hope that factors, when and if measured, would find great usefulness in the affairs of society. By the criterion of social usefulness, the multiple aptitude batteries have been found wanting. Now, I have no desire to furnish ammunition for those test critics who would have us stop all testing merely because they find a trivially faulty item in a standardized test. At a time when there is shouting about the tyranny of the testers and the brass of the brain watchers, at a time when school people are showing resentment at the disruption caused by too many national testing programs, at a time when federal and state legislators are all too willing to write legislation that places restrictions on the use of tests, and at a time when both majorities and minorities are being denied the benefits of test-based guidance because certain well-intentioned persons fail to realize that scores for the underprivileged minorities are useful indices of *immediate*, or present, functioning—at a time when all these and other forces are operating to throw out the tests, it is high time for the profession to establish a bureau of standards to test the tests instead of coasting down a road that is tinged with some of the trappings of Madison Avenue. Better to have informed internal control than ignorant, hostile, external control.

INTELLIGENCE ELSEWHERE?

Aside from the near loss of the idea that progress in school may depend on general intelligence, one wonders whether intelligence has come to be regarded as unimportant in other areas.

Any of you who have money invested in stocks and wish some reassurance regarding the intelligence level of business and industry managers should read Edwin Ghiselli's (1963) Bingham Lecture. His summary of his own work indicates that the average intelligence of those in the upper and middle management levels falls at the ninety-sixth percentile of the population. Thomas Harrell (1961) came to a similar conclusion. Furthermore, management level is correlated with intelligence—you can be too dumb to succeed as a manager. Also you can be too bright to be a managerial success! Now it must be admitted that little, if anything, is known about whether managament success might be better predicted by measures of factor-analytic defined abilities. On this you are free to guess—most of you will have already guessed my guess.

A one-by-one cataloguing of what we know or do not know about what abilities contribute to success within various occupational and professional groups would merely add to the dullness of this presentation, so let us turn to some of the more esoteric fields of psychology to see whether the concept of general intelligence has or has had any relevance. One such field, and a very broad one, is creativity. Anyone who peeks over the fence into this field is apt to be astonished at the visible chaos. The definition of creativity is confounded by the diversity of subareas within the field, the criterion problems are far from licked, and so little is known about the creative process that measuring instruments are, seemingly, chosen on a trial-and-error basis.

We might presume that the role, if any, of general intelligence in creativity would increase as we pass from art to music, to architecture, to literature and drama, to science. Your presumption about the ordering may be different and more nearly correct. I would like to discuss briefly the extremes of my ordering.

At the risk of being called a heretic and a has-been statistician, I would like first to resort to the single case of a painter, examples of whose works were reproduced in color recently by Desmond Morris (1962) in a journal called *Portfolio and Art News Annual*. To my uncultured eye these paintings have the general appearance of the so-called school of modern art, and the running comment on the paintings involves what I must presume is the jargon of contemporary art critics: talk about self-rewarding activities, compositional control, calligraphic differentiation, thematic variation, optimum heterogeneity, and universal imagery. Since authors may use pen names, I would guess that this painter is using "Congon" as a "brush" name. Supposedly by now some of you will be guessing that this single case is of interest in the context of this paper because of Congon's IQ. Well, because of this painter's underprivileged cultural background, no test scores are available. Congon, despite striking contribution to art, happens to be a chimp. Aside from a rather obvious conclusion, one wonders what would emerge from a blind (as to source) analysis of Congon's paintings by the personality boys. We might even tell them that Congon was breast fed.

Without in any way implying that creativity in the arts is unimportant, we hasten on to scientific creativity, a specific area in which it seems likely, because of the Sputnik-inspired spurt of interest, that we can learn something of the role, if any, of general intelligence. But immediately we encounter skulls that have been cracked on the criterion problem.

One elaborate study (C. Taylor, Smith, Ghiselin, & Ellison, 1961), on a sample of 166 physical scientists working at Air Force research centers, came up with 150, yes, believe it or not, 150 *criteria* of scientific productivity and creativity. By combining some scores and eliminating others, the number of criteria was reduced to 48. A factor analysis of the intercorrelations of the 48 reduced the number to 14 "categories." Apparently the 150 original criterion measures included everything except success at turning on a kitchen faucet, so one need not be surprised at the outcome of the factor analysis. For example, one factor-derived criterion of scientific productivity and creativity is "likableness," another is "status seeking," another is extent of membership in scientific and professional societies—the joiners, no doubt.

The fact that the intercorrelations among the 14 criterion categories, derived from factor analysis, range from −.08 to +.55, with a median of only .18, indicates either criterion complexity or else a whale of a lot of vagueness as to what is meant by productivity and creativity in science. Now this criterion mess emerged from a study of interview results of 166 "physical scientists," but nearly half of these so-called scientists were engineers, and the education of the total group indicates only 2 years of graduate work on the average; so when is a scientist a scientist a scientist?

The next step in this study was to collect data on 107 of these so-called scientists for a whopping total of 130 potential predictors, which, when pitted against 17 criterion measures, produced 2,210 "validity coefficients." The distribution of these, excluding 30 values involving un-cross-validated empirical keys, almost restores one's faith in the random-sampling distribution of correlation coefficients around zero! There were 16 predictors based on aptitude tests, hence 16×17, or 272, "validities" for this area. Since only 4% of them reach the 5% level, we can do no more than accept the null hypothesis: Aptitude ain't important in scientific productivity and creativity. The idea that some scientists are more equal in ability than others apparently is not true.

But this criterion-based study did not contribute to my worry about the role of general intelligence—the failure to include a general intelligence measure as a potential predictor may be interpreted as indicating that the authors already had the answer.

Let us turn to another criterion-based study (D. Taylor, 1961). The criterion measures for creativity and productivity were based on the checking by supervisors of statements that had been scaled by Thurstone's equal-appearing interval method. Creativity and productivity, so gauged, correlated .69 with each other on a sample of 103 researchers (electronic scientists and engineers). For this same group, intelligence, as measured by the Terman Concept Mastery Test (CMT), correlated only .20 or less with the criteria. Two Psychological Corporation tests and an American Institute for Research test did a little better. Creativity is slightly more predictable than productivity. Insofar as these two criteria are themselves valid, the findings indicate that within a group of research workers, precious little of the variance in creativity, and still less in productivity, can be predicted by the tests.

A third study (MacKinnon, 1962) based on criterion (rated) measures of performance was concerned with the creativity of architects. Although the author reports that *within* a creative sample the correlation is essentially zero between intelligence (CMT) and rated creativity, it is not clear from the context what is meant by "within" sample. If this means within the sample of 40 creative architects selected as the "most creative" in the country, then we indeed have such a drastic restriction in range on the *criterion* variable that little, if any, correlation can be expected for any and all predictors. Now the author says, without presenting any evidence, that "Over the whole range of intelligence and creativity there is, of course, a positive relationship between the two variables [p. 488]." One wonders just what is meant by creativity in architecture as rated either by fellow architects or by editors of architectural journals. If judged creativity reflects engineering-structural innovation, then intelligence would likely be a correlate; if judged creativity depends on new artistic designs, then the intelligence component would likely be of less importance. It would seem that when the author says we "may have overestimated . . . the role of intelligence in creative achievement [p. 493]," he should have included some marked qualifications as to what type of creativity he had in mind.

That such qualification is indeed necessary is supplied by a finding of still another investigator (Barron, 1963). For a group of highly creative writers it was estimated, by way of the Terman CMT, that their average IQ is about 140, which we interpret as meaning that a high IQ is a necessary, though not sufficient, condition for outstanding success as a writer. On the basis of his own studies and those of other persons, this same investigator suggests that "over the total range of intelligence and creativity a low positive correlation" of .40 probably obtains. This sweeping generalization is for all areas of creativity.

And speaking of sweeping generalizations, consider the suggestion in a 1961 study (Holland, 1961) that "we need to use nonintellectual criteria in the selection of students for scholarships and fellowships [p. 146]." The author did not say so, but presumably he meant in addition to intellectual ability; maybe he did not, since he had previously concluded that "intelligence has little or no relationship to creative performance in arts and science . . . [p. 143]" at the high school level. His data back up this conclusion, as might have been expected when correlations are based on groups restricted in range to the top 1%!

If the foregoing examples of criterion-based studies of creativity seem to indicate that general intelligence is relatively unimportant for creativity, it should be remembered that drastic but unknown or unspecified curtailment of range exists for both ability and criteria. Why do correlational studies under such adverse circumstances?

Next we turn to a few studies of creativity which cannot be criticized because of restriction of range on the criteria—these studies simply avoid this problem by never having actual criterion information. The approach is to claim that certain tests, which typically are scored for novel responses or novel solutions to problems, *are* measures of creativity, with no evidence whatsoever that the tests have predictive validity for nontest, real-life creative performance. This bit of ignorance does not prove to be a handicap to those who think that creativity can be studied without the nuisance of obtaining criterion measures. We reluctantly accept the test-based criteria solely for the sake of seeing what happens to general intelligence as a part of the picture. Time permits only three examples.

We first note that general intelligence has not manifested itself as a correlate of so-called creativity tests in the factor-analytic studies of creativity. The explanation for this is easily found—no measures of general intelligence are used in these studies. When discussing his plans for studying creativity, a certain author (Guilford, 1950) said that "we must look well beyond the boundaries of the IQ if we are to fathom the domain of creativity [p. 448]." He went on to say, the conception "that creative talent is to be accounted for in terms of high intelligence or IQ . . . is not only inadequate but has been largely responsible for lack of progress in the understanding of creative people [p. 454]." With a part of this one can agree, but does it follow that one should prejudge the role of general intelligence as a source of variance in creativity tests or factors derived therefrom? Does the failure to include an IQ test help one learn the extent to which one must go beyond the boundaries of the IQ to fathom creativity? Apparently the author, although willing to predict that the correlations between IQ and the many types of creativity tests "are only moderate or low," was unwilling to include an IQ test for the sake of finding out. However, negation by omission is not very convincing.

That at least one test bearing the label "creativity" is correlated more than moderately with IQ is evidenced by the value of .67 (average for boys and girls) for the carefully chosen sample of 15-year-olds in Project Talent (Shaycoft, Dailey, Orr, Neyman, & Sherman, 1963). This sample-stable r (based on a total N of 7,648) becomes .80 when corrected for attenuation.

In a recent extensive study (Getzels & Jackson, 1962), already extensively criticized, creativity is defined as the sum of scores on five tests (median intercorrelation of only .28). Although the investigators use the sum score for most of their analyses, they do not bother to report the correlation of creativity, so defined, with IQ. From the published report I have ascertained (via the correlation-of-sums formula) that creativity and IQ correlate to the extent of .40 for the total of 533 cases. Now this r of .40 has been greatly attenuated because of three things: first, the usual measurement errors; second, the cases were highly selected on IQ (mean of 132); third, the IQs are a mixture from the Stanford-Binet, Henmon-Nelson, and Wechsler Intelligence Scale for Children (the use of regression-estimated Binet IQs from the other two scales aggravates rather than improves the mixture). We deduce that intelligence and the creativity tests used here have far more common variance than the authors believe.

Much is made of the finding that the creativity tests tended to correlate higher than did IQ with verbal-content school achievements. Again the IQ comes in for an unfair drubbing because of the same mixture of IQ scores and, what is more pertinent, because of explicit selective curtailment on the IQ variable and only incidental selection on the creativity variable.

Of more importance to the present paper is the analysis, by these same authors, based on a high IQ group and a high creative group, these groups being selected as the top 20% for each variable but excluding those who were in the top 20% on both variables. These two selected groups were then contrasted on total school achievement (and a host of other variables that are of no interest here). The mean IQ for the high IQ group was 150 whereas the mean IQ for the high creative group was 127, yet the achievement means of the two groups were "unexpectedly" equally superior to the school population mean despite the 23-point difference in mean IQ. The authors say that it "*is* quite surprising" that the high creativity group achieved so well. From this it is concluded that the "creative instruments account for a significant portion of the variance in school achievement [p. 24]," and the subsequent argument implies that creativity is more important for ordinary school achievement than is the IQ. Now anyone who is at all familiar with a three-variate problem will not be "unexpectedly" surprised at the foregoing results

—indeed, if the authors had bothered to give the three basic correlations among the three variables (IQ, creativity, and total school achievement) for the entire group, any person versed in simple multivariate analysis could deduce the results. Furthermore, he could deduce a further result (and this one has been overlooked by the critics) which might be unpleasantly surprising to the thesis of these authors: namely, the high IQ and the high creative groups did equally well in school achievement despite an unreported difference in mean creativity that is of the same order as the much stressed difference in IQ.[2] Utilizing the half-blind logic of the authors, one can say that creative ability is not as important as IQ for school achievement—just the opposite of their position.

Now the fact that seven of nine replications of this study confirm the original findings merely indicates that repetition of the same faulty design and false logic will lead to the same false conclusions. The design being used is such that, if two variables are equally correlated with a third, the conclusion will be reached that the two are actually unequally correlated with the third. This is the neatest trick of the decade for supplying educationists with an antidote for the IQ virus. I cannot refrain from saying at this point that, although discouraged, I am still hopeful that people who do statistical studies will first learn a modicum of elementary statistics!

Time does not permit a discussion of other studies in which creativity is defined in terms of test performance instead of being based on actual creativity of the sort prized by society. In summary of this brief on creativity studies, I would like to offer a few dogmatic-sounding observations. First, one need not be surprised at the fact that so-called creativity tests do not yield high correlations with IQ tests—but the correlations are generally far higher than those found in typical studies with range restrictions. I would anticipate that for normalized scores, the uncurtailed scatters for IQ versus creativity tests will be bivariate normal. Second, if we have honest to goodness criterion measures of literary or architectural or scientific creativity, the scatter diagram between IQ and such creativity (not normalized, since it makes sense to expect a skewed distribution for actual creativity) will be triangular in shape for unselected cases. That is, at the high IQ levels there will be a very wide range of creativity, whereas as we go down to average IQ, and on down to lower levels, the scatter for creativity will be less and less. Having a high IQ is not a guarantee of being creative; having a low IQ means creativity is impossible. Third, it remains to be seen whether or not the so-called creativity tests and/or factors derived therefrom have appreciable value as predictors of actual creative performance. Such tests may or may not yield better predictions than a test of general intelligence. Fourth, as far as I am concerned, to claim factorial validity for creativity tests, along with definitions of creativity in terms of tests, is an unwarranted avoidance of the fundamental problem of validity.

The recently renewed interest in "gifted" children, along with the flurry of creativity studies, has led to a reexamination of methods for identifying the gifted. It has long been recognized that identification in terms of high IQ is too narrow—those gifted in such areas as art and music would be overlooked. The argument against the IQ is now (Torrance, 1962) being reinforced by the claim that the selection of the top 20% on IQ would mean the exclusion of 70% of the top 20% on tested creativity. This startling statistic, which implies a correlation of only .24 between IQ and creativity, is being used to advocate the use of creativity tests for identifying the gifted. Be it noted that these creativity tests will also miss those gifted in art and music.

We are being told that it is important "to identify creative talent early in life," hence you need not be surprised that the search goes down to the kindergarten level, with claims of successful identification. The creativity tests are presumed to be better for this purpose than the IQ tests because of the failure of the IQ to be constant, an argument that completely overlooks the fact that the IQ does have some constancy whereas absolutely nothing is known about the stability of standings on creativity tests. The IQ tests, known to be imperfectly valid as predictors of outstanding achievement in life, are to be replaced by the creativity tests, known to be of unknown validity as predictors. Anyway, progress, defined as change, is in the offing.

The IQ is being linked with *learning* as an outmoded educational objective; the new objective involves an emphasis on *thinking*. Somehow or other creativity, not general intelligence, is being associated with thinking. The horrible idea of underachievers and overachievers, in terms of expectancies based on the IQ, will be abolished. But no thought is given to the fact that the use of creativity tests will simply define a new crop of under- and overachievers.

In an apparent zeal to rid us of general intelligence, it is argued that measured creativity is significantly related to ordinary school achievement. Maybe so, but never, never does one find complete data reported as to the relative sizes of validity coefficients. And, as we have seen, the technique being used will show that equal coefficients are unequal. Why not the full facts, free of fantasy?

An additional difficulty is not being faced by those who would replace IQ tests by creativity tests, or creative-thinking tests. The factor-analytic studies indicate either no, or a trivially small, general creativity factor in these tests, yet these self-characterized "bold, adventurous" reformers (see Torrance, 1963) do not hesitate to advocate a total score which is nearly devoid of meaning. Changing the curriculum to the teaching of creativity and creative thinking will not overcome this measurement difficulty. Again, I express the hope that the IQ is replaced by something better rather than by something worse.

There are other areas, such as reasoning, problem solving, and concept formation, in which one might expect to find some consideration of intelligence as an aspect. One might also expect that investigators of thinking would have something to say about individual differenecs in thinking being dependent upon intelligence, but for some unintelligent reason these people seem never to mention intelligence. Surely, it cannot be inferred that thinking about thinking does not involve intelligence!

IN CONCLUSION

It has been the thesis of this paper that the concept of general intelligence, despite being maligned by a few, regarded as a second-order function by some, and discarded or ignored by others, still has a rightful place in the science of psychology and in the practical affairs of man. It has not been argued that the nature of general intelligence is well understood. Much, however, has been written about its nature. Over 40 years ago (Intelligence, 1921a, 1921b), an editor secured and published the reasoned views of 13 well-known test psychologists. Later, Spearman set forth his speculations about the nature of g. Prior to these, Binet had, of course, given much thought to the problem.

More recent discussions exist. Hebb (1949) has considered the problem from the viewpoint of neurology and brain functioning. Cyril Burt (1955), always a vociferous defender of the concept of general intelligence, has reviewed the evidence for a g and restated the idea, dreadful to some, that intelligence is innate. Perhaps it was inevitable that Raymond Cattell (1963), who has camped with the general intelligence contingent, should gaze into his crystal n-dimensional factor ball and find evidence for crystallized as opposed to fluid general intelligence. Joseph McVicker Hunt's (1961) book on *Intelligence and Experience* is in large part devoted to questions pertaining to the nature of intelligence.

By far the most provocative recent discussion that I have encountered is the closely reasoned 44-page paper by Keith Hayes (1962). He puts forth a motivational-experiential theory of intelligence. In essence, he presumes that there are hereditary differences in motivation. "Experience-producing drives" and environmental differences produce differences in experience, which in turn, by way of learning, lead to differences in ability. Therefore, differences called intellectual are nothing more than acquired abilities. I think that Hayes has ignored the possibility of individual differences in learning ability, but if such a formulation leads to experimental manipulation of variables, we may eventually make progress in an area that has too long been dominated by ever increasing fractionization by factor analysis, with little thought as to how the fractured parts get put together into a functioning whole.

Abilities, or capacities, or aptitudes, or intellectual skills, or whatever you choose to call them, are measured in terms of response products to standardized stimulus situations. The *stimulus* is presented to an *organism* which by some *process* comes up with a *response*; thus any attempt to theorize and/or study intellect in terms of a simple stimulus-response (S-R) paradigm seems doomed to failure unless drastically modified and complicated by the insertion of O for organism and P for process.

There have been thousands of researches on the multitudinous variations from organism to organism, and the results fill books on individual differences. These studies can be roughly classified into two types. First, those that ascertain the intercorrelations among scaled response products to various stimulus situations, known as tests, have to do with the structure of intellect; and whether the resulting factors are anything more than dimensions for describing individual differences need not concern us here. The second type of study seeks the nontest correlates of test performance, and whether or not any of the found correlates can be regarded as explaining individual differences is not of interest here. Both types of studies certainly force one to stress the overwhelming diversity exhibited among the organisms.

But these studies of individual differences never come to grips with the *process*, or operation, by which a given organism achieves an intellectual response. Indeed, it is difficult to see how the available individual difference data can be used even as a starting point for generating a theory as to the process nature of general intelligence or of any other specified ability.

As a basis for a little speculation, let us conceive of a highly hypothetical situation in which the two members of a pair of identical twins, with identical experiences, find themselves cast up on an uninhabited tropical island. Let us assume that they are at the supergenius level, far beyond that of your favorite man of genius. Let us also assume that, though highly educated in the sciences, they have been fortunate enough to have had zero exposure to psychology. In addition, we presume that, being highly involved and abstracted in the pursuit of science, they have never noticed what we call individual differences in abilities.

A quick exploration of the island assures them that food is plentiful, that shelter is available, and that clothing is not a necessity. To allay the boredom that they foresee as an eternity in this laborless heaven, they decide to spend their time in the further pursuit of science, but the lack of the wherewithal for constructing gadgets rules out any research in the physical sciences. Having had a college course in Bugs and Bites they proceed to study the life of the island's insects, then the habits of the birds, and the antics of a couple of monkeys. The manner in which the monkeys adjust to the environment leads them to set up some trial situations for more systematic observation. Needless to say, the monkeys show evidence of what we call learning and we call problem solving.

Eventually they decide that attempting to outwit each other might be more fun than being outwitted by the monkeys, so they begin to cook up and use games and problems for this purpose. This activity leads each to speculate and introspect about how problems are invented and how solved. Then by cleverly designed experiments, preceded of course by theory, they set forth highly developed laws and principles about what we call reasoning and problem solving. Incidentally, they switch back and forth between the roles of experimenter and subject, there being no college sophomores available. They continue for years the study of their own mental operations, constantly on the alert for new phenomena to investigate.

And now with apologies to the ancient Greeks, who did have some ideas along these lines, we leave with you the 64-million drachma question: Will our two identical supergeniuses, being totally unaware of individual differences, ever hit upon and develop a concept of intelligence?

NOTES

[1] Address of the President to the Seventy-Second Annual Convention of the American Psychological Association. Los Angeles, September 5, 1964.

[2] Since this was written, the replication study of Yamamoto (1964) gives data that corroborate this deduction.

REFERENCES

Barron, F. *Creativity and psychological health.* Princeton, N.J.: Van Nostrand, 1963.

Bennett, G. K., Seashore, H. G., & Wesman, A. G. *Differential Aptitude Tests, manual.* (2nd ed.) New York: Psychological Corporation, 1952.

Burt, C. L. The evidence for the concept of intelligence. *Brit. J. educ. Psychol.,* 1955, *25*, 158–177.

Cattell, R. B. Theory of fluid and crystallized intelligence: A critical experiment. *J. educ. Psychol.,* 1963, *54*, 1–22.

Cronbach, L. J. The two disciplines of scientific psychology. *Amer. Psychologist,* 1957, *12*, 671–684.

Getzels, J. W., & Jackson, P. W. *Creativity and intelligence.* New York: Wiley, 1962.

Ghiselli, E. E. Managerial talent. *Amer. Psychologist,* 1963, *18*, 631–642.

Guilford, J. P. Creativity. *Amer. Psychologist,* 1950, 5, 444–454.

Harrell, T. H. *Manager's performance and personality.* Cincinnati, O.: South-Western, 1961.

Hayes, K. J. Genes, drives, and intellect. *Psychol. Rep.,* 1962, *10*, 299–342.

Hebb, D. O. *The organization of behavior.* New York: Wiley, 1949.

Holland, J. L. Creative and academic performance among talented adolescents. *J. educ. Psychol.,* 1961, *52*, 136–147

Hunt, J. McV. *Intelligence and experience.* New York: Ronald Press, 1961.

Intelligence and its measurement: A symposium. *J. educ. Psychol.,* 1921, *12*, 123–147. (a)

Intelligence and its measurement: A symposium. *J. educ. Psychol.*, 1921, *12*, 195–216. (b)

MacKinnon, D. W. The nature and nurture of creative talent. *Amer. Psychologist*, 1962, *17*, 484–495.

Miles, T. R. On defining intelligence. *Brit. J. educ. Psychol.*, 1957, *27*, 153–165.

Morris, D. The biology of art. *Portfolio art News Annu.*, 1962, No. 6, 52–63, 122–124.

Segel, D. The multiple aptitude tests. *Personnel guid. J.*, 1957, *35*, 424–432.

Shaycoft, M. F., Dailey, J. T., Orr, D. B., Neyman, C. A., Jr., & Sherman, S. E. Project Talent: Studies of a complete age group—age 15. Pittsburgh: University of Pittsburgh, 1963. (Mimeo)

Taylor, C. W., Smith, W. R., Ghiselin, B., & Ellison, R. Explorations in the measurement and predictions of contributions of one sample of scientists. *USAF ASD tech. Rep.*, 1961 No. 61–96.

Taylor, D. W. Variables related to creativity and productivity among men in two research laboratories. In C. W. Taylor & F. Barron (Eds.), *Scientific creativity.* New York: Wiley, 1961.

Thurstone, L. L. *Primary mental abilities.* Chicago: Univer. Chicago Press, 1938.

Thurstone, L. L., & Thurstone, T. G. *Factorial studies of intelligence.* Chicago: Univer. Chicago Press, 1941.

Torrance, E. P. *Guiding creative talent.* Englewood Cliffs, N.J.: Prentice-Hall, 1962.

Torrance, E. P. *Education and the creative potential.* Minneapolis: Univer. Minnesota Press, 1963.

Yamamoto, K. Role of creative thinking and intelligence in high school achievement. *Psychol. Rec.*, 1964, *14*, 783–789.

Guilford, one of the leading advocates of the multi-factor concept
of intelligence, counters McNemar's position. He feels there is
sufficient evidence to reject the notion of general intelligence.

Is it possible that Guilford has the more accurate theoretical
model, but general intelligence tests are of more practical value?
If so, what position should educators take regarding this issue?

Intelligence Has Three Facets

J. P. GUILFORD

Many a layman who has taken a psychologist's intelligence test, especially if
he did not do as well as he thought he should, has the conviction that a score,
such as an IQ, does not tell the whole story regarding intelligence. In thinking so, he is absolutely right; traditional intelligence tests fall far short of
indicating fully an individual's intellectual status. Just how far short and in
what respects have not been well realized until very recent years during which
the whole scope of human intelligence has been intensively investigated.

This is not to say that IQ tests are not useful, for they definitely are, as
years of experience have demonstrated. Intelligence-quotient tests were originated more than 60 years ago for the purpose of determining which children
could not learn at normal rates. This meant that the content of IQ tests
weights heavily those intellectual abilities that are pertinent to school learning in the key subjects of reading and arithmetic, and other subjects that
depend directly upon them or are of similar nature psychologically. IQ
tests (and also academic-aptitude tests, which are essentially similar) predict
less well at educational levels higher than the elementary grades, for at
higher levels subject matter becomes more varied. Even at the elementary
level, predictions of achievement have been poor in connection with the
initial stages of learning to read, in spelling, and in the arts. The defender of
the IQ test might say that intelligence is not involved in such subjects. But he
would not only be wrong, he would also be dodging problems.

ONE INTELLIGENCE, OR MANY ABILITIES?

The father of IQ tests, Alfred Binet, believed firmly that intelligence is a
very complex affair, comprising a number of different abilities, and he manifested this conviction by introducing tests of many kinds into his composite

From *Science*, May 10, 1968, 160: 615–620. Copyright 1968 by the American Association
for the Advancement of Science. Reprinted with permission of author and publisher.

scale. He did not know what the component abilities are, although he suggested that there are several different kinds of memory, for example. He went along with the idea of using a single, overall score, since the immediate practical goal was to make a single administrative decision regarding each child.

Test-makers following Binet were mostly unconcerned about having a basic psychological theory for intelligence tests, another example of technology running far in advance of theory. There was some concern about theory in England, however, where Charles Spearman developed a procedure of factor analysis by which it became possible to discover component abilities (1). Spearman was obsessed with a very restricting conception that there is a universal g factor that is common to all tests that have any claim to the label of "intelligence tests," where each test has its own unique kind of items or problems. His research, and that of others in his country, found, however, that correlations between tests could not be fully accounted for on the basis of a single common factor (2). They had to admit the existence of a number of "group" factors in addition to g. For example, sets of tests having verbal, numerical, or spatial material, respectively, correlated higher within sets than with tests in other sets. The extra correlation among tests within sets was attributed to additional abilities each of limited scope.

Factor analyses in the United States have followed almost exclusively the multiple-factor theory of Thurstone (3), which is more general than Spearman's. In Thurstone's conception, a g factor is not necessary but analysis by his methods would be likely to find it if the intercorrelations warrant such a result. It is not necessary to know the mathematics basic to factor theory in order to follow the remaining content of this article, but for those who wish additional insights the next few paragraphs present the minimum essentials of a mathematical basis. To all readers it may be said that factor analysis is a sensitive procedure, which, when properly used, can answer the taxonomic questions of *what* intellectual abilities or functions exist and what their properties are.

The basic equation in multiple-factor theory, in matrix form, is $Z = FC$, where Z is a matrix of test scores, of order n by N, where N individuals have all taken n different tests. Z indicates that the scores are in standard form, that is, each element $z = (X - \overline{X})/s_x$, where X is a "raw" score on an arbitrary scale, $\overline{X}$ is the mean of the raw scores in the sample of N individuals, and s_x is the standard deviation. In the basic equation, F stands for the "complete factor matrix," which is of order n by $(r + n)$, where r is the number of *common* factors. The addition of n columns indicates that there are n *specific* factors or components, one for each test. In this matrix, f_{ij} is the loading or weight for test I in connection with factor J. C is of the order $(r + n)$ by N and represents the scores of N individuals on $(r + n)$ factors. The basic equation means that for each individual his standard score z_{ij} in a particular test is a weighted sum of his $(r + n)$ factor scores, each factor score also in standard form. An assumption for this form of the equation is that the factors are orthogonal (uncorrelated) variables.

The factor-analysis problem is to derive the matrix of common-factor loadings, A, given the score matrix for N individuals in n tests. The interest is in only the r common factors. The analysis ordinarily starts with intercorrelations among the n tests. The reduced (specifics ignored) intercorrelation matrix R is mathematically related to the factor matrix A by the equation $R = AA'$, where A represents only the common-factor components in F, and A' is the transpose of A. R can be computed from empirical data by the equation $R = ZZ'/N$. Starting with the computed correlation matrix R, the problem is to find the common-factor matrix A. Methods for accomplishing this operation are described by Harman (4).

Very rarely, indeed, does anyone using the multiple-factor approach find and report a g factor. The reason is that there are too many zero correlations among tests of intellectual qualities, where one genuine zero correlation would be sufficient to disallow a g factor that is supposed to be universal. My examination of more than 7000 intercorrelations, among tests in the intellectual category, showed at least 17 percent of them to be acceptable as zero correlations (5). The multiple factors usually found are each commonly restricted to only a few tests, where we may ignore factor loadings less than .30 as being insignificant, following common practice.

DISCOVERY OF MULTIPLE ABILITIES

Only a few events in discovering factors by the Thurstone approach will be mentioned. In Thurstone's first major study (6) as many as nine common factors were thought to be sufficiently interpretable psychologically to justify calling them "primary mental abilities." A factor is interpreted intuitively in terms of the apparent human resource needed to do well in the set of tests loaded strongly together on the mathematical factor. A distinction between mathematical factors and psychological factors is important. Surface features of the tests in the set may differ, but examinees have to perform well in some unique way in all of them. For example, Thurstone designated some of the abilities as being visual-perceptual, inductive, deductive, numerical, spatial, and verbal. Two others dealt with rote memory and word fluency. Thurstone and his students followed his 1938 analysis with others that revealed a few additional kinds of abilities.

Another major source of identified intellectual abilities was the research of aviation psychologists in the U.S. Army Air Force during World War II (7). More important than the outcome of adding to the number of intellectual abilities that called for recognition was the fact that where Thurstone had found one spatial ability, there proved to be at least three, one of them being recognized as spatial orientation and another as spatial visualization. Where Thurstone had found an inductive ability, there were three reasoning abilities. Where Thurstone had found one memory ability, there were three, including visual memory. In some of these cases a Thurstone factor turned out to be a confounding of two or more separable abilities, separable when more representative tests for each factor were analyzed together and when allowance was made for a sufficient number of factors. In other cases, new varieties of tests were explored—new memory tests, space tests, and reasoning tests.

The third major event was in the form of a program of analyses conducted in the Aptitudes Research Project at the University of Southern California since 1949, in which attention was first concentrated on tests in the provisional categories of reasoning, creative thinking, planning, evaluation, and problem-solving (8). Nearly 20 years later, the number of separate intellectual abilities has increased to about 80, with at least 50 percent more predicted by a comprehensive, unified theory. The remainder of this article is mainly concerned with that theory.

THE STRUCTURE-OF-INTELLECT MODEL

Two previous attempts to put the known intellectual abilities into logical schema had been made by Burt (9) and Vernon (10), with similar results. In both cases the models were of hierarchical form, reminiscent of the Linnaous taxonomic model for the animal kingdom. Following the British tradition of emphasis upon g, which was placed at the apex of the system, there were broad subdivisions under g and under each subdivision some sub-subcategories, on down to abilities that are regarded as being very narrow in scope.

My first attempts (11) found that the hierarchical type of model had to be discarded for several reasons. First, there had to be a rejection of g itself, for reasons mentioned earlier. Furthermore, most factors seemed to be of somewhat comparable level of generality, where generality is operationally defined in terms of the number and variety of tests found to represent each ability. There did appear to be categories of abilities, some concerned with discovery or recognition of information, memory for information, productive thinking, and evaluation, with a number of abilities in each category, but there are other ways of organizing categories of abilities. The most decisive observation was that there were a number of parallels between abilities, in terms of their common features.

Some examples of parallels in abilities will help. Two parallel abilities differ in only one respect. There was known to be an ability to see relations between perceived, visual figures, and a parallel ability to see relations between concepts. An example of a test item in the first case would be seeing that one figure is the lower-left half of another. An item in the second case might require seeing that the words "bird" and "fly" are related as object and its mode of locomotion. The ability to do the one kind of item is relatively independent of the ability to do the other, the only difference being that of kind of information—concrete or perceived in the one case and abstract or conceived in the other.

For a pair of abilities differing in another way, the kind of information is the same for both. One of the abilities pertains to *seeing* class ideas. Given the set of words *footstool, lamp, rocker, television*, can the examinee grasp the essence of the nature of the class, as shown by his naming the class, by putting another word or two into it, or by recognizing its name among four alternatives? The ability pertains to discovery or recognition of a class concept. In another kind of test we ask the examinee to *produce* classes by partitioning a list of words into mutually exclusive sets, each with a different class concept. These two abilities are relatively independent. The one involves a process of understanding and the other a process of production. These processes involve two psychologically different kinds of operation.

A third kind of parallel abilities has pairs that are alike in kind of information involved and in kind of operation. Suppose we give the examinee this kind of test item: "Name as many objects as you can that are both edible and white." Here we have given the specifications for a class and the examinee is to produce from his memory store some class members. The ability involved was at first called "ideational fluency." The more of appropriate members the examinee can produce in a limited time, the better his score. In a test for a parallel ability, instead of producing single words the examinee is to produce a list of sentences. To standardize his task for testing purposes and to further control his efforts, we can give him the initial letters of four words that he is to give in each of a variety of sentences, for example: W _____ c _____s _____d _____. Without using any word twice, the examinee might say, "Why can't Susan dance?," "Workers could seldom deviate," or "Weary cats sense destruction." The ability was first called "expressional fluency." The kind of information in both these tests is conceptual, and the kind of operation is production.

But the kind of operation in the last test is different from that for the classifying test mentioned before. In the classifying test, the words given to the examinee are so selected that they form a unique set of classes and he is so told. The operation is called "convergent production." In the last two tests under discussion, there are many possible responses and the examinee produces alternatives. The operation is called "divergent production." It involves a broad searching or scanning process. Both operations depend upon retrieval of information from the examinee's memory store.

The difference between the two abilities illustrated by the last two tests is in the nature of the things produced. In the first case they are single words that stand for single objects or concepts. The thing produced, the "product," is a *unit* of information. In the second case, the product is an organized sequence of words, each word standing for a concept or unit. This kind of product is given the name of "system."

In order to take care of all such parallels (and the number increased as time went on and experience grew), a matrix type of model seemed called for in the manner of Mendeleev's table of chemical elements. The differences in the three ways indicated—operation (kind of processing of information), content (kind of information), and product (formal aspect of information) —called for a three-dimensional model. Such a model has been called "morphological" (*12*). The model as finally completed and presented in 1959 (*13*) is illustrated in Fig. 1. It has five categories of operation, four categories of content, and six categories of product.

It is readily seen that the theory calls for $5 \times 4 \times 6$, or 120, cubical cells in the model, each one representing a unique ability, unique by virtue of its peculiar conjunction of operation, content, and product. The reader has already been introduced to three kinds of operation: cognition (discovery, recognition, comprehension), divergent production, and convergent production. The memory operation involves putting information into the memory store and must be distinguished from the memory store itself. The latter underlies all the operations; all the abilities depend upon it. This is the best logical basis for believing that the abilities increase with experience, depending upon the kinds of experience. The evaluation operation deals with assessment of information, cognized or produced, determining its goodness with respect to adopted (logical) criteria, such as identity and consistency.

The distinction between figural and semantic (conceptual) contents was mentioned earlier. The distinguishing of symbolic information from these two came later. Symbolic information is presented in tests in the form of letters or numbers, ordinarily, but other signs that have only "token" value or meaning can be used.

The category of behavioral information was added on the basis of a hunch; no abilities involving it were known to have been demonstrated when it was included. The basis was E. L. Thorndike's suggestion (*14*) many years ago that there is a "social intelligence," distinct from what he called "concrete" and "abstract" intelligences. It was decided to distinguish "social intelligence" on the basis of kind of information, the kind that one person derives from observation of the behavior of another. Subsequent experience has demonstrated a full set of six behavioral-cognition abilities as predicted by the model, and a current analytical investigation is designed to test the part of the model that includes six behavioral-divergent-production abilities. In a test for cognition of behavioral systems, three parts of a four-part cartoon are given in each item, with four alternative parts that are potential completions. The examinee has to size up each situation, and the sequence of events, correctly in order to select the appropriate part. As a test for divergent production of behavioral systems, the examinee is given descriptions of three characters, for example, a jubilant man, an angry woman, and a sullen boy, for which he is to construct a number of alternative story plots involving the characters and their moods, all stories being different.

The reader has already encountered four kinds of products: units, classes, relations, and systems, with illustrations. The other two kinds of products are transformations and implications. Transformations include any kind of change: movement in space, rearrangement or regrouping of letters in words or factoring or simplifying an equation, redefining a concept or adapting an object or part of an object to a new use, revising one's interpretation of another person's action, or rearranging events in a story. In these examples the four kinds of content are involved, from figural to behavioral, illustrating the fact that all six kinds of products apply in every content category.

Implied information is suggested by other information. Foresight or prediction depends upon extrapolating from given information to some naturally following future condition or event. If I make this move in chess, my knight will be vulnerable. If I divide by X, I will have a simpler expres-

Figure 1   The Structure-of-Intellect Model

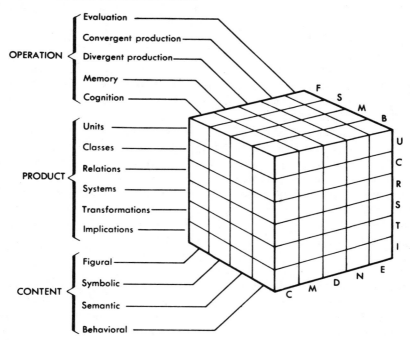

sion. If it rains tonight, my tent will leak. If I whistle at that girl, she will turn her head. The "If . . . then" expression well describes an instance of implication, the implication actually being the thing implied.

SOME CONSEQUENCES OF THE THEORY

The most immediate consequence of the theory and its model has been its heuristic value in suggesting where to look for still undemonstrated abilities. The modus operandi of the Aptitudes Research Project from the beginning has been to hypothesize certain kinds of abilities, to create new types of tests that should emphasize each hypothesized ability, then factor analyze to determine whether the hypothesis is well supported. With hypotheses generated by the model, the rate of demonstration of new abilities has been much accelerated.

At the time this article was written, of 24 hypothesized abilities in the category of cognition, 23 had been demonstrated. Of 24 expected memory abilities, 14 were recognized. In the other operation categories of divergent production, convergent production, and evaluation, 16, 13, and 13 abilities, respectively, were accounted for, and in all these categories 17 other hypotheses are under investigation. These studies should bring the number of demonstrated abilities close to the century mark. It is expected that the total will go beyond the 120 indicated by the model, for some cells in the figural and symbolic columns already have more than one ability each. These proliferations arise from the differences in kind of sensory input. Most known abilities are represented by tests with visual input. A few have been found in tests with auditory input, and possibly one involving kinesthetic information. Each one can also be placed in the model in terms of its three sources of specification—operation, content, and product.

Having developed a comprehensive and systematic theory of intelligence, we have found that not the least of its benefits is an entirely new point of view in psychology generally, a view that has been called "operational-informational." I have elaborated a great deal upon this view elsewhere (15). Information is defined for psychology as that which the organism discriminates. Without discrimination there is no information. This far, there is agreement with the conception of information as viewed by communication engineers, but beyond this point we part company. Psychological discriminations are most broadly and decisively along the lines of kinds of content and kinds of products, from which arise hiatuses between intellectual abilities. Further discriminations occur, of course, within the sphere of a single ability. I have proposed that the 4×6 intersections of the informational categories of the SI (structure of intellect) model provide a psychoepistemology, with 24 subcategories of basic information. I have also proposed that the six product categories—units, classes, relations, systems, transformations, and implications—provide the basis for a psycho-logic (16). Although most of these terms are also concepts in modern logic, a more complete representation appears in mathematics.

The operational-informational view regards the organism as a processor of information, for which the modern, high-speed computer is a good analogy. From this point of view, computer-simulation studies make sense. In addition to trying to find out how the human mind works by having computers accomplish the same end results, however, it might be useful, also, to determine how the human mind accomplishes its ends, then to design the computer that performs the same operations. Although a psychology based upon the SI concepts is much more complicated than the stimulus-response model that became traditional, it is still parsimonious. It certainly has the chance of becoming more adequate. The structure of intellect, as such, is a taxonomic model; it provides fruitful concepts. For theory that accounts for behavior, we need operational models, and they can be based on SI concepts. For example, I have produced such a model for problem-solving (17).

There is no one problem-solving ability. Many different SI abilities may be drawn upon in solving a problem, depending upon the nature of the problem. Almost always there are cognitive operations (in understanding the nature of the problem), productive operations (in generating steps toward solution), and evaluative operations (in checking upon both understanding and production). Memory operations enter in, to keep a record of information regarding previous steps, and the memory store underlies all.

There is something novel about producing solutions to problems, hence creative thinking is involved. Creative thinking depends most clearly upon divergent-production operations on the one hand, and on transformations on the other. Thus, these two categories have unique roles in creative problem-solving. There is accordingly no one unique ability to account for creative potential. Creative production depends upon the area in which one works, whether it is in pictorial art, music, drama, mathematics, science, writing, or management. In view of the relative independence of the intellectual abilities, unevenness of status in the various abilities within the same person should be the rule rather than the exception. Some individuals can excel in more than one art form, but few excel in all, as witness the practice of having multiple creative contributors to a single motion picture.

The implications of all this for education are numerous. The doctrine that intelligence is a unitary something that is established for each person by heredity and that stays fixed through life should be summarily banished. There is abundant proof that greater intelligence is associated with increased education. One of education's major objectives should be to increase the stature of its recipients in intelligence, which should now mean stature in the various intellectual abilities. Knowing what those abilities are, we not only have more precise goals but also much better conceptions of how to achieve those goals.

For much too long, many educators have assumed, at least implicitly, that if we provide individuals with information they will also be able to use that information productively. Building up the memory store is a necessary condition for productive thinking, but it is not a sufficient condition, for productive abilities are relatively independent of cognitive abilities. There are some revealing findings on this point (18). In a sample of about 200 ninth-grade students, IQ measurements were available and also the scores on a large number of tests of various divergent-production (DP) abilities. Table 1 shows a scatter diagram with plots of DP scores (19) as a function of IQ. The striking feature of this diagram pertains to the large proportion of high-IQ students who had low, even some very low, DP scores. In general, IQ appears to set a kind of upper limit upon DP performance but not a lower limit. The same kind of result was true for most other DP tests.

On the basis of present information, it would be best to regard each intellectual ability of a person as a somewhat generalized skill that has developed through the circumstances of experience, within a certain culture, and that can be further developed by means of the right kind of exercise. There may be limits to abilities set by heredity, but it is probably safe to say that very rarely does an individual really test such limits. There is much experimental evidence, rough though it may be, that exercise devoted to certain skills involved in creative thinking is followed by increased capability (15, p. 336). Although special exercises have their demonstrated value, it is probably better to have such exercises worked into teaching, whatever the subject, where there are opportunities. Informing individuals regarding the nature of their own intellectual resources, and how they enter into mental work, has also been found beneficial.

There is not space to mention many other problems related to intelligence—its growth and its decline, its relation to brain anatomy and brain functions, and its role in learning. All these problems take on new aspects,

TABLE 1   Scatterplot of Expressional Fluency (one aspect of divergent production) Scores in Relation to CTMM (California Test of Mental Maturity) IQ

DP score	Intelligence quotient								
	60–69	70–79	80–89	90–99	100–109	110–119	120–129	130–139	140–149
50–59					1		3		1
40–49						2	4	1	
30–39			2	3	4	11	17	6	2
20–29			1	3	10	23	13	7	
10–19	1	5	3	9	11	19	7	3	1
0– 9	1	3	1	4	10	11	2		

when viewed in terms of the proposed frame of reference. For too long, many investigators have been handicapped by using a single, highly ambiguous score to represent what is very complex but very comprehensible.

Without the multivariate approach of factor analysis, it is doubtful whether any comprehensive and detailed theory of the human intellect, such as the model in Fig. 1, could have been achieved. Application of the method uncovers the building blocks, which are well obscured in the ongoing activities of daily life. Although much has already been done by other methods to show the relevance and fruitfulness of the concepts generated by the theory (15), there is still a great amount of developmental work to be done to implement their full exploitation, particularly in education.

SUMMARY

In this limited space I have attempted to convey information regarding progress in discovering the nature of human intelligence. By intensive factor-analytic investigation, mostly within the past 20 years, the multifactor picture of intelligence has grown far beyond the expectations of those who have been most concerned. A comprehensive, systematic theoretical model known as the "structure of intellect" has been developed to put rationality into the picture.

The model is a cubical affair, its three dimensions representing ways in which the abilities differ from one another. Represented are: five basic kinds of operation, four substantive kinds of information or "contents," and six formal kinds of information or "products," respectively. Each intellectual ability involves a unique conjunction of one kind of operation, one kind of content, and one kind of product, all abilities being relatively independent in a population, but with common joint involvement in intellectual activity.

This taxonomic model has led to the discovery of many abilities not suspected before. Although the number of abilities is large, the 15 category constructs provide much parsimony. They also provide a systematic basis for viewing mental operations in general, thus suggesting new general psychological theory.

The implications for future intelligence testing and for education are numerous. Assessment of intellectual qualities should go much beyond present standard intelligence tests, which seriously neglect important abilities that contribute to problem-solving and creative performance in general. Educational philosophy, curriculum-building, teaching procedures, and examination methods should all be improved by giving attention to the structure of intellect as the basic frame of reference. There is much basis for expecting that various intellectual abilities can be improved in individuals, and the procedures needed for doing this should be clear.

REFERENCES AND NOTES

[1] C. Spearman, *Am. J. Psychol. 15*, 201 (1904).

[2] For the benefit of the uninitiated, a (positive) correlation between any two tests means that if certain individuals make high (low) scores in one of them they are likely also to make high (low) scores in the other.

[3] L. L. Thurstone, *Vectors of Mind* (Univ. of Chicago Press, Chicago, 1935).

[4] H. H. Harman, *Modern Factor Analysis* (Univ. of Chicago Press, Chicago, 1967).

[5] J. P. Guilford, *Psychol. Bull. 61*, 401 (1964).

[6] L. L. Thurstone, "Primary Mental Abilities," *Psychometric Monographs No. 1* (1938).

[7] J. P. Guilford and J. I. Lacey, Eds., *Printed Classification Tests* (Government Printing Office, Washington, D.C., 1947).

[8] We are indebted to the Office of Naval Research, Personnel and Training Branch, for continued support, and for additional support at various times from the U.S. Office of Education and the National Science Foundation, Biological and Medical Sciences Division.

[9] C. Burt, *Brit. J. Educ. Psychol. 19*, 100, 176 (1949).

[10] P. E. Vernon, *The Srtucture of Human Abilities* (Wiley, New York, 1950).

[11] J. P. Guilford, *Psychol. Bull. 53*, 267 (1956).

[12] F. Zwicky, *Morphological Analysis* (Springer, Berlin, 1957).

[13] J. P. Guilford, *Am. Psychologist 14*, 469 (1959).

[14] E. L. Thorndike, *Harper's Magazine 140*, 227 (1920).

[15] J. P. Guilford, *The Nature of Human Intelligence* (McGraw-Hill, New York, 1967).

[16] ———, *ibid.*, chap. 10.

[17] ———, *ibid.*, chap. 14.

[18] ——— and R. Hoepfner, *Indian J. Psychol. 41*, 7 (1966).

[19] Expressional Fluency is the sentence-construction test illustrated earlier.

In this article, Kuder presents twelve principles of interest measurement. Do you agree with all twelve? Would all twelve be applicable to vocational maturity inventories? Does Kuder present sufficient evidence for principle seven?

Some Principles of Interest Measurement

FREDERIC KUDER

Vocational interest inventories are intended to help young people find the occupations which will bring them the greatest satisfaction in their work. This statement of purpose carries the implication of two requirements which must

From *Educational and Psychological Measurement*, 1970, 30: 205–226. Copyright 1970 by Frederic Kuder. Reprinted with permission of publisher and author.

be met in the development of an inventory. One of these requirements is that an interest inventory must be valid with respect to the criterion of job satisfaction. The other is that the inventory must be usable in the counseling of people who may have quite limited backgrounds of training and experience.

Given these two requirements it is possible, with the aid of a few reasonable assumptions, to derive a number of principles appropriate to the development and use of an interest inventory. Some of the principles presented in the following pages may seem so obvious and well-established that they are hardly worth mentioning. Still, they should be on the record. On the other hand, some of the principles suggested are at considerable variance with established practice and, indeed, with a number of things the writer has done during a learning period of thirty-five years in the field.

Before getting into the list, it must be recognized that although the purpose of giving an interest inventory is to help get a person into the occupation he will find most satisfying, it is not adequate to present him with the name of a single occupation which is deemed to meet that requirement. For one thing, psychological measurement is not that precise. Any score has a degree of error in it so that there is some uncertainty whether the occupation with the highest score represents the "best" occupation. The problem then becomes one of giving the counselee a list of several occupations on which the very best occupation for him is likely to appear, even though it may not be the first on the list. In preparing this list, however, it should not be forgotten that, if the inventory has been well designed, the occupation with the highest score is the one which has the highest *chance* of being best for the counselee (from the standpoint of interests), that the occupation with the next highest score has the next highest chance of being best for him, and so on, so that in terms of giving appropriate time and attention to the consideration of specific occupations, the most useful form in which to present occupational scores is in order of magnitude. Just how far down the list it is worth going is a judgment which must be made in the light of the specific situation and a knowledge of the standard errors of the scores involved. In many cases, special circumstances, including the limitations of the individual's resources and the current supply of workers in various occupations, may necessitate going farther down the list than would be the case under more favorable conditions.

It is patently not possible for every member of society to attain that position for which he is best suited; it is too much to hope that the needs of society and of the individuals who constitute that society could ever mesh that well. Some modification of the requirements of the two must necessarily take place. Although society is not incapable of showing some flexibility over a period of years, it is the individual, needless to say, who must make the necessary accommodation in terms of planning for the near future. But this situation should not discourage one from doing the best he can. As a start, the individual needs a list of occupations which hold particular promise for him. The occupations should preferably be listed in order of probable suitability so that the counselee will have some basis for assigning priorities for his time and attention.

THE CRITERION

Since the purpose of vocational counseling in general and of vocational interest measurement in particular is to help the young person identify the career he will find most congenial, it might at first appear that degree of satisfaction should be set up as the criterion for developing a measure of suitability for each occupation. The resulting estimates of the absolute degree of job satisfaction which people could be expected to derive from various occupations would be designed to be comparable not only from one person to another in any occupation group, but also from one occupation to another for any one person.

If only the task were as simple as it sounds! This approach is impractical for a number of reasons. One of the difficulties in particular is serious enough to prevent a satisfactory solution. Even if the assumption is made that absolute and comparable estimates of the criteria can be obtained, the seemingly insurmountable problem of obtaining a good representation of the *possible* range of satisfaction from people actually engaged in an occupation remains.

The fact is that people in any one occupation are a highly selected group who represent adequately only a small part of the continuum which extends from high satisfaction to extreme dissatisfaction. There are a number of occupations—such as those of physician and minister—in which almost no one dislikes his work, and for which the range of job satisfaction is especially restricted. It can not be assumed for any occupational group, however, that those who say they dislike their work are close to the lower end of the continuum. After all, they are still engaged in the occupation. Those who can't stand it are gone!

Yet good representation is the first essential for developing a dependable prediction system. It is questionable practice to apply a formula to those ranges which are poorly represented in the criterion, and extrapolation beyond the limits of the sample studied is subject to even larger errors.

In the search for a feasible approach to the problem, it is helpful to keep in mind that it is not essential that absolute measures be used, or even that the measures be comparable from one person to another, in order for an inventory to be valid for use in counseling. After all, the purpose of using an interest inventory in counseling is not to rank a number of people, but to rank a multitude of occupations for a single person. The absolute degree of satisfaction derived from occupations may vary greatly from person to person, but the variation which is relevant for the individual is that variation which exists within himself. The criterion needed for standardizing an interest inventory or, indeed, a counseling program, is some index of the relative satisfaction which each participant in the study receives from many kinds of work.

On the face of it, obtaining measures of the relative degree of satisfaction to be expected from a number of jobs by the individual may appear to be just as impractical as attempting to use absolute measures. Of course, it would be very convenient if groups of people in each occupation could be identified as being without doubt in the very best occupation for them. In that case, the problem of the criterion would be solved, and the task would be reduced to developing a system designed to classify each of these people in his own occupation. The ideal population for this purpose would consist of a number of immortals who have had experience in all possible occupations and have finally settled upon the occupation which each of them liked best.

Fortunately, a more realistic solution to the problem is available. The approach described below rests on the plausible assumption that our present system of getting people into occupations, inefficient as it may sometimes be, is considerably more successful than random selection would be. Of course, it can not be assumed that everyone in a given occupation is in the very best one for him, or even that those who say they like their work are in the occupation they would find most satisfying. As noted by Clark (1961), there are no doubt some people who would not be satisfied with any job, while there are others who might really enjoy as many as fifty occupations. The fact that a person reports he likes his work is no guarantee that he could not find substantially greater satisfaction in a number of other kinds of work, nor can it be assumed that if a person dislikes his work he would like anything else better.

Nevertheless, it seems reasonable to assume that the members of an occupation who have stayed in an occupation long enough to give it a real trial and who report they like their work are better satisfied *on the average* than they would be if they were all in any other one occupation. It is assumed, for example, that if a large sample of carpenters were converted into barbers after suitable training, there would be a loss in the general level of job satisfaction; that is, they would be less satisfied as barbers, on the average, than they had been as carpenters. This assumption does not preclude the possibility that some of the carpenters might be better satisfied as barbers.

If the general assumption stated is true, trends observed for differences between occupational groups should give an indication of the direction of the larger differences to be expected from hypothetical "pure" groups, that is, groups composed entirely of people in the occupation they would have found most congenial if they had been able to try out all possible occupations. Since there is some error in the system of fitting people to jobs, a difference in the responses of carpenters and barbers, for example, to a specific item would not be as pronounced as the corresponding difference between pure groups, but the differences would be in the same direction. Scales based on a composite of items would also produce differences in the same direction as would scales based on groups composed only of carpenters and barbers who have found the most satisfying occupation for themselves. Therefore, a scale which is successful in differentiating between groups of carpenters and barbers as they occur in real life should reflect, with some degree of error, the extent to which a person resembles a hypothetical ideal group of carpenters more than he resembles a hypothetical ideal group of barbers, or vice versa. The extent to which the two real groups can be differentiated is an indication of how well this purpose is accomplished. Other things being equal, the less overlapping there is between two groups, the better the scale for that particular comparison, and the greater will be the confidence with which young people can be told they would probably like one more than another.

Thus the problem of establishing validity for counseling purposes becomes one of classification and the following principle may be stated:

> Principle 1. The capability of differentiating well between occupational groups is one of the essential characteristics of a vocational interest inventory.

In applying this principle, it appears desirable to restrict the occupational groups used to those who like their work from among those who have been in an occupation long enough to have a good basis for judging whether they like it. The system would probably work in any case but sharper differentiation can be expected if obvious mistakes are eliminated at the outset.

Principle 1 means that one of the fundamental questions in judging a vocational interest inventory is how well it differentiates among the specific occupational groups for which it is scored. This question makes sense in terms of the counseling situation. After all, the process of deciding upon a vocation consists of making a series of choices in which one specific occupation is compared with another specific occupation. It is also true that the more scales there are available for this purpose, the greater the usefulness of the instrument will be.

The task of finding out how well an inventory differentiates among occupational groups breaks down to one of finding out how well the two groups in each possible pairing of occupational groups are differentiated from each other. For each pair of groups, this differentiation can be expressed as the percentage of cases classified correctly. A summary figure can then be obtained for all of the pairings of the occupations for which the inventory is scored.

It has already been noted that it can not be assumed that everyone in an occupation is in the very best one for him. In any pair of occupational groups there are probably some people who would really enjoy the other occupation in the pair more than their own. This consideration means that ordinarily it is too much to expect perfect differentiation between any two groups. The differentiation can never be any higher than the imperfections of the criterion allow, but in any case, the higher it turns out to be, the better the instrument is for purposes of counseling. Within any pair of groups, the upper limit must surely depend on how similar the two occupations are, and the evidence so far collected appears to bear out this generalization.

Two quite different approaches to the problem of differentiating among occupational groups have been used over the years. When Moore (1921), for example, studied sales engineers and design engineers, his problem was the relatively simple one of differentiating between two groups. Other early investigators such as Ream (1924) and Freyd (1924) studied two groups, and Cowdery (1926) used three. However, when it came to dealing with many occupations, the task of developing a scale for each possible pair must have appeared to be preposterously impractical. Fortunately, Strong proposed the ingenious idea of using a general reference group as a basis for developing occupational scales. Not that such scales could be expected to differentiate as well between the occupations in each pair as would a series of scales made specifically for each pair, but at that time the use of a general reference group must have appeared to be the only practical way of dealing with the problem.

The use of a general reference group, while apparently solving one problem, raised another troublesome one that was what the composition of such a group should be. It might be supposed that a sample of the general population would be most logical, but Strong (1943) soon discovered that scales based on a reference group of this sort did not give good differentiation among professional groups. His studies indicate that there is no single reference group which is satisfactory for the whole range of occupations. He has demonstrated that a scale developed for a certain occupation with respect to one reference group may have little correlation with another scale developed for that same occupation with respect to another reference group.

Another disadvantage in the use of a general reference group is that sharpness of differentiation between specific occupations is sacrificed. The items which differentiate best between an occupational group and a general reference group are not likely to be the same as those which differentiate best between that same occupation and another specific occupation. Indeed, each comparison of one occupation with another will produce its own set of items, or its own set of weights, depending on the technique used.

After wrestling with this problem over a period of several years, the writer finally developed a rationale (1963) which is essentially a return to the early idea of differentiating between two occupations at a time. The advantage of the rationale is that it is possible to apply it to any number of occupations, and that it improves markedly accuracy of classification over the general reference group approach. The rationale of the system and the results of a comparative study, using cross-validation groups, have been presented in the literature (1963, 1968). Briefly, the new system produced 32 per cent fewer errors than the general reference group system. It is just as logical, of course, to make the comparison in the other direction. In that case, the general reference group system was found to produce 47 per cent more errors than the new system.

REPRESENTATION OF PERTINENT FACTORS

Good differentiation among occupational groups does not occur by accident. It is not enough for an investigator to assemble a collection of questions which he considers appropriate to the problem. If an effective instrument is to be developed, a series of studies involving the administration and analysis of a succession of experimental forms, with each study based on the experience and information previously gained, is essential. There was a time when it appeared that the number of interest factors pertinent to vocational choice might be as few as four or five (Thurstone, 1931). Now it appears it may well be several times that many. Obviously, the best possible differentiation between two groups can not be obtained if pertinent factors are not even represented in the inventory. The next principle may be stated as follows:

> Principle 2. The questions in a vocational interest inventory should be well distributed throughout the domain of interests relevant to vocational choice.

Ideally, the questions should be evenly distributed throughout factorial space, and they should have equal communalities. When these conditions exist, the centroid of the items which meet a certain standard of validity will necessarily coincide with the criterion. This situation is illustrated in Figure 1 for a two-space example. Let us suppose the items are evenly distributed with respect to the two factors and that item communalities are all the same. Economical coverage of the whole two-factor space can be facilitated by entering each possible answer twice—once when it is scored positively and once when it is scored negatively. Thus in the diagram, circles which are exactly opposite each other could represent the same response scored in opposite ways.

Let vector C represent the criterion, and suppose that all responses which correlate with the criterion in excess of a certain standard, designated by line s–s', are scored. Since line s–s' cuts off equal arcs on either side of vector C and since the items are evenly distributed in these arcs, it follows that the resulting score will coincide with vector C or at least will be very close to it. This line of reasoning holds true for any level at which the standard of validity may be set. It also holds true for any weighting system which assigns weights which are a function of validity.[1] Of course, the general principle illustrated here for two factors is applicable to any number of factors.

It must be recognized from the outset that there are bound to be differences between the ideal model and the results of efforts to achieve it. In order to make the task even possible, approximation procedures must be resorted to. For one thing, it is not possible to attain the intensive sort of coverage shown in Figure 1 in a relatively short inventory. The fact that it is much easier to construct reliable items in some areas than in others is another of the complications involved. Another is that it is more difficult to force coverage of some areas of factorial space with some forms of items than with other forms.

The development process inevitably requires a succession of laborious steps aimed at getting better approximations of the model. In actual practice,

Figure 1   Application of a Standard (s-s') in Selecting Items To Be Scored for a Test

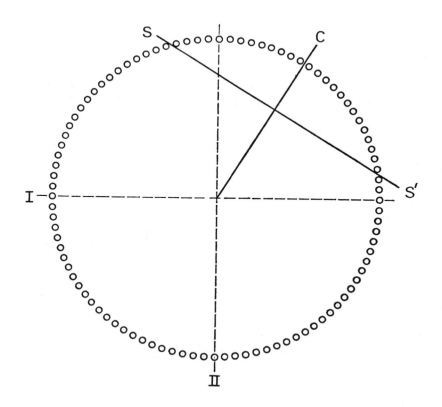

a shortage or even absence of items with certain required characteristics will be revealed as soon as the first item analysis is made, even if a large number of items are used in the first place and every effort is made to make the original coverage comprehensive. This situation means that new items must be written and possibly old items revised, and the new collection must be administered to a variety of new groups who must also be given the items already selected as well as older items which identify the frame of reference being used. After the next analysis, another set of experimental items must be administered in the effort to fill in gaps, and this process may be continued as long as necessary to achieve the standards desired, or until funds and the investigator are exhausted.

Nevertheless, as noted recently by Wright (1967), it is often possible to capitalize on the characteristics of a theoretical model even if the model is not achieved precisely. To draw on personal experience, the Kuder-Richardson formulas for estimating test reliability have turned out to be useful even though the assumptions on which they are based are seldom strictly fulfilled.

VOCABULARY LEVEL

From the standpoint of both validity and stability it is important that the questions in the inventory be well understood by the subjects. An answer has no validity if the counselee does not understand the question. The answer can hardly have stability, either, if it is likely to change over a period of time because of improvement in the counselee's comprehension of the content of the question. Furthermore, not only will some of the users of the inventory have very limited backgrounds, but many of the members of the groups on whom the inventory should be standardized are likely to be similarly limited. The following principle allows for both situations:

> Principle 3. The activities described in the questions must be clear and easily understood by the subjects, both by those who answer the inventory for their own guidance and by those who, as members of criterion groups, answer the inventory for the purpose of establishing occupational scoring systems.

ON THE COMPARABILITY OF TWO DOMAINS
OF INTERESTS

It has been noted that the validity of a vocational interest inventory rests on its ability to differentiate between specific occupational groups. It should be added immediately that ability to differentiate between groups is not the only essential requirement. In fact, it is possible to obtain excellent differentiation between occupational groups with questions it would be absurd to ask young people. It would probably be possible to differentiate almost perfectly between computer programmers and podiatrists by asking the straightforward question, "Would you rather be a computer programmer than a podiatrist?" Or two separate questions could be used: "Would you like to be a podiatrist?" and "Would you like to be a computer programmer?" Except for those who answered both questions the same way, differentiation would probably be close to perfect, although it can not be denied that a limited number of computer programmers might actually prefer to be podiatrists, and vice versa!

But what counselor would put such questions to a young person in search of an occupation? No counselor needs to be reminded that he must keep the conversation within the understanding of his counselee. Words which the counselee does not understand fully are equally inappropriate in an interest inventory, as suggested in Principle 3.

Two quite different domains of interest in activities can be identified. One is the domain of interests in activities which are generally well understood by people in general, including young people. The other is the domain of interests in activities which are understood best by people who have had experience in specific occupations. In general, almost everyone understands the former type of activity and relatively few fully understand the latter. No one is familiar with more than a small proportion of the activities of the latter type, a situation which would make it extremely difficult and complicated to work out a factor analysis in the second type of domain.

It might appear, on the surface, that it would not be possible to obtain an adequate picture of the interests of people in a specific occupation without resorting to questions about activities which are specific to the occupation and which are generally unfamiliar to people not in the occupation. However, there is really no reason to suppose that degree of familiarity affects the dimensions involved. Let us consider the possibility that the dimensions of interests in little-known activities are essentially the same as the dimensions of interests in well-known activities. If this is so, then it should be possible to generalize from one domain to the other. If the inventory is cast in terms of activities which are generally well understood, it should be possible to give a counselee estimates of the extent to which his interests correspond to the interests characteristic of people in a wide range of occupations, including occupations about which he knows nothing or even has erroneous ideas. After all, vocational counselors have been operating for years on the basis of assumptions similar to this one. The principle involved is as follows:

Principle 4. The use of an interest inventory in vocational counseling rests on the assumption that the domain of interests in generally well-understood activities is essentially the same as the domain of interests in activities which are not generally well-understood.

CONTEXT AND ITEM FORM

There are other ways in which the form of the item can be important. For example, there is the pertinent question of whether the context in which an item is placed is likely to affect the answers given to the item. The process of developing and improving an inventory calls for eliminating the less useful items and experimenting with new ones which are deemed to be promising. This procedure is not possible without changing the order of the items and the composition of the inventory. It seems quite likely that the degree of pleasantness associated with preceding questions could influence responses to some forms of items. There should be some assurance that the sort of item format used will continue to measure approximately the same thing even when the nature of the preceding items is changed considerably. The appropriate principle may be stated as follows:

> Principle 5. A form of item should be used which is known to be affected relatively little by changes in context.

RESPONSE BIAS

The next principle concerns response bias, namely, the effect which the form of a question may have on the answer given, quite apart from what the content of the question may be. It is now well established that check lists of questions cast in true-false, agree-disagree, or like-dislike form are particularly susceptible to such an effect as revealed by the early studies of Mathews (1929), Lorge (1937) and others. More recently, Jackson and Messick (1962) found that from one-half to three-fourths of the variance of a number of scales based on items of this type was "interpretable in terms of acquiescence and desirability." Dolliver's recent study (1968) is another of a long series by many different investigators which establish that items calling for the kinds of responses mentioned are subject to substantial response bias.[2]

It must be recognized that in the case of empirically derived scoring keys, validity is not destroyed by the fact that the items used are subject to response bias. Even so, the writer is inclined to believe that the effect of substantial response bias is to reduce the degree of validity attainable, and that the investigator who employs such items has yielded "hostages to fortune." As observed by Jackson and Messick, "one rapidly approaches an upper limit on the amount of information elicited by items which permit massive response-style effects like generalized acquiescence and desirability bias." The following principle is therefore advanced as a desirable one:

Principle 6. The form of question should be as free as possible from the effects of response bias.

ON THE USE OF OCCUPATIONAL TITLES
IN INTEREST INVENTORIES

The next principle bears indirectly on the question of face validity and the possibility that in the case of interest inventories face validity may actually be false validity. The fact that a form is classified as a vocational interest inventory does not mean it must include occupational titles in the items. As a matter of fact, there is something incongruous about asking a young person if he would like to engage in various occupations when the purpose is to help him find occupations worthy of his consideration. If a person really knows enough about occupations to answer questions about them, it is pertinent to ask whether he needs the information which the interest inventory is designed to yield. If he does not know enough to answer the questions intelligently, then his answers will only add to the error variance in his scores.

Often a child expresses a preference for a particular occupation because someone he admires is in it, or because schoolmates have mentioned it as their choice, or because it has acquired a pleasant association for some other reason which has nothing to do with the duties of the occupation. Changes in preferences are likely to be merely a reflection of one or more factors such as changes in the child's knowledge about occupations, new acquaintanceships, or other experiences which tend to affect the degree of pleasantness associated with the occupation. Nor is imperfect knowledge about occupations confined to the very young. Morris and Murphy (1959) found substantial evidence of misunderstandings and misconceptions by the general public as to what an individual actually does in any given occupation.

Another reason for avoiding occupational titles is found in a theory advanced by Bordin to the effect that a person answers an interest inventory in terms of his conception of an occupation with which he identifies himself. As a generalization, Bordin's idea is difficult to accept, since it does not appear likely that every young person in search of an occupation already identifies himself with an occupation, either consciously or unconsciously. As a statement of an influence which might operate to a greater or less extent in some cases, Bordin's idea appears more plausible. If a person has decided, for reasons which may or may not be pertinent, that he wants to be a physician, then he might conceivably tend to mark answers which he thinks a physician would mark and, if the specific question were one of the items, he would certainly mark that he would like to be a physician. To use his expressed preference for the occupation of physician to raise his Physician score is reasonable only if he knows enough about a physician's work to make a sound judgment.

Strong, in his book, *Vocational Interests of Men and Women*, (1943, p. 624) presents the hypothetical case of a young man "who actually ought to go into public accounting" but who marks that he is indifferent to the item, Certified Public Accountant, "because he had never heard of the occupation." In the face of situations of this sort, Strong raises the question of whether items should be weighted "as the statistics indicate in order to secure maximum differentiation of occupational groups or shall weights be reduced in order, on the one hand, to make it more difficult for someone to fudge the results or, on the other hand, to not penalize an honest person who doesn't happen to know the meaning of the items?"

Strong puts his finger on two big drawbacks of occupational titles in interest inventories: (1) answers to such items are particularly susceptible to faking, either consciously or unconsciously, and (2) young people may not be familiar with certain occupations, including those which may be suitable for the individual. In fact, the less a person knows about occupations, the more he is likely to need help in finding an appropriate one, and his answers to questions about specific occupations he does not know well are not likely to provide that help. These considerations suggest that it is better to avoid this type of item altogether, as stated in the following principle:

> Principle 7. Occupational titles should not be used in the items in an interest inventory intended for use in vocational counseling.

There was a time when the writer thought it permissible to use some of the more common occupational titles in items. Continued consideration of the problem, however, has led to the conclusion that, in the absence of evidence from young and unsophisticated subjects concerning the validity of specific items of this nature, it is more prudent to avoid the use of occupational titles entirely. It is quite possible that long-term follow-up studies of items answered by college upper-classmen and graduate students would show some degree of validity for items composed of the better-known occupational titles. The prospect of obtaining valid results would appear to be considerably less good for students at the high school level. In any case, whatever the group, the average validity obtained can not be taken as a true indication of validity for the less well-informed young people in the group.

The use of occupational titles is a tricky business which carries the risk of reducing validity in the counseling situation. After all, an occupational title is not an ordinary word. It can encompass a whole world of impressions and experiences for some and carry almost no meaning for others. Occupational titles give the appearance of validity, and they can actually be valid for those people who have a comprehensive knowledge of the terms. It does not follow that they are valid for young people who need good advice.

OBTAINING TRUE ANSWERS

Implicit in the use of interest scores in counseling is the assumption that the counselee has been completely cooperative and candid, and that he has understood the directions and questions. The next two principles deal with different aspects of this assumption. Principle 8 is concerned with keeping the process of answering the inventory as free of tension as possible, and keeping to a minimum those influences which might lead to invalid answers. Principle 9, on the other hand, is concerned with discovering, after the fact, whether anything has actually happened in answering the questions which might affect the usefulness of the scores in counseling. These principles are as follows:

> Principle 8. The questions should not be unpleasant or threatening.
> Principle 9. It is highly desirable that a means be available for checking on the confidence which can be placed in the answers to the inventory.

There is, of course, no way of compelling a person to answer questions carefully and sincerely and with understanding. Fortunately, however, it is possible to build into an inventory, devices which will identify most of the cases in which the answers are not true indications of a person's interests.

The earliest study of faking was made by Strong in 1927, although it was not reported in the literature until the publication of Strong's book in 1943. A later study by Steinmetz (1932) was actually the first to appear in the literature. Both studies demonstrated that Strong Vocational Interest Blank responses can be faked easily and scores shifted in the desired direction. Subsequent studies by other investigators have corroborated this finding and extended the conclusion to inventories in general.

There is room for differences of opinion as to whether one kind of item is more resistant to faking than another, but there is actually no experimental evidence that any one inventory is superior to others in this respect. It seems likely that fakability is more a matter of the content of the questions than of their form. Questions which are obviously related to occupations would presumably be more "transparent" than those which are not.

Although a subject *can* fake his answers in the desired direction, it does not follow that he will choose to do so. When he is taking an inventory for purposes of personal guidance, there is little reason to doubt that he will answer the questions carefully and sincerely. In such a case it may not be particularly important to check on faking. Even so, it would sometimes be helpful to the counselor to know whether there was a probability that some special circumstances—such as pressure to get through too quickly for reasonable consideration to be given the questions, or a distracting situation, or some influence which motivates the subject to conceal or distort his real preferences, or lack of understanding, or just plain carelessness—were operating to prevent the scores from reflecting a true picture of the counselee's interests.

SHOULD THE SAME INVENTORY BE USED FOR BOTH SEXES?

As time goes on, women are breaking into more and more occupations previously considered to be the exclusive domain of men. In view of this accelerating trend, it becomes more and more desirable that the same interest inventory be usable for both men and women.

This situation means that young women must often be counseled about the possibility of entering an occupation for which a scale for women workers has not been developed because of the lack of women in the field. This situation immediately stimulates the question of using masculine scores for such occupations. A study by Hornaday and Kuder (1961) and a more recent study by the writer (1966) have indicated the feasibility of such an approach. However, if women's inventories are to be scored for masculine scales, the questions answered must be the same as those used in collecting data from male occupational groups. Ergo:

Principle 10. It is highly desirable to use the same inventory for both sexes.

It is logical that feminine scores could be used in a similar manner in the guidance of young men. This question deserves further exploration, although it must be recognized that there appears to be little interest in such an application at the moment.

RELIABILITY AND STABILITY

It is sometimes overlooked that an inventory intended to discriminate within-the-person has its own special requirements which are not necessarily the same as those for a measure intended to discriminate among people. A single test which differentiates well among persons is useless in itself for differentiating within the person, and scores which are comparable within-the-person are not necessarily comparable from person-to-person. One important area in which the difference is particularly apparent is that of reliability and stability, which can be thought of as short-term and long-term consistency. The important information needed, as applied to counseling, is how reliable and stable the set of scores is for each subject. An appropriate measure of this consistency might well be a correlation computed between two sets of scores from the same subject. This correlation will vary from person to person, of course, and will no doubt depend somewhat on the length of the interval between testings. In our present state of knowledge, there is no way of knowing in advance what it will be for a specific counselee. However, it is possible to get a general idea of the consistency of sets of scores by studying a distribution of the correlations obtained from a representative group of subjects.

The stability of the answers to an item is undoubtedly influenced by quite a number of characteristics of both the items and the subjects who answer them. Some of these influences have already been touched upon. For example, subjects with extremely limited education and experience can not be expected to be as consistent in their responses to questions about a complicated activity as subjects whose backgrounds encompass the activity involved. If an inventory is to be generally useful, it must consist of items which are stable for the vast majority of the subjects for whom it is intended.

The general principle toward which this discussion has been leading is as follows:

> Principle 11. The set of scores from a vocational interest inventory must have high reliability and stability, and these characteristics should be measured in terms of reliability and stability within-the-person.

A corollary of this principle is that the items of an interest inventory should be unaffected by age. This objective may appear almost hopeless of accomplishment, and in practice it may have to be modified to apply to groups of items in the same general area rather than to single items, or applied in the sense that the relation of age to time response should be kept to a minimum. Nevertheless, the ideal model should be kept in mind.

It may be that an alternative approach to the age problem is to develop corrections for differences in age. The practical obstacles to such a solution are greater than might at first appear, but it remains as a possibility.

THE QUESTIONS OF REPORTING SCORES FOR FAMILIES OF OCCUPATIONS

For many years it has been common practice to present vocational interest scores grouped in families of similar occupations, and the writer accepted this practice as a reasonable one, without giving it particular thought. In the course of time, however, it became necessary to face the question of how scores from the Occupational Interest Survey should be presented, and an intensive study of the problem led to the decision to present scores in order of magnitude rather than by occupational families.

The main objection to listing scores by job families is that doing so has the effect of allowing information known about average relationships existing in groups to influence individual decisions more than specific information about the individual himself. It is true that a knowledge of average group relationships can be useful in counseling, but inferences based on data from groups of people should not be allowed to outweigh conflicting data known about the individual. Yet there is a marked tendency for people to think that if they obtain high scores on most of the occupations listed in a family they should consider all occupations in that family regardless of the score. It may be true that all occupations in a family are about equally attractive to most people, but there are important individual exceptions to the rule. Not all professors of psychology would enjoy being practicing clinical psychologists, and not all mathematicians would enjoy being statisticians. In the counseling situation, large differences in scores should not be ignored for the individual simply because the corresponding differences are small on the average for people in general. The listing of occupations in families on the report of scores makes it easy for the subject to ignore evidence concerning important ways in which he differs from the group, and in this way it defeats to some extent the purpose of providing information about individual differences. The principle involved is:

> Principle 12. The most useful form in which to report scores from an interest inventory is in order of magnitude.

SUMMARY

The following twelve principles are proposed as being of importance in the development and use of a vocational interest inventory:

1. The capability of differentiating well between occupational groups is one of the essential characteristics of a vocational interest inventory.
2. The questions in a vocational interest inventory should be well distributed throughout the domain of interests relevant to vocational choice.
3. The activities described in the questions must be clear and easily understood by the subjects, both by those who answer the inventory for their own guidance and by those who, as members of criterion groups, answer the inventory for the purpose of establishing occupational scoring systems.
4. The use of an interest inventory in vocational counseling rests on the assumption that the domain of interests in generally well-understood activities is essentially the same as the domain of interests in activities which are not generally well-understood.
5. A form of item should be used which is known to be affected relatively little by changes in context.
6. The form of question should be as free as possible from the effects of response bias.
7. Occupational titles should not be used in the questions in an interest inventory intended for use in vocational counseling.
8. The questions should not be unpleasant or threatening.
9. It is highly desirable that a means be available for checking on the confidence which can be placed in the answers to the inventory.

10. It is highly desirable to use the same inventory for both sexes.
11. The set of scores from a vocational interest inventory must have high reliability and stability, and these characteristics should be measured in terms of reliability and stability within-the-person.
12. The most useful form in which to report scores from an interest inventory is in order of magnitude.

A person who follows these principles should not be surprised if he produces a deceptively simple questionnaire which looks like something a junior high school student might have thrown together on a rainy Saturday afternoon. That's the way it *should* look!

NOTES

[1] Of course different cutting points and different weighting systems will not produce identical reliabilities, although it may be noted that apparently there is ordinarily a fairly wide range of possibilities within which there is not much difference in the reliabilities obtained (Kuder, 1957).

[2] These words are written in full knowledge of the article by Rorer (1965) in which he purports to demolish what he breathlessly calls the "great response-style myth." It may be noted that Rundquist (1966) has written a comprehensive and thoughtful comment which demonstrates the inappropriateness of Rorer's title.

REFERENCES

Bordin, E. S. A theory of vocational interests as dynamic phenomena. *Educational and Psychological Measurement*, 1943, *3*, 49–65.

Clark, K. E. *Vocational interests of non-professional men.* Minneapolis: University of Minnesota Press, 1961.

Cowdery, K. M. Measurement of professional attitudes. Differences between lawyers, physicians, and engineers. *Journal of Personnel Research*, 1926, *5*, 131–141.

Dolliver, R. H. Likes, dislikes, and SVIB scoring. *Measurement and Evaluation in Guidance*, 1968, *1*, 73–80.

Freyd, Max. The personalities of the socially and mechanically inclined. *Psychological Monographs*, 1924, *33* (Whole No. 151), 101 pp.

Hornaday, J. A. and Kuder, G. F. A study of male occupational interest scales applied to women. *Educational and Psychological Measurement*, 1961, *21*, 859–864.

Jackson, D. N. and Messick, S. Response styles and assessment of psychopathology. In *Measurement in personality and cognitition*, edited by S. Messick and J. Ross, 1962, John Wiley and Sons.

Kuder, G. F. A comparative study of some methods of developing occupational keys. *Educational and Psychological Measurement*, 1957, *17*, 105–114.

Kuder, G. F. A rationale for evaluating interests. *Educational and Psychological Measurement*, 1963, *23*, 3–12.

Kuder, G. F. *Manual, occupational interest survey.* Chicago: Science Research Associates, 1966, 1968.

Lorge, I. Gen-like: Halo or reality? *Psychological Bulletin*, 1937, *34*, 545–546.

Mathews, C. O. The effect of the order of printed responses on an interest questionnaire. *Journal of Educational Psychology*, 1929, *20*, 128–134.

Moore, B. V. Personnel selection of graduate engineers. *Psychological Monographs*, 1921, 30 (Whole No. 138), 85 pp.

Morris, R. G. and Murphy, R. J. The situs dimension in occupational structure. *American Sociological Review*, 1959, *24*, 231–239.

Ream, M. J. *Ability to sell: It's relation to certain aspects of personality and experience.* Baltimore: Williams & Wilkins, 1924.

Rorer, L. G. The great response-style myth. *Psychological Bulletin*, 1965, *63*, 129–156.

Rundquist, E. A. Item and response characteristics in attitude and personality measurement: A reaction to L. G. Rorer's "the great response-style myth." *Psychological Bulletin*, 1966, 66, 166–177.

Steinmetz, H. L. Measuring ability to fake occupational interest. *Journal of Applied Psychology*, 1932, *16*, 123–130.

Strong, E. K., Jr. *Vocational interests of men and women.* Stanford, California: Stanford University Press, 1943.

Thurstone, L. L. A multiple factor study of vocational interests. *Personnel Journal*, 1931, *10*, 202–206.

Wright, B. D. Sample-free test calibration and person measurement. Invitational conference on testing problems, Educational Testing Service, 1967.

The abstract by the authors precludes the need for an editor's introduction. Prediger and Hanson do an excellent job of discussing a "hot" topic. Relate this article to Kuder's principle ten. Other articles pertinent to this issue are AMEG Commission (1973), Campbell (1973), and Harmon (1973). See the recommended reading for Unit IV for the complete references.

The Distinction between Sex Restrictiveness and Sex Bias in Interest Inventories

DALE J. PREDIGER
GARY R. HANSON

Authors' abstract   Recent definitions of sex bias in interest inventories focus on factors related to sex which limit the career options considered by persons taking the inventories. This article proposes that these sex-limiting or sex-restrictive effects of interest inventories do not necessarily constitute sex bias and that sex restrictiveness is an important characteristic of interest inventories that should be considered separately from sex bias. Tentative definitions of sex-restrictive and sex-biased reporting procedures are provided and applied to three interest inventories for purposes of illustration. The types of evidence these definitions require of publishers are also discussed and parallels with the Equal Employment Opportunity Commission guidelines on test bias are drawn. The authors maintain that unless a distinction between sex-restrictive and sex-biased reporting procedures is made, current definitions of sex bias in interest inventories (e.g., the AMEG and NIE definitions) can and will be successfully challenged by inventory authors, and delays in eliminating biased reporting procedures will result.

Two recent definitions of sex bias in interest inventories (AMEG Commission on Sex Bias in Measurement 1973; National Institute of Education 1974) both focus on the sex-limiting (sex-restrictive) effects of inventories. This article proposes that:

1. Sex-restrictiveness is an important characteristic of interest inventories in its own right.

2. A sex-restrictive inventory is not necessarily sex biased. Hence, sex restrictiveness should be considered separately from sex bias.

3. The publisher of a sex-restrictive inventory must demonstrate that

From *Measurement and Evaluation in Guidance*: Vol. 7, No. 2, July 1974, pp. 96–104. Copyright (1974) American Personnel and Guidance Association. Reprinted with permission of author and publisher.

sex restrictiveness is a necessary concomitant of validity in order for the inventory to be called "sex fair." That is, if an interest inventory discriminates between the sexes in the career options it suggests, it must do so only as a requirement of validity.

Tentative definitions of sex-restrictive and sex-biased reporting procedures for interest inventories are provided and applied for purposes of illustration and clarification to the following three interest inventories: Holland's Self-Directed Search (1972), Holland's Vocational Preference Inventory (1965), and the American College Testing Program Interest Inventory (ACT 1974; Hanson 1974). These instruments were chosen because they measure highly similar dimensions of interest. However, the proposed definitions can be applied to other instruments as well. Because this article was written to help clarify issues involved in defining sex bias rather than to assert conclusions, selection of the three interest inventories for purposes of illustration does not imply that they are either sex biased or sex fair.

The definitions in this article focus on what an interest inventory reports to a person, i.e., scores, suggestions of occupations for exploration, etc. Hence, no specific requirements with respect to same or separate forms for men and women, separate norms, use of masculine or feminine pronouns in inventory items, etc., are implied by the definitions. Although these may be important concerns in their own right, they are involved here only to the degree that they affect what is reported.

SEX RESTRICTIVE INTEREST INVENTORIES

As already noted, the recent definitions of sex bias in interest inventories formulated by the NIE (1974) and the AMEG Commission on Sex Bias in Measurement (1973) both appear to focus on a separate but related characteristic of interest inventories, i.e., sex restrictiveness. The two definitions are presented below:

NIE Working Definition: "Within the context of career guidance, [sex bias results from] any factor that might influence a person to limit—or might cause others to limit—his or her consideration of a career solely on the basis of gender [1974, p. 1]."

AMEG Commission Definition: "Within the context of career guidance, sex bias is that condition or provision which influences a person to limit his or her consideration of career opportunities solely on the basis of that person's sex [1973, p. 172]."

In elaborating on this definition, AMEG Commission members stated that their primary concern ". . . is that neither sex be limited in occupational options on the basis of interest inventory results [p. 172]."

Operational Definition of Sex Restrictiveness

If consideration of career options is systematically limited on the basis of sex, then the distributions of suggested career options will differ for representative samples of males and females for whom the inventory is intended. Hence, the following operational definition of sex-restrictive interest inventories is proposed:

> An interest inventory is sex restrictive to the degree that the distribution of career options suggested to males and females is disproportionate. Conversely, an interest inventory is not sex restrictive if each career option covered by the inventory is suggested to similar proportions of males and females. (Although interest inventories should cover the full range of career options in American society, the degree of coverage must be considered independently of the degree of sex restrictiveness.)

In the above definition, "suggested career options" result from the application of scoring or interpretation procedures used or advocated by the interest inventory publisher. Implementation of the definition would require publishers to develop and report the distributions of career options suggested by their inventory to a cross section of males and females. This is not an unreasonable requirement since most publishers have or can obtain norm group data for use in developing the distributions.

The Definition of Sex Restrictiveness Illustrated by Data

The definition of sex restrictiveness may be applied to scores for different types of interests (e.g., mechanical, social, artistic) when these interest types are suggestive of career options and to the career options suggested directly by an interest inventory score report (e.g., by high scores for an accountant scale or a machine trades "job family," etc.). Some inventories report the former, some the latter, and some report both. Inventories in the third category include Holland's Self-Directed Search (SDS), Holland's Vocational Preference Inventory (VPI), and the ACT Interest Inventory (ACT-IV).

Because the ACT-IV uses same-sex norms, males and females automatically receive highly similar mean profiles for the six types of interests that are assessed (e.g., social service, creative arts). That is, the mean standard scores of males and females on all scales are approximately the same. Thus, according to the definition, this reporting procedure would not be sex restrictive. The mean raw score profiles for males and females on Holland's SDS, however, are substantially different as illustrated by data in the SDS manual (Holland 1972). Raw scores rather than scores based on norms are used in reporting SDS results.

The distributions of several career options for males and females suggested by the SDS and ACT-IV are shown in Table 1. Each of the two-letter codes in the table characterizes a group of occupations, as determined and listed by Holland (1973). The distributions of suggested career options (groups of occupations) were formed by finding, for each member of the specified samples, the person's two highest scores from among the six that are reported for both inventories. Scale titles corresponding to the letter codes are shown in the table footnotes.

As noted, the ACT-IV uses same-sex norms in reporting interest scores. Distributions based on this reporting procedure are provided in the columns at the right of Table 1. However, for comparative purposes, Holland codes based on ACT-IV raw scores are also reported, even though this procedure is not used in scoring the ACT-IV. As with the SDS, the two highest raw scores were used to determine the two-letter Holland code for each person in the samples.

The two samples for which SDS results are available are described in the SDS manual (Holland 1972). The urban high school sample consisted of 435 males and 298 females attending four high schools. The college student sample consisted of 4,074 males and 4,283 females attending 31 colleges. The latter students had taken Holland's VPI, a forerunner of the SDS and currently part of the SDS.

ACT-IV results are reported for a nationally representative sample of 10,169 ninth graders (ACT 1974) and a 2.5 percent random sample drawn from approximately 400,000 college-bound high school seniors who completed the ACT-IV as part of the ACT Assessment in October and December of 1973.

Inspection of Table 1 shows substantial differences for males and females in the distribution of career options (occupations) associated with common two-letter Holland codes when Holland's scoring and reporting system is used. The attention of females, as a group, is directed to occupations such as home economist, elementary school teacher, receptionist, and telephone operator, while males, as a group, are encouraged to explore occupations such as surgeon, electrical engineer, air traffic controller, and machinist. However, when same-sex norms instead of raw scores are used to report ACT-IV results, systematic differences between the career options suggested to males and females disappear. (See columns at right of Table 1.) Similar data are available from the authors for each of the 30 possible two-letter Holland codes.

Application of the definition of sex-restrictive interest inventories to the data in Table 1 may result in different conclusions with respect to the two reporting procedures that were used. However, a judgment that either or both of the reporting procedures are sex restrictive does not necessarily mean that the procedures are sex biased. As Holland (1974) has maintained, sex

TABLE 1 Percentage of Women and Men Receiving Selected Holland Two-letter Codes through Use of Two Procedures for Reporting Interest Inventory Results

Holland two-letter code group	Examples of occupations in Holland code group ("Suggested career options")	Holland SDS & VPI (Score reports based on raw scores)[a]				Holland two-letter code group	ACT Interest Inventory[b]							
		Urban H.S. students (SDS)		College students (VPI)			Score reports based on raw scores[a]				Score reports based on same-sex norms			
							9th graders nationwide		H.S. seniors college-bound		9th graders nationwide		H.S. seniors college-bound	
		W (N=298)	M (N=435)	W (N=4283)	M (N=4074)		W (N=4827)	M (N=5342)	W (N=5127)	M (N=4117)	W (N=4827)	M (N=5342)	W (N=5127)	M (N=4117)
IR	Surgeon, zoologist, biochemist, X-ray technician, electrical engineer, dentist, computer programmer, airplane pilot	0.3	11.5	0.7	13.5	IR	0.2	6.0	0.3	9.5	3.9	3.9	6.4	5.2
SA	Home economist, speech teacher, cosmetologist, manicurist, elementary teacher, librarian, dental assistant, LPN	19.8	3.4	25.1	3.6	SA	28.8	3.5	29.7	7.6	4.5	3.4	4.3	5.3
CS	Business teacher, personnel clerk, receptionist, telephone operator, bookkeeper, secretary (NEC), cashier	14.4	2.8	2.7	1.0	CS	6.2	0.4	4.7	1.6	3.8	2.1	1.4	1.3
RI	Dental technician, forester, electrician, baker, civil engineer, air traffic controller, jeweler, draftsman, machinist, upholsterer, dry cleaner, printer	0.3	10.1	0.0	7.8	RI	0.1	11.3	0.1	5.3	4.3	4.5	4.6	5.2
AS	English teacher, journalist-reporter, drama teacher, art teacher, music teacher, foreign language instructor	6.7	3.7	18.0	4.0	AS	20.9	4.6	8.8	4.6	5.2	4.5	4.4	6.3

Note.—The scale titles used by Holland (1973) are abbreviated as follows: R=Realistic, I=Investigative, A=Artistic, S=Social, E=Enterprising, and C=Conventional. These titles can also be used to represent ACT-IV Scales.

[a] Raw scores are used to determine a person's highest interest areas on Holland's SDS. Raw scores are not used in reporting Holland code groups for the ACT-IV. However, the results of using this reporting procedure are shown for purposes of comparison.

[b] Students with tied scores, typically 6%-10% of the total group, were excluded from the analyses.

restrictiveness may result from factors in society that interest inventories must reflect in order to be valid (e.g., sex role stereotyping as a socialization process). Nevertheless, sex restrictiveness may be an important consideration for many in the evaluation of an interest inventory.

In fact, sex-restrictive interest inventories, especially those which reinforce sex role stereotypes, pose a dilemma for society. One of the major and commonly acknowledged functions of interest inventories is to encourage career exploration. If boys and girls are not encouraged to explore nontraditional occupations, few are likely to enter these occupations. Hence, one might argue that even when the validity of an interest inventory is partially dependent on reflecting sex role stereotypes, a society in a state of change may be justified in sacrificing some degree of validity for the purpose of broadening the scope of career exploration. Exploration, after all, does not imply commitment. If an interest inventory is used early in the career decision making process, as career development theory and decision making theory suggest (Prediger 1974), boys and girls (men and women) will have ample time to explore the personal consequences of making nontraditional career choices—to decide what is "valid" for them.

The question of sex bias in interest inventories has not yet been directly addressed. However, according to Holland's definition of sex bias (Holland 1974), the data in Table 1 indicate that the SDS may be sex biased. Holland defines sex bias in tests and inventories as resulting from those practices which ". . . depend primarily on the sex . . . of the recipient rather than on a comprehensive and valid assessment of his or her assets and liabilities, including life situation [p. 211]." Holland does not define the phrase "depend primarily on the sex of the recipient." However, it is apparent from Table 1 that the probability that a person's attention will be directed to a particular occupation (e.g., elementary school teacher, surgeon, engineer) is highly dependent on the sex of the person. Whether it is "primarily" dependent on sex is open to debate, of course.

SEX-BIASED INTEREST INVENTORIES

The authors propose that sex restrictiveness is a potential indicator of sex bias and, because of its serious social implications, the publisher of a sex-restrictive inventory must demonstrate, in order for the inventory to be called "sex fair," that sex restrictiveness is a necessary concomitant of validity. That is, if an interest inventory discriminates between the sexes in the career options it suggests, it must do so only as a requirement of validity. Hence, sex restrictiveness does not necessarily indicate sex bias. In the definition of sex bias proposed below, attention is focused on the reason for sex restrictiveness.

An interest inventory that is sex restrictive, as previously defined, can be considered to be sex biased when the publisher uses or advocates arbitrary rules or procedures (rules or procedures unsupported by empirical evidence) for determining which career options will be suggested to an individual. Conversely, in order for a sex-restrictive inventory to be called sex fair, the publisher must demonstrate that sex restrictiveness is a necessary concomitant of validity as commonly defined [American Psychological Association 1966]. The burden of proof is on the publisher.

Because the interest score distributions for males and females in an occupation are crucial in demonstrating sex fairness, these distributions should be provided for selected occupations and their implications for reporting procedures discussed. For example, if males and females, as groups, receive substantially *different* scores on an interest inventory yet the same *score* profiles are used to characterize male and female members of an occupation, then the publisher of an interest inventory that uses a profile matching system to identify career options should show that the interest score distributions of male and female members of the occupation are, in fact, the *same*. Similar documentation would be required when other criteria for identifying career options are involved.

In many ways, the proposed definitions of sex restrictiveness and sex bias in interest inventories parallel the Equal Employment Opportunity Commission (1970) guidelines for the use of tests in employee selection. Data on the rejection rates for minority and nonminority job applicants must be provided. If differential rates (restrictiveness) are indicated, the employer must show that restrictive employment practices are justified on the basis of validity evidence in order to avoid the charge of discrimination.

Sex Bias Definition Illustrated by Data

The scoring and reporting procedures regularly used with the ACT-IV result in it being relatively free of sex restrictiveness. Validity data for the ACT-IV (Hanson 1974) also show that college senior women and men enrolled in various majors receive essentially the same ACT-IV score profiles when same-sex norms are used. At the same time, profile differences across majors are in hypothesized directions. Although data for occupational groups are not yet available for the ACT-IV, analyses of Project TALENT five-year follow-up data show that the use of same-sex norms results in similar Project TALENT interest profiles for males and females employed in several different occupations (Roth, Hanson & Cole 1973). Raw score profiles for males and females in these occupations differ substantially, however (Flanagan et al. 1971). Considered together, these findings support the use of same-sex norms in reporting ACT-IV results. This is important since the above definition of sex bias does not eliminate the need for validity evidence for interest inventories that are not sex restrictive.

In order to understand the implications of the proposed definition of sex bias for the SDS, one must recall that men and women receive characteristically different interest profiles on the SDS (i.e., women tend to score high on the Social and Artistic Scales and men tend to score high on the Investigative and Realistic Scales). Yet, the same profile (expressed as a Holland code) is used to represent members of an occupational group, *regardless of sex*, in determining suggested career options (Holland 1972). In order for this to be fair to members of both sexes, the publisher must show that male and female members of the occupation do indeed obtain the same or highly similar Holland codes.

Although evidence on this point is not available for the SDS, data based on vocational plans are available for the VPI (Holland et al. 1969), the forerunner of the SDS. Inspection of Table 2 shows several discrepancies in the Holland codes for males and females in nontraditional occupations. Additional evidence related to this point is available for the six General Occupational Theme Scales on the new Strong-Campbell Interest Inventory (Campbell 1974). These scales, which are based on Holland's typology, have titles identical to those used by Holland in the SDS (e.g., Investigative, Social,

TABLE 2   Holland Two-letter Codes for College Males and Females in Selected Occupational Plan Groups

Occupational Plan Group	Males Two-Letter Code	N	Group[a]	Females Two-Letter Code	N	Group[a]
Agronomist	RE	166	4	IA	15[b]	4
Architectural draftsman	RI	237	2	AS	14[b]	2
Aviation worker	RI	149	2	SA	10[b]	2
Mathematician	IR	74	2	SC	36	2
Medical technologist	IR	53	2	IS	127	2
Dentist	IE	120	4	SA	32	4
Nurse	SI	34	2	SI	952	2
Elementary teacher	SI	117	4	SA	1497	4
Social worker	SI	19	4	SA	140	4
Buyer	EC	16	4	SE	55	4
Lawyer	EA	288	4	SA	32	4
Secretary	ES	15	2	SC	1024	2

Note: Holland codes are based on the mean VPI score profiles of two-year and four-year college students with various vocational plans as described by Holland et al. (1969). Selected occupational plan groups are arranged according to the first letter of the Holland code for males.

[a] 4 = 4-year college students; 2 = 2-year college students.

[b] Although these samples are small, they are the largest of the 10 occupations listed for women that correspond to occupations with a first letter code of R listed for men (N = 27). Out of a total of 121 occupational groups listed for women, none received a first letter code of R.

Artistic, etc.) and scores reflect essentially the same sex differences as were noted for the SDS.

Campbell (1974) has provided high point codes similar to Holland codes for more than 200 occupational samples. Whenever possible, data for men and women in the same occupation were analyzed separately in developing these codes. The resulting codes for many occupations differ for men and women. For example, more than 60 percent of 63 realistic and investigative occupations were assigned different codes on the basis of sex (e.g., dietitian was coded REC for men and IC for women). Campbell (1974) noted that men and women in the same occupation sometimes have similar code types and sometimes do not. He concluded that "although such sex differences add considerable complexity to the occupational-classification system, they are important and empirically documented, and should not be ignored [p. 89]."

If similar sex differences for occupations characterize SDS scales, then representing an occupation by a Holland code that ignores these differences may be unfair to one or both sexes. The proposed definition of sex bias would require validity evidence justifying the use of the same occupational codes for both sexes. If this evidence can be provided, then sex restrictiveness in the SDS would not be indicative of sex bias. That is, it would be a necessary concomitant of validity.

CONCLUSION

The purpose of this discussion has been to clarify some of the issues involved in defining sex bias in interest inventories. While there may be problems with the definitions offered here, readers will hopefully see the importance of distinguishing between questions of sex bias and sex restrictiveness. Unless this distinction is made, the authors believe that identifying biased career interest inventory reporting procedures will be a difficult task at best. The current AMEG and NIE definitions can and will be successfully challenged by inventory authors. At worst, enough dust and smoke will be raised to obscure the real issues and to cause protracted delays in eliminating biased reporting procedures.

REFERENCES

AMEG Commission on Sex Bias in Measurement. Report on sex bias in interest measurement. *Measurement and Evaluation in Guidance*, 1973, 6, 171–177.
American College Testing Program. *Handbook for the Career Planning Program, Grades 8–11*. Iowa City, Iowa: Author, 1974.
American Psychological Association. *Standards for Educational and Psychological Tests and Manuals*. Washington, D.C.: Author, 1966.

Campbell, D. P. *Manual for the Strong-Campbell Interest Inventory.* Stanford, Calif.: Stanford University Press, 1974.

Equal Employment Opportunity Commission. Guidelines on employment selection procedures. *Federal Register,* 1 August 1970, *35,* 12,333.

Flanagan, J. C.; Shaycoft, M. F.; Richards, J. M., Jr.; & Claudy, J. C. *Five Years after High School. Appendix II.* Palo Alto, Calif.: American Institutes for Research, 1971.

Hanson, G. R. Assessing the interests of college youth: Summary of research and applications. *ACT Research Report No. 64.* Iowa City, Iowa: American College Testing Program, 1974, in press.

Holland, J. L., *Manual for the Vocational Preference Inventory.* Iowa City, Iowa: Educational Research Associates, 1965.

Holland, J. L. *Professional Manual for the Self-Directed Search.* Palo Alto, Calif.: Consulting Psychologists Press, 1972.

Holland, J. L. *Making Vocational Choices: A Theory of Careers.* Englewood Cliffs, N.J.: Prentice-Hall, 1973.

Holland, J. L. Some guidelines for reducing systematic biases in the delivery of vocational services. *Measurement and Evaluation in Guidance,* 1974, *6,* 210–218.

Holland, J. L.; Whitney, D. R.; Cole, N. S.; & Richards, J. M., Jr. An empirical occupational classification derived from a theory of personality and intended for practice and research. *ACT Research Report No. 29.* Iowa City, Iowa: American College Testing Program, 1969.

National Institute of Education. *Proposed Guidelines for Assessment of Sex Bias and Sex Fairness in Interest Inventories.* Washington, D.C.: Author, 1974.

Prediger, D. J. The role of assessment in career guidance. In E. G. Herr (Ed.), *Vocational Guidance and Human Development.* Boston: Houghton Mifflin, 1974. Pp. 325–349.

Roth J. D.; Hanson, G. R.; & Cole, N. S. Relating high school interests to occupations five years after high school. In G. R. Hanson and N. S. Cole (Eds.), *The Vocational Interests of Young Adults* (Monograph 11). Iowa City, Iowa: American College Testing Program, 1973. Pp. 109–125.

Goldberg discusses the trends of personality assessment under the headings, "Why Measure That Trait?", "How Measure That Trait?", and "How Use That Measure?". However, which trait is chosen to be measured depends upon the ultimate use of the measures of individual differences. Goldberg dismisses as "poppycock" the idea that all behavior is situational. The opposite viewpoint is discussed in the second and third chapters of the Mischel (1968) reference given at the end of Goldberg's article.

Are the findings Goldberg presents regarding the superiority of general predictors over differential predictors related to the issue McNemar and Guilford discussed?

Can you explain the rather consistent finding that actuarial prediction is more accurate than clinical prediction? Can you affectively accept such a finding?

Some Recent Trends in Personality Assessment

LEWIS R. GOLDBERG

Author's abstract   Some past and current research in personality assessment is discussed and evaluated, including such topics as (*a*) the exploitation of the natural language to construct descriptive personality taxonomies, (*b*) the search for trait-by-treatment interaction effects, (*c*) the relative validity of different strategies of personality inventory construction, (*d*) the comparative utility of nonlinear prediction schemes, (*e*) the quest for models of the judgments of expert decision makers, and (*f*) the utility of substituting judgmental models for human judges in applied contexts.

Individuals obviously differ in a host of ways, not all of which are of equal importance to themselves or to others. Tom can wiggle his ears like hummingbird wings, while elaborate electronic sensors detect no movement in Mary's. While Tom and Mary may fall at the top and bottom percentile of the world's population on ear-wiggling skill, this particular difference between them is not nearly as important as the fact that Mary is female and Tom is not. The first basic goal of psychological assessment is to identify the most important individual differences from the enormous variety which are manifested.

While most of us might agree that sex is a more important human dif-

From *Journal of Personality Assessment*, December 1972, 36, 6: 547–560. Reprinted with permission of author and publisher.

ference than skill at ear-wiggling, it is far less likely that we will agree on the relative importance of many other sorts of individual differences. The concept of importance implies a value hierarchy, and scientists—no less than nonscientists—have widely differing ones. However, any evaluation of the relative importance of various individual differences ultimately depends on one's intentions. What do we want to *do* with our measures of these differences?

It is traditional in psychological discourse to distinguish between two apparently disparate uses of assessment tools. Assessment constructs (and the resulting instrumentation) are typically viewed as having rather unique significance either for the development of psychological theories ("basic" science) or for the forecasting of critical outcomes demanded by societal decision-makers ("applied" science). Fortunately, these two uses of assessment instruments are not as disparate as was once believed; today many psychologists make at least an implicit assumption that theoretically meaningful variables, when reliably measured, can be used to predict important societal criteria, and conversely that those individual differences which turn out empirically to be the most useful in the prediction of significant human outcomes are the variables which an eventual theory of individual differences will have to include.

Viewed in this light, then, it is apparent that trait discovery is intimately concerned with test utilization—via the process of measurement. Once one has decided on the particular individual differences one wants to tap, one is faced with the more technical (psychometric) problem of measuring these differences in as precise and reliable a fashion as possible. The resulting measures must then be combined in some manner so as to generate nontest predictions, which in turn must be compared with expectations from some theory or validated against some set of external criteria. The results of these operations bear on the construct validity of the entire system: the choice of particular individual differences, the subsequent measurement of these differences, and the combination function which links the measures in some overall predictive expression.

The field of psychological assessment, then, has three major goals: (*a*) the discovery of the most important individual differences, (*b*) the optimal measurement of these critical dimensions, and (*c*) the most effective utilization of the resulting measures for both theoretical and applied purposes. I will discuss some recent trends in personality assessment by focusing on each of these three goals in turn.

WHY MEASURE *THAT* TRAIT?

While the most critical question we can ask of any test constructor is why he chose to measure *those particular attributes*, it is a rare test manual that includes any rationale for this choice. Two psychologists, Raymond Cattell and Harrison Gough, stand out as the major exceptions to this generalization. Since each has propounded a general rationale for selecting the most important individual differences from the much larger total set, let us briefly consider their positions.

Both rationales share a core assumption, namely that *those individual differences which are of the most significance in the daily transactions of humans with each other will become encoded into the natural language as single-word trait-descriptors.* This powerful theoretical position, which was once propounded by Gordon Allport, has been stated more recently by Warren Norman:

> Attempts to construct taxonomies of personality characteristics have ordinarily taken as an initial data base some set of perceptible variations in performance and appearance between persons . . . . By far the most general efforts to specify the domain of phenomena on which to base such a system have proceeded from an examination of the natural language. The argument in its essential form has been that perceptible differences between persons in their characteristic appearance or manner of behaving . . . become codified as a subset of the descriptive predicates of the natural language in the course of its development [Norman, 1963; p. 574].

That is, the "importance" of an individual difference is given operational definition as its probability of occurrence in the natural language. The more important the difference, the more will people notice it, wish to talk of it, and eventually invent a word for it. Since one can see this process exemplified in the evolution of nouns in the natural language (e.g., snow, of more importance to Eskimos than to Englishmen, has led to more words in Eskimo dialects than in English), one can assume that a similar process operates for adjectives, including those describing differences among individuals. Moreover, one might also assume that the more important individual differences within any linguistic culture would have more synonyms associated with them (thereby providing more nuances of meaning), and that these synonyms in turn would be shorter and more phonetic than those associated with the less important individual differences. To return to an earlier example, there is no single word in English which refers to "ear-wiggling skill," while there are a number of words which refer to gender.

While both Cattell and Gough have started with the natural language, their positions diverge from this point on. To Gough, the most important individual differences are those he calls "folk concepts," which he has defined as: "variables used for the description and analysis of personality in everyday life and in social interaction. It is theorized that such folk concepts, viewed as emergents from interpersonal behavior, have a kind of immediate meaningfulness and *universal relevance* . . . [Gough, 1965; p. 295]."

"The goal . . . is to measure those traits of character which arise directly and necessarily from interpersonal life, and which should therefore be relevant to the understanding and prediction of social behavior in any and all situations and *in any culture* . . . 'folk concepts' are *culturally universal* [Gough & Sandhu, 1964; p. 544]." (Italics added) Thus, to Gough, "importance" gains operational currency by reference to the set of all natural languages: the more languages which have one or more trait-descriptive terms for a particular kind of individual difference, the more universal, and hence more important, is that difference. While Gough did not utilize any cross-cultural linguistic studies in order to initially select the traits he included in his *California Psychological Inventory*, it is clear that this might have been a logical starting place for the development of such an inventory. On the other hand, of all inventory constructors, Gough has been among the most active in carrying out cross-cultural studies of his inventory scales, after their construction.

To Cattell, on the other hand, the natural language merely provides a starting point—rather than an ultimate destination. Allport and Odbert (1936) originally culled 17,954 trait names from *Webster's Second Unabridged Dictionary*, some 4,504 of which they deemed descriptive of "real traits." Cattell (1950, 1957) further reduced the set to 171 terms, by eliminating words which he considered synonomous with others in the set, and he collected peer ratings based upon these 171 terms. A cluster analysis of these ratings yielded 36 clusters or "surface traits," ostensibly the most important phenotypic individual differences in mankind. Factor analyses from a series of peer-rating studies led Cattell to the conclusion that between 15 and 20 distinct factors were necessary to account for the covariance among the surface traits; these latter became the "primary personality factors" in Cattell's taxonomic schema. Since these factors were themselves oblique, Cattell was able to continue factoring and thus arrive at four broad second-order factors. Consequently, one can view the distillation process as progressing from roughly 18,000 concepts to 4,500, and then from 170, to 35, to 15, and finally to 4.

Recently, the original Allport-Odbert list of trait descriptors has been expanded by Warren Norman, on the basis of a comprehensive survey of *Webster's Third Unabridged Dictionary*. A new pool of approximately 40,000 trait-descriptive terms has been identified and classified by Norman, and a subset of approximately 2,800 terms, hopefully providing comprehensive coverage of the stable and specific "biophysical" traits encoded in the English language, is presently under investigation (Norman, 1967).

In contrast to Gough and Cattell, most other test developers have never discussed their rationales for trait selection. Consequently, to uncover some of the rationales implicit in the work of other psychologists, I have recently reviewed the history of personality scales and inventories (Goldberg, 1971). Most of the published personality measures have been developed as a response to applied societal pressures, namely to forecast (*a*) personal or social adjustment, (*b*) satisfaction and success in vocational choice, or (*c*) academic achievement. Many of the remaining measures, which were less directly stimulated by applied demands, include those scales and inventories directed at two extraordinarily popular targets for structured measurement, namely (*d*) introversion-extroversion and (*e*) masculinity-femininity, and at two influential "theories" of individual differences, namely (*f*) Spranger's (1928) schema for classifying "personal values" and (*g*) Murray et al.'s (1938) classification of "manifest needs."

During the past few decades, the intuitive taxonomies devised by Freud, Jung, Rosanoff, Spranger, Murray, and Allport have been supplemented by the empirical schemas developed by Thurstone, Cattell, Guilford, Eysenck, Comrey, and Edwards. Moreover, future research based upon the Norman (1967) list of 2,800 trait descriptors should encourage another round of taxonomic ventures. However, if the future is anything like the past, new personality measures are at least as likely to be targeted upon constructs arising out of applied societal pressures as upon any new theoretical schemes.

In fact, the most potent factor in the determination of the targets for past personality measures has been sheer historical precedence. For better or for worse, psychologists have tended to utilize those constructs already identified by their predecessors. Moreover, this general "law of least effort" has also led inventory developers to borrow heavily from past item pools. Items devised around the turn of the century may have worked their way via Woodworth's *Personal Data Sheet*, to Thurstone and Thurstone's *Personality Schedule*, hence to Bernreuter's *Personality Inventory*, and later to the *Minnesota Multiphasic Personality Inventory*, where they were borrowed for the *California Psychological Inventory*, and then injected into the *Omnibus Personality Inventory*—only to serve as a source of items for the new *Academic Behavior Inventory*. As a result of the widespread practice of item borrowing, there is substantial item overlap between a number of present inventories (one result of which is that convergent validity coefficients computed between scales from two inventories, generally lamented as being too low, may in fact be spuriously high).

Moreover, among those inventory developers who have eschewed past constructs or past item pools, another trend is equally clear. Each original individual difference has been gradually split into smaller and smaller constructs. As an example, Introversion-Extroversion was later divided into three components, one of which was social extroversion; the latter, in turn, has been fractionated into at least five components, one of which was dominance; and recently, dominance has been shattered into 30 to 40 "facets" by Butt and Fiske (1968, 1969). Adjustment was once just that—a single global construct; over the years, the construct has been shredded so finely that Jackson and Messick's new *Differential Personality Inventory* purports to measure some 28 varieties of maladjustment. Analogously, anxiety has been dichotomized into general anxiety and test anxiety, and the former, which was construed as five independent factors in the *16 Personality Factor Questionnaire* (16 PF), has more recently detonated into myriads of "person-by-situation interactions" in the hands of Endler, Hunt, and Rosenstein (1962).

This last effort reflects an evergrowing tendency to minimize and/or belittle the transsituational generality of individual differences (e.g., Mischel, 1968). The recent explosion of interest in the newest paradigm in the personality arena, namely social learning theory, has led some psychologists to switch "disciplines"—in the language of Cronbach's (1957) classic APA presidential address, from correlational psychology to experimental psychology—from a focus upon individual differences to a focus on situational influences on behavior. In the name of science, an enormous amount of poppycock has recently been expressed to the effect that (*a*) all behavior is "situational" in character, and/or (*b*) that psychometricians and/or trait theorists have never considered situational influences on human behavior. In fact, the classic psychometric position has been that situations "constrain" individual differences—that they profoundly affect both the mean and the variance of these differences, though the rank order of individuals on the "trait" should remain relatively invariant across those situations which permit sizeable trait variation to occur. The most extreme form of the social learning viewpoint not only posits that situations are moderator variables (affecting the rank order of individuals on the trait across situations) but that the correlations across individuals in all pairs of situations are near zero for all classes of behaviors. Such an extreme S-R viewpoint, which was decried by Cronbach (1957) and before him Dashiell (1939), seems patently absurd in 1971.

Cronbach (1957) has probably expressed the issue most articulately:

> A true federation of the disciplines is required. Kept independent, they can give only wrong answers or no answers at all regarding certain important problems. It is shortsighted to argue for one science to discover the general laws of mind or behavior and for a separate enterprise concerned with individual minds, or for a one-way dependence of personality theory upon learning theory [p. 673].

> In both applied work and general scientific work, psychology requires combined, not parallel, labors from our two historic disciplines. In this common labor, they will almost certainly become one, with a common theory, a common method, and common recommendations for social betterment [p. 683].

While the arguments advanced by Cronbach have inspired others to begin the search for trait-by-treatment interaction effects, the journey has barely begun. For example, in my own review of literally hundreds of adjustment scales and inventories (Goldberg, 1971), I could uncover very few instances in which adjustment measures were explicitly constructed to predict differential responses to different treatments—ostensibly the *raison d'etre* for clinical diagnosis. Moreover, of the dozens of vocational inventories developed over the years, few—if any—have been focused on the prediction of differential responses to different types of work settings. It is only in the area of scholastic prediction—and then only recently—that psychologists have begun to develop measures to produce trait-by-treatment interaction effects (Siegel & Siegel, 1964, 1965, 1967). And in this type of setting, the road has proved incredibly rocky. Recent reviews of trait-by-treatment interaction research by Bracht (1969), Cronbach and Snow (1969), and Goldberg (1972b) have revealed very few replicated effects.

In one large-scale investigation of trait-by-treatment interactions in a college setting (Goldberg, 1972b), we found that for four different instructional treatments and three different classes of criteria, when the best of the general predictors were compared with the best of the differential predictors, the general predictors produced by far the largest effects. That is, if one were to make differential predictions for these three criteria using the most significant interaction effects, in no case would one's resulting predictions be as valid as simply using a single general predictor and thus ignoring all experimental variations in teaching methods. About twice as much criterion variance was predictable by the best of the general predictors as by the best of the differential predictors, in spite of the fact that the most powerful general predictors of one of the criteria were not included in these analyses. These poignant findings suggest that the significant interactions we discovered in this project—even if replicated at the very same strength in future studies—are unlikely to lead to differential predictions which are more valid than those achievable by general predictors alone. Clearly, one of the most tantalizing problems in the field of psychological assessment is the discovery of those traits and those situations which do produce reliable interaction effects. In the interim, Cronbach's clear vision of a "common theory" still appears hyperopic.

HOW MEASURE THAT TRAIT?

Let us turn now to the second major goal of personality assessment, the optimal measurement of those individual differences previously discovered or conceptualized. The assessment enterprise differs from such other endeavors as astrology, palm reading, and tea-leaf gazing—all of which also try to predict important human outcomes—by its reliance on scientific methods of verification, and by its use of samples of human behavior as raw data. The constraints placed on such behavior by the psychologist can obviously vary from none to high. At one extreme of this continuum are all relatively "unobtrusive" measures (Webb, Campbell, Schwartz, & Sechrest, 1966), including behavior observations and sociometric techniques, while at the other extreme are highly structured tests, scales and inventories. In the middle of the distribution are the procedures most favored by many clinicians, namely the interview and the projective techniques.

One important recent trend in the personality assessment literature has been an enormous shift in emphasis away from the middle and towards the two extremes of this distribution. Specifically, a host of studies stemming from the "social learning" paradigm, as well as those from the "ecological" movement stimulated by Roger Barker and his students, have redirected research attention to L-data (Cattell, 1957), to behavior which is relatively unconstrained by any interventions of the psychologist. And, at the other extreme, there has been a rapid proliferation of research on structured scales and inventories (Goldberg, 1971). While interviews and projective techniques have been gradually losing favor among psychometric researchers (Buros, 1970; Damarin, 1971), if not among clinical practitioners, this trend probably represents a reaction to the transducer involved. For raw behavior, of whatever type and under whatever degree of constraint, must be transduced—either automatically or through some human cognitive processing—before measurement may be said to have occurred. In the coding or scoring of behavior observations, interviews, and projective techniques, another man operates as the transducer; in personality scales and inventories, the transduction is automated, and man is not needed in this role. Some problems endemic to the use of man as transducer have been widely discussed of late, and I will return to this issue in a later section of this paper.

In a sense, all psychometric problems can be divided into two types, namely those concerned with the specification of optimal test *stimuli* or the most appropriate classes of *responses* to be recorded or coded, and those concerned with the selection of an optimal strategy for grouping these responses to produce an aggregate test or scale *score*. At this point, I will focus solely on the second class of psychometric problems, namely those concerned with strategies and tactics of personality scale construction.

While various strategies of scale construction have proliferated over the years under a number of names, they can all be divided into three main types, which can be labeled *External*, *Internal*, and *Intuitive*. The *External* strategy derives its name from the fact that some nontest reference groups are used to determine an item's scale membership and direction of keying, and this strategy has consequently been referred to as the "criterion-group" or "empirical" strategy. The second major strategy of inventory construction has been labeled *Internal*, since the internal structure of the item pool is the sole determiner of an item's scale membership and its direction of keying. The third major strategy of inventory construction, labeled *Intuitive*, relies on the cognition of the test developer for judgments regarding the suitability of an item for inclusion (and direction of keying) in a scale. While the earliest Intuitive scales were constructed from the judgments of a single individual, more recent ones have sometimes been based on the pooled judgments of a number of individuals, in an attempt to attenuate the idiosyncratic features of any single judge. Moreover, recent proponents of this general strategy of inventory construction—which has often been referred to under such labels as the "rational" or "theoretical" approach—have tended to use a mixture of two strategies, typically beginning scale construction by the intuitive assembly and keying of items, then later "purifying" the resulting scales through internal consistency analysis (e.g., discarding items with low, or negative, correlations with a priori scale scores). Let us look at the origins of these and other strategies.

The earliest means for gauging the extent to which an individual manifested some phenotypic trait was to ask him for a self-estimate. Since the form of the question and the conditions under which the question was asked might affect the reply, psychologists began to develop rating scales in order to standardize the process of self-estimation. However, early investigators quickly noted some characteristics of self-ratings that appeared to limit their usefulness. In the first place, such ratings turned out to be only moderately reliable when the same individuals were assessed on two or more occasions. In addition, it seemed likely that subjects might have difficulty estimating their status on any rather complex or global trait, since they would not know how much to weight each of the trait elements in order to arrive at a composite rating; moreover, it is probable that individuals would differ in the weights they assigned.

To solve these problems, early investigators attempted to break up the self-rating task into more molecular units, and the Intuitive scale construction strategy was born. The burden of proof that the scale measured the trait fell squarely on the shoulders of the test constructor, who ideally would have to demonstrate that (*a*) all of the items in the scale were related to the trait, (*b*) no set of items tapping important elements of the trait were not included in the scale, and (*c*) the method of combining or weighting items to obtain a scale score was appropriate for the trait (Loevinger, 1957).

By the late 1930s, a number of psychologists began to argue that psychology had not yet reached the stage where trait relevance could be reliably and validly intuited. Therefore, they argued, only the empirically-determined effectiveness of each item should legitimately influence the decision as to whether it belonged in a scale. Moreover, if one could locate two groups of subjects, each of whom logically could be seen as falling at one of the two poles of a trait, then the differential item response frequency of the two criterion groups could provide a nonsubjective index of item validity (Meehl, 1945). So was born the External strategy, and with it two of today's most popular personality inventories, the MMPI and the CPI.

Over the years, personality scales began to proliferate so hardily that they threatened to outnumber the available supply of people. Clearly, some method of birth control seemed called for, and factor analysis appeared to some psychologists as the final solution to this problem. For example, Cattell (1950, 1957) warned that there was virtually no limit either to the number of traits that personality theorists could invent or to the number of criteria psychologists might be asked to predict, and, therefore, that if a separate scale had to be devised for every trait and every criterion, the public would be swamped in a sea of test booklets. To solve this dilemma, Cattell proposed a systematic search for the most salient and important individual differences in mankind. Cattell's goal has been to provide a comprehensive battery of factor scales which could be used empirically via multiple-regression techniques to predict any trait or criterion of interest.

In assessment controversies, as in wars, there are always hostile armies waiting to ravage both sides, and in the 1950s a new force entered the fray. Many psychologists have long had a dim view of personality scales constructed by any strategy, since all self-report measures seemed too easily amenable to various forms of impression management. While test constructors have long sought methods of controlling dissimulation and image enhancement (e.g., Meehl & Hathaway, 1946), only recently have such tendencies—now reconceptualized as "social desirability response set"—been considered to account for the major portion of the variance in Intuitive, Internal, and External scales (e.g., Edwards, 1957). What scale variance remains has been viewed as being largely determined by another such bias, namely "acquiescence response style" (e.g., Jackson & Messick, 1958). As one might guess, it was not long before some investigators sought to measure these putative biases directly (e.g., Jackson & Messick, 1961, 1962)—and so was born the Stylistic strategy of scale construction.

While no one has yet argued for the use of Stylistic scales as direct predictors of important societal criteria, their proponents have advocated the elimination of various types of response bias, either during the original scale construction process (e.g., Jackson, 1971) or through the addition of Stylistic scales as potential suppressor or moderator variables in prediction functions which include scales constructed by other strategies. Interestingly, the seemingly plausible hypothesis that the use of Stylistic scales might improve the validity of other measures, either in a suppressor or a moderator role, has never been confirmed. In fact, none of the investigators of this issue has as yet discovered any Stylistic scale which generally served either as a suppressor variable in multivariate prediction functions (e.g., Dicken, 1963; Goldberg, Rorer, & Greene, 1970), or as a moderator of the validity of other sorts of personality scales (e.g., Goldberg, Rorer, & Greene, 1970).

While the relative merits of the various strategies have been heatedly argued over the years, only recently have any empirical comparisons among strategies been reported (Butt & Fiske, 1968; Hase & Goldberg, 1967). In my own comparative validity project (Goldberg, 1972a), five strategies of scale construction were used to construct nine different 11-scale "inventories" from the CPI item pool, five inventories based on the three major strategies (*External, Internal,* and *Intuitive*) and four inventories based on two control strategies (*Stylistic* and *Random*). The average cross-validities of each inventory were compared across 13 criterion indices. My findings suggest that while the inventories constructed by the three major strategies produced quite similar average cross-validities, there was a sizeable criteria-by-strategies interaction effect. Specifically, the External strategy appeared to produce a broader band-width but lower fidelity inventory than did either the Internal or the Intuitive strategies. However, a subset of five Rational scales provided average cross-validities at least as high as those produced by any of the other strategies and tactics under study.

This later finding suggests that some of the strongest criticisms of the Intuitive strategy may have been unfounded. For, of the three major strategies, it is only the Intuitive which does not capitalize on sample-specific characteristics, and it may be for this reason that the Intuitive inventories performed as validly as they did in our project. That is, the very characteristic of both the External and Internal strategies which gives them their power also provides their Achilles heel: namely, their dependence upon—and vulnerability to—characteristics of the particular samples used in their construction. On the other hand, the validity of inventories constructed by intuitive procedures is dependent upon the wisdom of the particular judge, or the sample of judges, used to construct the scales. In the past, the sampling of judges has generally been considered to be more crucial than the sampling of subjects, and thus the Intuitive strategy has lost some favor in the psychometric community. One of the main lessons from recent assessment research may be that such judgmental biases are not as critical as has previously been believed.

In an important theoretical article, Jackson (1971) has forcefully made this point by issuing the following provocative challenge:

> For any trait for which substantive definition is possible, let the most elaborate empirical item-selection procedures using criterion groups be pitted against two hours of work by a couple of good item writers . . . . One might extend this challenge even further. It might even be possible to use unselected item writers. It might be interesting, for example, to have an introductory class of psychology students write one item each with regard to a defined dimension, with perhaps just a bit of screening for substantive cogency and clarity of style, and conduct the comparison on that basis. The comparison proposed would be, of course, that of the empirical validity against a criterion relevant to the construct in question. The author would fully expect under cross-validation that even an inexperienced item writer would be superior to empirical item selection with a typical heterogeneous item pool [pp. 237–238].

While the findings from my own comparative validity project should not encourage those empiricists who would leap to take up Jackson's gauntlet, it is important to realize that Jackson's challenge was specifically directed at scale *fidelity*, and that he made no specific claims for *band-width*. Yet, the most surprising aspect of my own work is the finding that the External strategy produced an inventory of slightly broader band-width than those produced by either the Internal or Intuitive strategies. This tantalizing finding is, at first blush, majestically counter-intuitive. One might well predict that inventories produced by the External strategy should be relatively valid solely for those target criteria used to develop the scales (and thus be relatively narrow in band-width across a range of nontarget criteria), while the more homogeneous and independent sets of scales produced by the Internal and Intuitive strategies should possess relatively wider band-width when these scales are combined via multiple-regression procedures. Yet, our findings suggest that the less homogeneous scales produced by the External strategy may include some personologically relevant variance which is not included in those constructed by the Internal and Intuitive strategies, and that this type of variance may permit slightly higher cross-validities against precisely those criteria which are generally the least predictable. Clearly this finding now demands replication in other settings.

HOW *USE* THAT MEASURE?

Measures of individual differences are developed in order that they be used. Specifically, just as item responses must be amalgamated to produce scale scores, so scale and test scores must be combined in some manner to generate optimal predictions for the multidimensional types of criteria psychologists are typically called upon to forecast. And, in general, this score combination process can be carried out in one of two ways, either actuarially (i.e., mechanically, statistically) or via the use of a human as an information processor. As virtually all psychologists are now aware, the relative merits of these two modes of data processing have been hotly debated of late, and the resulting "clinical vs. statistical prediction controversy" (e.g., Gough, 1962; Meehl, 1954; Sawyer, 1966) has produced a flurry of recent experimental studies.

I can summarize this ever-growing body of literature by pointing out that over a rather large array of judgment tasks, rather simple actuarial formulae have typically performed at a level of validity no lower than that of the human expert. Consequently, it now seems safe to assert rather dogmatically that when acceptable criterion information is available, the proper role of the human in the decision-making process is that of a scientist: discovering or identifying new cues which will improve predictive accuracy, and constructing new sorts of systematic procedures for combining predictors in increasingly more optimal ways. Let us now examine some recent research bearing on, in turn, (*a*) actuarial models, (*b*) human judgments, and (*c*) the amalgamation of these two data processing modes.

Actuarial Models

One of the most central questions to be addressed by investigators in applied settings concerns the nature of the mathematical prediction function they will utilize. Specifically, they must ascertain whether some nonlinear or configural function will provide more valid predictions than the classical linear regression equation, and if so, which of the many varieties of nonlinear functions should be so employed. Over the years, a number of nonlinear and configural techniques have been proposed for psychometric use, but only rarely has anyone assessed their incremental utility over the linear model. I conducted one such comparison a few years ago (Goldberg, 1969). It was inspired by a prediction by Paul Meehl (1956) that the relationships between MMPI scores and the diagnostic classification of psychosis vs. neurosis should be highly configural in character, and, therefore, that no linear combination of MMPI scores should be able to differentiate neurotic from psychotic patients as accurately as configural actuarial techniques. After ten years of research on this question, I can now assert that neither moderated regression analyses, profile typologies, the Perceptron algorithm, density estimation procedures, Bayesian techniques, nor sequential analyses—when cross-validated —have been able to improve on a simple linear function.

However, one might justifiably remain skeptical of any single set of empirical findings, if they stood alone. Yet, over the past few years a number of extensive, systematic, and methodologically sophisticated attempts to uncover configural relationships between predictors and *other* criteria have been reported, and virtually all of them have presented a similar tale. For example, Stilson and Astrup (1966) reported a comparison between linear and nonlinear methods for long-term prognosis among psychotic patients. They used large samples, good clinical data, and reasonably clean criteria. They concluded,

> The gains resulting . . . from the use of a nonlinear procedure are almost entirely lost in cross-validation. This indicates that the simple additive formula based on the number of symptoms will prove to be about as good as the nonlinear procedures . . . if prognoses are to be made for new patients [p. 472].

This study should be examined carefully, since pattern analysis, profile coding, and other nonlinear classification techniques are presently so fashionable in clinical circles.

As one further example, Lunneborg and Lunneborg (1967b) reported a study of a randomly-selected group of 3,000 high school seniors. A series of aptitude, interest, and achievement tests was used to predict academic success in four college areas—English, mathematics, foreign language, and the physical sciences—as well as a dichotomous criterion, satisfactory vs. unsatisfactory progress toward a degree. A number of sophisticated pattern-analytic systems were investigated. The Lunneborgs concluded their report with the following disturbing passage:

> The failure of pattern information to aid prediction confirms the negative results of earlier attempts to use patterns and is all the more poignant a failure because of the attention paid to the selection of differentiated criteria and relevant predictors. There are even well-developed ideas throughout the educational literature as to the different configurations of abilities intuited behind different achievement criteria. In response to similar speculations in the counseling literature regarding patterns of personality needs associated with academic achievement, a study of reliable, frequent EPPS need patterns demonstrated the same lack of predictive stability (Lunneborg & Lunneborg, 1967a). Given the content similarity in the present study between predictors and criteria, the use of only reliable patterns, and the refinement of criteria, there would seem to be small room for continuing the conjecture that patterns can go above and beyond prediction from simple linear functions of original variables (Lunneborg & Lunneborg, 1967b, [p. 951]).

One of the great challenges of future assessment work must be to show how—and under what conditions—these conclusions are wrong.

Human Judgment

Interestingly, the picture remains much the same when we turn to recent research on judgmental processes. Just as the linear model has proved remarkably robust as an actuarial tool, so the same model has proved equally powerful in predicting, or representing, human judgments themselves. Over the years, the research focus among judgmental investigators has changed dramatically, from the early studies of judgmental accuracy (e.g., Holtzman & Sells, 1954) to more recent attempts to simulate (or "model" or "capture the policies of") professional decision-makers (Goldberg, 1968).

An investigator of the clinical judgment process might express his aims through the following question: By what mathematical model can one use the data available to a judge so as to simulate most accurately the judgments he actually makes? To answer this question, one must (a) discover some formal (i.e., specifiable) model, which (b) uses as its "input" the information (data, cues, symptoms, etc.) initially presented to the judge, and (c) combines the data in some optimal manner, so as to (d) produce as accurately as possible a copy of the responses of the judge—(e) regardless of the actual validity of those judgments themselves. Note that such a model is always an intraindividual one; that is, it is intended as a representation of the responses of a single judge, and the test of the model is how well it predicts these judgments.

What sort of judgmental model should one try? Since introspective accounts describe the judgment process as curvilinear, configural, and sequential (e.g., McArthur, 1954; Meehl, 1954, 1960; Parker, 1958), one possible strategy is to begin with fairly complex models, perhaps with an eye to seeing how they may eventually be simplified. The research of investigators at two major centers for research on human inference—Oregon Research Institute and the Behavior Research Laboratory of the University of Colorado—has proceeded from a diametrically opposite strategy (Hammond, Hursch, & Todd, 1964; Hoffman, 1960), namely to start with a linear regression model and then to proceed to introduce complications only so far as is necessary to reproduce the responses of a particular judge.

Since experts generally describe their cognitive processes as complex ones involving the curvilinear, configural, and sequential utilization of cues, one might expect that the linear model would provide a rather poor representation of their actual judgments. Consequently, we might anticipate the need to introduce new terms into the model to represent these more complex processes. While the introduction of such terms can never serve to decrease accuracy in the sample of judgments used to derive the regression weights, these extra terms may simply serve to explain the vagaries of the particular judgments from the derivation sample and thus can severely attenuate the accuracy of the resulting model upon its cross-validation in another sample of judgments. However, when the judge is actually using the cues in a curvilinear or in a configural manner, then the introduction of the mathematical approximations of these processes should serve to improve the model.

In study after study, however, the accuracy of the linear model has been at approximately the same level as the reliability of the judgments themselves, and—no doubt because of this—the introduction of more complex terms into the basic equation has rarely served to increase the cross-validity of the more complex model. Hammond and Summers (1965) and Slovic and Lichtenstein (1971) have reviewed a series of studies in which the same general finding has emerged: for a number of different judgmental tasks and across a considerable range of judges, the simple linear model appears to predict the judgmental responses quite adequately, in spite of the reports of the judges that they are using cues in a highly configural manner. This is not to say that human judges behave like linear data processors, but only that the power of the linear regression model is so great that it serves to obscure most of the configural processes in judgment.

Amalgamating Man and Machine

There is an old psychometric axiom that validity is constrained by reliability, specifically that the correlation between a measure and any criterion cannot be higher than the square root of the reliability of that measure. While we routinely use that axiom to guide our thinking about test construction procedures, the same axiom can also be applied to the predictions from human judgments. For we know that the expert is not a machine. While he possesses his full share of human learning and hypothesis-generating skills, he lacks the machine's reliability. He "has his days." Boredom, fatigue, illness, situational and interpersonal distractions all plague him, with the result that his repeated judgments of the exact same stimulus configuration are not identical. He is subject to all those human frailties which keep the reliability of his judgments below unity. And, if the judge's reliability is less than perfect, there must be error in his judgments—error which can serve no other purpose than to attenuate his accuracy. If we could remove some of this human unreliability by eliminating the random error in his judgments, we might thereby increase the validity of his predictions. The problem, then, is to separate the expert's judgmental unreliability from his—hopefully, somewhat valid—judgmental strategy.

As I have already noted, ten years of research on the judgment process have demonstrated that for many types of common clinical decisions and for many sorts of expert judges, a simple linear regression equation can be constructed which will predict the responses of a judge at approximately the level of his own reliability (Hoffman, 1960; Hammond, Hursch, & Todd, 1964; Naylor & Wherry, 1965; Goldberg, 1968). While the regression model has been utilized (probably inappropriately) to explain the manner in which experts combine cues in making their diagnostic and prognostic decisions (Green, 1968; Hoffman, 1968), there is little controversy about its power as a predictor of these judgments. In addition, of course, such a model possesses at least one asset which humans typically lack: perfect reliability.

Now, how would such models fare as predictors themselves? That is, if the set of regression weights generated from an analysis of the judgments of an expert were used to make predictions for each target individual, would these predictions be more valid, or less valid, than the original judgments from which the weights were derived? To the extent that the model fails to capture valid nonlinear variance in the judge's decision processes, it should perform less creditably than the judge. To the extent that it eliminates the random error component in human judgments, it should perform more validly than the judge. Which of these counteracting factors is more important in typical clinical decision-making? Can we construct a mathematical representation of a judge—without any recourse to criterion information—which is more valid as a decision maker than the human we have used as a model?

Fortunately, the answer to this last question appears to be "Yes." I described the mathematics of the situation in a recent paper (Goldberg, 1970), and presented the results of an illustrative study comparing man and his model. Specifically, I compared the validity of 29 clinical psychologists with their linear models as predictors of the diagnostic classification, psychosis vs. neurosis, from the MMPI profiles of 861 psychiatric patients. I found that, in general, models of the judges were slightly more valid than the judges themselves. Moreover, this slight incremental validity of model over man persisted even when the models were constructed on a small set of cases, and then man and model competed on a completely new and much larger set. Dawes (1971) has extended the generality of these conclusions by demonstrating that a linear model of the decisions made by the graduate admissions committee of a university psychology department is a more valid predictor of graduate achievement than the committee's decisions themselves. An even more impressive demonstration of the same phenomenon has been reported by Wiggins and Kohen (1971), who asked 98 graduate students in psychology to predict the grade point average of 100 other psychology graduate students. The average judge obtained a validity coefficient of .33 on this task, as compared to a value of .50 for the average model. Moreover, for every one of the 98 judges, the model of the judge was more valid than were the judgments themselves!

Proponents of actuarial prediction have repeatedly emphasized the lower cost of such procedures when compared to the cost of human experts. Analogously, one should realize that the use of judgmental models is inherently less costly than the use of human experts, for after a judge has been used to derive his model he is free to perform other activities. Therefore, if cost is a factor in deciding between the use of men or their models, then in many situations judges would have to be substantially more valid than their models before the overall utilities would favor the continued use of expensive professional time. So far, however, there have been no reports of any substantial incremental validity of man over his model. Consequently, if these findings can be generalized to other sorts of judgmental problems, it would appear that only rarely—if at all—will the utilities favor the continued employment of a man over an actuarial—or a judgmental—model.

A CONCLUDING NOTE

While the three central questions in psychological assessment (Why measure *that* trait?, *How* measure that trait?, How *use* that measure?) are still far from answered, a common thread in all future answers might well involve a reconception of the optimal roles for man's judgment and for his empirical techniques. In the past, it has been customary to pit "reason" against "facts," to debate the relative virtues of (a) the intuitive taxonomies (e.g., Freud) vs. the empirical ones (e.g., Cattell), (b) the Intuitive strategy of scale construction vs. the empirical strategies (External and Internal), and (c) the use of clinical intuition vs. actuarial modes of information processing. However, "intuition" and "facts" must both be deployed, although at different stages of the scientific process. Intuition is an absolute necessity at the earliest stages (e.g., perception and concept formation), while empirical analyses are equally necessary in later stages. To deny the roles of either intuition or data is to court disaster. To establish their proper roles in trait discovery, psychometrics, and test usage is perhaps the greatest unfinished business of the next decade.

REFERENCES

Allport, G. W., & Odbert, H. S. Trait-names: A psycho-lexical study. *Psychological Monographs*, 1936, *47*, (1, Whole No. 211).

Bracht, G. H. The relationship of treatment tasks, personological variables, and dependent variables to aptitude-treatment interactions. Unpublished doctoral dissertation, University of Colorado, 1969.

Buros, O. K. (Ed.) *Personality tests and reviews.* Highland Park, N.J.: Gryphon Press, 1970.

Butt, D. S., & Fiske, D. W. Comparison of strategies in developing scales for dominance. *Psychological Bulletin*, 1968, *70*, 505–519.

Butt, D. S., & Fiske, D. W. Differential correlates of dominance scales. *Journal of Personality*, 1969, *37*, 415–428.

Cattell, R. B. *Personality: A systematic theoretical and factual study.* New York: McGraw-Hill, 1950.

Cattell, R. B. *Personality and motivation: Structure and measurement.* New York: World Book, 1957.

Cronbach, L. J. The two disciplines of scientific psychology. *American Psychologist*, 1957, *12*, 671–684.

Cronbach, L. J., & Snow, R. E. Individual differences in learning ability as a function of instructional variables. Office of Education Final Report No. OEC 4-6-061269-1217, March 1969.

Damarin, F. A special review of Buros' *Personality tests and reviews. Educational and Psychological Measurement*, 1971, *31*, 215–241.

Dashiell, J. F. Some rapprochements in contemporary psychology. *Psychological Bulletin*, 1939, *36*, 1–24.

Dawes, R. M. A case study of graduate admissions: Application of three principles of human decision making. *American Psychologist*, 1971, *26*, 180–188.

Dicken, C. Good impression, social desirability and acquiescence as suppressor variables. *Educational and Psychological Measurement*, 1963, *23*, 699–720.

Edwards, A. L. *The social desirability variable in personality assessment and research.* New York: Dryden, 1957.

Endler, N. S., Hunt, J. McV., & Rosenstein, A. J. An S-R inventory of anxiousness. *Psychological Monographs*, 1962, *76* (17, Whole No. 536).

Goldberg, L. R. Simple models or simple processes? Some research on clinical judgments. *American Psychologist*, 1968, *23*, 483–496.

Goldberg, L. R. The search for configural relationships in personality assessment: The diagnosis of psychosis vs. neurosis from the MMPI. *Multivariate Behavioral Research*, 1969, *4*, 523–536.

Goldberg, L. R. Man vs. model of man: A rationale, plus some evidence, for a method of improving on clinical inferences. *Psychological Bulletin*, 1970, *73*, 422–432.

Goldberg, L. R. A historical survey of personality scales and inventories. In P. McReynolds (Ed.), *Advances in psychological assessment: Volume Two*. Palo Alto, Calif.: Science and Behavior Books, 1971.

Goldberg, L. R. Parameters of personality inventory construction and utilization: A comparison of prediction strategies and tactics, *Multivariate Behavioral Research Monographs*, 1972, *7*, No. 72-2.(a)

Goldberg, L. R. Student personality characteristics and optimal college learning conditions: An extensive search for trait-by-treatment interaction effects. *Instructional Science*, 1972, *1*, 153–210.(b)

Goldberg, L. R., Rorer, L. G., & Greene, M. M. The usefulness of "stylistic" scales as potential suppressor or moderator variables in predictions from the CPI. *Oregon Research Institute Research Bulletin*, 1970, *10* (No. 3).

Gough, H. G. Clinical versus statistical prediction in psychology. In L. Postman (Ed.), *Psychology in the making*. New York: Knopf, 1962.

Gough, H. G. Conceptual analysis of psychological test scores and other diagnostic variables. *Journal of Abnormal Psychology*, 1965, *70*, 294–302.

Gough, H. G., & Sandhu, H. Validation of the CPI socialization scale in India. *Journal of Abnormal and Social Psychology*, 1964, *68*, 544–547.

Green, B. F., Jr. Descriptions and explanations: A comment on papers by Hoffman and Edwards. In B. Kleinmuntz (Ed.), *Formal representation of human judgment*. New York: Wiley, 1968.

Hammond, K. R., Hursch, C. J., & Todd, F. J. Analyzing the components of clinical inference. *Psychological Review*, 1964, *71*, 438–456.

Hammond, K. R., & Summers, D. A. Cognitive dependence on linear and nonlinear cues. *Psychological Review*, 1965, *72*, 215–224.

Hase, H. D., & Goldberg, L. R. The comparative validity of different strategies of deriving personality inventory scales. *Psychological Bulletin*, 1967, *67*, 231–248.

Hoffman, P. J. The paramorphic representation of clinical judgment. *Psychological Bulletin*, 1960, *57*, 116–131.

Hoffman, P. J. Cue-consistency and configurality in human judgment. In B. Kleinmuntz (Ed.), *Formal representation of human judgment*. New York: Wiley, 1968.

Holtzman, W. H., & Sells, S. B. Prediction of flying success by clinical analysis of test protocols. *Journal of Abnormal and Social Psychology*, 1954, *49*, 485–490.

Jackson, D. N. The dynamics of structured personality tests: 1971. *Psychological Review*, 1971, *78*, 229–248.

Jackson, D. N., & Messick, S. Content and style in personality assessment. *Psychological Bulletin*, 1958, *55*, 243–252.

Jackson, D. N., & Messick, S. Acquiescence and desirability as response determinants in the MMPI. *Educational and Psychological Measurement*, 1961, *21*, 771–790.

Jackson, D. N., & Messick, S. Response styles on the MMPI: Comparison of clinical and normal samples. *Journal of Abnormal and Social Psychology*, 1962, *65*, 285–299.

Loevinger, J. Objective tests as instruments of psychological theory. *Psychological Reports*, 1957, *3*, 635–694.

Lunneborg, C. E., & Lunneborg, P. W. EPPS patterns in the prediction of academic achievement. *Journal of Counseling Psychology*, 1967, *14*, 389–390.(a)

Lunneborg, C. E., & Lunneborg, P. W. Pattern prediction of academic success. *Educational and Psychological Measurement*, 1967, *27*, 945–952.(b)

McArthur, C. Analyzing the clinical process. *Journal of Counseling Psychology*, 1954, *1*, 203–208.

Meehl, P. E. The dynamics of "structured" personality tests. *Journal of Clinical Psychology*, 1945, *1*, 296–303.

Meehl, P. E. *Clinical versus statistical prediction: A theoretical analysis and a review of the evidence.* Minneapolis: University of Minnesota Press, 1954.

Meehl, P. E. Clinical versus actuarial prediction. *In Proceedings of the 1955 Invitational Conference on Testing Problems.* Princeton: Educational Testing Service, 1956.

Meehl, P. E. The cognitive activity of the clinician. *American Psychologist*, 1960, *15*, 19–27.

Meehl, P. E., & Hathaway, S. R. The K factor as a suppressor variable in the MMPI. *Journal of Applied Psychology*, 1946, *30*, 525–564.

Mischel, W. *Personality and assessment.* New York: Wiley, 1968.

Murray, H. A., et al. *Explorations in personality.* New York: Oxford, 1938.

Naylor, J. C., & Wherry, R. J., Sr. The use of simulated stimuli and the "JAN" technique to capture and cluster the policies of raters. *Educational and Psychological Measurement*, 1965, *25*, 969–986.

Norman, W. T. Toward an adequate taxonomy of personality attributes: Replicated factor structure in peer nomination personality ratings. *Journal of Abnormal and Social Psychology*, 1963, *66*, 574–583.

Norman, W. T. 2800 personality trait descriptors: Normative operating characteristics for a university population. Office of Research Administration No. 08310-1-T, 1967, University of Michigan, NIMH Grant No. MH-07195.

Parker, C. A. As a clinician thinks . . . *Journal of Counseling Psychology*, 1958, *5*, 253–262.

Sawyer, J. Measurement *and* prediction, clinical *and* statistical. *Psychological Bulletin*, 1966, *66*, 178–200.

Siegel, L., & Siegel, L. C. The instructional Gestalt: A conceptual framework and design for educational research. *AV Communication Review*, 1964, *12*, 16–45.

Siegel, L., & Siegel, L. C. Educational set: A determinant of acquisition. *Journal of Educational Psychology*, 1965, *56*, 1–12.

Siegel, L., & Siegel, L. C. A multivariate paradigm for educational research. *Psychological Bulletin*, 1967, *68*, 306–326.

Slovic, P., & Lichtenstein, S. Comparison of Bayesian and regression approaches to the study of information processing in judgment. *Organizational Behavior and Human Performance*, 1971, *6*, 649–744.

Spranger, E. *Types of men (Lebensformen)*. Halle: Niemeyer, 1928.

Stilson, D. W., & Astrup, C. Nonlinear and additive methods for long-term prognosis in the functional psychoses. *Journal of Nervous and Mental Disease*, 1966, *141*, 468–473.

Webb, E. J., Campbell, D. T., Schwartz, R. D., & Sechrest, L. B. *Unobtrusive measures: A survey of nonreactive research in social science.* Chicago: Rand McNally, 1966.

Wiggins, N., & Kohen, E. S. Man versus model of man revisited: The forecasting of graduate school success. *Journal of Personality and Social Psychology*, 1971, *19*, 100–106.

RECOMMENDED READING FOR UNIT IV

AMEG Commission on Sex Bias in Measurement. "Report on Sex Bias in Interest Measurement." *Measurement and Evaluation in Guidance*, 1973, 6: 171–177.

Backman, M. E. "Patterns of Mental Abilities: Ethnic, Socioeconomic and Sex Differences." *American Educational Research Journal*, Winter 1972, 9: 1–12.

Buros, O. K. (ed.). *The Nineteen Thirty-eight Mental Measurements Yearbook.* New Brunswick, N.J.: Rutgers University Press, 1938.

Buros, O. K. (ed.). *The Nineteen Forty Mental Measurements Yearbook.* New Brunswick, N.J.: Rutgers University Press, 1941.

Buros, O. K. (ed.). *The Third Mental Measurements Yearbook.* New Brunswick, N.J.: Rutgers University Press, 1949.

Buros, O. K. (ed.). *The Fourth Mental Measurements Yearbook.* Highland Park, N.J.: Gryphon Press, 1953.

Buros, O. K. (ed.). *The Fifth Mental Measurements Yearbook.* Highland Park, N.J.: Gryphon Press, 1959.

Buros, O. K. (ed.). *The Sixth Mental Measurements Yearbook.* Highland Park, N.J.: Gryphon Press, 1965.

Buros, O. K. (ed.). *The Seventh Mental Measurements Yearbook.* Highland Park, N.J.: Gryphon Press, 1972.

Buros, O. K. (ed.). *Tests in Print.* (2nd edition). Highland Park, N.J.: Gryphon Press, 1974.

Campbell, David P. "Reactions to the AMEG Commission Report on Sex Bias in Interest Measurement." *Measurement and Evaluation in Guidance*, 1973, 6, 3: 178–181.

Harmon, Lenore W. "Sexual Bias in Interest Measurement." *Measurement and Evaluation in Guidance*, 1973, 5: 496–501.

Hathaway, Starke R. "MMPI: Professional Use by Professional People." *American Psychologist*, 1964, 19: 204–210.

REPORTING AND USING RESULTS

unit

V

Educational decisions should be based on relevant information. Educators have the responsibility of determining what information needs to be obtained, obtaining it, using that information wisely in their own decision making, and imparting it in readily understood terms to others responsible for making educational decisions. What information should be gathered, how or whether it should be used, and how or whether it should be imparted to others are questions on which reasonable men have differed. The articles in this unit present some thoughtful views on these issues.

Few, if any, educators doubt the wisdom of determining what and how well students have learned. Not to do so would mean we could not evaluate schools' effectiveness or the students' progress. However, how to record what students have learned, in what fashion, and who should receive such information are more debatable issues. Alphabetical or numerical grades are the most frequent means of reporting. These symbols attempt to convey an overall impression of a student's total performance in a subject matter area. This method has been under attack. Several formal and informal surveys suggest that many students and teachers would prefer abolishing grades. Holt (1971) and Melby (1966) present two strongly-worded articles against grading. Ebel (1974) is a most able spokesman in favor of grading. Millman (1970) builds a case for a criterion-referenced marking system. Comparing different reporting procedures should not be on an either-or basis; more than one procedure can be used in a school system. Measurement experts do not deny the usefulness of highly detailed and specific information, but they do feel that grades serve useful functions. Feldmesser delineates some of these functions in the first article of this unit. McMahon reports on a school system that attempted a procedure different from the traditional grading method. One interesting phenomenon in higher education is the inflation of grades. *Time* (Nov. 11, 1974) reports for example that at Yale 42 percent of all undergraduate 1974 spring term grades were A's and 46 percent of the senior class graduated with honors. Other colleges and universities report similar grading patterns. If this continues to occur, grades will surely lose their meaning and no longer serve the functions Feldmesser mentions.

The public has legitimate conflicting concerns regarding dissemination of test data. Parents want reports on their children to assist them in educational decisions. The public also wants to judge schools' performances and feels the schools should release data to facilitate correct judgements. On the other hand, the public is concerned about releasing information to the wrong people. Thus, schools have to tread carefully between releasing information to those who should have it and withholding it from those who should not. The Russell Sage Foundation has published a set of *Guidelines for the Collection, Maintenance, and Dissemination of Pupil Records.* Excerpts from it are presented in this unit. The full document is the report of a work conference whose participants included educators, psychologists, sociologists, lawyers, a judge, and a state senator. The "Family Educational Rights and Privacy Act of 1974" (Section 438 of Public Law 93-380) is also reproduced in this unit. As of the time of this writing, there is much concern over the interpretation of this act, although most educators support the intent behind it.

Although there are restrictions with respect to releasing individual scores, why not release district or building results. The push for accountability (see also Unit VI) has resulted in more districts announcing their scores to the public. Hawes discusses whether it is urgent or unthinkable and suggests twelve ways to announce test results.

To release district or building scores to the public is reasonably threatening to educators. For a teacher to have his/her effectiveness judged by a superintendent, personnel director, or school board solely on the basis of standardized achievement test results is extremely threatening to teachers and they correctly reject the legitimacy of such a procedure. Should test results play any role in evaluating teachers? The Ebel editorial in this unit provides a controversial, but in my view correct, answer to that question. But the answer is more philosophical than practical. He does not really tell us *how* we can equitably use test results to help evaluate teachers, only that it is *philosophically* sound to do so.

One of the factors that somewhat limits the usefulness of standardized achievement test scores is that the content of such tests never exactly matches the curricular goals of a local school district or individual classroom teacher. Cox and Sterrett suggest a procedure which recognizes the lack of a perfect match and therefore provides more meaningful information.

Feldmesser argues that grades can be useful by providing unique and useful information to the student and by generating other kinds of evaluation and enhancing their effectiveness. He builds a powerful case by refuting many of the arguments that have been made against grading. See Ebel (1974) for another discussion of grades.

Feldmesser focuses on college grading. Can his arguments be extended to the secondary and elementary schools?

You are encouraged to read the McMahon article immediately following Feldmesser's. It describes what occurred in a junior high school when traditional letter grades were discontinued.

The Positive Functions of Grades

ROBERT A. FELDMESSER

The custom of giving grades in college courses, recording them in permanent form, and calculating a grade point average is clearly under attack. A survey conducted by the American Council on Education in fall 1970 found that 44 percent of entering freshmen favored abolishing grades.[1] Many faculty members find merit in the objections of students, and many institutions are, indeed, modifying their grading practices.

Yet there is general agreement that it is educationally beneficial for a college student to receive some evaluation of his work, that is, some judgment about the quality of his academic performance which he can use to guide his future academic behavior. A grade is essentially one form of evaluation: specifically, a form so highly condensed or abstracted that it can be expressed as a number, or as a letter that can be converted into a number, and entered on a permanent record. Admittedly, all forms of evaluation may not be equally beneficial, and some may not be beneficial at all. The controversy about grades, therefore, resolves into the issue of the worth of this particular kind of evaluation.

Do grades serve any evaluative function that cannot be served, or served better, by some other form of evaluation? It is the contention here that they do. Grades have the first-order function of providing unique and useful information to the student, and second-order functions of generating other kinds of evaluation and enhancing their effectiveness. Grades *can* be justified on the basis of their contributions to student learning, apart from their putative usefulness to administrators, graduate schools, employers, or society in general. To support the benefits of grades *for the student* is to meet the opponents of grades on their most defensible ground.

Reprinted from *Educational Record*, Winter 1972, pp. 66–72, with permission of the author and the American Council on Education, Washington, D.C.

Grades here mean the familiar A-F or 4-0 systems and their variants, as distinguished from both total abolition of grades and pass-fail and similar arrangements that allow no differentiations among students who meet minimum course requirements and which are advocated as a way to relieve the pressure of conventional grades. Although a position supporting grades bucks a strong tide, one may hope that, in the long run, rationality can be made to prevail over the whims of fashion.

The kind of evaluation most widely favored is one highly detailed and specific, giving the student a maximum of information about his performance along each of the relevant dimensions of a course. This sort of feedback, it is said, helps him identify his strengths and weaknesses so he can most wisely allocate his time and energy in his future academic work. There is no quarrel here with the argument that this type of evaluation is indeed useful.

SUPPLEMENTARY ROLE

There is, nevertheless, an important role to be played by the summative evaluation called a grade. This role does not preclude a multidimensional evaluation but supplements it. A grade should be considered an effort to put back together, to synthesize, the separate judgments about a student's work. It gives the student some sense of the quality of his performance *on the whole*. To a student in a biology course, for example, it is not enough to know that his lab work was weak while his grasp of abstract concepts was strong, and that he was high on understanding of cell structure but low on understanding of ecological relationships and middling on understanding of reproductive systems. He will also want to know what it all adds up to: whether, all things considered, he did well or poorly or something in between. The grade thus satisfies a natural curiosity, but, while that seems like a virtue in itself,[2] the grade does more. It helps a student decide whether, taking one thing with another, biology is a field in which further inputs of his resources are likely to be productive for him, or whether he should switch to another field. In other words, if it is useful to him to have judgments about one aspect of his course work as distinguished from other aspects, it is also useful to him to have judgments about one course, holistically considered, as distinguished from other courses.

This same logic can and should be applied to the infamous grade point average. It helps a student to know how well he is doing in higher education generally, all *courses* considered, so that he can make a more informed decision about whether further study is the right thing for him and, if it is, what sorts of institutions would be most suitable. In the absence of this information, he may waste his time by pursuing his studies or waste his talents by not pursuing his studies. Calculation of a grade point average obviously requires grades, as they have been defined above.

Educational researchers, above all, should appreciate this function of grades, for they often find it useful to know not only a subject's response to a particular item of a scale, or his score on several subscales, but also his total score on the scale as a whole. Each of these kinds of information is appropriate to different purposes and none can be substituted for another. Isn't it the same for the student? Wouldn't he, too, find information on different levels of generality or abstraction, ranging from an instructor's comments on an exam to a course grade and a grade point average, equally and uniquely useful but for different purposes?

SECOND-ORDER FUNCTIONS

The second-order functions of grades derive from another need: the need to report evaluations to a central agency of authority within the educational institution. If a central agency is to receive evaluations of all students in all courses during the entire time they are in college, the evaluations must be highly condensed—preferably to a single symbol—so the central agency does not have to devote an inordinate amount of resources to record keeping—which is to say that if evaluations are to be reported, they must take the form of grades. Thus, to establish the functional necessity of reporting is to establish by implication the need for grades.

Why, then, is reporting a functional necessity? In particular, why is it important to the student's learning, since that is the criterion here? There are two basic arguments:

The first has been surprisingly neglected in discussions of grading. As mentioned, there is agreement that a student benefits from receiving an evaluation of his performance. But a question that no one seems to have asked is, Why should an instructor bother to furnish an evaluation to his students? This is not an idle question. Many instructors are dilatory about providing evaluations even where conventional grading practices are in force. Given the pressures that divert faculty from their teaching, as well as the difficulty of making evaluations, it is highly probable that many faculty members would be happy to abandon the evaluative role altogether. At two institutions—Brandeis University and the University of California at Santa Cruz—where pass-fail grading was instituted under conditions that allowed instructors to know which students were receiving P-F grades, those students complained, said a Brandeis observer, that

> instructors often took fewer pains in evaluating their submitted work than they did with those taking the course for a letter grade.[3]

At Santa Cruz, where most courses are offered only on a P-F basis but instructors are supposed to provide detailed evaluations, several students said they were very unhappy with their instructors for not having completed evaluations for their files. One is quoted as saying

> With a few exceptions, they don't give a goddamn.[4]

REPORTING REQUIREMENT

These comments hint at what could well happen if instructors did not have to report grades at all. In short, the reporting requirement exercises a coercive force on the instructor in behalf of his students. At the very least, it compels him to make some minimal evaluation—the minimum represented by the grade itself.

But in most cases, the reporting requirement probably prods the instructor to make more than a minimal evaluation. If he has to submit a grade, he will probably feel an obligation to develop some reasonable basis for it, if only so he can defend it if questioned. Hence, he will set up more or less detailed evaluative procedures; and if he is going to do that anyway, it takes little extra effort to inform his students of the results as his course progresses. This step also helps avoid a situation in which students could claim that their grade was unfair because it took them by surprise or that they could have taken corrective action if they had been informed earlier. Moreover, the reporting requirement has a quality-control function, analogous to that of the requirement for public trials: it restrains the instructor from making evaluations that merely reflect his ideological or punitive inclinations, lest he be called upon to justify his grade. In the absence of this requirement, some instructors would probably be quite ruthless about "maintaining academic standards."[5]

BASIS FOR DECISIONS

After asking why an instructor should bother to evaluate his students, the second question is, Why should students pay any attention to an evaluation? The usual answer is that the evaluation helps the student learn, and the student is in college for the sake of learning, so naturally he will take evaluations of his work seriously. That answer is not convincing; some have expressed the suspicion that many students are in college not to learn but to get a degree. And students, like faculty, are presented with many distractions from what is supposed to be their central task.

Aside from that, however, many students—and their number is, if anything, increasing—deliberately decide, on what seem to them sufficient grounds, that the content of a particular course, or particular parts of a course, is irrelevant to their needs and, therefore, should *not* be learned. It can be said that that is their business; if they choose not to learn, they will and should bear the consequences of their decision. But this attitude amounts to a shirking of the faculty's educational duty, if not to a denial of its educational pretensions.

The student, after all, is young, and his very presence in a course indicates that he knows relatively little about the field. Consequently, he does not necessarily know what parts of a course will be relevant to his needs over the long run. His teachers claim more foresight in such matters; if they are unwilling to make that claim, they should not be his teachers. Thus, instructors are entitled—and obliged—to exert some pressure on the student to induce him to learn material whose importance he is not yet in a position to perceive. One effective and appropriate way to apply this pressure is to make it in the student's immediate interest to take his instructors' evaluations seriously. This step can be accomplished, in turn, by using those evaluations as the basis for important short-run decisions about the student, for example, decisions about further study or employment. Finally, if evaluations are to be the basis for such decisions, the evaluations must be reported to some central agency with the authority to make those decisions or to transmit the information to others who can. The knowledge that important decisions will be based on a student's grade is another force compelling instructors, too, to take more care with grades than they otherwise might.

REINFORCING EFFECT

Something more is involved here than the familiar motivational function of grades (though it may be noted that students do have difficulty generating their own motivation in the absence of grades).[6] Students, like other people, interpret the significance of communications in part by the significance attributed to them by others. If no one else cared what evaluations had been made of his work, why should the student care? If no one else based any important decisions on those evaluations, wouldn't the message to the student be that the evaluations were, in fact, not important? Why, then, should he allow them to influence his academic behavior? It is apparent, then, that grades reinforce the feedback function of other evaluations.

In grading, however, there is no reason to reject a student's perceptions of his own needs and interests completely; surely he knows some things about himself which his instructors do not and cannot know. A proper grading system will take this into account, for example, by providing for student participation in determining the components of a grade and by permitting students to assign varying weights to their grades in the calculation of their GPA.[7] Also, allowing a student's grades to be used in too many or excessively threatening ways impairs rather than enhances their motivational function.

Whatever the merits of the preceding arguments, a great many criticisms of grades continue to be made.[8] It may be a plausible hypothesis that the dysfunctional outweigh the functional consequences of grades. However, some criticisms of grades are totally unwarranted, suffering from defects in logic. Others are more properly directed at the *misuse* of grades rather than at grades per se, or at evaluation generally rather than at grades specifically.

A few do refer to the technical deficiencies of grades themselves. Most valid criticism can be met by institutional changes.

REWARDS FOR LEARNING

One common objection to grades is that they are extrinsic rather than intrinsic rewards. In the minds of many people, a moral stigma is attached to the pursuit of learning for the sake of external rewards. But, why is it so heinous to learn as a means toward an end? How well would college faculty fare on this test of academic purity: how much of a faculty member's time is spent acquiring new knowledge for the sheer delight of it, and how much to be a better teacher, or to contribute to the solution of a social or technological problem, or to dazzle students, or to have something to publish? This is not simply an ad hominem thrust; the model offered by the faculty is probably more powerful than the grading system in influencing attitudes toward learning.

In any case, if students have internalized the attitude that learning is "merely" instrumental rather than an end in itself, college would seem a rather late stage at which to try to initiate a change. If one nevertheless wishes to make the effort, what better way to begin than by establishing firm clear bonds between learning and valued external rewards? Indeed, there is no other way, since—except for the satisfactions connected with a few primitive biological urges, such as eating—all intrinsic rewards of necessity begin as extrinsic.[9] If this principle seems not to have operated prior to college, it is most likely because the act being rewarded was not *learning* as most prefer to define it. But what is crucial about rewards, in the last analysis, is not whether they are intrinsic or extrinsic, but what kinds of behavior they induce, and, in the present instance, that is a matter of the validity of grades as measures of academic performance.

GRADES VS. SUCCESS

It is also said that there must be something wrong with grades because they are not good predictors of "success" in later life. But, as Donald P. Hoyt has suggested, that is not necessarily a condemnation. Grades should measure learnings; success is in large part a result of what has been done with the learning.[10] Moreover, it is not completely clear that knowledge and understanding are ingredients necessary to success in society. Assuming they are, one might urge that, if the employment of cognitive learnings in the scramble for success were inhibited by certain *affective* learnings, for example, sensitivity to the needs and rights of others, and if grades were valid measures of both, their lack of correlation with success might be cause for gratification.

PROMOTING COMPETITION

A third unwarranted criticism is that grades foster competitive attitudes. This criticism applies to grades only insofar as it applies to evaluations of human performance generally, because a comparison with the performance of other humans is usually the most meaningful frame of reference, if not the only one, for such evaluations.

Furthermore, a certain kind of competitive perspective is actually quite desirable. In considering his future, a student should take into account his comparative advantages vis-à-vis others in his field so he can better determine where he can make his most satisfying contribution. Thus, he might want to choose a field in which other people would work less effectively than he. At the very least, a student deserves the information about which fields those are, and grades provide a convenient way to tell him. This aspect of grades has nothing to do with inducing men to cut each other's throats, or even with preparing them to live in a competitive world—the implications and justifications of grades which students are increasingly resisting. In the perspective suggested here, grades foster a competitive attitude only by spurring students to realize that their own talents and energies compete with each other in the sense that resources put to one use cannot be put to another.

Another unwarranted criticism is that a low grade discourages a student from further study of a subject. Isn't that exactly what a low grade should do? If, despite efforts to learn, a student is performing poorly in, say, math, he *should* be discouraged from taking further math courses; this action is an aid to his education, not a detriment, for he might learn more in art history or economic theory. Letting a student know that he is performing poorly is preferable to permitting him to entertain an illusion about himself.

A student can be given a negative evaluation in a course, however, without having it broadcast to the world, that is, without having it entered on his transcript and incorporated into his GPA. This permanent record, it is complained, does the damage. Since the GPA is important to students, even a slight decline is said to arouse inordinate anxiety, and students will go to great lengths to avoid it, for example, confining themselves to courses in which they are confident they can earn high grades.[11] That undesirable by-product implies a misuse of grades. (Interestingly enough, studies of pass-fail grading have shown that it does not substantially alter students' course elections, although that is supposed to be one of its main purposes.[12])

FUNCTION OF ANXIETY

The anxiety aroused by fear of a low grade is but the obverse side of the motivational coin. If a grade is to motivate, then a high grade must be a never-guaranteed but ever-possible outcome; a low grade, therefore, must be an avoidable but also ever-possible outcome. If the possibility of a low grade creates anxiety in the student, he should be able to reduce that feeling by studying to avoid the low grade. That is one way in which the motivational function is served, and evidence indicates that it works, when the anxiety is *moderate.*[13]

Anxiety interferes with learning only when it becomes excessive, and— neurotic personalities aside—that happens when too much importance is attributed to a single grade. There are several ways to prevent excessive anxiety.

DIMINISHING PRESSURES

First, a student should be allowed to weight his grades differentially, so he can give low weight to grades in those courses that arouse the most anxiety in him. Second, he should be helped to understand that a grade is not a judgment of his moral worth, but merely an informational statement, and a tentative and fallible one at that. Third, there should be strict limitations on the use of a student's grade record. While it must be available to college authorities, for reasons stated above, these officials should adopt explicit restrictions on its use. It should not be a basis for determining financial aid or participating in extracurricular activities. Certainly it should never have been given to draft boards without the student's permission. Indeed, beyond its use by the college itself, in admitting students to honor sections or in dismissing them for unsatisfactory academic work, the grade record should be regarded as the property of the student alone, so he can prevent its use as a threat. This rule would not defeat the reporting function. If graduate schools or employers wanted to see a student's grade record, they should be required to obtain it through the student, and he should have the right of refusal. He would be quite aware of the significance that would be attached to his exercise of that right. If he gave permission for his record to be sent outside the institution, the "authority" of the college would become simply the capacity to certify that the grade record was accurate.

A different problem is presented by the student who receives many low grades. These, it is said, not only deter him from further academic work but also may injure his self-esteem. Assuming that these grades are valid evaluations, discouraging the student from further academic work may, again, be the best thing for him, although it is doubly important to assure him that one can be a worthy human being without a bachelor's degree. If his self-esteem is nevertheless injured, that is surely a result chiefly of the negative evaluations themselves; it is doubtful that reporting them as grades adds much to the damage. But if one believes that every individual has the capacity for success in some subject, even at the college level, then it follows that the harm lies not in the concept of grading but either in poor teaching that failed to develop any capacity, or in inaccurate evaluations that failed to register successful performance when it occurred.

In the end, it is their lack of validity that emerges as the most legitimate criticism of grades. Whatever valuable functions they could perform in the abstract will not be performed if grades are not valid measures of learning; and all too often, they are not. Lack of validity is alluded to when it is charged that grades displace learning as the goal of study; that grades tend to reward memorization and other low-level academic skills rather than understanding and creativity; that grades make the student a slave to his instructor, fearful of offending him or disagreeing with him. If understanding, originality, initiative, and rational skepticism of authority are among the proper objectives of education—and certainly they should be—then grades that fail to reflect these qualities are not valid grades, by the very definition of *validity*.[14] The same is true of all educational evaluations, of which recorded grades are but a final distillation.

ACCURATE EVALUATION

This, however, is a remediable defect. Valid educational evaluations are difficult but not impossible to arrive at; certainly they can be far more closely approached than at present. If they are rare in the experience of most college students, the main reason is that the overwhelming majority of college faculty have had no training whatsoever in making them. Evaluations of academic performance, including grades, are being made by instructors who, typically, have not formulated their teaching objectives in any deliberate way; do not understand, and may not even have thought about, the relationships of objectives to the manner in which they conduct classes, make assignments, or give examinations; and have never learned anything about the techniques of measuring attainment of those objectives. As McGeorge Bundy said years ago:

> The ordinary college teacher, giving out grades in the ordinary way on the basis of a few special papers or tests and a single final examination, is a fountain of error, and everyone knows it except the man himself.[15]

Ultimately, training in evaluation should be the responsibility of the graduate schools that produce college teachers. Meanwhile, each college could well undertake to fill the gap itself. It could, for one thing, publish a clear statement about grading policies and practices;[16] faculty and students should naturally participate in drawing it up—an instructive experience in itself. For another thing, a college could conduct a seminar on evaluation at the opening of each academic year, with all faculty members expected to attend in their first year and perhaps every third or fourth year thereafter to keep up to date on theories and technologies. It would be highly desirable for students to attend this seminar, too. Exposure to the mundane procedures involved in evaluation would help students appreciate the fallibility of evaluative instruments, would tend to divest grades of their moral overtones, and might thereby lead to a more relaxed attitude. Furthermore, knowledge on the part of faculty that their students were moderately sophisticated in the matter of grades would be an efficacious way to enforce good practices. These steps would help overcome the evil that grades can do, allowing everyone to take full advantage of their positive functions.

NOTES

[1] Staff of the Office of Research, *National Norms for Entering College Freshmen—Fall 1970* (Washington: American Council on Education, 1970), p. 43.

[2] Melvin M. Tumin, "Evaluation of the Effectiveness of Education: Some Problems and Prospects," *Interchange*, 1 (1970): 96–109.

[3] Mathew R. Sgan, "Letter Grade Achievement in Pass-Fail Courses," *Journal of Higher Education*, November 1970, p. 639.

[4] Memo to the Santa Cruz faculty from the chancellor's office, 6 January 1970, p. [4].

[5] Burton R. Clark, *The Distinctive College: Antioch, Reed, Swarthmore* (Chicago: Aldine, 1970), p. 131.

[6] William R. Torbert and J. Richard Hackman, "Taking the Fun Out of Outfoxing the System," in *The Changing College Classroom*, ed. Philip Runkel, Roger Harrison, and Margaret Runkel (San Francisco: Jossey-Bass, 1969), pp. 167–76; Robert A. Feldmesser, *The Option: Analysis of an Educational Innovation* (Hanover, N.H.: Dartmouth College, 1969), pp. 70–87.

[7] Feldmesser, *The Option*, pp. 145–51

[8] Jonathan R. Warren, *College Grading Practices: An Overview* (Washington: ERIC Clearinghouse on Higher Education, George Washington University, 1971); Sidney B. Simon, "Grades Must Go," *School Review*, May 1970, pp. 397–402.

[9] Robert L. Ebel, *Measuring Educational Achievement* (Englewood, N.J.: Prentice-Hall, 1965), p. 400.

[10] "The Relationship Between College Grades and Adult Achievement, A Review of the Literature," *ACT Research Reports* (Iowa City, Iowa: American College Testing Program, 1965), p. 46.

[11] Howard S. Becker, Blanche Geer, and Everett C. Hughes, *Making the Grade: The Academic Side of College Life* (New York: John Wiley, 1968).

[12] Feldmesser, *The Option*, pp. 53–55; Marvin Karlins, Martin Kaplan, and William Stuart, "Academic Attitudes and Performance as a Function of Differential Grading Systems: An Evaluation of Princeton's Pass-Fail System," *Journal of Experimental Education*, Spring 1969, pp. 39–40, 44; Ward Cromer, "An Empirical Investigation of Student Attitudes Toward the Pass-Fail Grading System at Wellesley College," an address before the Eastern Psychological Association in Philadelphia, 1969, p. 2; "Pass/Fail Study Committee Findings," *Key Reporter*, Winter 1969-70, p. 2; Richard

M. Gold et al., "Academic Achievement Declines Under Pass-Fail Grading," *Journal of Experimental Education*, Spring 1970, p. 20.

[13] Norman E. Wallen and Robert M. W. Travers, "Analysis and Investigation of Teaching Methods," in *Handbook of Research in Teaching*, ed. N. L. Gage (Chicago: Rand McNally, 1963), p. 496.

[14] Ebel, *Measuring Educational Achievement*, pp. 400–401.

[15] "An Atmosphere to Breathe: Woodrow Wilson and the Life of the American University College" (New York: Woodrow Wilson Foundation, 1959), p. 19. See also Becker, Geer, and Hughes, *Making the Grade*, p. 140.

[16] George R. Bramer, "Grading and Academic Justice," *Improving College and University Teaching*, Winter 1970, pp. 63–65.

McMahon reports on a school system that dropped the traditional grading procedure. Do you think the experiences he describes are typical? Was the new technique continued long enough to be given a fair trial?

A, B, C Grades? Don't Knock It!

WILLIAM E. McMAHON

Instead of allowing unsuccessful experiments to fade quietly away, what is needed is an official burial to crack the veil of silence which surrounds them. By way of contributing to this hard core of truth, I would like to report on an educational experiment in which I was recently involved: for it was educational in more ways than one.

The grading techniques of Garmisch Junior High School were completely revised in the fall of 1969. The Garmisch Plan was only a modified version of what is known as non-gradedness. As explained by the principal: "We are a non-graded school in that we don't give the A to F grades and are not hung up on what grade-level work a particular student is doing." We did not modify anything really except the method of reporting to parents. Instead of letter grades we were to rely completely on conferences and written evaluations.

The revisions seemed simple enough and above all desirable. Doing away with report-card grades promised to relieve the teachers of what is generally felt to be a hateful task. "Unfair," "meaningless," "capricious," even "undemocratic" are all words used to describe the traditional grading system. Some specific objections are:

Preoccupation with grades inhibits learning.

Grading is actually inimical to recognizing individual differences.

Reprinted by permission from the April, 1971 issue of *The Clearing House*, Vol. 45, pp. 465-467.

Grades can give a false self-image, either too inflated or (more often) too deflated.

Grading is impossibly subjective.

There are many more objections. It is no wonder, then, the teachers responded to the proposal with interest. Every child learning at his own rate, at his own level, because he wanted to learn, without fear of failure or hope of any reward other than the natural satisfaction of setting a goal and then attaining it—all this could be had by the simple expedient of dropping that evil grading system.

As a theory it sounded impeccable. "If a teacher needs grades to get a kid to work, he's a pretty lousy teacher," argued one supportive parent. "He obviously doesn't know how to involve students in the learning process."

We had been warned there would be a transformation in the school spirit when we did away with grades. There *was* a transformation, all right, but not the kind we had expected. Almost immediately, it seemed, the students began to dislike the teachers, openly criticizing them. This had not happened to us before. It was puzzling, but a letter from a parent gave us a clue: "This new system," he wrote, "is entirely for the convenience of the teachers, so you won't have to do the work of figuring out grades."

We were stunned. The new system was in reality more work (writing detailed comments and holding long conferences consumed many extra hours), but the students and their parents did not see it that way. They thought we were just being lazy, and they resented us for it.

Nine weeks went by. The first "report" card came out. When the students saw that everyone received the same grade, that every grade was an "S," they thought, "So why work? The ones who study and learn a lot get the same grades as those who don't." Morale sagged.

At this same time the teachers began to realize how *un*specific written evaluations really are. "Don't tell me my daughter is well-adjusted," warned one grim father. "I happen to know she has the temperament of a wet wasp. I just want to know how she stands in solving equations."

"Oh, she's good at solving equations," I assured him. "She can do some of the most difficult ones."

"But does that mean she's high, or just average," he persisted.

"I'd say she's a little better than average."

The parent went away muttering, "Why doesn't he say she's a B-student and get it over with?"

We found ourselves engaged in similar guessing games with the students:

Student: How did I do on the German test?
Teacher: Your work in German is fine. It was a good test.
Student: Was it an "A" or a "B"?
Teacher: I don't know what grade it would be, but you really zapped it.
Student: Did anyone in the class do better?

Teacher: No-o-o. I don't think . . .
Students (Exultantly) Then it was an "A"!
Teacher: (Desperately) But it's a low class!

And so on.

"Grades didn't give us much to go on," another parent complained, "just a tiny crumb. Now you've taken even that away."

By the end of the first semester our experiment was failing fast. The kids despised us and the system. When the principal suggested that along with "S" and "I" (improvement desired), some few students should be given an "O" for truly outstanding work, one of the teachers remarked, "Why don't we give 'S-plus' and 'S-minus' and we'll be right back where we started with five different grades?"

After the first semester we returned to the usual A-to-F grading system. This time the change in the school atmosphere was not so dramatic. Only gradually did the morale of students and teachers start to revive. But by the end of March the trend was clear: apathy was losing out to hustle; hostility was slowly giving way to friendliness. What promised to be a disastrous school year ended on an almost joyous note.

Out of this experience have come certain reflections:

(1) *The possibility of failure was seen to be what makes success meaningful.* The "successful" students were more hostile to the experiment than any other group. This fact is borne out by the research of J. W. Atkinson on programmed learning. There he showed that better students soon reject any 100 per cent reward system. Potential failure, therefore, is often an important part of a learning situation.

(2) *If the student is working on an appropriate level, "bad" grades happen only if they be richly deserved.* When mediocre efforts are given the same recognition as excellent ones, it is confusing for a young person, whether he be a high-achiever or a low-achiever. (One of the good results of the experiment was to emphasize once again the tremendous importance of individualizing instruction so that every student who wants to do well can do well.)

(3) *Conferences and written evaluations are of no use as motivation and of limited value as communication.* They were never meant to be motivators, but even as communication they fall short. If a person is able to capture in words the actions and processes, in short, the *essence*, of another human being, such an achievement is not called evaluation; it is poetry!

(4) *Even though the traditional grading system has its drawbacks, it does act as a real motivator.* Until something better is found, therefore, it is probably a mistake to drop it. Grades do not seem as important for motivating young children. Our elementary students are getting along fine without

the traditional grading. There is, however, a change around age eleven. It may be that the child by this time has mastered enough of his environment for minimal survival, and the inner drive to know *every*thing—so powerful in younger children—begins to lessen. Then it is that artificial motivators, such as letter grades, have their place in education.

Admittedly, these reflections are based on only one experiment. But it was *our* experiment. It has an immediacy, therefore, which casts doubt on some of the more exhaustive studies. Having once learned that eliminating grading, an idea which came to us highly recommended, does not work (at least, not for us), I have come to suspect that most educational theories have noisy births, rapid proliferation, and unattended funerals. No one hears of their demise. If non-grading has been tried in a number of places and then quietly dropped, as seems to be the case in some high schools, it would be a great help to hear about it.

The Russell Sage Foundation has published a set of *Guidelines for the Collection, Maintenance, and Dissemination of Pupil Records*. Excerpts from it are presented here. For data collection purposes they differentiate between data which require only representational (e.g., Board of Education) consent and data collection which should proceed only with individual consent. They describe three classes of data that require different arrangements for security and access. Finally they suggest guidelines for the dissemination of information. The paper following this one on the rights and privacy of parents and students should be read in conjunction with these excerpts.

Proposed Principles for the Management of School Records

RUSSELL SAGE FOUNDATION

Schools typically maintain extensive and intimate information about pupils and their families for legitimate educational purposes including instruction, guidance and research. Necessarily, the collection and maintenance of any information about a pupil or his family constitutes a potential intrusion on

Excerpts from *Guidelines for the Collection, Maintenance, and Dissemination of Pupil Records*, © 1970 Russell Sage Foundation. Reprinted with permission of the publisher.

privacy. At the same time, society, by its approval of our educational institutions, legitimizes such intrusions, at least in those cases where the information collected can be demonstrated to be necessary for the effective performance of designated educational functions.

There are clear indications, however, that current practices of schools and school personnel relating to the collection, maintenance, use, and dissemination of information about pupils threaten a desirable balance between the individual's right to privacy and the school's stated need to know. Specifically, we may point to the following examples of *potential* abuse:

Information about both pupils and their parents is often collected by schools without the informed consent of either children or their parents.

Pupils and parents typically have little or, at best, incomplete knowledge of what information about them is contained in school records and what use is made of this information by the school.

Within many school systems few provisions are made to protect school records from examination by unauthorized school personnel.

Access to pupil records by nonschool personnel and representatives of outside agencies is, for the most part, handled on an *ad hoc* basis. Formal policies governing access by law enforcement officials, the courts, potential employers, colleges, researchers, and others do not exist in most school systems. For example, in many school systems a police official may obtain access to a pupil's record file.

It is our opinion that these deficiencies in record-keeping policies, taken together, constitute a serious threat to individual privacy in the United States.

COLLECTION OF DATA

We begin, and urge school authorities to begin, from the fundamental principle that no information should be collected from students without the prior informed consent of the child and his parents.

Such consent may be given either individually or through the parents' legally elected or appointed representatives (for example, the Board of Education) depending on the nature of the information to be collected.

. . . representational consent will, for example, ordinarily be sufficient in situations involving aptitude and achievement testing . . .

On the other hand, we believe that programs of personality testing and assessment, for example, should proceed only with the informed individual consent of each child and/or his parents. . . . Moreover, individual consent should be an absolute requirement before information, other than that required for pupil identification, concerning a pupil's family is obtained (for example, ethnic origin, religious beliefs, income and occupational data, husband-wife relations, and the like), or before any information not directly relevant for educational purposes is solicited from the pupil or his parents.

In all situations where individual consent is to be obtained, it should be in writing.

We recognize that certain special problems are presented by data gathering in individual situations. Illustrative here are interviews or diagnostic tests by the school counselor, social worker, nurse, psychologist, school principal, etc. . . . In most of this class of situations, the requirement of enforced consent cannot be met, perhaps because of the age of the student, or the unforeseeable course of the interview process. Moreover, in many schools there is an element of duress in that the student feels obliged to participate in the situation. The principles advanced by the conferees for these situations are as follows:

> The professional should inform the student as fully as possible, consonant with his professional responsibility and the capacity of the student to understand the implications of the situation, about the data that are likely to be obtained;
> and
> should stress the voluntary character of the student's participation.
>
> Where reasonable doubt exists about the capacity of the student to understand the implications of the situation, either because of the student's age or other circumstances, parental permission should be sought first. Moreover, where a student clearly in need of intervention declines to participate, the professional should seek parental consent.

CLASSIFICATION AND MAINTENANCE OF DATA

The total set of student personnel data extant in a school at a given time ranges from tentative uncorroborated reports on alleged student behavior to highly stable information. . . . These differing kinds of data require differing arrangements for security and access.

Category "A" data: Includes official administrative records that constitute the *minimum* personal data necessary for operation of the educational system. Specifically we take this to mean identifying data (including names and address of parents or guardian), birth date, academic work completed, level of achievement (grades, standardized achievement test scores), and attendance data.

> These records should be maintained in perpetuity, subject to the conditions set forth below. . . .

Category "B" data: Includes verified information of clear importance, but not absolutely necessary to the school, over time, in helping the child or in

protecting others. Specifically, scores on standardized intelligence and aptitude tests, interest inventory results, health data, family background information, systematically gathered teacher or counselor ratings and observations,
and verified reports of serious or recurrent behavior patterns are included in
this category.

> Great care must be exercised by the school to ensure the accuracy of Cate-
> gory "B" data. . . .
>
> School systems should give serious consideration to the elimination of
> unnecessary Category "B" data at periodic intervals; for example, at points
> of transition from elementary to junior high school and from junior high to
> high school. . . .
>
> . . . Parents should be periodically informed of the content of these
> records and their right of access to these data.

Category "C" data: Includes potentially useful information but not yet verified or clearly needed beyond the immediate present; for example, legal or
clinical findings including certain personality test results, and unevaluated
reports of teachers, counselors, and others which may be needed in ongoing
investigations and disciplinary or counseling actions.

> Such data should be reviewed at least once a year and destroyed as soon as
> their usefulness is ended; or transferred to Category "B." Transfer to Cate-
> gory "B" may be made only if two conditions are met; namely, (1) the
> continuing usefulness of the information is clearly demonstrated and (2) its
> validity has been verified, in which case parents must be notified and the
> nature of the information explained. . . .

ADMINISTRATION OF SECURITY

It is recommended that schools designate a professional person to be responsible for record maintenance and access, and to educate the staff about
maintenance and access policies. All school personnel having access to records
should receive periodic training in security, with emphasis upon privacy
rights of students and parents.

Records should be kept under lock and key at all times, under the supervision of the designated professional.

Formal procedures should be established whereby a student or his
parents might challenge the validity of any of the information contained in
Categories "A" or "B."

DISSEMINATION OF INFORMATION REGARDING PUPILS

The school may, without consent of parents or students, release a student's
permanent record file, including Categories "A" and "B" defined above, to:

other school officials, including teachers, within the district who have a legitimate educational interest. . . .

the state superintendent and his officers or subordinates, so long as the intended use of the data is consistent with the superintendent's statutory powers and responsibilities.

to officials of other primary or secondary school systems in which the student intends to enroll, under the condition that the student's parents be notified of the transfer, receive a copy of the record if desired, and have an opportunity to challenge the record's content via a specified judicial-like procedure. . . .

The school or any school personnel *may not* divulge, in any form, to any persons other than those listed above, any information contained in school records except:

with written consent from the student's parents,
. . . or
in compliance with judicial order, or orders of administrative agencies where those agencies have the power of subpoena. Parents and/or students should be notified of all such orders and the school's compliance.

School districts often face instances in which governmental agencies, local, state, and federal, mandate the release of information on individuals. The principle of informed consent should apply in all cases except those involving school responsibilities under existing child abuse or neglect statutes, and the conferees recommend that governmental agencies, in mandating the provision of information, abide by the recommendations herein contained to assure the rights of privacy. Where identification of individuals is nevertheless legally required, with or without consent, we recommend that written protest be made by the local educational agency to the requesting agency, that parents be informed of the specific information which has been provided, and that legislative redress be sought.

The following public act became effective in November, 1974. It prohibits giving federal funds to schools that deny parents (or students over eighteen) the right to inspect, review, and challenge the content of their child's (or their own) school records. As of this writing there is much concern over the interpretation of this act. For example, college placement files often contain letters of recommendation that were supposedly confidential. Has the right of the writer been violated if the student sees these letters? If high school students or their parents challenge, and have removed, various test data and grades what inferences will prospective employees and college admissions officers make? Would it not be reasonable to infer the removed data were negative? Would that benefit the student?

Family Educational Rights and Privacy Act of 1974

SECTION 438 OF PUBLIC LAW 93-380

PROTECTION OF THE RIGHTS AND PRIVACY OF PARENTS AND STUDENTS

Sec. 438. (a) (1) No funds shall be made available under any applicable program to any State or local educational agency, any institution of higher education, any community college, any school, agency offering a preschool program, or any other educational institution which has a policy of denying, or which effectively prevents, the parents of students attending any school of such agency, or attending such institution of higher education, community college, school, preschool, or other educational institution, the right to inspect and review any and all official records, files, and data directly related to their children, including all material that is incorporated into each student's cumulative record folder, and intended for school use or to be available to parties outside the school or school system, and specifically including, but not necessarily limited to, identifying data, academic work completed, level of achievement (grades, standardized achievement test scores), attendance data, scores on standardized intelligence, aptitude, and psychological tests, interest inventory results, health data, family background information, teacher or counselor rating and observations, and verified reports of serious or recurrent behavior patterns. Where such records or data include information on more than one student the parents of any student shall be entitled to receive, or be informed of, that part of such record or data as pertains to their child. Each recipient shall establish appropriate procedures for the granting of a request by parents for access to their child's school records within a reasonable period of time, but in no case more than forty-five days after the request has been made.

(2) Parents shall have an opportunity for hearing to challenge the content of their child's school records, to insure that the records are not inaccurate, misleading, or otherwise in violation of the privacy or other rights of students, and to provide an opportunity for the correction or deletion of any such inaccurate, misleading, or otherwise inappropriate data contained therein.

(b) (1) No funds shall be made available under any applicable program to any State or local educational agency, any institution of higher education, any community college, any school, agency offering a preschool program, or any other educational institution which has a policy of permitting the release of personally identifiable records or files (or personal information contained therein) of students without the written consent of their parents to any individual, agency, or organization other than to the following—

(A) other school officials, including teachers within the educational institution or local educational agency who have legitimate educational interests;
(B) officials of other schools or school systems in which the student intends to enroll, upon condition that the student's parents be notified of the transfer, receive a copy of the record if desired, and have an opportunity for a hearing to challenge the content of the record;
(C) authorized representatives of (i) the Comptroller General of the United States, (ii) the Secretary, (iii) an administrative head of an education agency (as defined in section 409 of this Act), or (iv) State educational authorities, under the conditions set forth in paragraph (3) of this subsection; and
(D) in connection with a student's application for, or receipt of financial aid.

(2) No funds shall be made available under any applicable program to any state or local educational agency, any institution of higher education, any community college, any school, agency offering a preschool program, or any other educational institution which has a policy or practice of furnishing, in any form, any personally identifiable information contained in personal school records, to any persons other than those listed in subsection (b) (1) unless—

(A) there is written consent from the student's parents specifying records to be released, the reasons for such release, and to whom, and with a copy of the records to be released to the student's parents and the student if desired by the parents, or
(B) such information is furnished in compliance with judicial order, or pursuant to any lawfully issued subpoena, upon condition that parents and the students are notified of all such orders or subpoenas in advance of the compliance therewith by the educational institution or agency.

(3) Nothing contained in this section shall preclude authorized representatives of (A) the Comptroller General of the United States, (B) the Secretary, (C) an administrative head of an education agency or other records which may be necessary in connection with the audit and evaluation of Federally-supported education program, or in connection with the enforcement of the Federal legal requirements which relate to such programs: Provided, that, except when collection of personally identifiable data is specifically authorized by Federal law, any data collected by such officials with respect to individual students shall not include information (including social security numbers) which would permit the personal identification of such students or their parents after the data so obtained has been collected.

(4) (A) With respect to subsection (c) (1) and (c) (2) and (c) (3), all persons, agencies, or organizations desiring access to the records of a student shall be required to sign a written form which shall be kept permanently with the file of the student, but only for inspection by the parents or student, indicating specifically the legitimate educational or other interest that each person, agency, or organization has in seeking this information. Such form shall be available to parents and to the school official responsible for record maintenance as a means of auditing the operation of the system.

(B) With respect to this subsection, personal information shall only be transferred to a third party on the condition that such party will not permit any other party to have access to such information without the written consent of the parents of the student.

(c) The secretary shall adopt appropriate regulations to protect the rights of privacy of students and their families in connection with any surveys or data-gathering activities conducted, assisted, or authorized by the Secretary or an administrative head of an education agency. Regulations established under this subsection shall include provisions controlling the use, dissemination, and protection of such data. No survey or data-gathering activities shall be conducted by the Secretary, or an administrative head of an education agency under an applicable program, unless such activities are authorized by law.

(d) For the purposes of this section, whenever a student has attained eighteen years of age, or is attending an institution of postsecondary education the permission or consent required of and the rights accorded to the parents of the student shall thereafter only be required of and accorded to the student.

(e) No funds shall be made available under any applicable program unless the recipient of such funds informs the parents of students, or the students, if they are eighteen years of age or older, or are attending an institution of postsecondary education, of the rights accorded them by this section.

(f) The Secretary, or an administrative head of an education agency, shall take appropriate actions to enforce provisions of this section and to deal with violations of this section, according to the provisions of the Act, except that action to terminate assistance may be taken only if the Secretary finds there has been a failure to comply with the provisions of this section, and he has determined that compliance cannot be secured by voluntary means.

(g) The Secretary shall establish or designate an office and review board within the Department of Health, Education, and Welfare for the purpose of investigating, processing, reviewing, and adjudicating violations of the provisions of this section and complaints which may be filed concerning alleged violations of this section, according to the procedures contained in sections 434 and 437 of this Act.

(b) (1) (i) The provisions of this section shall become effective ninety days after the date of enactment of section 438 of the General Education Provisions Act.

(2) (i) This section may be cited as the Family Educational Rights and Privacy Act of 1974.

In response to the demands for accountability (see Unit VI) more school districts are releasing their test scores to the public. In this article Hawes discusses some possible dangers of such releases, presents some examples of reporting procedures, suggests twelve sound ways to announce test results, and tells what to do if the scores are low.

Releasing Test Scores: Urgent or Unthinkable

GENE R. HAWES

Release student test scores to the public?

Ten years ago, the idea was enough to make most superintendents shake. Not any more, however. In growing numbers, school officials not only are thinking seriously about releasing scores for their districts but are actually doing it. Some even release results in a way once considered more inflammatory than any other—by individual school rather than by district.

Why has it become suddenly urgent for these schoolmen to do what is

From *Nation's Schools*, April 1972, 89, 4: 41–55. Reprinted with permission from Nation's Schools, April 1972. Copyright 1972, McGraw-Hill, Inc., Chicago. All rights reserved.

still deemed unthinkable by some of their colleagues? One reason, mainly: to satisfy mounting public needs and demands for accountability and for hard data on what schools are accomplishing with public monies.

It is essentially for this reason, too, that state legislatures and state education departments have begun to require public release of test results annually. California introduced public reporting of results for each of its 1,100 school districts in 1965 when the state first mandated reading achievement testing in Grades 1 to 3. Four years later it extended the release requirement to cover basic achievement and academic ability (or IQ) testing mandated for both Grades 6 and 12.

Virginia's state board of education similarly introduced public announcement of achievement and academic ability results in its state testing program for Grades 4, 7 and 11 late last summer. Mean scores are reported for every grade in each of the state's 133 school districts.

One of the most striking developments in the trend toward public release, which began in big city school systems, has been the voluntary decision by individual superintendents to announce test results. Extensive reports of test results and related factors for each school building, for example, recently were introduced by the school districts of Tulsa, Okla.; Columbus, Ohio; and New Rochelle, N.Y. Each superintendent in these districts decided independently of any external requirement to make the results regularly available as an important step in public accountability.

In spite of the decisions reached in Tulsa, Columbus and New Rochelle, however, many schoolmen continue to consider public release of test scores hazardous.

Possible dangers: Foremost among possible dangers in releasing test scores is public misunderstanding. The grade-equivalent scores most commonly used to express achievement tend to leap out at the typical taxpayer or newsman, overshadowing any dry but essential qualifications given with them.

Says Elma Armistead, assistant superintendent of the Lindbergh School District in St. Louis County, Mo., who prepares test result reports distributed internally to district principals every year: "There would be real concern and fear if these were used publicly because we have different programs in different buildings. We feel some real dangers would result if the community started comparing schools or grades by average test standings. Teachers in the low-scoring schools especially would feel that they were on the firing line." It's hard enough, she finds, to have professionals use the results with necessary insight. "Even when I give the report to the principals," she notes, "I caution them to be careful not to use the results in isolation to compare either teachers or youngsters."

Objections in Virginia: In Virginia, many superintendents have serious reservations about the state's recent decision to release results for each district. Hermann Lee, who heads the Rockbridge County schools, states that among superintendents he knows "there was considerable opposition to having this done." Among Lee's own misgivings: Tests used in the state testing program are normatively referenced while they should instead be criterion-referenced; test results reflect the work of the schools only in the cognitive domain, neglecting their work in the psycho-motor and affective domains. Still, Lee believes that "the time to hide information about the schools is long since past," and that the release stirred a new resolve to improve in certain "pockets" of his district.

"What you really have to do is explain the whole situation to the public," he declares. "Tell them everything—or tell them nothing." Accordingly, soon after release of the results, he held an open discussion meeting with the public, explaining tests and test scores generally, discussing differences in the results due to widely varying per pupil expenditures and other factors, and giving his recommendations for district action in areas where the Rockbridge schools appeared weak.

In the Roanoke schools, approaching release of test results spurred special efforts "to acquaint the public with the nature of test scores and possible pitfalls and misinterpretations in using them," Superintendent Roy Alcorn says. Prior to announcing the results, Roanoke's school board issued background news statements and held informal press briefings explaining how to interpret test results. "With these advance preparations, no special difficulty developed after the results were actually released," Alcorn comments.

For the future, Alcorn states, "We'll be putting more emphasis on regular reports of how well the schools are doing." One large project now under way: an overall assessment report in which test scores will serve as only one of several means of evaluation. Others may include a retention-rate profile, a profile of graduates who enter post-high school programs, and perhaps longitudinal data on graduates' progress in employment or college.

Eighteen years of releasing: In the few individual districts that have long made test results routinely available to the public, enthusiasm runs high. Such is the case in Springfield, Mo., where annual districtwide results have been reported for 18 consecutive years at open school board meetings, most recently last July with achievement test standings for each K-12 grade (see Display 1).

Among scores on 50 different subtests covered in that report, only three fell below corresponding national norms. "The community takes pride in our test results," comments Superintendent J. E. Kuklenski. "Test scores represent just one means of evaluation," he emphasizes, "but to some of our publics, this is the thing they want to see." Results for individual schools in the district are not made public.

Rationale for releasing by schools: Superintendents who recently have decided to release results on their own initiative, however, have deliberately

Display 1 Reporting—Springfield style: Using this simple form of report for each districtwide K-12 grade, the Springfield, Mo., school system makes its test results public annually at an open school board meeting. The report gives only the Springfield median with third and first quartile points, compared to corresponding points nationally.

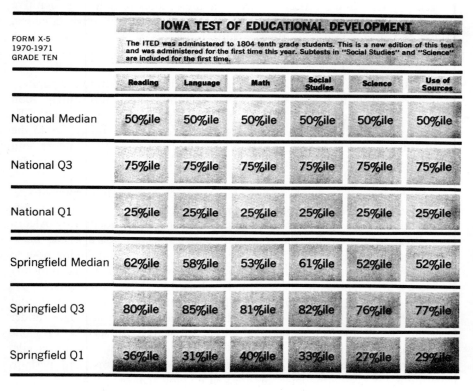

FORM X-5 1970-1971 GRADE TEN	IOWA TEST OF EDUCATIONAL DEVELOPMENT					
	The ITED was administered to 1804 tenth grade students. This is a new edition of this test and was administered for the first time this year. Subtests in "Social Studies" and "Science" are included for the first time.					
	Reading	Language	Math	Social Studies	Science	Use of Sources
National Median	50%ile	50%ile	50%ile	50%ile	50%ile	50%ile
National Q3	75%ile	75%ile	75%ile	75%ile	75%ile	75%ile
National Q1	25%ile	25%ile	25%ile	25%ile	25%ile	25%ile
Springfield Median	62%ile	58%ile	53%ile	61%ile	52%ile	52%ile
Springfield Q3	80%ile	85%ile	81%ile	82%ile	76%ile	77%ile
Springfield Q1	36%ile	31%ile	40%ile	33%ile	27%ile	29%ile

chosen to give them school by school as well as districtwide. Tulsa Superintendent Gordon Cawelti tells why in saying his release of testing and related data in October 1970 "was an attempt to focus the attention of the staff and the public on the work of the schools for accountability."

That attempt took the form of a scrupulously detailed, 134-page book, *Profiles of achievement in the Tulsa Public Schools: a school-by-school report of achievement test results and related factors for the 1969–1970 school year.*

Cawelti sees a good chance that similar decisions to release school-by-school test scores will be made in time by many more school systems across the country. "It's been very slow in coming voluntarily," he observes, "but I think that it probably will grow to be a fairly typical practice nationally."

The kind of accountability Tulsa hopes to achieve by releasing school-by-school test scores relates directly to cost-effectiveness. In his preface to the *Profiles* report, Cawelti wrote:

"As school dollars have become increasingly scarce, educators are going to be compelled to develop and operate a *systems approach* to learning. Although this is a very complex procedure, it means, very simply, that *all* components of an instructional process be considered and evaluated in program development with particular emphasis on the relative *cost* of particular components. We need to move toward a cost-effectiveness approach to program development in larger school systems, and the full *disclosure* of performance is a very necessary first step."

Cawelti's position rests on the premise that a school system can run greater dangers of public misunderstanding by keeping important information from the public than by disclosing it. At the same time, he realizes the limitations of test scores. General explanation and qualification occupy the first 22 pages of *Profiles*, and each school profile also reports data on qualifying "input" factors related both to pupils and community and to educational resources. Cawelti recognizes, too, that "standardized tests reflect a narrow definition of the goals of the schools, but a concrete one."

To improve future test result reports, Cawelti hopes to add statistics on "residual achievement"—the amount by which actual achievement stands above or below predicted expectancies. "This is the best way to do it," he says, but he has not yet decided on exactly how to gather the information.

Although release of test scores in Tulsa brought on no major problems, it did create some minor ones: Principals in the lower-achieving schools found it difficult to explain their low standing in relation to average achievement, even with accompanying data showing handicaps such as pupils' low socioeconomic levels, low median IQ (given for elementary schools), and high mobility. And the one input factor local newspapers chose to report along with median results by school was the percentage of black pupils rather than pupils' socioeconomic levels. "This didn't go over at all well in the black community," Cawelti says, "and rightfully so."

Because test results change little from one year to the next, future Tulsa *Profiles* probably will be issued every two years.

Paul I. McCloud, who played a leading role in developing and preparing the report as Tulsa's director of instructional research, observes that, "We've received many compliments on the report, and on the superintendent's courage in issuing it." Its general reception by the public, he says, was "very positive."

"Some patrons criticized it because they thought it reflected on low-achieving schools," McCloud adds. "In a follow-up survey we made, however, the bulk of our principals reacted favorably." Major responsibility rests with principals, he says, for explaining the results for individual schools, and for initiating short-term efforts to improve student achievement.

One deplorable misuse of the report, he notes, has been its extensive application by real estate dealers in selling homes near what they assume to be the best schools. Nevertheless, the report intentionally makes no attempt to interpret its factual data on individual schools or to give any kind of rank-order listing. Rather, it portrays a school's grade-level performance by showing the full score ranges and the 25th, 50th and 75th percentile levels within them (see Display 2).

Pioneering by Columbus: Predominantly favorable reaction also followed another, still earlier independent decision to release test results for individual schools in Columbus, Ohio. Made in 1968 by former Superintendent Harold E. Eibling, the decision led to annual issuance of *The Columbus School Profile* starting in May 1969.

When it appeared, Eibling declared that the Columbus schools had "achieved national leadership in public accountability." At that time the report was the most extensive in the country to be made public on test results and related factors for individual schools.

Information released in the Columbus *Profile* is even more voluminous than that given by Tulsa. The full 1970 Columbus report is an 11 by 17 inch book running to nearly 190 pages. Each school's profile graphs the range of test performance in each of two years for eight achievement areas, shows two-year distributions of academic aptitude scores, and gives graphed data on each of 17 "school factors" (see Display 3).

"Generally positive" is the way that Howard O. Merriman characterizes the overall reactions to the report in Columbus. As executive director of evaluation, research and planning, he led the work of designing the complex announcement program.

"There were lots of predictions beforehand that the release would stir up a furor," Merriman says. "But the reactions probably have been more positive than if we'd continued to keep scores confidential."

Extensive press coverage of the *Profile* was "fairly well handled," Merriman judges. It included advance stories on the coming test score release, and accounts of Eibling's press conference announcing the first *Profile*. Some news stories reported expressions of shock by various leaders, especially from the black community, at the low average scores of inner-city schools. These criticisms, however, were not aimed at Columbus' action of releasing results by school.

Current plans call for the annual *Profile* to give a three-year span of test results. New *Profile* editions will reflect a broadened definition of accountability being developed by Superintendent John Ellis.

Quiet debut in New Rochelle: Superintendent Robert R. Spillane of New Rochelle, N.Y., thought so highly of the Columbus *Profile* that he decided to follow its format when making school-by-school data public for the first time last spring.

Viewing the test score release as a "first step toward accountability," Spillane says he "felt it certainly would be important for the district to know what we were accomplishing, building by building." He gave *The New Rochelle School Profile* an effective though quiet debut, sending copies to

Display 2 Reporting—Tulsa style: Test results for each school in Tulsa are released in this graphic form portraying the full range of scores for the selected school grade plus median and third and first quartile points, compared to (1) the citywide score distribution for that grade and (2) the national median. Data on related "input" factors is given at bottom.

Elementary School: CARNEGIE

Membership (November 5, 1969): 816

Principal and Teachers (K-6)	25
Special Education Teachers	2
Corrective Reading Teachers	0
Guidance Counselors	0
Total Staff	27

STANFORD ACHIEVEMENT TEST
INTERMEDIATE II
GRADE 5—APRIL, 1970

"National" Norm Median Grade Equivalent=5.7 (Shown by dotted line)

Q3 Median Q1	PARAGRAPH MEANING		SPELLING		ARITHMETIC APPLICATIONS		SOCIAL STUDIES		SCIENCE		Q3 Median Q1
Q3	6.5	7.0	6.8	7.4	6.2	7.8	6.3	6.4	6.3	6.9	Q3
Median	5.3	6.2	5.5	6.4	5.3	6.3	5.2	5.7	5.0	6.0	Median
Q1	4.3	5.0	4.4	5.2	4.2	5.4	4.3	4.8	4.0	4.7	Q1
	All-City	This School	All-City	This School	All-City	This School	All-City	This School	All-City	This School	

RELATED "INPUT" FACTORS

Pupils and Community				Educational Resources		
Factor	All-City	This School		Factor	All-City	This School
Economic Level	Average	High		Teachers with Advanced Degrees	23.8%	34.6%
A.F.D.C. Pupils	9.5%	0.0%		Teachers New to This Building	21.6%	15.4%
Negro Pupils	13.9%	0.0%		Average Years Teaching Experience	12.6	13.6
Pupil Mobility	33.7%	14.3%		Average Homeroom Size	26.0	30.1
Average Attendance	94.4%	96.2%				
Median I.Q. (Grade 3)	101	112				

247

Display 3 Reporting—Columbus style: This graphic report of input factors and test results made public by the Columbus, Ohio, schools is now the country's most elaborate form of report on results for individual schools. Report shown for an elementary school gives a two-year comparison of results, to be expanded to a three-year comparison in the future.

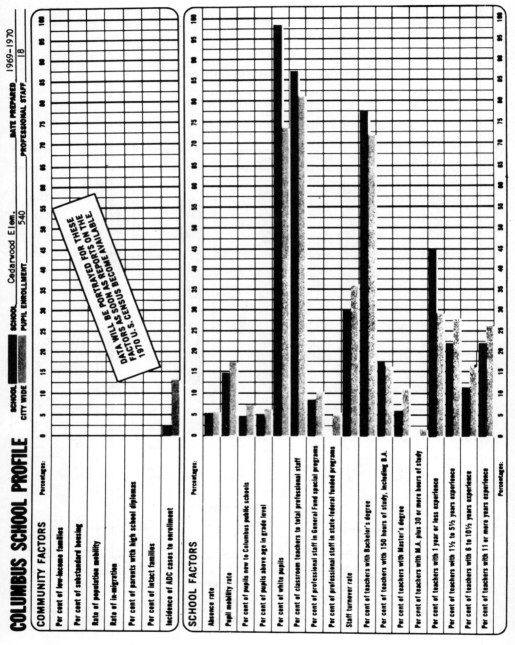

HOW TO READ THE COLUMBUS SCHOOL PROFILE CHARTS

ACADEMIC APTITUDE

In the *academic aptitude* section, if the median on the school bar or on the city bar occurs at a standard score of 50, the students as a group performed at the national norm. If the median occurs at a number greater than 50, the group performed *above* the national norm. If the median occurs at a number *less* than 50, the group performed *below* the national norm. The example below shows how the four parts of the bars under *academic aptitude* should be read:

QUARTILE I	QUARTILE II	QUARTILE III	QUARTILE IV
Performance of the lower ¼ of all students tested	Performance of the lower-middle ¼ of all students tested	Performance of the upper-middle ¼ of all students tested	Performance of the top ¼ of all students rated

MEDIAN

(Half of the pupils scored below and half scored above this point)

ACHIEVEMENT

In the *achievement section*, the school bars and the city bars can be compared to National Norm Grade Placements. If the test was given at Grade 6 it is expected that the median performance on the school and city bars will occur at the National Norm Grade Placement of Grade 6. If the test was given at Grade 8, the median performance should occur at Grade 8 National Norm Grade Placement.

Each of the four parts of the school and city bars may also be compared to National Norm Grade Placements. For example, if the test was given in Grade 6 and the break between the first and second parts of the school bar occurs at Grade 4, then one-fourth the students in Grade 6 at that school scored two grade levels below the national norm. The example below shows how the bars under *achievement* should be read:

National Norm Grade Placements are based on the scores of a large representative group of students across the country, called the norming group. Each grade placement represents the average performance of students in the norming group who were at that grade level when tested. For example, a placement of Grade 6 on any of the subtests means that on that test the median number of items answered correctly by Columbus students was the same as for the Grade 6 students in the norming group.

270 East State Street
Columbus, Ohio 43215

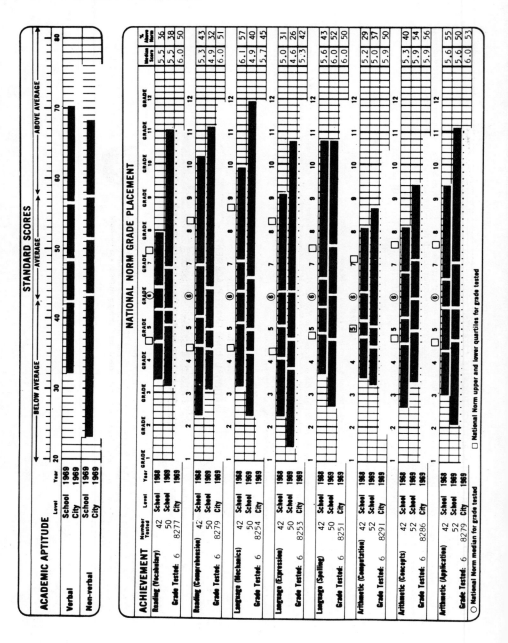

libraries and interested community organizations, and placing reference copies at the reception desk in each school. Local newspapers, preoccupied with controversies over finance and busing, hardly mentioned the report.

"Community reaction was mixed," Spillane observes. "Some parents with youngsters in open classroom programs felt the *Profile* didn't reflect what their children were doing. Some administrators had to be restrained from using it as a club over teachers' heads." He's pleased to see it cited at meetings by persons representing both sides of school issues, however, and sums up by saying, "Overall, I see that it's brought some very positive steps."

Easing tensions in California: Following California's decision seven years ago to announce districtwide test results, considerable tension developed among the state's educators. Teachers in low-achieving schools felt threatened by the step, and some teachers even refused to give the state-mandated tests. San Francisco school authorities originally fought the decision but became enthusiastic supporters after gaining experience with test score release.

"Usually we'll have some bombs that fall somewhere in the state," says William P. Baker about reaction to test announcements in recent years, "but I'm not aware of any serious problems that occurred this year." Baker, deputy superintendent of East Side Union High School District in San Jose, is chairman of the test advisory committee for the state board of education.

In his own and surrounding districts, the public by now has become "rather sophisticated" about test results, Baker observes. People in his district started developing their sophistication in 1955, he explains, when the district first made test results for each school available at open school board meetings. It is not uncommon, he adds, for districts to release school-by-school results, though they are required by law to give districtwide scores only.

In California, substantial responsibility rests with the individual district for interpreting local test results. The latest central report giving results for each district statewide was nearly 600 pages long, Baker observes, and future reports may run still longer. (See Display 4)

"An excellent start on the problem of making such a complex body of information understandable has been made by the California State Education Department," he says. In addition to medians in achievement and academic aptitude testing, the department gives per pupil data on ten background factors such as expenditures, socioeconomic level, and ethnic composition. Each district interprets its own results when presenting them to the local school board as required by law.

Another California superintendent, L. Edward Holden of San Leandro Unified School District, sees no grave problems raised for a district by the state-mandated release. "The schools belong to the public," he says. "The public has a right to know."

In his district's K-12 schools, Holden points out, "We have some schools with lower test results than others. If we seem to have problems in

Display 4 Reporting—California style: Complex chart on facing page shows how the California State Department of Education releases scores for all districts in the state. The test reports enable each district to compare its median achievement scores and various other characteristics with those of all other districts in the state, as well as with districts similar in type of organization and number of pupils.

> Columns in the chart:
> *Factor value:* the "raw" numerical value for each input and output factor.
> *Group rank:* percentile ranks that compare each district with others having similar organization (unified, elementary or high school) and daily attendance.
> *State rank:* how a district compares with all other California districts, regardless of type of organization or ADA.
> Additional columns (not shown): *'Z' score* and *deviations from state mean* provide data for overcoming the unequal internal limitation of percentile rankings.

> The California report actually is divided into three sections: Part I, a statewide analysis and summary; Part II, percentile ranks and normalized standard scores for achievement test scores and other school district factors (the example on facing page is drawn from this section); and Part III, prediction of achievement test scores for each California school district. According to Alex Law, chief of the California education department's Office of Program Evaluation, Part III was designed to assist school personnel in analyzing the data secured from the state testing program.

those schools, we push harder to help them cope with problems by giving them more instructional support."

But other California districts apparently need to do more in applying their results to improve learning. State Superintendent Wilson C. Riles recently declared that the state testing program now "serves more as fodder in political and legislative wrestling matches than it does as a source of improved instruction for the child." He sees it being used "more for comparative than diagnostic purposes."

In spite of Riles's distress, the experiences of the Springfields, Columbuses, Tulsas and other districts in diverse parts of the country indicate that test results can be released to the public, even school by school, with more helpful than harmful effects. As William Baker of San Jose puts it:

"Perhaps school officials have been defensive about test results for too long. I'm not sure myself what it is they're trying to protect. Of course schools with underprivileged pupils will have depressed scores. In our district, though, we think that some of our best schools are ones below the median. Knowing test results can help the public first see where steps need to be taken, and then see where gains have been made."

TWELVE *SOUND* WAYS TO ANNOUNCE TEST RESULTS

If you're thinking about releasing test results to the public, make sure the scores are carefully presented and explained. Otherwise, they'll seem like

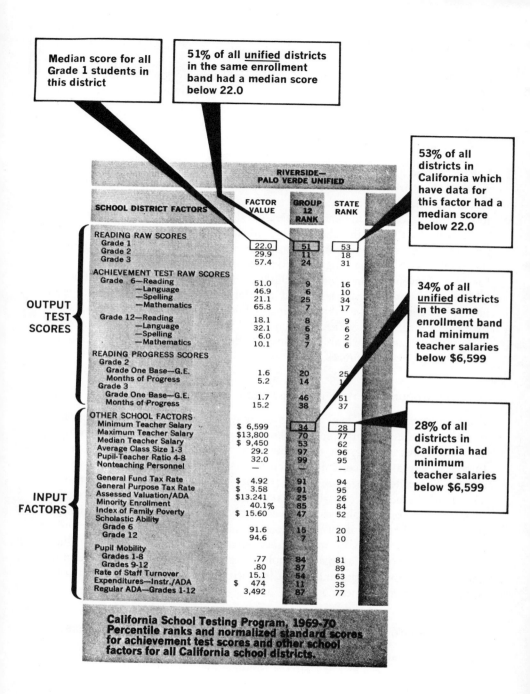

Median score for all Grade 1 students in this district

51% of all **unified** districts in the same enrollment band had a median score below 22.0

53% of all districts in California which have data for this factor had a median score below 22.0

34% of all **unified** districts in the same enrollment band had minimum teacher salaries below $6,599

28% of all districts in California had minimum teacher salaries below $6,599

RIVERSIDE—
PALO VERDE UNIFIED

SCHOOL DISTRICT FACTORS	FACTOR VALUE	GROUP 12 RANK	STATE RANK
READING RAW SCORES			
Grade 1	22.0	51	53
Grade 2	29.9	11	18
Grade 3	57.4	24	31
ACHIEVEMENT TEST RAW SCORES			
Grade 6—Reading	51.0	9	16
—Language	46.9	6	10
—Spelling	21.1	25	34
—Mathematics	65.8	7	17
Grade 12—Reading	18.1	8	9
—Language	32.1	6	6
—Spelling	6.0	3	2
—Mathematics	10.1	7	6
READING PROGRESS SCORES			
Grade 2			
Grade One Base—G.E.	1.6	20	25
Months of Progress	5.2	14	1
Grade 3			
Grade One Base—G.E.	1.7	46	51
Months of Progress	15.2	38	37
OTHER SCHOOL FACTORS			
Minimum Teacher Salary	$ 6,599	34	28
Maximum Teacher Salary	$13,800	70	77
Median Teacher Salary	$ 9,450	53	62
Average Class Size 1-3	29.2	97	96
Pupil-Teacher Ratio 4-8	32.0	99	95
Nonteaching Personnel	—	—	—
General Fund Tax Rate	$ 4.92	91	94
General Purpose Tax Rate	$ 3.58	91	95
Assessed Valuation/ADA	$13.241	25	26
Minority Enrollment	40.1%	85	84
Index of Family Poverty	$ 15.60	47	52
Scholastic Ability			
Grade 6	91.6	15	20
Grade 12	94.6	7	10
Pupil Mobility			
Grades 1-8	.77	84	81
Grades 9-12	.80	87	89
Rate of Staff Turnover	15.1	54	63
Expenditures—Instr./ADA	$ 474	11	35
Regular ADA—Grades 1-12	3,492	87	77

OUTPUT TEST SCORES

INPUT FACTORS

California School Testing Program, 1969-70 Percentile ranks and normalized standard scores for achievement test scores and other school factors for all California school districts.

just so much mish-mash. To get off on the right foot, follow this compendium of advice from test experts and schoolmen actually involved in releasing test scores.

1. Don't spring the report on the public.

Let the public and press know ahead of time that test results are going to be released. Use briefing sessions and school publications to explain the concept and nature of testing and to share portions of the district's agenda of work to be done before results can be released. (The schedule for the first public test release by Columbus schools listed 30 steps, ranging from preparing copy for the printer to distributing the test report to schools.) When acquainting the public with testing, suggests Nicholas Criscuolo, supervisor of reading for New Haven, Conn., public schools, "It's important to stress that, in addition to standardized tests, the district administers diagnostic tests to identify strengths and weaknesses in specific skills that cannot be measured by standardized tests." Information of this sort, adds Criscuolo, assures parents that teachers are able to pinpoint deficiencies in students' skills and redirect teaching procedures.

2. Introduce the results with a basic explanation.

Lead off reports with explanations of why the results are being released, what tests were administered, and how to understand the information given. The Columbus *Profile* not only identified the tests used but went a step further to explain the content of each test. An example: "Language (Expression)—These items measure the correctness and effectiveness of expression. The items, based on a classroom dialog and a paragraph, require the student to select the word or phrase which correctly fits the blank or the underlined passage." Background information on explaining test scores can be found in standard testing textbooks and in users' manuals provided by test publishers.

Points out New Haven's Criscuolo: "Release of naked scores is nebulous and does not develop the understanding citizens need concerning what standardized scores really mean."

3. Prepare a tabular summary of test results for the local press.

Although less satisfactory than the full data display given in the actual report, a press summary might head off the publication of misleading or ineffective summaries prepared by newspapers themselves. Tables made by the Tulsa newspapers gave only two not too useful items for each school: median scores and percentage of black pupils. A better summary might have resulted had the press been supplied by the school district with tables showing the full score range, followed by the median in parentheses, and the socioeconomic background of the school population with percentage of black pupils in parentheses.

4. Consider ways to report separate scores for special samples.

When deciding how results will be presented, be alert to special possibilities available through advanced data processing analyses made by the school system or the test publisher. A simple analysis of pupil mobility, for example, can give separate test results for pupils enrolled for at least two or three consecutive years and for pupils more recently enrolled (the accomplishments of the school program will be better reflected for the former group). With proper advance preparation, separate results can be obtained for almost any defined group. Breakdowns of separate scores should supplement, not replace, the general test report on school-by-school results.

5. Shy away from composite scores for each school.

Composite scores invite misinterpretation and misuse by encouraging arbitrary rankings of schools. Most schoolmen experienced in releasing test scores agree that scores which give a single index for overall performance in reading, math or language arts can be convenient when used internally by people knowledgeable about testing and learning. Used externally, however, composites can give the mistaken impression of packing everything about a school into one rank number.

6. Don't limit yourself to medians.

Whether a district announces test results on a districtwide or school-by-school basis, reporting only the median or mean scores for each grade tested is grossly inadequate. Average scores alone lead citizens to forget that any grade or school includes both high and low-achieving pupils. Districts that inform the public with special success commonly give, in addition to mean scores, each grade's first and third quartile points (25th and 75th percentiles) and sometimes its full range of scores as well (see Displays 2 and 3 for examples).

7. Avoid using grade-equivalent scores if possible.

These scores, the type most often used for releasing achievement test results, are likely to be misunderstood by both the informed and uninformed. Burton Faldet, educational assessment director for Science Research Associates, declares: "The grade-equivalent score can be a very misleading index of test performance to present to the public." Reason: The public assumes that the purely descriptive levels indicated by the score are desirable objectives or standards. For example, says Faldet, the widely stated aim of "reading at grade level," as defined by grade-equivalent scores, is far too often simply assumed to be a reasonable goal. Since "grade level" by definition is the median score on the national norms, however, half of all students necessarily read "below" grade level. A readily available and more understandable form in which to release results publicly, he advises, is the percentile-in-grade type of achievement test score beginning to gain in use. Still better, he adds, would be a score that shows longitudinal growth.

8. Avoid implying that national norms are desirable standards.

Almost every announcement now cites "national norms" as reference points, with results above implied to be good and results below to be poor. It would be far more realistic and informative, however, to use performance in previous years, or expectancies, or performance criteria (when available) as the reference points. Nicholas Criscuolo notes that New Haven, now in its fourth year of publicly reporting reading scores, uses both national averages and previous performance. "To draw any conclusions concerning the effectiveness of the system's reading program," he adds, "tests need to be the same from year to year. If this year's test is a complete revision of last year's, few meaningful conclusions can be drawn." Perhaps the best reference points of all would be learning goals, however defined, that had been realistically developed and validated by the schools and accepted by the community in advance.

9. For school-by-school release, report on related factors whenever possible.

When releasing results for individual schools, it is essential to announce data on "input factors," such as absence rate, staff experience, and pupil-teacher ratio, that influence learning and help account for differences in schools' test results (see Display 5). Because no satisfactory systematic method of connecting test results and input factors has been developed, however, avoid interpretation. Leave it to the reader to connect specific factors with specific results intuitively.

10. Sum up what the results mean.

Accompany your district's test announcement with a separate statement briefly summarizing the practical significance of results. Otherwise, the dis-

GOING BEYOND SCORES: REPORTING WHAT AFFECTS LEARNING

If Johnny can't learn, there may be many reasons why. He could be attending his fourth school in two years, or sitting in a class with 45 other students, or missing school frequently.

Because standardized tests don't take any of this into account, many districts feel they must. They supplement test scores with data on widely varying factors that affect learning.

The data simply alerts the public to consider more than scores when judging school performance. It appears without interpretation because, as the Columbus public schools explain in their latest test report, "exact effects of factors which precede or intervene in the educational process are not specifically known." The Columbus report adds, however, that "the relationship of certain factors to educational success has been fairly well established. For example, poverty is a high correlate of low achievement. As the incidence of low-income families rises, it is rather simple to predict the increase of low achievement."

To get an idea of the kind of input factors reported, look at this list compiled from the California, Columbus and Tulsa test reports:

California

minimum teacher salary
maximum teacher salary
median teacher salary
average class size
pupil-teacher ratio
non-teaching personnel
general tax fund rate
general purpose tax rate
assessed valuation per
    unit of average daily
    attendance
minority enrollment
index of family poverty
scholastic ability
pupil mobility
rate of staff turnover
instructional expenditures
    per ADA unit
regular average daily
    attendance

Columbus

per cent of substandard
    housing
per cent of intact families
incidence of ADC cases
    to enrollment
absence rate

pupil mobility rate
per cent of pupils new to
    Columbus public schools
per cent of pupils above
    average in grade level
per cent of white pupils
per cent of classroom
    teachers to total
    professional staff
per cent of professional
    staff in General Fund
    special programs
per cent of professional
    staff in state-federal
    funded programs
staff turnover rate
per cent of teachers with:
bachelor's degree
150 hours of study
    including B.A.
master's degree
M.A. plus 30 or more
    hours of study
1 year or less experience
1½ to 5½ years'
    experience
6 to 10½ years' experience
11 or more years'
    experience*

Tulsa

economic level
AFDC pupils
black pupils
pupil mobility
average attendance
median IQ (Grade 3)
teachers with advanced
    degrees
teachers new to this
    building
average years' teaching
    experience
average homeroom size

* Initially, Columbus
planned to include four
additional variables (per
cent of low-income families,
rate of population mobility,
rate of in-migration, and
percent of parents with
high school diplomas) but
later dropped them when
sufficient information could
not be obtained from the
1970 Census.

trict risks having erroneous—and possibly damaging—interpretations made by community leaders or newsmen. The statement should assess not only the results' broad significance in the community but their specific significance in each area of potentially serious controversy as well. It might tell, for example, that certain low-achieving schools are lower because of their high concentration of disadvantaged pupils, or that low scores in math can be attributed to introduction of a new program. It also should mention any steps the district intends to take toward improvement in areas where the schools appear weak. The summary should be released separately by the superintendent, not included in the basic report of results. The impartial explanation in the basic report, rather than drawing conclusions, should enable the reader to understand the factual data.

11. Explain the need for special evaluation of innovative programs.

Widely used achievement tests are designed to assess learning in established curriculums and may not adequately reflect achievement in a school district's innovative programs. For this reason, in announcing achievement results, it may be advisable to explain briefly that certain innovative programs require special evaluation. New Rochelle's Supt. Robert Spillane notes, for example, that special evaluation is being arranged for the extensive "open education" program in his district. The public should be made aware that current assessment techniques may not apply at all well to new programs.

12. Ideally, report by 'residual achievement.'

The most meaningful and realistic way to release test results would be by showing the extent to which the district's efforts changed what pupils would otherwise have been expected to accomplish. That change is what Tulsa Supt. Gordon Cawelti calls "residual achievement" and views as the best form of release. Schools can be held accountable only for change above or below expected achievement, Cawelti maintains. Apparently no district has yet released results in this form, although techniques for doing it have become available. One technique—a form of score called "growth scale values"—is explained by SRA's Faldet: Growth scale values extend in one continuous scale from Grades 1 through 12 and range from zero to more than 800. They can depict the steady educational growth of a pupil or pupil group.

SRA, which produces these scales, also provides computer-produced plots of progress in past grades on growth scale charts and predicted expectancies in learning growth for the coming year. With these predicted expectancies, a district can show how actual achievement stands above or below expected achievement. The expectancies, Faldet says, "serve as a gauge against which to decide what to expect, whether to intervene, and by how much intervention has been effective."

WHAT TO DO IF SCORES ARE LOW

Nobody wants to see headlines that illuminate poor test scores. Nevertheless, they typify the kind of trouble you can find yourself in when test scores fall below national norms.

If your district appears headed for unfavorable headlines, how you release scores can be more critical than ever. So pay attention to the suggestions earlier and especially to the six that follow. They won't get you off the hook—they're not designed to. But if you think your district is doing better than national norm comparisons show, they may help you get that message across to the public.

1. Explain what national norms are and what they do and don't mean. Point out that the particular achievement test used was administered by its publisher to a national sample of the student population. Resulting scores placed each student at some point on a line between the highest and lowest scores. A percentile rank was then assigned to each score. The median score (or 50th percentile or norm) for each grade in the sample is the score above and below which half the students in that grade fell. It is also the score your district compares its results against. When the local median is higher than the national, your district is "above the norm"—lower, and it's below.

Don't hesitate to mention that a district whose median scores fall below the medians on national norms may be doing a bang-up job, all things considered. Likewise, a district with median scores above national norms may not be doing as well as it should. By all means explain that, although every parent wants his child to be above the norm, it's statistically possible for only half the children in any given grade to be there.

2. If current test results, though low compared to national norms, are better than those of previous years, say so. That indicates improvement.

3. Outline new programs (or types of increased instructional support) that would be needed to improve performance in problem grades or schools if plans for such strengthening have been made. Costs of these new efforts might be stressed to develop public support.

4. Report on special national norms that match grades or schools in your district more closely than general national norms (national norms for ESEA Title I pupils, for example).

5. Stress and document important learning outcomes not measured by standardized tests (as in your physical education, art, music, health, vocational and citizenship programs).

6. Develop and announce with test results other long-range measures of school system accomplishment—such as graduates' occupations and starting salaries or percentage of students going on to college.

How Columbus tells what testing is all about

Look to Columbus for ideas on how to get across the meaning and usefulness of test scores.

Since 1969 when they publicly released their first *School Profile* of school-by-school test results (see Display 3), Columbus school officials have distributed truck loads of explanatory and informational materials to parents, community groups, and school staff. One of the first items: a 5 by 7 inch take-home leaflet used as a report card stuffer prior to release of the maiden report. The leaflet asked and answered five basic questions: What is the *Columbus School Profile*? What information does it provide? Why was it developed? How is it related to individual pupil test scores? and Where can citizens get more information?

Another item, distributed mainly to principals and teachers, gave 14 reasons why the test report would be useful to them. An example of one cited use: "For identification of schools where special programs would be very appropriate, whether they are reading programs for the educationally deprived or advanced math courses for very able students."

Still another item, a single sheet telling how to use the report and describing input and output factors, was attached to the individual school profile taken home by each elementary and junior high student.

In addition to these and other items, then Superintendent Harold H. Eibling made the public statement shown in Display 6 when the first test report was released. He explained the purpose of the report, told what it revealed about Columbus schools, and indicated how the new information would be used. Citizens who wanted further clarification of testing procedures or results were urged to attend special briefings.

Display 6   Statement made by Columbus Supt. Harold H. Eibling at press conference held the day the first *Columbus School Profile* was released.

The Columbus public schools today are releasing publicly for the first time the results of a comprehensive study conducted in all 124 elementary and all 27 junior high schools in the school system.

The report, called the *Columbus School Profile*, graphically portrays information about community and school conditions and the results of academic aptitude tests and achievement tests in reading, arithmetic and language.

The tests were given to approximately 8,200 sixth-graders and approximately 7,000 eighth-graders in September and October of 1968.

The report is presented on a school-by-school basis with a separate profile for each of the participating schools. The community and school factors provide background in understanding the total teaching-learning situation in each school.

In looking at the report, four questions immediately come to mind:

1. What is the purpose of the *School Profile?*
2. What does it show about each school, its students, its staff, and the entire school district?
3. How will *School Profile* information be used?
4. Will such a program be continued in the future?

Let's take these questions in order.

The purpose of the *Columbus School Profile* is really three-fold: to strengthen the accountability of the school system to the public; to improve communications between the school system and the people it serves; and to provide a common factual basis for identifying problems, setting priorities, carrying out improvements, and reviewing results.

It is obvious that the public is today demanding more accountability from all public agencies. People want to know what kind of results they are getting from their investment of tax dollars. The release of the *Columbus School Profile* puts the Columbus public schools in the forefront of public agencies in responding to this urgent demand.

The release of this information opens new avenues of communications between the schools and parents, as well as with the community at large. It offers concrete information which can be the basis for discussion on the future course of our educational programs, and it provides a vast reservoir of information which will be invaluable in planning future programs to meet pupil needs.

Now, what does the information contained in these *Profiles* tell us about our schools? Briefly told, it reveals that:

1. Sixth-graders and eighth-graders in Columbus exhibit virtually the same aptitude for academic achievement as do sixth and eighth-graders throughout the nation.

2. When comparisons were made between the achievement of Columbus pupils and pupils in New York City, Philadelphia, and San Francisco, the only school systems for which achievement results were available, it was found that Columbus pupils performed as well or better. As an example, Columbus eighth-graders scored 1.1 years higher than Philadelphia eighth-graders in reading achievement.

3. The range of pupil performance within each school was much greater than the difference in performance between any two schools.

4. The percentage of Columbus sixth-graders who scored above the median grade-level based on national norms in each subtest is as follows: reading (vocabulary), 49.7; reading (comprehension), 48.5; arithmetic (computation), 41.1; arithmetic (concepts), 43.9; arithmetic (application), 49.2; language (mechanics), 43.9; language (expression), 40.7; and language (spelling), 48.9. Nationally, 50 per cent of the pupils taking the tests are expected to score above the median and 50 per cent below.

5. The percentage of Columbus eighth-graders who scored above the median grade-level based on national norms in each subtest is as follows: reading (vocabulary), 45.9; reading (comprehension), 46.4; arithmetic (computation), 43.4; arithmetic (concepts), 49.8; arithmetic (application), 47.7; language (mechanics), 49.0; language (expression), 49.5; and language (spelling), 41.0.

A summary of the report is attached to provide a broader picture of the test results as well as school and community information.

There really are no surprises in this report. It has become common knowledge during this decade that pupil performance in large city school districts lags behind national norms. The encouraging thing to note is that Columbus pupils achieved so close to national norms on several subtests. For example, 49.8 per cent of Columbus eighth graders scored at or above the national norm on the arithmetic concepts subtest. This means that only 14 more pupils, out of the 7,000 tested, would have had to score at or above the national norm for the median of the entire grade to have been at the national norm.

However, there are clear indications of room for improvement in such areas as the performance of Columbus pupils, staff recruitment and assignment, coping with such problems as pupil mobility and poverty, and the preservice and inservice training of professional personnel.

I am pleased to note, however, many of these areas of need are already being improved through programs financed by the 8.2 mill levy passed last November. We have, of course, just gotten under way with these programs since January 1.

Among the most vital provisions of the levy are the employment of reading-improvement teachers and arithmetic-improvement teachers, the employment of teacher aides to relieve teachers of non-instructional duties, the establishment of libraries in all elementary schools, and the strengthening of curriculum development and supervision. The expansion and conversion of the summer program to a tuition-free basis also appears to be a judicious move, in view of the information contained in the *Profile Report*.

Since we now have this wealth of information, how will it be used?

First, the *Profile* of a school will be sent home with each pupil attending that school by Wednesday, May 28.

Second, we are holding special orientation meetings with all members of the professional staff.

Third, an orientation meeting has been scheduled for 7:30 p.m., Tuesday, May 27, at Mohawk High School for representatives of interested civic organizations.

Fourth, the complete report is being distributed to each school and all public libraries today for anyone to see and study.

Fifth, copies of the report are being mailed to persons who have previously expressed an interest in this type of information about our schools.

Sixth, follow-up meetings to answer questions or clarify specific points will be scheduled after parents and the community have had an opportunity to see the profiles and study the report.

I would caution each person studying these *Profiles* and the report, however, to be careful in making comparisons of any sort.

Preferably, these *School Profiles* will be used to understand where a school, or the school system, is at this point in time.

Education is a complex process. The reader should exercise caution in making simplistic comparisons and should avoid ranking schools on any one factor. In fact, we must be skeptical of any such ranking, or simple cause-effect explanations. In addition, comparisons with other school districts are at best difficult. For in such comparisons, as it is within a school district, there are many factors which go into producing an environment for teaching and learning.

In addition to making the *Profile* report available to all segments of the community, this information is, of course, vital to our educational planning.

The *Profile* report and Neighborhood Seminar recommendations will be studied carefully during the summer. Many areas of school operation will require additional research.

We envision the future of releasing test data as an extension of what we have begun here today. Granted, this first attempt is limited in its scope, dealing only with few academic and achievement factors at just two grade levels. However, it is our plan to expand the program so that in future years we will have information to permit a year-to-year comparison of changes in pupil performance within each school.

Ebel suggests that standardized test results are relevant to assist in evaluating teachers. Do you accept this premise? If so, how can we avoid misusing such results? If you reject Ebel's position what is your counterargument?

Use Standardized Tests in Evaluating Teachers?

ROBERT L. EBEL

Recently a number of advanced graduate students in education were asked to comment on the problem of evaluating teacher competence. The problem was put to them in terms of this situation: A superintendent had lost confidence in his ability to evaluate teachers on the basis of direct observation of their work. He proposed to use standardized tests of pupils achievement as

Reprinted from *Instructor*, copyright © November 1973 by the Instructor Publications, Inc., used by permission.

an alternative source of evidence of their competence. The question thus became: Was the superintendent's decision a sound one? Or, perhaps, was there at least some merit in his decision?

A number of the graduate students gave inadequate answers. Many of them recognized the complexity of the problem of evaluating teacher competence. But far too many said—or implied by their rejection of all suggested solutions—that it was a problem for which no solution exists. Yet every school and college has, and uses, procedures for discriminating between the better and the poorer teachers. Surely these procedures are far from perfect, but if they are worthless—if a good teacher is in fact indistinguishable from a poor one—what rational basis exists for specially planned programs of teacher education, for certification requirements, for selective employment, for periods of probation, or for salary differentials?

A few of the students said correctly that the superintendent should use all of the relevant information he could lay his hands on in forming judgments about the competence of teachers. Such information would include not only his own impressions from classroom visits, but also the opinions of supervisors, of fellow teachers, of pupils, and of parents. All this is true and relevant. But the weakness in many of the students' answers was their inclination to state or to imply that standardized tests of student achievement could provide *no valid evidence whatsoever* of teacher competence.

Now it is quite proper to recognize the limitations of standardized tests as measures of pupil achievement, and their limitations as bases for inferring teacher competence. Many of the students did a thorough job on this aspect of their answers. But is it proper to then conclude, as a majority of them did, that these limitations of standardized tests are so serious, so intractible, that no valid judgments can be made on the basis of scores they yield, however sophisticated, reasonable, and otherwise well-informed the superintendent may be?

If a superintendent notes low achievement test scores for a class and immediately concludes, on this evidence alone, that the teacher is incompetent, he would be no wiser than a physician who hears a patient's complaint of pains in the lower abdomen and immediately concludes, on this evidence alone, that the patient has appendicitis. Is it not equally foolish to deny the possibility that poor pupil achievement *might* be the result of poor teaching, just as pain in the lower abdomen *might* be the results of appendicitis? If we concede that pupil achievement is influenced by teaching then we must also concede that standard test scores have something useful to contribute to the complex process of evaluating teacher competence.

If the education we offer is good, we ought to be able to provide some evidence to show that it is. We ought not to camouflage incompetence or excuse mediocrity by asserting that the important results we are getting defy detection.

One factor limiting the usefulness of standardized achievement tests is that the content of such tests never exactly matches the curricular goals of a local school district or individual classroom teacher. Cox and Sterrett suggest a procedure which recognizes this lack of a perfect match and therefore provides more meaningful information.

A Model for Increasing the Meaning of Standardized Test Scores

RICHARD C. COX
BARBARA G. STERRETT

Authors' abstract   The model which is proposed to increase the meaningfulness of standardized test scores includes the following steps: (a) a precise description of curriculum objectives and a specification of pupil achievement in reference to these objectives; (b) the coding of each item on a standardized test with reference to the curriculum, and (c) the assignment of two scores to each pupil, one reflecting his achievement on items that test content to which he has been exposed; the other his achievement on items that test content beyond his present status in the curriculum or not represented in the curriculum at all.

Scores from standardized tests are typically interpreted in a norm-referenced sense. That is, raw scores are converted to certain normative standard scores such as percentile ranks, age or grade equivalents, and/or stanines which indicate the relative order of individuals. These norm-referenced scores are then used to make comparisons of individuals, classes, schools, or school systems by ranking the individual or group in relation to the norm group.

Chief among the disadvantages or criticisms of standardized achievement tests is that since they cover broad areas of content, none is totally appropriate to any one specific curriculum. Standardized tests which are designed to be comprehensive enough for all curricula may be useful to none. Thus the normative scores which pupils receive on these tests may have little or no relation to performance in their own curriculum. If a teacher is concerned with pupil achievement in a specific content area, a norm-referenced score is not the most appropriate measure. What is needed is a criterion-referenced test which reflects the degree to which an individual's achievement corresponds to some desired performance standard. Criterion-referenced test scores indicate whether or not essential behaviors have been achieved; they

From *Journal of Educational Measurement*, Winter 1970, 7, 4: 227–228. Reprinted with permission of author and publisher.

provide information as to what the pupil does or does not know with reference to a well specified criterion (Popham & Husek, 1969).

What is being proposed is a method for obtaining criterion-referenced information from standardized tests. The model includes (a) a precise description of curriculum objectives and a definition of pupil achievement in relation to these objectives, (b) the coding of each standardized test item with reference to the curriculum, and (c) the scoring of the standardized test in accordance with pupil position in the curriculum.

The first step in the procedure is to specify curriculum objectives and to define pupil achievement with reference to these objectives. It is necessary to have a clear description of the curriculum through which pupils proceed so that each pupil's level of achievement can be determined according to a specified criterion. This criterion could be the number of skills a pupil has been exposed to, the number of units of work he has achieved, or any other measure of actual performance in the curriculum. This first step in the model may be difficult to apply in instructional programs if curriculum objectives are not specified or if achievement criteria are not clear.

Step two of the procedure is the coding of each standardized test item with reference to the curriculum objectives. Each item on the test or on a particular subtest of interest must be examined for content in order to compare it with the curriculum objectives. Occasionally a test item may not correspond to any objective, or a curriculum objective may not be tested by any item. At this point the available information consists of the coded test items and the position of each pupil in the curriculum. With these data it is possible to determine which of the items validly tests each pupil in the sense that an item covers objectives to which that pupil has been exposed.

Step three in the procedure is the scoring of the standardized test separately for each pupil, taking into account his placement in the curriculum. The model is appropriate, in fact easier to apply, for group instruction, since placement in the curriculum is uniform. It is possible to assign each pupil a score on those items which test objectives he has studied. In addition, it is possible to provide a score on the remainder of the test which combines testing objectives beyond the student's present level of achievement or objectives excluded from the curriculum. It would be possible, for example, to report that a given pupil has correctly answered 80% of the items he was expected to know and 30% of the remaining items. Not only are these new scores more meaningful with reference to the curriculum, but they also provide data which are different from the typical standardized test scores.

REFERENCES

Popham, W. J., & Husek, T. R. Implications of criterion-referenced measurement. *Journal of Educational Measurement*, 1969, 6, 1–9.

RECOMMENDED READING FOR UNIT V

Badal, Alden W., and Larsen, Edwin P. "On Reporting Test Results to Community Groups," *Measurement in Education*, 1970, 1, 4: 1–12.

Clark, D. Cecil. "Competition for Grades and Graduate-Student Performance." *The Journal of Educational Research*, 1969, 62, 8: 351–354.

Ebel, Robert L. "Should School Marks Be Abolished?" *Michigan Journal of Secondary Education*, 1964, 6: 12–18.

Ebel, Robert L. "Shall We Get Rid of Grades?" *Measurement in Education*, 1974, 5, 4: 1–5.

Gold, Richard M. "Academic Achievement Declines under Pass-Fail Grading." *Journal of Experimental Education*, 1971, 39, 3: 17–21.

Holt, John. "I Oppose Testing, Marking and Grading." *Today's Education*, March 1971, 60: 28–31.

Melby, Ernest O. "It's Time for Schools To Abolish the Marking System." *Nation's Schools*, 1966, 77: 104.

Millman, Jason. "Reporting Student Progress: A Case for a Criterion-Referenced Marking System." *Phi Delta Kappan*, 1970, 52: 226–230.

Ricks, James H., Jr. "On Telling Parents about Test Results." *Test Service Bulletin No. 54. The Psychological Corporation*, 1959.

Stallings, William H., and Lesslie, Edwood K. "Student Attitudes toward Grades and Grading." *Improved College and University Teaching*, Winter 1970, 18: 66–68.

Wesman, Alexander G. "Testing and Counseling: Fact and Fancy." *Measurement and Evaluation in Guidance*, 1972, 5, 3: 397–402.

TRENDS AND ISSUES
IN EVALUATION

Of the numerous topics that are classified as trends or issues in evaluation, some have already been dealt with in previous units. The role of measurement in Unit I is somewhat of an issue. The structure of intelligence discussed by McNemar and Guilford in Unit IV represents another issue. Releasing test scores (Unit V) classifies as both a trend and issue. In this final unit the other trends or issues covered are: the social consequences of testing, criterion-referenced testing, program evaluation, accountability, the etiology of intelligence, and definitions of test fairness.

Ebel's article discusses possible social consequences of testing. He acknowledges some dangers of testing and suggests how they may be minimized. In conclusion, he examines the social consequences of not testing. This aspect of the issue deserves careful consideration. Historical evidence would support him and most, if not all, measurement specialists would agree.

Classical theory and techniques of test construction were developed on the assumption that the purpose of testing is to differentiate among individuals with respect to the degree to which they possess a certain characteristic. The interpretation of an individual's score on such a test may be based on its relation to the scores of other individuals, or norm-referenced. For some purposes of testing comparisons among individuals may be irrelevant. Instead each person is compared to a standard or a set of standards. Interpreting a score in this way is called criterion-referenced interpretation. (Some writers use the phrase content-referenced.) In education, recent support for criterion-referenced measurement has originated largely from the emphasis on behavioral objectives, sequencing and individualization of instruction, development of programmed materials, a learning theory that suggests time is the important variable in the degree of learning, and a belief that norm referencing promotes unhealthy competition to achieve excellence. Klein and Kosecoff discuss some of the major issues in constructing tests appropriate for criterion-referenced interpretation.

Within the past decade educators have utilized an increased number of different programs. Many of the new programs were funded externally with the stipulation that careful evaluations be conducted to ascertain their effectiveness. Although educators have always made implicit evaluations of their programs (i.e. they have made decisions about them), formal explicit program evaluation is reasonably new and fraught with difficulties. Renzulli discusses some of the major problems and issues of program evaluation in his article.

Recently, an enlarged concept of accountability has entered the educational world. Certainly, program evaluation is related to, and perhaps grew out of, the idea of accountability. But accountability is broader in concept, more controversial, and even more difficult to implement. Evaluation hopefully determines whether a program is effective; accountability, to some critics, is a move to fix the blame for any perceived educational inadequacies. Teachers generally fear accountability programs because they suspect a general tendency to blame teachers for educational shortcomings. The articles by Ornstein and Talmage, and Wrightstone et al. discuss some of the rhetoric, realities and measurement problems of the accountability movement.

One of the most long standing controversies in psychology is the heredity-environment debate. With respect to intelligence test score performance the debate, although not resolved, has become more sophisticated. The original question, "Which factor affects intelligence test scores?", was replaced by "What is the proportionate contribution of each?". A more recent question is "How do heredity and environment interact to affect test scores?" Since the publication of several papers by Jensen (e.g. 1968, 1969, 1970) some psychologists have returned to the second question. The article by Anastasi clears up some of the common fallacies regarding the heredity-environment issue. Many, but not all, psychologists would agree with most of the points she makes. Other articles on this hotly debated subject are listed in the references at the end of the this unit.

The issue of test fairness to minority groups is another very controversial topic. Flaugher's article presents a very good nontechnical discussion of it. The papers referenced at the end of his article are some of the very best in print and interested readers could well profit from reading all of them.

In this article Ebel presents possible social consequences of testing and not testing. It is true that parents can and do misuse test scores. But as Ebel states: "We do not flatter our fellow citizens when we tell them, in effect, that they are too ignorant, or too lacking in character to be trusted with the knowledge of their children, or of themselves, that we possess." Critics of Ebel's position would likely respond by saying we are not in the business of flattery. Does the quote above seem inconsistent with Ebel's statement about laymen's interpretation of IQ scores?

Compare his position on the concept of the IQ and aptitude tests with Dyer's (Unit I), McNemar's (Univ IV), and Guilford's (Unit IV). Which side of the heredity-environment controversy (see Anastasi, this unit) would appeal more to him? Note Ebel's position about releasing test scores to the layman. Would he be in substantial agreement with Hawes (Unit V)?

I believe the last paragraph of Ebel's article to be of utmost importance. He is most likely correct that without tests "educational opportunities would be extended less on the basis of aptitude and merit and more on the basis of ancestry and influence; social class barriers would become less permeable." Those members of minority groups who are hostile to testing would do well to consider that prognostication.

The Social Consequences of Educational Testing

ROBERT L. EBEL

Tests have been used increasingly in recent years to make educational assessments. The reasons for this are not hard to discover. Educational tests of aptitude and achievement greatly improve the precision, objectivity and efficiency of the observations on which educational assessments rest. Tests are not alternatives to observations. At best they represent no more than refined and systematized processes of observation.

But the increasing use of tests has been accompanied by an increasing flow of critical comment. Again the reasons are easy to see. Tests vary in quality. None is perfect and some may be quite imperfect. Test scores are sometimes misused. And even if they were flawless and used with the greatest skill, they would probably still be unpopular among those who have reason to fear an impartial assessment of some of their competencies.

From *School and Society*, Vol. 92, No. 2249, Nov. 14, 1964, pages 331–334. Reprinted with permission of authors and *Intellect Magazine*.

Many of the popular articles critical of educational testing that have appeared in recent years do not reflect a very adequate understanding of educational testing, or a very thoughtful, unbiased consideration of its social consequences. What appears in print often seems to be only an elaboration and documentation of prejudices and preconceptions, supported by atypical anecdotes and purposefully selected quotations. Educational testing has not fared very well in these articles.

Among the charges of malfeasance and misfeasance that critics have leveled against the test makers there is one of nonfeasance. Specifically, they are charged with having shown lack of proper concern for the social consequences of educational testing. These harmful consequences, the critics have suggested, may be numerous and serious. The more radical among them imply that, because of what they suspect about the serious social consequences of educational testing, the whole testing movement ought to be suppressed. The more moderate critics claim that they do not know much about these social consequences. But they also suggest that the test makers don't either, and that it is the test makers who ought to be doing substantial research to find out.

Perhaps so, but it is worth noting that the scarcity of formal research on the social consequences of educational testing does not mean that there is no reliable knowledge about those consequences, or that those engaged in educational testing have been callously indifferent to its social consequences. Further, scientific research on human behavior may require commitment to values that are in basic conflict with our democratic concerns for individual welfare. If boys and girls are used as carefully controlled experimental subjects in tough-minded research on social issues that really matter, not all of them will benefit, and some may be disadvantaged seriously. Our society is not yet ready, and perhaps should never become ready to acquiesce in that kind of scientific research. Finally, and unfortunately, research seldom if ever reveals clearly what society *ought* to do about a particular problem.

Before proceeding further, let us mention specifically a few of the harmful things that critics have suggested educational testing may do:

1. It may place an indelible stamp of intellectual status—superior, mediocre or inferior—on a child, and thus predetermine his social status as an adult, and possibly also do irreparable harm to his self-esteem and his educational motivation.
2. It may lead to a narrow conception of ability, encourage pursuit of this single goal, and thus tend to reduce the diversity of talent available to society.
3. It may place the testers in a position to control education and determine the destinies of individual human beings, while, incidentally, making the testers themselves rich in the process.
4. It may encourage impersonal, inflexible, mechanistic processes of evaluation and determination, so that essential human freedoms are limited or lost altogether.

Consider first, the danger that educational testing may place an indelible stamp of inferiority on a child, ruin his self-esteem and educational motivation, and determine his social status as an adult. The kind of educational testing most likely to have these consequences would involve tests purporting to measure a person's permanent general capacity for learning. These are the intelligence tests, and the presumed measures of general capacity for learning they provide are popularly known as IQ's.

Most of us . . . are well aware of the fact that there are no direct, unequivocal means for measuring permanent general capacity for learning. We know that all intelligence tests now available are direct measures only of achievement in learning, including learning how to learn, and that inferences from scores on those tests to some native capacity for learning are fraught with many hazards and uncertainties.

But many people who are interested in education do not know this. Many of them believe that native intelligence has been clearly identified and is well understood by expert psychologists. They believe that a person's IQ is one of his basic, permanent attributes, and that any good intelligence test will measure it with a high degree of precision. They do not regard an IQ simply as another test score, a score that may vary considerably depending on the particular test used and the particular time when the person was tested.

One of the important things test specialists can do to improve the social consequences of educational testing is to discredit the popular conception of the IQ. Wilhelm Stern, the German psychologist who suggested the concept originally, saw how it was being overgeneralized and charged one of his students coming to America to "kill the IQ." Perhaps we would be well advised, even at this late date, to renew our efforts to carry out his wishes.

If human experience, or that specialized branch of human experience we call scientific research, should ever make it quite clear that differences among men in achievement are largely due to genetically determined differences in talent, then we ought to accept the finding and restructure our society and social customs in accord with it. For the present, it will be more consistent with the facts as we know them, and more constructive for the society in which we live, to think of talent, not as a natural resource like gold or uranium to be discovered, extracted and refined, but as a synthetic product like fiberglass or D.D.T.—something that, with skill, effort and luck, can be created and produced out of generally available raw materials to suit our particular needs or fancies.

This means, among other things, that we should judge the value of the tests we use not in terms of how accurately they enable us to *predict* later achievement, but rather in terms of how much help they give us to *increase* achievement by motivating and directing the efforts of students and teachers. From this point of view, those concerned with professional education who have resisted schemes for very long-range predictions of aptitude for, or success in, their professions have acted wisely. Not only is there likely to be much more of dangerous error than of useful truth in such long-range predictions, but also there is implicit in the whole enterprise a deterministic conception of achievement that is not wholly consistent with the educational facts as we know them, and with the basic assumptions of a democratic, free society.

Consider next the danger that a single widely used test or test battery for selective admission or scholarship awards may foster an undesirably narrow conception of ability and thus tend to reduce diversity in the talents available to a school or to society.

Here again, it seems, the danger is not wholly imaginary. Basic as verbal and quantitative skills are to many kinds of educational achievement, they do not encompass all aspects of achievement. Overemphasis on a common test could lead educators to neglect those students whose special talents are neither linguistic nor mathematical.

Those who manage programs for the testing of scholastic aptitude always insist, and properly so, that scores on these tests should not be the sole consideration when decisions are made on admission or the award of scholarships. But the question of whether the testing itself should not be varied from person to person remains. The use of optional tests of achievement permits some variation. Perhaps the range of available options should be made much wider than it is at present to accommodate greater diversity of talents.

The problem of encouraging the development of various kinds of ability is, of course, much broader than the problem of testing. Widespread commitment to general education, with the requirement that all students study identical courses for a substantial part of their programs, may be a much greater deterrent of specialized diversity in the educational product. Perhaps these requirements should be restudied too.

What of the concern that the growth of educational testing may increase the influence of the test makers until they are in a position to control educational curricula and determine the destinies of students?

Those who know well how tests are made and used in American education know that the tests more often lag than lead curricular change, and that while tests may affect particular episodes in a student's experience, they can hardly ever be said to determine a student's destiny. American education is, after all, a manifold, decentralized, loosely organized enterprise. Whether it restricts student freedom too much or too little is a subject for lively debate. But it does not even come close to determining any student's destiny, not nearly as close as the examination systems in some other countries, ancient and modern.

But test makers have, I fear, sometimes given the general public reason to fear that we may be up to no good. I refer to our sometime reluctance to take the layman fully into our confidence, to share fully with him all our information about his test scores, the tests from which they were derived, and our interpretations of what they mean.

Secrecy concerning educational tests and test scores has been justified on several grounds. One is that the information is simply too complex for untrained minds to grasp. However, essential information revealed by the scores on most educational tests is not particularly complex. If we understand it ourselves, we can communicate it clearly to most laymen without serious difficulty. To be quite candid, we are not all that much brighter than they are, much as we may sometimes need the reassurance of thinking so.

Another justification for secrecy is that laymen will not use test scores properly. It is true that test scores can be misused. They have been in the past and they will be in the future. But does this justify secrecy? Can we minimize abuses due to ignorance by withholding knowledge? We do not flatter our fellow citizens when we tell them, in effect, that they are too ignorant, or too lacking in character to be trusted with the knowledge of their children, or of themselves, that we possess.

Seldom acknowledged, but very persuasive as a practical reason for secrecy regarding test scores, is that it spares those who use the scores from having to explain and justify the decisions they make. Preference is not, and should not, always be given to the person whose test score is the higher. But if score information is withheld, the disappointed applicant will assume that it was because of his low score, not because of some other factor. He will not trouble officials with demands for justification of a decision that, in some cases, might be hard to justify. But all things considered, more is likely to be gained in the long run by revealing the objective evidence used in reaching a decision.

If specialists in educational measurement want to be properly understood and trusted by the public they serve, they will do well to shun secrecy and to share with the public as much as it is interested in knowing about the methods they use, the knowledge they gain, and the interpretations they make. This is clearly the trend of opinion in examining boards and public education authorities. Let us do what we can to reinforce the trend. Whatever mental measurements are so esoteric or so dangerous socially that they must be shrouded in secrecy probably should not be made in the first place.

Finally, let us consider briefly the possibility that testing may encourage mechanical decision making, at the expense of essential human freedoms of choice and action.

Those who work with mental tests often say that the purpose of all measurement is prediction. They use regression equations to predict grade point averages, or expectancy tables to predict the chances of various degrees of success. Their procedures may seem to imply not only that human behavior is part of a deterministic system in which the number of relevant variables is manageably small, but also that the proper goals of human behavior are clearly known and universally accepted.

In these circumstances, there is some danger that we may forget our own inadequacies and attempt to play God with the lives of other human beings. We may find it convenient to overlook the gross inaccuracies that plague our measurements, and the great uncertainties that bedevil our predictions. Overestimating our own wisdom and virtue, we may project our particular value systems into a pattern of ideal goals and behavior for all men.

If we do this, if we ignore our own limitations and those of our tests, if we undertake to manage the lives of others so that they will qualify as worthy citizens in our own particular vision of utopia, we do justify the concern that one harmful social consequence of educational testing may be mechanistic decision making and the loss of essential human freedoms.

A large proportion of the decisions affecting the welfare and destiny of a person must be made in the midst of overwhelming uncertainties concerning the outcomes to be desired and the best means of achieving those outcomes. That many mistakes will be made seems inevitable. One of the cornerstones of a free society is the belief that in most cases it is better for the person most concerned to make a major decision affecting him, and to take the responsibility for its consequences.

The implications of this for educational testing are clear. Tests should be used as little as possible to *impose* decisions and courses of action on others. They should be used as much as possible to provide a sounder basis of *choice* in individual decision making. Tests can be used and ought to be used to support rather than to limit human freedom and responsibility.

Let us now have a brief look at the other side of the coin—the social consequence of *not* testing. If the use of educational tests were abandoned, the encouragement and reward of individual efforts to learn would be made more difficult. Excellence in programs of education would become less tangible as a goal and less demonstrable as an attainment. Educational opportunities would be extended less on the basis of aptitude and merit and more on the basis of ancestry and influence; social class barriers would become less permeable. Decisions on important issues of curriculum and method would be made less on the basis of solid evidence and more on the basis of prejudice or caprice. These, it seems to us, are likely to be the more harmful consequences, by far. Let us not forego the wise use of good tests.

Klein and Kosecoff discuss some of the major issues and procedures in constructing tests appropriate for criterion-referenced interpretation. Compare the purpose offered here for criterion-referenced tests with the purposes discussed by Airasian and Madaus in Unit I.

Some advocates of criterion-referenced testing seem to imply that once objectives have been delineated appropriately the task of item writing becomes trivial. Klein and Kosecoff correctly rebut that implication. Of the great number of possible items for even highly specific objectives, only a small sample is chosen from this large pool. Further, multiple-choice item difficulty depends a great deal on the homogeneity of the alternatives (note the example in the article). This complicates the interpretation of the scores and makes uncertain the meaning of mastery.

After reading the section on content validity recall the Lennon article (Unit II). Can you now answer question four in the editor's introduction to that article?

Finally, consider the authors' point that for parents to interpret "satisfactory progress" they must use as a frame of reference the rate of progress of other students (a norm-referenced interpretation).

Issues and Procedures in the Development of Criterion Referenced Tests

STEPHEN P. KLEIN
JACQUELINE KOSECOFF

PREFACE

A visitor to our planet Earth surveying the current state of educational testing would very likely be confused by what he found. He would observe, for

The report upon which this article is based was funded by the ERIC Clearinghouse on Tests, Measurement and Evaluation. The Clearinghouse operates under contract with the National Institute of Education, U.S. Department of Health, Education and Welfare. Contractors undertaking such projects under government sponsorship are encouraged to express freely their judgment in professional and technical matters. Points of view or opinions do not therefore represent official National Institute of Education position or policy.

example, the increasing use of tests in all phases and facets of the educational process including the evaluation of instructional personnel. He would learn, too, about the great technological improvements that have been made in tests and in their administration, scoring, and reporting procedures. All of these factors would tend to support the notion that tests are fulfilling an important and vital role. On the other hand, this same observer might also hear the valid complaints of the growing cadre of test critics. These critics complain that present tests are inappropriate for most educational decision making and, if a test is not going to be used for decision making, why bother giving it in the first place?

Perhaps one of the quickest ways of alleviating our visitor's confusion is to point out to him certain changes that have been occurring in education and testing during the past few years. For example, most expert test construction in the past has focused upon a relatively few kinds of assessment instruments, such as those that are used to decide whether a student should be accepted for college. Comparatively little help has been given to the classroom teacher to diagnose individual student needs or assess the outcomes of particular instructional programs. Now, however, there is growing desire to individualize instruction, to assess validly the outcomes of instructional programs, and to hold teachers and administrators responsible for actual gains in student performance. These trends have increased the demand on test developers for appropriate tools to facilitate the measurement process, because existing measures are useful for some important educational decisions but are not designed to meet all needs. It is evident, therefore, that test critics are complaining not about tests per se, but about the need for certain kinds of quality measures that are not currently available.

It is within this context of increased need for and reliance on valid test results that the movement towards so-called "criterion referenced tests" (CRT) has been given new impetus. A criterion referenced measure is essentially "one that is deliberately constructed so as to yield measurements that are directly interpretable in terms of specified performance standards."[1] (Glaser & Nitko, 1971). The pertinent question is whether or not the individual has attained some significant degree of competence on an instructional performance task (Harris, 1972).

Measures with these characteristics are, of course, not new to education. What is new is the range of importance of the decision areas for which they are being employed or emphasized and the attention they are being given by measurement and curriculum experts alike (Airasian & Madaus, 1972; Baker, E., 1972; Keller, 1972; Davis, 1972, 1973; Hawes, 1973). It would not be surprising, therefore, for us to witness during the next few years a number of major contributions to testing theory and methodology arising from the use of criterion referenced tests. Further, the improvement of such measures is likely to have many ramifications for instructional practice, since with improved tools even more reliance is likely to be placed upon the results obtained. For example, a bill is now pending before the United States Congress that would require criterion referenced test data to make funding decisions affecting thousands of schools and involving several million dollars (Quie, 1973).

It is appropriate at this point in time, therefore, for us to examine how criterion referenced tests are constructed and, more importantly, the basic issues and procedures associated with these steps. It is hoped that such an appraisal will clarify some of the basic methodological and theoretical concerns associated with criterion referenced tests that will be examined during the next few years.

This paper is divided into two parts. In the first section the major issues and steps in the development of CRTs are considered. In the second section representative CRT systems in mathematics, as well as important efforts in other content areas, have been selected for review.[2] [The second section is not included here.]

MAJOR ISSUES AND STEPS IN CRT DEVELOPMENT

This section of the paper provides a review of the basic steps in the development of CRTs and the major issues associated with these steps. Although many of the steps and issues have their counterpart in classical test development, the present focus is upon those considerations unique to CRT, and especially those relating to the development of such measures in mathematics. It should be kept in mind, however, that the method chosen to resolve a particular issue at one stage in the development of a CRT is likely to have ramifications for other stages in the developmental process as well as in the interpretation of the scores obtained. In addition, the most important but not necessarily self-evident of these implications are noted, and the primary techniques and procedures that have been used as well as their most important advantages and limitations are identified.

Purpose and Defining Characteristics of CRTs

It is a generally accepted principle that somewhat different kinds of measures have to be constructed for different purposes. This principle also appears to carry over into the development of CRTs. For example, to ensure an adequate level of test reliability, a CRT or series of CRTs that will be used in making a decision about an individual's level of performance will need to be longer than one used for group assessment. Similarly, the focus of the CRTs used for managing an individualized learning segment of a small mathematics unit would be narrower than that used to measure end-of-year performance of all students in a classroom. The characteristics of the target audience, such as their ages and ethnic backgrounds, are also likely to influence the test construction process in terms of the appropriateness of various kinds of stimuli and response formats. Further, the anticipated number of students to be tested and the context in which the testing will occur influence test format, production, distribution, administration, scoring, and analysis.

Figure 1 lists some of the basic purposes that have been noted for using CRTs in terms of the decisions to be made and the focus of the testing (Harris, 1973; Skager, 1973). Three major kinds of decisions have been identified. Decisions relating to the organization of an instructional program are classified as planning decisions. Validating the quality and competency of a program is encompassed by certification decisions. Decisions based on additional investigation of the instructional program are included in a research category. With respect to the focus of the testing program, three classifications are considered. First, a CRT can be primarily involved with the individual student. Second, groups of students such as a classroom or ethnic group can be the focus. And third, the instructional program itself might be the primary unit of concern.

Figure 2 illustrates how differences in the target audience would result in different test items for the same objective. From an inspection of these figures and the foregoing discussion it is apparent that the different uses of CRTs may require different kinds of measures and test models. The fundamental issue underlying these differences is the degree to which the CRT or set of CRTs will provide precise and reliable information about student per-

FIGURE 1   Purposes for Criterion Referenced Tests

Focus of the Testing Program	Type of Decision		
	Planning	*Certification*	*Research*
Student	Diagnosis, Prediction, and Placement	Determination of "mastery," grades, and success of placement	Interactions between the student, the group, and the program
"Group" (Classroom, ethnic, SES cultural, or geographical groups)	Classroom management Curriculum selection	Instructional and administrative accountability	Interactions between group(s) and program, e.g., do students with certain characteristics function better than others in a given situation?
"Program" (A program may be used with one or more groups)	Organization and sequencing of instruction, Curriculum and product development, Needs Assessment	Program Evaluation Analysis of subject matter domain	Comparisons between types of programs Analysis of program components Development of measurement methodology

FIGURE 2   Comparison of General Item Formats for the Same Objective at Different Grade or Age Levels

---

Objective

The student will indicate by marking the appropriate choices on an attitude scale his/her appreciation of the importance of mathematics in everyday life.

	First Graders	*Twelfth Graders*
Format	The student is given a test booklet. Each page is a different color and has a familiar symbol at the top of the page, such as a rabbit. Each page also has the words "Yes" and "No." Directions are provided to the student so that he/she understands to mark the choice that answers the question that is read by the teacher.	The student is given a set of statements and a series of choices ranging from "Strongly Agree" to "Strongly Disagree." The student marks the number of his choice on a machine-scorable answer sheet.
Sample Items	The teacher reads the following kinds of directions and questions: "Now turn to the red page with the rabbit at the top. . . . Now I am going to read you the next question. 'Do you have to know how to work with numbers to tell time?' . . . Now turn to the yellow page with the duck at the top. . . . 'Do you have to know how to add and subtract numbers to catch a ball?' . . . . Now turn to the page with the table at the top. . . . 'Do you have to know how to work with numbers to buy something at the store?' . . . and so forth.	The following kinds of items might appear on a scale to measure the objective: 1. Persons who fill medical prescriptions need to use mathematics frequently in their work. 2. Only a very small part of a carpenter's job requires him to use mathematics. 3. It is more important for a bank teller to make friends easily than it is for him or her to make arithmetic computations accurately. 4. In order to be a good plumber, one would have to be able to do basic arithmetic computations with fractions.
Comments	Note that the child does not have to read the questions, the questions are asked about him or herself rather than some other person, and that the language level and activities are within the students' repertoire of experiences.	The statements are balanced with respect to being positive or negative regarding the importance of mathematics so as to reduce any irrelevant tendencey to agree or disagree.

---

formance relative to various feasibility constraints associated with gathering this information, such as costs and testing time.

Objectives Chosen

As noted in the preface to this paper, one of the essential features of CRTs is their foundation in clearly defined educational objectives. There are, however, a number of issues associated with how these objectives should be developed and stated. The essence of these issues may be summarized by the question: "What kinds of objectives should form the basis for a CRT system?"

Almost all developers of CRTs agree that to assess performance within a given area requires the construction of a set of CRTs rather than a single measure. The problem then arises as to which objectives within an area should become the basis for the CRTs and how broadly or narrowly these objectives should be stated, that is, the extent of each *objective's coverage*. The statement of an objective may be further delineated by defining the *conditions* under which the measurements are made (e.g., open vs. closed book, with or without the aid of a sheet containing needed formulas, and so forth) and/or the *standards* of performance to be reached in order for the objective to be achieved (e.g., "80 percent correct," "in less than 2 minutes," and so forth) (Mager, 1962; Popham, 1965). Implicit or explicit assumptions about the *relative importance* of the objectives and the *characteristics of the area* to be assessed (such as the logical and/or sequential organization of the objectives in it) also influence decisions as to which objectives should form the basis for a CRT system (Popham, 1972).

The resolution of the issues associated with choosing a set of objectives usually hinges upon the anticipated purpose(s) of the CRT system. Thus, there is a consideration of the degree of precision needed relative to various practical considerations. This balance is illustrated by the IOX Criteria for Objective Selection (Popham, 1972).

Some of the procedures that have been used to develop the objectives bases for CRTs systems are described briefly below:

1. *Expert Judgment.* A small group of experts within the area to be assessed meet and, on the basis of their knowledge and experience in the field, jointly decide which objectives are the most important to measure. These objectives are then screened to determine the feasibility of measuring them and, where necessary, to clarify and/or redefine them. This is probably the most common approach.

2. *Consensus Judgment.* Various groups such as community representatives, curriculum experts, teachers, and school administrators decide which objectives they consider to be the most important. A measurement and/or curriculum expert is then responsible for defining and stating these objectives in a way that would permit them to be assessed (Klein, 1972; Wilson, 1973).

3. *Curriculum Analysis.* A team of curriculum experts analyzes a given set of curriculum materials such as textbooks in order to identify, and where necessary infer, the objectives that are the focus of these materials (Baker, R. L., 1972).

4. *Analysis of the Area To Be Tested:* An in-depth analysis is made of an area such as mathematics in order to identify all contents (such as single-digit numerals) and behaviors (such as multiplication with replacement)

that are included in that area (Glaser & Nitko, 1971; Nitko, 1973). The objectives associated with these contents and behaviors are then organized in some systematic fashion, such as in terms of a hierarchy and/or sequence of objectives for the components of the subject area (in mathematics usually referred to as "strands") (Nitko, 1971; Roudabush, 1971; Popham, 1972).

Item Construction and Selection

Once the purpose(s) and the objectives for the CRT system have been delineated, the next step is to construct and/or select test items or tasks to measure the objectives chosen. This is one of the most difficult steps in the total developmental process because of the vast number of test items or tasks that might be constructed for any given objective, even those that are relatively narrowly defined. For example, consider the following objective: "The student can compute the correct product of two single digit numerals greater than 0 where the maximum value of this product does not exceed 20." The specificity of this objective is quite deceptive since there are 29 pairs of numerals that meet this requirement and at least 10 different item types that might be used to assess student performance (see Figure 3). Further, each of the resulting 290 combinations of pairs and item types could be modified in a variety of ways that might influence whether the student answered them correctly. Some of these modifications are:

Vary the sequence of numerals (e.g., 5 then 3 versus 3 then 5).
Use different item formats (e.g., multiple choice versus completion).
Change the mode of presentation (e.g., written versus oral).
Change the mode of response (e.g., written versus oral).

It soon becomes evident that even a highly specific objective could have a potential item pool of well over several thousand items (Hively, 1970, 1973; Bormuth, 1970).

The number of items to construct for each objective is influenced by several factors. Some of these factors are the amount of testing time available and the cost of making an interpretation error, such as saying that a student has achieved mastery when he has not. A survey of current measures reveals that the usual practice is to use about three to five items per objective. This practice appears to stem more from feasibility constraints than any sound foundation in psychometric theory or technology.

The particular item construction and selection approach or combination of approaches chosen to define a CRT program is a major consideration. One reason for this is that the methods used have a direct bearing on the utility and content validity of the CRTs developed and the interpretation of their scores. For example, if there is a hierarchy of objectives and if a CRT is to be based on an objective at a given level of generality in this hierarchy, then

FIGURE 3   Item Types Using the Content of Numerals 3 and 5 for the Objective

The student can compute the correct product of two single digit numerals greater than 0 where the maximum value of this product does not exceed 20.

a. $\begin{array}{r} 5 \\ \times 3 \\ \hline \end{array}$

b. $\overline{5 \times 3} =$

c. $(5)\ (3) =$

d. $5 \cdot 3 =$

e. 5 times $3 =$

f. The product of 5 and $3 =$

g. $5 \times \underline{\quad} = 15$

h. If $x = 5$ and $y = 3$, what is the value of xy?

i. What numeral multiplied by 3 will equal 15?

j. John has 5 apples. Sally has 3 times as many apples as John. How many apples does Sally have?

---

it is likely that the items used will be sampled from the relevant subobjectives. Unless there is a specified hierarchy or an organization of objectives, such systematic sampling is impossible. When this latter situation occurs, one has much less confidence that the measure(s) developed really assess the whole objective. One reason for this concern is that without a systematic plan for guidance, it is very easy to just construct items for those aspects of an objective that are most amenable to measurement rather than those aspects that might be considered most germane or critical. On the other hand, it also seems likely that responsible test developers working without an overall plan are more likely to focus their attention on the most salient (and perhaps most frequently taught) facets of an objective than on those aspects that may be just tangential to what a student must really know or be able to do. Thus, the best compromise between systematic sampling (and thereby improved content validity) and potential instructional relevance is to first develop a provisional systematic plan and then assign items to some or all the components of this plan based upon their perceived relative importance. This latter approach is the one most frequently adopted by major test publishers (Wood, 1961).

A related issue in construction and selection of CRT items is the degree to which the items should be sampled with respect to their relative difficulty within an objective. It is a well known and frequently used principle of test construction that slight changes in an item can affect its difficulty. This is most readily accomplished by varying the homogeneity of the alternatives in a multiple choice item, such as in the two examples below:

Eight hundredths equals
   a. 800
   b. 80
   c. 8
   d. .08

Eight hundredths equals
   a. 800
   b. .80
   c. .08
   d. .008

The extent to which the items within an objective are sampled with respect to difficulty has, of course, a direct bearing on the interpretation of the scores obtained. In other words, if only the most difficult items are used, then the phrase "mastery of the objective" has a very different meaning than if the items were sampled over the full range of difficulties. The fact that the difficulties of items on CRTs (and thus their scores) can be influenced so easily poses real problems to CRT users. To blindly assume that the scores obtained indicate an accurate appraisal of the degree of mastery achieved, merely because a measure is called a "CRT" is an exercise in self-deception.

A third consideration influencing the construction and selection of items is the degree to which an item is dependent upon or related to a particular set of curriculum or institutional materials and techniques (Baker, R., 1972; Skager, 1973). For example, if the instruction only gave students practice in solving multiplication problems in the form used in item types a-e in Figure 3, and if the CRT for this unit only used these same item types, then the CRT would be said to be "instructionally dependent" or biased. It is readily apparent that the more instructionally dependent the CRT, the more likely the effects of instruction would be evidenced in the scores obtained with it and the less generality one could draw from these scores regarding the student's mastery of the objective. On the other hand, instructionally independent tests are more likely to reflect a student's general ability. Thus, an instructionally biased test might be preferred for such purposes as teacher accountability, while an instructionally independent test might be preferred for school accountability and for evaluation studies comparing the effects of different programs.

A fourth issue, and one which has perhaps not received as much attention as it should, is the potential interaction between the objective and how it is measured. It is often assumed, for example, that selected response items (e.g., multiple choice) serve as an effective proxy for constructed response items (e.g., completion or short answer) because the performance of students on the two kinds of items are highly related. Although this may be generally true, it may not be true for certain kinds of objectives; and further, the degree of mastery required to answer a constructed response item is usually greater than it is to answer the selected response item. The relative scoreability of the latter format, however, has led to its use almost exclusively in published measures, including CRTs. It should be recalled that anything affecting item difficulty on a CRT will influence the total score on it and thereby the interpretation of that score.

The foregoing considerations have led to a number of different methods of selecting and constructing items for CRTs. The general features of these methods are described below, but it should be remembered that each of these approaches begins with or involves the development of well-defined statements of the educational objective (s) to be measured.

1. *Panel of Experts.* A group of measurement and curriculum "experts" decide which items to use based on their knowledge and experience of the field (Zweig, 1973). When the experts involved are classroom teachers, this approach may lead to highly instructionally dependent measures.

2. *Systematic Sampling.* This approach is basically a variation of the classical test construction technique. It involves developing for each objective a matrix of contents and behaviors (or tasks) to be assessed. Items are then systematically sampled within this matrix and perhaps along a third continuum of item difficulty as well (Wilson, 1973; CTB/McGraw-Hill, 1973).

3. *Systematic Item Generation.* This is the most sophisticated of the various approaches and starts with the assumption that all the relevant contents, behaviors (or tasks), stimulus and response characteristics, and related factors can be defined for a given domain or universe of objectives (Hively, 1970, 1973; Cronbach, 1971; Skager, 1973). Basic item forms or "shells" are then constructed. Various techniques can then be used to generate the necessary items, including the use of a computer (especially in the field of mathematics) to meet certain prespecified criteria for coverage of the objectives (Kriewall & Hirsch, 1969).

It is evident from these descriptions that as the sophistication of the method improves, generality of the results and the costs of test construction tend to increase. Further, the particular method chosen will be influenced by the nature of the efforts that have been devoted to the generation of the objectives on which the CRTs are based and the purposes for which they will be used. Finally, the degree of sophistication may be limited still further by the clarity of the domain to be assessed, such as mathematics versus "citizenshsip" and the measurement technology available for constructing measures in that domain (e.g., academic achievement versus personality development).

Improving Item Quality

It is axiomatic that all tests and measures be field tested prior to basing decisions upon them. Although it appears that this axiom is often ignored, there are a number of methods that have been suggested for analyzing CRT items in order to identify those that are "faulty." It should be noted, however, that an item that is considered "faulty" or "good" using one method of analysis may not be identified as such using another method (Popham & Husek, 1969). This is illustrated in Table 1. It is apparent, therefore, that the final version of a test may be influenced greatly by the method of item analysis chosen for its construction (Cox & Vargus, 1966; Roudabush, 1973).

There are two basic concepts underlying the item analysis techniques associated with CRTs and at least one of these constructs is present in each analysis method. These two constructs are as follows:

1. An item is considered "good" if it is *sensitive* to instruction, that is, if performance on it is related to the degree of instruction obtained. The methods that rely heavily on this construct are usually used when there is little or no variation in student scores at any one testing. There are problems with such methods, however: they assume that the instruction was indeed effective; they tend to produce instructionally dependent measures; and they are biased by maturation and other irrelevant systematic factors that might tend to improve scores over time. Further, the use of a technique emphasizing sensitivity could easily lead to some rather interesting circular reasoning if one tried to improve the test and an instructional program at the same time.

2. An item is considered "good" if it *discriminates* between those who did well versus those who did poorly on the test as a whole or some "outside" criterion, such as performance in the next step in a sequence of instruction. This involves all the classical item analysis approaches and as such one must accept all the assumptions, advantages, and disadvantages that are normally associated with these techniques (especially item and test variance).

The kinds of analysis methods and their variations that have been suggested are listed below:

1. *Comparison Group.* Give the test to two groups who are known to possess different degrees of skill with respect to the objective(s) measured. One way of doing this is to give the test to those who have versus those who have not received instruction dealing with the objective. A second method is to give the test to those whose normal activities require different levels of attainment of the skill measured (e.g., carpenter versus auto mechanic for an objective dealing with computing the size of various geometric objects).

TABLE 1   Results of Different Item Analyses

Item No.	Item Difficulty		Possible Point Biserial r with Score on Test	Possible Sensitivity to Instruction
	Pretest	*Posttest*		
1	0%	100%	0	High
2	50%	50%	1.00	Low

The next basic step is to identify those items that discriminate best between the groups in the desired direction (that is, the presumably more able should do better). It is important for the purposes of CRT interpretation that if two separate groups are involved, they have the same general intellectual ability or other characteristics that might bias the test results.

2. *Single Group, Pre- and Posttest.* Give the test to the same group twice, once before instruction and again after instruction. Identify those items that discriminate between the two test sessions. A number of item analysis techniques designed specifically for CRTs have used this approach (Popham, 1970; Ozenne, 1971; Kosecoff & Klein, 1973; Roudabush, 1973).

3. *Single Group, Posttest Only.* Give the test to one group of individuals after a fixed period of instruction, that is, all examinees have had the same amount of opportunity to achieve the objective. If the time allotted is somewhat less than that needed for *all* the students to achieve the objective and the students are somewhat heterogeneous in their ability as is common in most classrooms, then the typical item analysis procedures such as computing point biserial correlation coefficients may be employed to identify faulty items. An internal criterion (total score on test) or an external criterion (success in achieving a more advanced skill) may be used (Glaser, 1963). One weakness in this approach is that items having very high or low difficulties will tend to have low biserial coefficients even though they may be very sensitive to instruction. An extreme case would be an item that would be failed by everyone prior to instruction but passed by everyone after instruction. A second weakness is that general intellectual ability as well as the effects of instruction may influence the results and there is no way of cleanly separating these influences.

4. *Single Group, Repeated Measures.* Each student periodically takes the complete test until he is able to achieve mastery. A record is kept of the number of times the student passes and fails each item. Analysis is then made to determine whether the item generally exhibits the desired pattern of failure then success (with no reversals), i.e., a desired pattern would be FFPP and an undesirable pattern would be PFFP. This approach is only applicable where there are no carry-over effects from test session to test session or where truly parallel items may be constructed for each test session and then systematically counterbalanced across sessions and examinees. The advantages of this approach are that it permits relevant scaling of an item within an objective and the analysis is made after all students have become "masters." The labor involved in this approach and the likelihood of finding items that scale well, however, have not contributed to this method's popularity.

One issue that is related to item analysis procedures and that seems to be neglected with respect to CRTs is the problem of knowing whether the final set of items provides adequate coverage of the objective. In other words, how many items are really needed to sample sufficiently a given objective? Further, a procedure is needed for determining whether some of the items are redundant. Although these kinds of issues have been examined in part with the more traditional kinds of tests, the unique demands of CRTs will correspondingly require new ways of dealing with this general problem of knowing when one has appropriate and efficient coverage.

Content Validity

A major concern of CRT developers is in establishing the content validity of their instruments. The three most common ways that have been used to do this are as follows:

1. *Systematic Test Development.* This approach involves presenting the rationale for the systematic procedure employed in terms of why it should result in a content valid test (Hively, 1970, 1973).

2. *Expert Judgment.* Content experts are given a variety of objectives and the items used to measure them. They are then asked to assign the items to their "appropriate" objective. The degree to which they are able to do this accurately reflects on item-objective consistency and thereby on content validity; that is, is a given item really measuring the objective for which it has been constructed? (Dahl, 1971).

3. *Item Analysis.* It is possible to compute internal consistency indices for a CRT and/or see whether an item on a given objective correlates more highly with other items for this objective than it does with items on other objectives. These approaches are limited by all the dangers of internal consistency validation techniques plus the potential problem of no variance on the measures (that is, the students all receive the same score). The latter problem, however, usually appears to be more theoretical than actual, because students do vary in their performance. This variation may be due to a number of factors including the students' general intellectual ability, cultural and environmental backgrounds, and the quality of instruction they receive. If enough students are tested, then one will discover sufficient variance in the levels of performance and/or in the time it takes to achieve a given level. Reports of "no variance" usually stem from failure to sample enough students and/or from the failure to examine the rate at which students master items and objectives. Thus, although one might conceive of a situation in which no variance might occur in a given classroom, it is hard to imagine how this might arise across a variety of classrooms—unless, of course, the test was totally inappropriate for the full range of examinees for whom it was constructed. The real problem, therefore, is not in finding variance but in identifying just that portion of the variance that is due to the student's degree of mastery of the particular objective on which the CRT is based rather than variance due to some extraneous influence.

Item and Test Bias

"Item bias" may be defined as a group by item interaction; that is, the profiles of performance of different groups (such as males versus females) across all items in the test are not parallel. "Test bias" is defined as a group by test interaction; that is, groups do not have the same shaped profile of scores across the various tests being considered (Cleary, 1966; Cleary & Hilton, 1968). Little attention has been paid to CRTs with respect to these kinds of biases, although they have become important topics within the general measurement field.

It should be noted, however, that the identification of a test or set of tests as being "biased" with respect to certain groups does not necessarily mean that the measures should be revised. The reason for this is that such "bias" may only mean that the educational and cultural experiences of the groups taking the tests are systematically different and the basis for these differences and how to deal with them should be examined. It is entirely likely, for example, for a test to appear biased simply because it draws more on the vocabulary from certain texts than it does from others, and the use of the more test-dependent texts is not random in the population of examinees. Wider use of the more dependent texts would, therefore, remove the supposed "bias" in the test; changing the test to be more representative of the texts used would also achieve the same result.

Test Scores

As noted in the preface to this paper, one of the two essential features of a CRT is that an individual's or a group's score on it is interpreted in terms of the level of performance obtained with respect to the achievement of the objective(s) on which the CRT is based. This type of score reporting is contrasted to the norm referenced approach in which a student's or a group's score is interpreted with respect to the performance of other individuals or groups (Popham & Husek, 1969). The primary advantage of the CRT approach is, therefore, its ability to provide a means for describing what the student (or group) can do or what it knows or how it feels without having to consider the skills, knowledge, or attitudes of others.

There is some question, however, as to whether a CRT can really do this (Klein, 1970; Davis, 1971; Ebel, 1972). For example, if parents are told that their child has mastered a given objective or set of objectives, their first question is "Is this performance satisfactory?" In other words, they are asking whether the child is progressing satisfactorily and the only frame of reference one can give in this situation is the rate of progress of other students. The fact that such a normative frame of reference can easily be provided also points out that one can make norm referenced interpretations of

CRT scores. The distinctive feature of a CRT score must, therefore, lie in its *emphasis* on describing the absolute rather than the relative level of performance with respect to an objective or skill. Because of this emphasis, different kinds of scores are generally reported for CRTs than for norm referenced measures. Some of the different kinds of scores that can be reported for CRTs that reflect emphasis on objectives are listed below:

1. The number or percent correct on a given objective or set of items that encompass a few highly related objectives.
2. "Mastery" of a given objective or set of items where "mastery" is defined in terms of a certain level of performance such as 90 percent correct.
3. The time it takes (such as in class hours of calendar days) for an individual to achieve a given performance level (including what has been defined as "mastery") (Harris, 1973).
4. The time (in minutes or hours) it takes a student to perform a certain task or set of tasks related to an objective (such as correctly computing the product of all single digit numerals).
5. The probability that the student is ready to begin the next level of instruction (this may be based on both the number of items correct and the pattern of answers given to these items).
6. The percentage of students who "pass" each item; that is, the item's difficulty. This kind of score is used exclusively in program evaluation where each item or task is considered important in itself.

Of all the scores listed above, the ones that have been the focus of most discussion are those that imply that the student has achieved "mastery" (Millman, 1972). The reason for this attention is that while such a score comes closest to the underlying spirit of a CRT, there is rarely a good way of defining exactly what is meant by "mastery." Arbitrary definitions, such as 85 percent correct, are rampant; but there is rarely any satisfactory criterion for setting such standards of performance. Further, a mastery score often hides the true level of student performance. In other words, if the student failed to achieve mastery did he miss by a little or miss by a great deal; or if he made it, did he just squeak by? Finally, the problems inherent in the construction of items for a CRT and especially those dealing with the defining of the acceptable item types, item selection procedures, and item difficulty severely limit the interpretation of what is meant by "mastery."

Packaging and Other Considerations

How a CRT is finally put together and packaged is again a function of the purpose(s) for which it will be used relative to the various kinds of constraints imposed on its development and use. When there is a vast number of objectives to be assessed and it is not considered reasonable to develop a separate CRT for each, one or more of the following techniques are used:

1. Combine objectives that are considered highly related to one another into a single measure.
2. Select a group of objectives from the total pool of objectives based on a set of appropriate criteria.
3. Limit the scope of each objective so as to reduce the potential number of items and/or tasks that might be needed to measure it.

All of these techniques do, of course, require the use of experts in the fields of measurement and curriculum in order to make sound compromises from both content and methodological points of view.

The methods of packaging and distributing CRTs are quite varied. One of the potentially most functional techniques involves printing tests on spirit masters so that each teacher can duplicate the copies needed for a given class without having to purchase large numbers of test booklets. A second innovation that appears to have promise is referencing the objective and even the test item to specific instructional materials. In one such case, the test form was printed in such a way that the teacher was told immediately whether the student passed the item, and in the event of a failure a manual then directed teachers to materials for additional instruction.

NOTES

[1] These performance standards are usually behaviorally stated, for example: "The student will be able to perform all fundamental mathematical operations involving single-digit integers."

[2] The intended focus of this paper was to be CRTs in mathematics; however, a review of the relevant literature disclosed relatively few references dealing exclusively with this field. Further, those articles pertaining specifically to mathematics mainly describe the development of particular instruments in certain contexts. They do not consider the general concerns associated with the development and use of CRTs in mathematics nor do they examine the vast array of situations for which they might be applicable. Therefore, it was decided to focus this paper on concerns central to CRTs in general, with special emphasis and examples coming from mathematics.

REFERENCES*

Airasian, P., & Madaus, G. Criterion referenced testing in the classroom. *Measurement in Education*, 1972, 3 (4), 1–8.

Baker, E. L. Using measurement to improve instruction. Paper presented at Convention of American Psychological Association. Honolulu, Hawaii, 1972. ED 069 762.

Baker, R. L. Measurement considerations in instruction product development. Paper presented at Conference on Problems in Objectives Based Measurement, Center for the Study of Evaluation, University of California, 1972.

* Items followed by an ED number (for example ED 069 762) are available from the ERIC Document Reproduction Service (EDRS). Consult the most recent issue of *Research in Education* for the address and ordering information.

Bormuth, J. P. *On the theory of achievement test items.* Chicago. University of Chicago Press, 1970.

Cleary, T. Test bias: Validity of the scholastic aptitude test for negro and white students in integrated colleges. Research Bulletin 66-31. Princeton, New Jersey: Educational Testing Service, 1966. ED 018 200.

Cleary, T., & Hilton, T. An investigation of item bias. *Educational and Psychological Measurement,* 1968, 28 (1), 61–75.

Cox, R., & Vargus, J. C. A comparison of item selection techniques for norm referenced and criterion referenced tests. Pittsburgh: Center for the Study of Instructional Programs, Learning Research and Development Center, University of Pittsburgh, 1966.

Cronbach, L. J. Test validation. In L. Thorndike (Ed.), *Educational Measurement* (2nd ed). Washington, D.C.: American Council on Education, 1971.

Dahl, D. A. The measurement of congruence between learning objectives and test items. Unpublished doctoral dissertation, University of California, Los Angeles, 1971.

Davis, F. B. Criterion referenced tests. Paper presented at Annual AERA Meeting, New York, 1971. ED 050 154.

Davis, F. B. Criterion referenced measurement. 1971 AERA Conference Summaries, ERIC/TM Report 12, 1972. Princeton, New Jersey: ERIC Clearinghouse on Tests, Measurement, and Evaluation, 1972. ED 060 134.

Davis, F. B. Criterion referenced measurement. 1972 AERA Conference Summaries, ERIC/TM Report 17, 1973. Princeton, New Jersey: ERIC Clearinghouse on Tests, Measurement, and Evaluation, 1973. ED 073 143.

Ebel, R. L. Evaluation and educational objectives: Behavioral and otherwise. Paper presented at the Convention of the American Psychological Association, Honolulu, Hawaii, 1972.

Glaser, R. Instructional technology and the measurement of learning outcomes: Some questions. *American Psychologist,* 1963, 18, 519–521.

Glaser, R., & Nitko, A. Measurement in learning and instruction. In R. L. Thorndike (Ed.), *Educational Measurement* (2nd ed.). Washington, D.C.: American Council on Education, 1971. Pp. 652–670.

Harris, C. Comments on problems of objectives based measurement. Paper presented at Annual AERA meeting, New Orleans, 1973.

Hively, W. Introduction to domain referenced achievement testing. Symposium presentation, AERA, Minnesota, 1970.

Hively, W., Maxwell, G, Rabehl, G., Sension, D., & Lundin, S. Domain referenced curriculum evaluation: A technical handbook and a case study from the MINNEMAST project. CSE Monograph Series in Evaluation, Volume 1. Center for the Study of Evaluation, University of California, Los Angeles, 1973.

Keller, C. M. Criterion referenced measurement: A bibliography, Princeton, New Jersey: ERIC Clearinghouse on Tests, Measurement, and Evaluation, 1972. ED 060 041 . . . bibliography. ERIC/TM Report 7, 1972.

Klein, S. P. Evaluating tests in terms of the information they provide. *Evaluation Comment,* 1970, 2 (2), 1-6. ED 045 699.

Klein, S. P. An evaluation of New Mexico's educational priorities. Paper presented at Western Psychological Association, Portland, 1972. TM 002 735. (ED number not yet available.)

Kosecoff, J. B. & Klein, S. P. Analyzing tests and test items for sensitivity to instructional effects. CSE Working Paper No. 24, Center for the Study of Evaluation, University of California, Los Angeles, 1973.

Kriewall, T. E., & Hirsch, E. The development and interpretation of criterion referenced tests. Paper presented at Annual AERA Meeting, Los Angeles, California, 1969. ED 042 815.

Mager, R. F. *Preparing instructional objectives.* San Francisco: Fearon Publishers, Inc., 1962.

Millman, J. Passing scores and test lengths for domain referenced measures. Paper presented at Annual AERA Meeting, Chicago, 1972. ED 065 555.

Nitko, A. J. A model for criterion referenced tests based on use. Paper presented at Annual AERA Meeting. New York, 1971. ED 049 318.

Nitko, A. J. Problems in the development of criterion referenced tests. Paper presented at Annual AERA Meeting. New Orleans, 1973.

Ozenne, D. O. Toward an evaluative methodology for criterion referenced measures: Test sensitivity. CSE Report 72, Center for the Study of Evaluation, University of California, Los Angeles, 1971. ED 061 263.

Popham, W. J. *The teacher-empiricist; A curriculum and instruction supplement.* Los Angeles: Lennox-Brown, Inc., 1965.

Popham, W., & Husek, T. R. Implications of criterion referenced measurement. *Journal of Educational Measurement,* 1967, 6 (1)), 1–9.

Popham, W. Indices of adequacy for criterion referenced test items. Presentation at Joint Session of NCEM and AERA, Minneapolis, Minnesota, 1970.

Popham, W. J. Selecting objectives and generating test items for objectives based tests. Paper presented at Conference on Problems in Objectives Based Measurement, Center for the Study of Evaluation, University of California, Los Angeles, 1972.

Roudabush, G. Some reliability problems in a criterion referenced test. Paper presented at Annual AERA Meeting, New York, 1971. ED 050 144.

Roudabush, G. E. Item selection of criterion referenced tests. Paper presented at Annual AERA Meeting, New Orleans, 1973. ED 074 147.

Skager, R. Generating criterion referenced tests from objectives based assessment systems: Unsolved problems in test development, assembly and interpretation. Paper presented at Annual AERA Meeting, New Orleans, 1973.

Wilson, H. A. A humanistic approach to criterion referenced testing. Paper presented at Annual AERA Meeting, New Orleans, 1973.

Zweig, R., & Associates. Personal communication, March 15, 1973.

Selected References on Test Item Construction

Ebel, Robert L. *Essentials of educational measurement.* Englewood Cliffs, New Jersey: Prentice-Hall Inc., 1972.

Gronlund, N. E. *Constructing achievement tests.* Englewood Cliffs, New Jersey: Prentice-Hall, 1968.

Wood, Dorothy A. *Test construction.* Columbus, Ohio: Merrill, 1961.

Renzulli presents an overview of major problems and issues of program evaluation. Relate the Ornstein and
Talmage article in this unit to Renzulli's section on the politics of educational evaluation; the Wrightstone et al. article, also in this unit, to the section on evaluation versus research; and both the Ebel, and Cox and Sterrett articles from Unit V to the section on standardized tests.

The Confession of a Frustrated Evaluator

JOSEPH S. RENZULLI

Author's abstract   Although a great deal has been written in recent years about the emerging science of program evaluation, certain basic and essentially unresolved problems continue to plague the work of the evaluator. This article attempts to point out the main dimensions of four problem areas commonly encountered by persons engaged in evaluation of educational programs: the politics of educational evaluation, the conflict between the behavioral objectives model and growing humanistic concerns in education, the distinction between research and evaluation, and the use of standardized tests in evaluation.

Anyone planning to deal with a theoretical or practical problem in educational evaluation these days cannot help but be overwhelmed by the massive and often conflicting body of literature that has grown up around this topic. With the possible exception of the three subjects—segregation, sex education, and student power—it is difficult to find an educational issue that has generated more rhetoric and greater controversy than the current concern for *evaluation* and the related issue of *accountability*.

As educators with dollar signs in their eyes busily scrambled to scoop up their fair share of the federal windfall that began with the enactment of the National Defense Education Act (NDEA), only the very foolish were not haunted by the inescapable realization that sooner or later they would be held accountable for the brave but often vague promises and grandiose schemes that were unblushingly written into thousands of proposals by well-intentioned but often starry-eyed educators who gave little or no serious attention to the problems of evaluation. Thus, the schemes that promised to provide solutions to schoolmen's prayers turned out, in most cases, to have

From *Measurement and Evaluation in Guidance*, Vol. 5, No. 1, April 1972. Copyright (1972) American Personnel and Guidance Association. Reprinted with permission of author and publisher.

little or no significant impact on the education system in general; and although the trimmings in today's schools may be a little fancier, the main course that is served to most youngsters is not very different from the educational menu of two or three decades ago. The main question is, of course, why is this so? Why in the face of unprecedented financial support for educational programs and projects have we been unable to demonstrate in any definitive fashion the effectiveness of proposed innovations in the system? The challenge of answering this question must be laid squarely at the feet of the educational evaluator. Although great strides have been made in the science of evaluation in recent years, our inability to master certain basic problems still prevents us from bringing about the often discussed but still illusive transformation of the schools.

The early chaos and misapplication of many federally financed programs have undoubtedly contributed to our heightened concern for evaluation and accountability, and this concern has given rise to a new methodology or second generation of educational evaluation. Unlike the first generation that seemed to be hung up on psychometrics and problems related to the measurement of individual differences, the second generation is concerned with system or program evaluation, and its main purpose is simply to find out how specific modifications in system inputs will bring about specific changes in system outputs. Although this methodology has focused so far mainly on special projects and externally financed programs, it does not take a great deal of imagination to envision the day when this rapidly expanding technology is refined to the point where it can be brought to bear on virtually every activity that parades under the banner of education.

But before we can reach the seemingly impossible dream of isolating cause-effect relationships in education, certain basic and essentially unresolved problems in evaluation must be mastered. This article attempts to provide a structural overview of some of the major problems and issues that continue to plague educational program evaluation. By isolating and pointing out the main dimensions of these problems, we hope to provide some direction for future efforts and to bring the problems into sharper focus so that the second generation of evaluators will be better able to resolve them.

POLITICS OF EDUCATIONAL EVALUATION

The first problem is concerned with the relationship that exists between the evaluator and the program being evaluated—that is, the politics of educational evaluation. Educational enterprises, and especially those that involve large amounts of funds from external sources, are managed by people and institutions that stand to gain certain benefits if their projects prove successful.

Although the main criteria for the success of any educational program should be in terms of benefits realized by students, we cannot deny that institutions stand to gain such benefits as continued funding and prominence from a successful program, and that the persons operating these programs stand to gain job security, prestige, and power in the form of decision-making authority. With these stakes consciously or unconsciously in mind, the administrators of programs and projects seek personnel who are euphemistically dubbed "independent external evaluators." In most cases the project managers have complete freedom in selecting the evaluator, and it is from their budget that the costs of evaluation are paid.

Notwithstanding the fact that project administrators are genuinely interested in finding ways in which their programs can be improved, we would be deluding ourselves if we believed that they are not primarily interested in getting a good overall evaluation, or at least avoiding an evaluation that might conclude with such statements as: "This project is a complete waste of time and money, and shows no noticeable benefits for the students" or "The project director is incompetent and should be fired immediately." Please remember that this is the same project director that hired the evaluator, squired him through several three-martini lunches, and suggested that he publish the results of his evaluation in a professional journal.

If project administrators' motives, so far as evaluation is concerned, appear to be somewhat less than virtuous, we should keep in mind that they have been forced into a situation over which they have had little control. In most cases, program evaluation is mandated by higher-level administration or funding agencies, and as such, is usually considered a necessary evil by project administrators and staff members who are asked to avail themselves of the evaluator's instruments of oppression so that their competence can be judged.

A few years ago I was involved in the evaluation of a large compensatory education program for inner city youngsters. On one occasion a large group of teachers and administrators were called together for a briefing on evaluation and the distribution of evaluative materials. As the group began to leave the auditorium, a quiet chant began to reverberate throughout the room—"Two, four, six, eight—we don't wanna evaluate!" That was among some of the kinder things that were said throughout the course of this particular evaluation.

It is difficult to understand how the need for evaluation is almost universally accepted at the cognitive level, and yet the efforts of the evaluator are likely to be greeted with all the warmth and understanding of a husband who finds his wife in bed with his best friend. Where have we gone wrong? Must practitioners feel threatened by evaluators and ambivalent about taking part in an evaluation? Must the role of the evaluator bring him into conflict with the role of the practitioner? If the answers to these questions are anything less than a resounding "No," what can we do to gain the understanding and support of persons on whom we must eventually pass judgment? A closer look at the evaluator may help us isolate a few more problems.

First, the evaluator usually stands to make a financial gain from his involvement with a funded project. While there is nothing inherently evil about turning a reasonable profit from one's labors, there are a few inherent subtleties that all of us who have played the evaluation game are aware of. If we come up with a generally favorable evaluation we are likely to be rehired and under these circumstances it is difficult to dismiss from our minds the great temptation on the part of the evaluator to report some needed improvement in minor areas while at the same time pointing out the general value and effectiveness of the bulk of a program.

A second problem is somewhat less embarrassing to talk about; however, it certainly must be considered as a source of evaluative bias. Good evaluation theory tells us that the evaluator should be involved in a project from the outset. He should work closely with the administrators and staff from the proposal-writing stage to the preparation of the final report. He is a full-fledged member of the team and, as such, he is quite likely to develop both a close personal relationship with project personnel and a strong emotional tie with the project itself. He starts to talk about *our* students, and *our* control group, and how much money we have left in *our* budget. Under these circumstances, we must raise the question: Is the independent external evaluator sufficiently detached from the project to take an objective look at it, or is he likely to approach evaluation with some of the same positive biases as a person who sets out to evaluate his own program?

We have somewhat of a dilemma here. If we were able to create a completely independent cadre of external evaluators—political untouchables with all the consumer concerns of a group like Nader's Raiders, would we not also widen the gap between the evaluator and the people whose honesty, trust, and cooperation are needed to mount an effective evaluation? In one situation where this kind of independence existed, teachers prepared students for a post-test by teaching lessons directly from the test booklet.

As long as factors such as funding, prestige, and power are involved, the political relationship between the evaluator and those being evaluated will not be an easy problem to solve.

ONE IRRESISTIBLE FORCE MEETS ANOTHER

Two irresistible forces in education seem hell-bent on a collision course, and I am afraid that our friend the evaluator is going to be caught squarely at the point of impact. The first irresistible force is the *behavioral objectives movement*. Although there is some growing controversy about the role of behavioral objectives in curriculum planning and evaluation, one cannot deny the value that it has had in helping to build evaluation and accountability models and to advance the science of education beyond the vagueness and lack of specificity that seems to have made us the step-child of the sciences. Further, some of the new experiments in education such as performance contracting and the voucher plan, and systems analysis approaches such as the planning, programming, and budgeting systems (PPBS) could not have been implemented had we not been able to specify in precise behavioral terms the objectives toward which our efforts are directed. Some educators, however, may be carrying their concern for behavioral objectives a bit too far. Nevertheless, this movement has been nothing less than a blessing to the evaluator who must know what is *supposed* to happen before he can begin figuring out how to measure it.

There is still another irresistible force growing in education today—a renewed concern for the total development of the individual as a human being, dealing with such difficult-to-measure objectives as self-actualization, consciousness III, and sociability. This force is somewhat more obscure than the behavioral objectives movement, but is nevertheless growing in force and magnitude.

As youngsters on college campuses across the country began to revolt against curricular irrelevance and lack of concern for the affective domain, educators from primary grades through graduate school began to give serious attention to the benefits that might be realized from a much more informal and humanistic education—one that replaces punch-card relationships with primary-group experiences, classroom activities and didacticism with experiences in the real world, and punitive testing and grading practices with concerns that focus on individual satisfaction. Supporters of this humanistic point of view remind us that a large proportion of man's behavioral repertoire is *not* acquired in formal learning situations, and that although the school can claim credit for giving youngsters the three R's and other skills and information, they have done so at the expense of other equally important objectives. Another argument is that this lack of humanistic concern for individuals has made schools essentially oppressive places and learning essentially coercive. Education, the humanists say, has degenerated to a process of conformity-oriented hurdle-jumping, and they point accusingly to the behavioral objectivists for making the process even more mechanistic.

Those with a humanistic orientation are also concerned with the objectives of education, but they do not agree with the behaviorally oriented about the precision with which the objectives can be measured. How can we determine in an objective and scientific manner, argue the behaviorists, when an educational experience has contributed to the development of a fully functioning, self-actualized, socially conscientious human being?

Herein lies the problem for the evaluator. Some truly relevant experiments are taking place in education today—experiments such as open classrooms modeled after the British primary system, alternate learning centers that do not have a formal curriculum, and experiences in group dynamics that are designed to improve race relations and to narrow the generation gap. Recently I read a very exciting Title III proposal designed to advance innovation and creativity in education. The guidelines for evaluating this proposal had a strong behavioral-objectives orientation, and, using these criteria, I was forced to give the evaluation design of this particular project a very low rating. Although objective tests were written into the evaluation design of the proposal, what was clearly written *between* the lines was a ritualistic compliance with state department of education regulations, a compliance that I believe would yield little useful information about the true objectives of the proposed program. Further, if this proposal should be funded, determining its effectiveness will be nothing less than an evaluator's nightmare.

I wish that I could offer some concrete suggestions for softening the impact of the collision between the two forces. The usual impassioned plea for research into the measurement of affective processes can only be reiterated, but perhaps we should also make a plea to funding agencies that will result in some relaxation of the rigid behavioral-objectives model that governs so much of the thinking so far as evaluation is concerned.

WHAT IS WAGGING WHAT?

Another major problem with which the front-line evaluator is concerned is the distinction between *evaluation* and *research*. How much of the rigor and control that one finds in traditional research design is necessary in order to carry out a "respectable" evaluation? Like the researcher, the evaluator does not want to be accused of employing an inappropriate or sloppy design, and since many second generation evaluators have entered this field with a strong research background, they are constantly haunted by the fear that they will lose the respect of their more rigorous colleagues.

Unfortunately, the theorists and model builders in evaluation have shown us little consistent direction in this regard. For example:

> One of the more obvious blots on the otherwise nearly-clean escutcheon of the educational research community stems from its ill-fated involvement with evaluation. In responding particularly to Federal mandates for better evidence of program success, educational practitioners have sought the assistance of educational researchers in designing and carrying out evaluative studies. The resulting effort has been a failure so conspicuous that I regard it as unnecessary to attempt to document it. That failure, I contend, has, as one of its chief (but not only) roots, the mistaken assumption that the research paradigm is appropriate to evaluative inquiry. Nothing could be further from the truth. The unfortunate marriage produced by this error in judgment has left irremedial scars on both parties [Guba, 1969, p. 4].

Contrast this statement with the following comments in a recent issue of the *Urban Review* (1969) which was devoted solely to program evaluation:

> Both [research and evaluation] should be serving the same function of supplying information to planners and policy makers about what does and does not work . . . but accurate information can stem only from rigorous experimental design and data collection techniques, whether in research or evaluation (Hawkridge & Chalupsky, 1969, p. 8].

> There are no formal differences between "basic" and "applied" research or between "research as such" and "evaluation research." Research designs, statistical techniques, or data collection methods are the same whether applied to the study of the most basic principles of human behavior or to the most prosaic of social action programs [Rossi, 1969, p. 17].

> From a technological viewpoint evaluation is a fundamental research activity. It can be conducted with as much precision as any other form of research, though it presents certain specialized problems such as controlling for the amount of attention given to the experimental group or that of executing a scientific design under naturalistic conditions [Mann, 1969, p. 12].

These last three statements are in sharp contrast to the first by Guba, and his divergence of opinion raises some significant problems for the evaluator. Should the evaluator insist on research that is rigorous in helping people to evaluate educational programs or should he evaluate the program in its naturalistic setting? Is the tail not wagging the dog when we change a program so that it will conform with an experimental design?

Some prominent researchers (Mackie & Christensen, 1967; Ottinger, 1969) have told us that "a very small percentage of findings from leading research studies are useful, in any direct sense, for the improvement of training and educational practice" (Mackie & Christensen, 1967, p. 5) because conditions employed by the research bear no determinable relationship to conditions outside the research setting. Commenting in a similar fashion in a recent issue of the *Review of Educational Research*, Cohen has expressed the opinion that:

> Experiments with decentralization, tuition vouchers, doubling per-pupil expenditures, and radical changes in secondary education have two salient attributes in common: to have meaning they would have to be carried out in existing schools, and few schools would be likely to oblige [Cohen, 1970, p. 233].

Thus we are faced with another dilemma. If our evaluations do not respect some of the mandates of good educational research, then they are unlikely to hold any water and the evaluator may be accused of not *really* demonstrating the effectiveness of the program under consideration. This is especially true when the evaluator depends heavily on soft data such as interviews and observations, data that usually cannot be treated with sophisticated statistical techniques as easily as hard data. Although the soft-nosed evaluator does not completely negate the value of statistics, he argues with great vehemence that the sights, sounds, and smells of the real classroom are easily hidden by statistics. Further, if the evaluator imposes strict controls over the program he is evaluating, he may be accused of ignoring the real world in favor of a design that has scientific respectability. Not only may the tail be wagging the dog in this case, but we must also question the impact that three-decimal research has had in bringing about major changes in education to decide whether or not the evaluator with a research bent wants to play the same game. Change is often governed by the heart as well as the head and, whether we like it or not, I think that much of the impact of a book like *Crisis in the Classroom* is the result of its heart-rending anecdotes rather than tables of means, standard deviations, and correlation coefficients.

WHEN IN DOUBT—GIVE ANOTHER TEST

The last problem discussed here concerns the role of testing and especially achievement testing in the evaluative process. If we were fortunate enough to have at our disposal a series of standardized measures that accurately reflect the stated objectives of our program, the problem would be quickly solved. But because of the vast changes that are taking place in the curriculum these days this is seldom the case. Thus we are left with the choice of either using standardized tests that are inappropriate in varying degrees, or attempting to develop our own tests. The latter choice, however, presents us with another kind of problem. If we are going to build our own measuring instruments, we must also deal with the psychometric problems with which the first generation of educational evaluators were concerned. Without some assurances that our homegrown instruments possess reliability, validity, objectivity, and practicality, our results are likely to be viewed with suspicion. Building in these scientific requirements is of course within the realm of possibility; however, it is often a luxury that the evaluator of a relatively small project cannot afford.

The use of standardized tests in evaluation also poses another kind of problem. A growing body of research findings indicates a somewhat limited relationship between the typical achievement criteria for program success and the presumed adult consequences of education, such as better jobs, and higher income. This nonrelationship is particularly apparent among black students. A study by Blau and Duncan (1968) showed that once inherited status is controlled for, years of school completed is only moderately related to adult occupational status, and the relationship between education and occupation is much weaker for blacks than for whites.

It appears then that a word of caution is in order here for at least the evaluators of compensatory programs who use school achievement as a proxy for the long-range criteria of success in adult life. We might even raise the question of whether standardized achievement batteries have outlived their usefulness, a usefulness that a few brave souls in education have always questioned. With the trend moving away from grouping (one of the major uses of standardized achievement tests), the limited relationship between these tests and curricular experiences, and the dangers of self-fulfilling prophecies always hanging over our heads, perhaps the evaluator can take the lead in questioning the usefulness of those tests.

REFERENCES

Blau, P. & Duncan, O. *The American occupational structure.* New York: Wiley, 1968.

Cohen, D. Politics and research: Evaluation of social action programs in education. *Review of Educational Research,* 1970, *40,* 213–238.

Guba, E. G. Significant differences. *Educational Researcher,* 1969, *20,* 4–5.

Hawkridge, D. G., & Chalupsky, A. B. Evaluating educational programs: A symposium. *Urban Review,* 1969, *3,* 8–10.

Mackie, R. R., & Christensen, P. R. *Translation and application of psychological research.* Goleta, Calif.: Human Factors Research, 1967.

Mann, J. Evaluating educational programs: A symposium. *Urban Review,* 1969, *3,* 12–13.

Ottinger, A. G. *Run, computer, run.* Cambridge, Mass.: Harvard University Press, 1969.

Rossi, P. H. Evaluating educational programs: A symposium. *Urban Review,* 1969, *3,* 17–18.

Silberman, C. E. *Crisis in the classroom.* New York: Random House, 1970.

The field of education has become the object of demands for accountability. While most professional educators would favor the concept of accountability many would be concerned about how it is implemented. Ornstein and Talmage discuss some of the rhetoric and realities of accountability. They point out that many educators object to the notion that a child's education is solely the responsibility of the teacher or principal, while ignoring family and community characteristics. Dyer (1970) discusses this same point as do Wrightstone et al. in the following article. Ornstein and Talmage also mention the testing instruments problem with respect to accountability. Stake (1971) and Wrightstone et al. discuss this issue in more detail.

    The questions at the end of the article are important to keep in mind when implementing any accountability model.

The Rhetoric and the Realities of Accountability

ALLAN C. ORNSTEIN
HARRIET TALMAGE

Surely, most people agree that everyone, including teachers and school administrators, should be held accountable for their work. But what many educators object to, even fear, is the oversimplified concept that defines accountability as the sole responsibility of the teacher or principal.

    Numerous other people bear some responsibility for student performance, and they should also be held accountable if we are going to employ a constructive model. These include parents, community residents, school board members, taxpayers, government officials, and the student himself—for the learner's state of health, cognitive abilities, motivation, self-concept, family background, and even age all affect learning.

    Accountability advocates often tell us that we must disregard family characteristics because they are used to alibi student failure. This ignores a wealth of research data which consistently shows that the family is the most important variable associated with student achievement scores.[1] Another large fraction of the variation associated with student learning depends on

Reprinted from *Today's Education*, journal of the National Education Association, © 1973, September-October, pp. 70–80. Reprinted with permission of Dr. Harriet Talmage and Dr. Allan C. Ornstein—Associate Professor of Education, Loyola University, Author of *Race and Politics in School/Community Organizations* (Goodyear, 1974) and *An Interdisciplinary Analysis of American Education* (Goodyear, 1975).

the characteristics of the student's classmates.[2] Only a small fraction of the variation is explained by school variables. Yet the current implication of accountability holds the teacher responsible for student performance—connoting, at best, the lay public's oversimplification or ignorance of the learning process and, at worst, the rise of politics in education and the antiteacher syndrome that is spreading across the nation.

Accountability, however we describe the concept, in its simplest form means to hold someone (or some group or agency) accountable for certain behavior or actions. Although accountability is a relatively new concept in the educational literature, the original idea dates back to the ancient Greek philosophers who stressed accountability through their words and actions.

As the cup of hemlock touched Socrates' lips back in 339 B.C., history recorded perhaps for the first time the act of holding a teacher accountable for what he was teaching. Four hundred years later, Jesus Christ was to be held accountable for what He taught. Then in 1925, John Scopes was tried and convicted for teaching about the theory of evolution.

Each of us is able to recall recent cases, even closer to home, concerning the dismissal of a teacher on the grounds that his reading list, learning activities, or political, moral, or religious interpretations ran contrary to the values of the community. This concept of accountability (holding a teacher responsible for the views he expresses) is certainly not new.

A somewhat different view of accountability also has a history going back into time, that is, accountability not only for what should be taught but for how it is taught. In the medieval universities, professors and tutors were paid directly by the students. The law students at Bologna during the middle of the thirteenth century extracted this form of accountability: Writes Friedrich Heer, "The students, who had the whip hand, kept their professors to a punctual observance of the lecture timetable, under threat of financial penalties, and revenged themselves on unpopular teachers by boycotts."[3]

On still another level, there has always been an implied form of accountability in terms of educational goals, compulsory attendance, student assessment, teacher ratings, evaluation of programs, duties of school administrators, and budget costs. As HEW Assistant Secretary for Education Sidney Marland puts it: ". . . accountability has always been with us. Until now it did not have a name."[4]

In the past, teachers and/or the schools were held responsible by those they served for what should or should not be taught, but responsibility for learning what was taught resided with the learner. The concept of accountability based on the ability of the educational delivery system to assure successful student learning is a product of our times.

Americans have long put great faith in the ability of the environment to shape our lives and in the extent to which changes in it can improve man and society. Both equal educational opportunity and institutional responsibility found support in the prevailing psychological theories of environmentalism and behaviorism. The early compensatory programs of the 1960's, followed by the Elementary and Secondary Education Act (ESEA) of 1965, served as outlets for the environmentalists' theory of intellectual development and the behaviorists' theory of changing human characteristics.

To help increase the federal commitment to compensatory education, the Johnson Administration commissioned James Coleman[5] to conduct a nationwide study on the lack of equal educational opportunity for minorities. This was the largest educational research enterprise ever conducted (the final report alone ran to some 1,300 pages, including 750 pages of statistics) to find out what was considered obvious: that there was a vast difference in the quality of schools attended by nonwhites and whites. "You know yourself," Coleman said to an interviewer, "that the difference is going to be striking."

He was wrong and was, in the words of one of his associates, staggered to find the *lack* of difference. In essence, Coleman found that the effects of the home environment on school achievement far outweighed those of the school program. The Office of Education issued a communication stating that the survey had been "carried to its logical conclusion; the Coleman Report is out of print." This, in effect, obscured the findings.

When Christoper Jencks[6] published his research on *Inequality*, he invited attacks from both the political left and right. He was branded both as an advocate of "racism" and of "mediocrity." On the basis of his data, Jencks contended that the most important factor related to school success was the student's characteristics and concluded that as long as everyone had an equal chance there would always be inequality. Compensatory education, heralded as a vehicle to redress the imbalance, had failed; no amount of educational spending could make a significant difference in bringing about equality. To support his egalitarian views, Jencks suggested redistribution of national income to achieve economic equality, regardless of ability.

Findings from both liberal and conservative sources documented minimal and sometimes zero returns from compensatory education spending.[7] President Nixon vividly illustrated the conservative push toward accountability. In his 1970 educational message, he related dollars spent to the results in student accomplishment: "From these considerations we derive another concept: *Accountability*. School administrators and schoolteachers alike are responsible for their performance, and it is in their interest as well as in the interest of their pupils that they be held accountable." Three years later, he defended his budget cuts in educational and social programs on the basis that many of these programs were "poorly conceived and hastily put together."

Despite reservations and despite the pitfalls of accountability, state legislatures and state offices of public instruction have moved forward with accountability plans of their own, apparently with little caution or a clear understanding of the implications.

In response to the demand for accountability, state legislators have enacted numerous statutes in the last several years. The Cooperative Accountability Project (CAP), a seven-state repository for accountability projects,[8] reports that as of 1972, 23 states had enacted some kind of accountability legislation (some states have passed more than one law). Seven of these states were anticipating the introduction of additional legislation in 1973 and nine others were planning to introduce bills for the first time or to reintroduce measures that did not pass before.[9]

In addition, many state educational agencies are developing their own testing and evaluation programs that are, in effect, accountability plans. As CAP notes, "It should not be assumed that states without legislation are not, in fact, establishing and implementing programs in these areas."[10]

The majority of the 23 states included in the CAP analysis have taken the position that accountability should be mandatory, leaving the specifics to the discretion of local districts. The laws range in content from definite and explicit to vague and broad guidelines, and it is difficult to categorize them. Not only do stated sections of the law sometimes have multiple requirements, but how to interpret the legislation is not always clear. With this in mind, it appears that 13 of the 23 states call for the assessment of students; 10 require management goals and methods of evaluation; and one established an advisory body to recommend a plan; eight require cost performance analysis; eight require evaluation of professional personnel (with only two giving personnel the right to appeal); and five require citizen involvement.

The California, Colorado, Florida, Maryland, and Michigan laws are often considered to contain some of the jargon commonly found in the accountability literature. The most comprehensive accountability legislation is included in California's Stull Act, the first law in the nation to require that competence of certificated personnel be measured in part in terms of student performance. The evaluation process in each school district must include (a) establishment of standards of expected student progress in each area of study and methods for assessing that progress; (b) assessment of personnel in relation to such standards of expected student progress; (c) assessment of personnel in their performance of other duties adjunct to their regular assignment; and (d) assessment of their effectiveness in maintaining control and preserving a suitable learning environment. When a certificated employee's performance is inconsistent with the standards prescribed by his school board, the employing authority must tell him so in writing, make specific recommendations as to how he can improve his performance, and assist him in doing so. The California Education Code also provides that any charges leading to dismissal procedures and revocation of certificates for incompetence or unprofessional conduct must be accompanied by an evaluation.[11]

Events in Florida are even more disturbing for educators. As part of the accountability spin-off, a bill has been introduced in the legislature that would wipe out all tenure and continuing contracts. The measure is being advocated for purposes of facilitating accountability plans.[12]

The implications should be obvious to both professors of education and teachers alike. If the bandwagon picks up in tempo, political fighting should intensify. And if a large number of teachers and professors find themselves driving trucks or farmed out to Siberia, we will have learned who lacks political clout.

The NEA itself maintains that the accountability movement is a "warped attempt to apply business-industrial models to learning," and that it threatens "more and more students and teachers" with "punitive, ill-conceived, and probably inoperable legislation and directives." Accountability misapplied, the organization continues, can lead to "a closed system—to educational fascism—compelling . . . educators and students to comply with inhumane, arbitrarily set requirements. . . ."[13]

Many educators and citizens alike are confused about what accountability means. For this reason, it is easy to get different answers from various people to the same question on accountability, which, in turn, confuses the original intent and the issues related to the question.

At this juncture in history, the concept of accountability has become linked to many evolving educational trends. In fact, it has become a unifying theme related to management by objectives, cost-effectiveness audits, system analysis, performance contracting, voucher plans, community participation and community control, consumer education, competency-based training, assessment of teacher performance, bilingual and bicultural education, program evaluation, and a host of other trends. This umbrella aspect of accountability makes for easy public acceptance.

To date, the most comprehensive accountability models appear to have been developed by Stephen Barro,[14] Henry Dyer,[15] and Frederick McDonald and Garlie Forehand.[16] All three models stress the complexity of the data-gathering process and analysis methods needed to assign responsibility properly.

All the authors contend that it is difficult, if not impossible, to disentangle the effects of several contributions to student learning. For this reason, Dyer and McDonald and Forehand suggest that no one individual should be held accountable; the school is matched with similar schools, and the entire staff of the school is held collectively responsible. *Interestingly, all the authors seem to have serious doubts about the actual implementation of any accountability plan in the real world.*

Briefly, Dyer advances the concept of "joint accountability," where the entire school staff is held accountable to some higher authority for its own operations, while the higher authorities are, in turn, held accountable for supplying appropriate information and facilities that each school staff requires to operate effectively. He divides his model into four variables: (a) input (characteristics of the students), (b) educational process (activities in the school organized to bring about desirable changes), (c) surrounding conditions (school, home, and community), and (d) output (characteristics of students as they emerge from a particular phase of their schooling).

These four variables contain several subvariables and are interrelated and measured to form a School Effectiveness Index (SEI) by which to judge whether or not the staff is producing hoped-for changes. With this profile, Dyer claims, a school can discern in which areas of student progress it is more or less effective compared to similar schools.

The McDonald-Forehand model also envisions each school as a unit of analysis for comparing student progress and includes provisions for community input that corresponds with the school's present system of community control.

The authors present a seven-stage model: (a) identifying meaningful student performance, (b) identifying achievement goals and discrepancies in achievement, (c) diagnosing causes of achievement and nonachievement, (d) obtaining information about likely causes of discrepancies in achievement, (e) developing a plan for corrective action, (f) implementing the plan, and (g) evaluating the plan. The model is cyclical and yields an ongoing Student Development Index (SDI) for schools to use and make comparisons.

Although there are several specific problems with both models, on a general level both are using pre- and post-test student scores and controlling for the differences in pretest scores to determine which schools are more effective. This approach has many inherent pitfalls, as the test specialists know all too well.

In comparing schools, it seems reasonable to adjust for student-teacher-community characteristics. But exactly what characteristics are controlled and what weights are to be applied to each characteristic is highly subjective. How one controls or considers the impact of racial tensions or political factors of the schools and community on performance is a difficult problem as yet unresolved. Controlling for teacher turnover and pupil turnover, especially in inner-city schools, is a problem of concern in any accountability model. Taking corrective action following evaluation can easily lead to conflict and confrontation between the teachers and community.

Advocates of accountability usually subscribe to the environmental theory of intellectual development. Good. But accountability advocates either have not done their homework or ignore the fact that most environmentalists subscribe to Benjamin Bloom's series of longitudinal studies[17] as the most important piece of research in this area.

On the basis of his research, Bloom points out that 50 percent of the child's general intelligence is developed by age four, another 30 percent by the age of eight, and the remaining 20 percent by age 17. He estimates that about one-third of general learning growth as based on achievement indices takes place between birth and age six; that 17 percent of this growth takes place between the ages of four and six; and that still another 17 percent of growth takes place between ages six and nine. Thus, the most important growing period for intellectual development and academic learning is before school age.

It appears, then, that educators are working against overwhelming odds to effect changes with students who show deficits in learning, since much of their potential has already been developed before they come to school. Also, the change problems become increasingly difficult as we progress through the grades and attempt to hold teachers and administrators accountable for older students. Thus, a ninth grade class with a two year average deficit in reading provides a more difficult change problem than a sixth grade class with a two year deficit. Similarly, two seventh grade classes with the same reading average but with different ranges in test scores are not evenly equated, although one might assume so since the averages are the same. The class with the wider range presents a more difficult change problem.[18] With extreme cases, we would need a powerful environment to effect positive changes.

In addition to the environmental factors impacting on learning and, in turn, compounding the problem of assessing student achievement, the test instruments used to measure achievement are subject to question.

Most standardized achievement and reading tests given to students contain about 30 to 50 questions. The students who score low on the tests obviously have answered few questions correctly. If a student answered only 10 questions correctly on the initial test, being able to answer an extra five questions on the post-test is easier for him (because of chance variation) than for someone who had almost all the items correct on the first test. The relative gain of a student whose score rose from 10 to 15 (50 percent) would be very much higher than that of a student whose score rose from 20 to 25 (25 percent).

In this connection, Ralph Tyler[19] points out that when the slow or less able student is pre- and post-tested, changes in his standardized test scores may largely be due to chance variations, since both scores are based on very small samples of knowledge, abilities, or skills.

As a further problem in correlating pre- and post-test scores, Stephen Klein[20] and Robert Stake[21] point out the need to take into consideration "regression" effects, where the low scores tend to increase and the high scores tend to decrease on second testing. Post-test scores, relative to their corresponding pretest scores, tend to change in the direction of the mean. Regression effects make the low-achieving students look better the next time around.

Robert Soar[22] calls our attention to another problem. Students who initially make low scores gain little on post-tests, as do students who initially have high scores. However, students who initially test toward the middle tend to gain on the second test. One possible reason is that the change situation may not be as much a matter of testing as of learning rate. Given the regression effects and Soar's findings, if students are ability-grouped, teachers assigned one ability group rather than another will be found to be more "effective" teachers despite the fact that the pre- and post-test results may have little bearing on the teachers' effectiveness.

According to Roger Lennon[23] a raw score gain of not more than two or three points is sufficient to account for an improvement of one grade level placement, say from 9.0 to 10.0, as measured by most reading tests for the secondary level. And Robert Stake[24] reports that a range of three to eight items is sufficient to account for an improvement of one grade level placement for most of the popular batteries used in elementary schools. Indeed, testwise students can easily guess a few items correctly on the second test. Even without coaching, this change is well within the error of measurement of an individual score.

A change in one grade level, in other words, may be a direct indicator of the probable extent of error in *any* test score, even among highly reliable measurements. Even with measures that have reliability coefficients of, say, the .90 range, which is as high a level as is reached by most commonly used batteries, the reliability of gain from pre- and post-measures comes from two fallible scores, and the error variances from them summate.

Overriding the above concerns is the problem of differential growth rates, that learning does not occur in equal units of time. Learning does not take place at a constant rate, age, or grade level; thus, the equality of instruction is not always the major factor involved. Yet we almost always assume the opposite when we interpret pre- and post-test scores. We fail to recognize that some teachers may be penalized by students who are within their slow period of development, while other teachers may be at an advantage because they are working with students of the same grade level who are developing at a faster rate.

Similarly, it is possible that students in a given period of human development, slow or fast, may be ready to learn one subject more rapidly than another because different learning skills and maturation abilities are required. Randomly assigning students to teachers may reduce this problem; however, it would negate the advantages that may accrue in matching learning styles and rates with specific teaching styles.

We are further hampered by the fact that we do not have test measurements that can appraise reliable change scores over a brief period, say in nine months, from September to June. Besides the variations in the rate of learning, with short intervals of time, the increments of change are small. Put in a different way, the effect on student learning that a teacher or school has in a year is usually too small to measure with accuracy. Nevertheless, most accountability plans include pre- and post-testing at the beginning and end of the school year so as to evaluate teacher performance or school effectiveness.

Then there is the temptation of teaching to the test, given a system where jobs or money are involved with extraneous factors such as test results. In fact, we know this has already occurred in Florida's teacher accountability program and with some performance contracts. The person held accountable has a choice: teaching what students should learn *or* what they must know to pass a particular test.

What does all this mean? In simple terms, scores on pre- and post-tests vary for a number of reasons that have nothing to do with the quality of instruction or the school program but, rather, with a host of technical and human considerations. The above discussion gives only a brief sample of the problems associated with pre- and post-tests. Actually, there are hundreds of other problems related to test design and format, test conditions, reliability, and validity—all of which have resulted in the publication of several texts.

Some accountability advocates argue that *criterion-referenced* tests should be used in measuring for accountability. Their reason is that most existing standardized tests are *norm-referenced*, and norm-referenced tests are constructed to measure the status of an individual or group at a particular time in relation to a large norm group. They do not accurately measure changes in learning, nor do they contain a sufficient number of questions covering the material on which the student was working to furnish a dependable answer to the question of how much he was taught—or to serve as indicators of teacher accountability.

Criterion-referenced tests can be constructed for the competencies to be learned, and then we can include a much larger sample of appropriate answers. In theory this is true. But most of these types of tests are in the infancy stages of development and are only now being discussed in the psychometric literature. More important, the problems associated with pre- and post-testing still remain unsolved.

Test specialists are well aware of the many problems related to accountability schemes and realize that simple pre- and post-tests cannot accurately evaluate the effect of treatment. We should be careful to adopt more sophisticated measures, which would take several years to work out. But we are not heading in this direction.

Liberal groups who advocate accountability often reject test experts as caretakers of the establishment, and black educators increasingly look upon these experts with suspicion and distrust, often condemning them for being victimized by their own Anglo-western history and culture. On the other hand, the conservative community is generally looking to save money and may not be interested in paying for the research required to develop adequate tests.

You can't have testing both ways. First, accountability advocates want to use tests to validate accountability while disregarding cautions by scholars in the field; then they dismiss the test data when this serves their ideological purpose.

There is also a concern that accountability encourages instruction toward narrowly defined behaviors that are the immediate target outcomes presumably forming the basis of assessment. If so, the things we can measure are what becomes important in instruction. Cognitive thinking of a higher order and affective objectives are often neglected because they are difficult to assess, although they may be just as important as learning how to count or read.

The accountability system using behavioral objectives as a focal point ignores the reality of human interaction: that much teaching and learning has little to do with intended goals and quantifiable outcomes. As Dennis Adams points out, the whole process of channeling learning to preconceived objectives "may very well waste the best human powers to learn" and may hamper much of what "is creative, imaginative, and innovative" in teaching and learning.[25] According to Henry Dyer, we may wind up teaching children "to pass tests at the expense of learning to hate the subject in which we test them. . . ."[26]

This does not mean that behavioral objectives have no place in education but that they should never become an all-embracing idea system which rewards or penalizes school people. When we combine behavioral objectives with teacher assessment and tie them up with jobs, the whole teaching process becomes, at best, rigid and compulsive and, at worst, politically oriented and somewhat reminiscent of the Orwellian 1984, where deviations from intended goals are treated as heretical. Under the guise of making education more scientific, we may be creating a scientific nightmare.

Since the implications of accountability for the selection of curriculum, instructional design, and evaluation practices are overwhelmingly evident, let us turn to the political implications.

Anyone who views accountability solely in terms of educational reforms is either naive or is masking his real intentions. The process of schooling is largely political and is linked to economic considerations—to jobs.

When we talk about accountability, especially in large cities, we are also talking about who will make decisions about who will be held accountable and whether those in power or those vying for power will use it for their own self-interests.

Initially, accountability was a tool of the political right in response to what appeared as reckless government spending on compensatory programs, but now it is a catchword of the political left. For the critics of compensatory spending, accountability is a way of raising educational productivity, of finding out what they are getting for their money, of establishing modes of proof, and of holding down taxes. For compensatory advocates, accountability serves as a second chance to prove the value of compensatory education to the many detractors who were feeling the cost of such government spending in taxes and rising inflation.

Accountability and community control have become companion slogans in many places. Almost all the demands for community control are accompanied by demands to hold professionals accountable.[27] For many of these proponents of reform, accountability has very little to do with good teaching and administrative abilities; it is a potential weapon that can be used by local community boards for or against specific groups or individuals—to hire, promote, or discharge.

When we talk about accountability, we are also talking about licensing procedures, what determines professional competence, and what power groups set performance standards.

When we talk about accountability, we are referring to which teachers and administrators should be hired, promoted, fired, or not employed when teaching jobs are difficult to come by. We are talking about who gets top administrative jobs that pay up to $30,000 and $40,000; in short, who runs the nation's largest school systems. Are we not, therefore, talking about power as well as professional competence?

Many educators advance the concept of accountability because they advocate change for the sake of change. According to Donald Robinson, today it seems there is "a heightened respect for change, per se, quite apart from any presumption of progress or improvements."[28]

While the serious authors of accountability models stress the need for research, experimentation, and verification for their approaches (or for any approach to accountability), this does not seem to be the trend. The general demand is to implement accountability on a mass scale, to ignore pilot testing ideas, and to worry later about the consequences.

Reformers argue for accountability as though it is guaranteed to improve education, yet they have no research evidence and they fail to point out the political and economic implications.

Given the usual discrepancies between rhetoric and reason, between promise and reality, it would be canny of accountability advocates to limit evaluation. Lack of data and concrete evidence tends to work in favor of those who advocate change and end up controlling new policies.

Without research, claims for accountability based on intuition and logic can continue to be voiced, and testimonials from the advocates of change can always be found. As long as there is no adequate research on the effects of accountability, the bite of the opponents' criticism is reduced. Moreover, they are put on the defensive: criticized for resisting change, branded as pro-establishment and as representing forces of stagnation.

As the schools proceed to implement accountability programs, questions arise that need answering. Can we accurately measure changes in learning? How do we translate generalities into specifics? How do we replace emotionalism with rationalism? Who should be held accountable, and for what? How can we safeguard teachers against scapegoating? Dare teachers and administrators state the simple truth: that the students, parents, and community are also accountable? Are we concerned with power or with effective instructional systems? Before we march madly in many directions singing education's latest popular tune, let us consider where we should go from here.

Unless and until we answer most of these questions satisfactorily, accountability may never have a chance to enhance the teaching profession. Too quick adoption of the concept, coupled with failure to work out inherent problems, may lead to quackery and chaos and, even worse, to punishment of educators by placing on them total blame for poor student performance.

Accountability, like so many other educational ideas, can be used by individuals who wish to attack and divide the educational system, and it can be used to advance the interests of self-serving groups. On the other hand, at least in theory, it can be used by educators to think more clearly about the goals of reform and methods for achieving these goals.

It must be understood that the schools, especially the public schools, have been increasingly burdened with the tasks and responsibilities that other social institutions no longer do very well or do not care to do. The schools have been asked to develop the child's human potential regardless of his background or ability, to educate him as well as possible, to make him into a healthy and responsible citizen. As Frank Jennings pointed out, society, having directed to the schools the responsibility of educating the child, now envisions school people "as ideal agents to be made accountable to the rest of society for the quality and quantity of educational results."[29]

It must be constantly reemphasized that distinguishing the multiple causes affecting student learning is nearly impossible and that attributing all of a child's success or failure in school to his teacher or principal is certainly wrong and unfair. Similarly, there is need to point out again that family characteristics have the greatest influence on most student learning. No one, including teachers and school administrators, should be held accountable for something he has little control over. The most that school people can be reasonably held responsible for is continually trying to better the quality of education for all children in all schools, within the limits imposed by the abilities of the child and conditions of the school.

Few people would disagree with the theory of accountability. Teachers do not fear evaluation; in fact, most of them welcome it and prefer that supervisors observe, evaluate, and make recommendations in a constructive manner. What they object to is that accountability systems carry with them a presumption of guilt and negative reasons for implementation. In addition, many of the systems border on narrow and misguided practices and seem to be influenced by hidden agendas.

But accountability is here to stay, at least for the foreseeable future. With this in mind, we present a set of questions to help safeguard professional integrity.

Does the proposed accountability plan:

1. Impose moderating restraints and regulating activities to prevent scapegoating of educators?
2. Define the relationships between lay people and educators?
3. Provide for the involvement of teachers and school administrators in all stages of development and coordination of the plan?
4. Reflect the school district's philosophy of education?
5. Call for a careful pilot testing period prior to mass-scale implementation?
6. Allow for professional evaluation and self-evaluation?
7. Provide comparative data with similar schools for self-study and improvement?
8. Contain grievance and appeal procedures with adequate professional representation in cases where teachers and administrators are evaluated in terms of student performance?
9. Include equal employment opportunity for all educational personnel?
10. Protect personnel against intimidation from local groups and prevent favoritism toward one group?
11. Guard against the possible danger of pitting human beings against each other, whether this involves students against students or teachers against teachers?
12. Have the support of state agencies in providing guides or data for professionals and lay people alike about test problems and errors of measurement scores?
13. Provide adequate time intervals between pre- and post-testing?
14. Take into consideration the multiplicity of variables associated with learning?
15. Include learning outcomes beyond narrowly defined behavioral objectives?

Ironically, the concept of accountability is spreading across the country. This is happening regardless of the fact that there are several problems inherent in the models, the least of which is a lack of understanding that different models of accountability make different sets of demands on different groups.

In addition, accountability is plagued by difficulties with measuring learning, with lack of evidence that it benefits students, and with few plans for formally evaluating these models on a pilot basis before plunging ahead. Mass implementation without verifications is absurd, and it reflects left and right ideology and educational bandwagonism.

What we need is a common language and some comparisons that permit self-examination and openness on both sides of the philosophical and political dividing lines. We need to put away our political and economic motives, to talk to one another as persons concerned for the welfare of all students. We need to advocate the importance of research, not rhetoric. We must provide a forum that permits us to understand fully such issues as the concept of accountability before advocating any one idea as a certain cure-all.

NOTES

[1] James C. Coleman and others, *Equality of Educational Opportunity* (Washington, D.C., U.S. Government Printing Office, 1966).

George W. Mayeske and others, *A Study of Our Nation's Schools* (Washington, D.C., U.S. Government Printing Office, 1970).

Christopher Jencks and others, *Inequality: A Reassessment of the Effect of Family and Schooling in America* (New York, Basic Books, 1972).

[2] Coleman, op. cit.

[3] Friedrich Heer, *The Medieval World* (New York, New American Library, 1961).

[4] Sidney P. Marland, "Accountability in Education," *Teachers College Record*, Vol. 73, No. 3 (February 1972) p. 345.

[5] Coleman, op. cit.

[6] Jencks, op. cit.

[7] Charles L. Schultze and others, *Setting National Priorities: The 1973 Budget* (Washington, D.C., The Brookings Institution, 1972), p. 357.

Harvey A. Averch and others, *How Effective Is Schooling? A Critical Review and Synthesis of Research Findings* (Santa Monica, California, Rand Corporation, January 1972).

Peter F. Drucker, "Can the Businessman Meet Our Social Needs?" *Saturday Review of the Society*, Vol. 1, No. 3 (April 1973), p. 42.

Daniel P. Moynihan, "Equalizing Education: In Whose Benefit?" *Public Interest*, No. 29 (Fall 1972), p. 73.

[8] Colorado, Florida, Maryland, Michigan, Minnesota, Oregon, and Wisconsin.

[9] Phyllis Hawthorne, *Characteristics of and Proposed Models for State Accountability Legislation* (Denver, Colorado, Cooperative Accountability Project, April 1973), p. 2.

[10] Ibid, p. 4.

[11] Assembly Bill 293 (July 1971), Assembly Bill 2999 (October 1971).

Phyllis Hawthorne, *Legislation by the States: Accountability and Assessment in Education* (Denver, Colorado, Cooperative Accountability Project, April 1973).

George B. Redfern, "Legally Mandated Evaluation," *National Elementary Principal*, Vol. LII, No. 5 (February 1973), pp. 45–50.

[12] "Tenure, Certification Battles Are Shaping Up in Florida," *Phi Delta Kappan*, Vol. LIV, No. 8 (April 1973), p. 561.

[13] NEA Press Release, January 4, 1973.

[14] Stephen M. Barro, "An Approach To Developing Accountability Measures for the Public Schools," *Phi Delta Kappan*, Vol. LII, No. 4 (December 1970), pp. 196–205.

[15] Henry S. Dyer, "Toward Objective Criteria of Professional Accountability in the Schools of New York City," *Phi Delta Kappan*, Vol. LII, No. 4 (December 1970), pp. 206–211.

[16] Frederick J. McDonald and Garlie A. Forehand, "A Design for Accountability in Education," *New York University Education Quarterly*, Vol. IV, No. 2 (Winter 1973), pp. 7–16.

[17] Benjamin S. Bloom, *Stability and Change in Human Characteristics* (New York, Wiley, 1964).

[18] Hulda Grobman, "Accountability for What: The Unanswered Question," *Nation's Schools,* Vol. 89, No. 5 (May 1972), pp. 65–68.

[19] Ralph W. Tyler, "Testing for Accountability," *Nation's Schools*, Vol. 86, No. 6 (December 1970), pp. 37–39.

[20] Stephen M. Klein, "The Uses and Limitations of Standardized Tests in Meeting the Demands for Accountability," *UCLA Evaluation Comment*, Vol. II, No. 4 (January 1971), pp. 1–7.

[21] Robert E. Stake, "Testing Hazards in Performance Contracting," *Phi Delta Kappan*, Vol. LII, No. 10 (June 1971), pp. 583–589.

[22] Robert S. Soar, "Accountability: Problems and Possibilities," paper presented at the annual American Educational Research Association conference (New Orleans, February 1973).

[23] Roger T. Lennon, "To Perform and To Account," *Journal of Research and Development in Education*, Vol. 5, No. 1 (Fall 1971), pp. 3–14.

[24] Stake, op. cit.

[25] Dennis M. Adams, "Some Questions Concerning Behavioral Objectives," *Journal of Teacher Education*, Vol. XXIII, No. 1 (Spring 1972), p. 26.

[26] Henry S. Dyer, "The Role of Evaluation in Accountability," paper presented at the Conference on Educational Accountability sponsored by the Educational Testing Service (Chicago, June 1971).

[27] Stokely S. Carmichael and Charles V. Hamilton, *Black Power: The Politics of Liberation*, (New York, Vintage Books, 1967).

Mario D. Fantini, Marilyn Gittell, and Richard Magat, *Community Control and the Urban School* (New York, Praeger, 1970), p. 192.

[28] Donald W. Robinson "Scraps from a Teacher's Notebook: Change for Its Own Sake," *Phi Delta Kappan*, Vol. LIII, No. 9 (May 1972), p. 587.

[29] Frank G. Jennings, "For the Record," *Teachers College Record*, Vol. 73, No. 3 (February 1972), p. 333.

This article covers some of the same concerns as the previous article by Ornstein and Talmage but it primarily focuses in on five measurement problems associated with accountability: (1) the definition of normal growth, (2) the reliance on interpolated norms, (3) interlevel and interform equivalence, (4) the reliability of difference scores, and (5) regression toward the mean. Terms such as "interpolated norms" or "regression toward the mean" may be unfamiliar to you at the present time. However, they are defined and explained in the article. It is not essential, or even expected, that you understand all the terms or problems prior to reading the article. Unfortunately, many accountability programs have been implemented by people who did not understand these problems, or realize they existed.

Accountability in Education and Associated Measurement Problems

J. WAYNE WRIGHTSTONE
THOMAS P. HOGAN
MURIEL M. ABBOTT

ACCOUNTABILITY IN EDUCATION

What Is Accountability

A recent development in the field of education has been the emergence of the concept of "accountability." This concept denotes that whoever is given a task to perform should be held responsible or "accountable" for the results of his performance. This, then, implies that those assigned the task of educating children should be held responsible for their performance with respect to the education of those children. There is nothing especially new in this concept of responsibility in education. Educators have always been concerned with pupil performance in academic as well as in personal and social areas and have accepted responsibility for change in that performance. What is novel is the increased attention to the possibility of determining the cost-

From *Test Service Notebook* 33. Issued by the Test Department, Harcourt Brace Jovanovich, Inc. Reprinted with permission of author and publisher.

effectiveness of any such change: that is, the relating of change in pupil achievement to the costs of producing that change. Another related new element is the use of the "systems approach" in which all phases of an educational program are planned and carried out as a whole rather than in segments. It is the purpose of this article to describe some of these new elements and to explore some of the measurement problems which have become associated with them.

Much of the impetus to the emergence of the accountability concept in education has come from questions raised regarding the cost-effectiveness of various educational programs. The ever increasing requests for additional funds have raised questions concerning whether these expenditures really resulted in better education. Until recently, much of the appraisal of educational programs had been in terms of input; for example, in terms of improved instructional materials, increased expenditures, decreased class size, or the institution of programs aimed at reducing the number of dropouts. The new approach holds that those assigned the task of educating children should be held accountable for results in terms of the output of the educational program; for example, in terms of change in student learning or reduction in the number of dropouts. Appraisal in terms of input or expenditures provides little evidence of pupil performance resulting from an educational program. Appraisal in terms of output permits the assessment of educational programs in terms of changes in student behavior. If cost-effectiveness is to be determined, then change in student behavior must be interpreted in terms of expenditures; that is, how much change in pupil learning or achievement results from specified expenditures for a program, such as professional staff, materials, capital outlay, etc.

In order to apply the concept of accountability in the field of education, it is suggested that certain components must be present. There must be measurable objectives in terms of output or pupil behavior, what the pupil should learn or become able to do. A second component consists of a program, usually a learning program, designed to lead to the achievement of these measurable behavioral objectives. A third is the evaluation of the achievement of these objectives; a determination of how successfully the objectives are realized, together with an assessment of the cost of the program. The fourth component is a systematic method of feedback to the ultimate decision makers, or those to whom the school personnel are accountable, so that the appropriate revisions in the program may be made to improve future pupil performance. The innovative element is the combining of all these tasks into a unified whole or into what may be called a "systems approach" to education. Because this is an integrated approach, the contention is that it promotes more efficient planning and carrying out of an educational program and also is conducive to determination of the cost-effectiveness of a program.

To date, in addition to the above necessary components, any implementation of the concept of accountability usually includes certain conditions, such as specified hours of pupil exposure to the instructional program, or a specified time limit in which objectives are to be met, as well as a defined target group of pupils. This means that the determination of "accountability," as it is presently advocated, usually requires that there be evidence of achievement of stated objectives for a particular group of students, using clearly identified procedures over a specified period of time, together with a determination of the cost of the program.

Emergence of Accountability in Public Education

Perhaps the earliest evidence of widespread attempts to apply the concept of accountability in education occurred in the 1920s with the introduction and use of nationally standardized achievement tests in various subject areas. These tests provided school systems with a new and easily interpreted kind of evidence of pupil performance. By means of the average grade scores achieved by pupils in a community, a school system was able to report to that community the educational progress of its students. In the main, the early reporting of these results was in the form of city-wide or community-wide averages. Implicitly or explicitly, such reporting of average test scores may be viewed as initial acts by school administrators and school boards in accounting for their performance in educating the pupils in their schools.

Although for many years local community groups, in cooperation with local school administrators, had requested and received achievement data for individual schools, these school-by-school results did not become a major issue until the late 1960s. At that time in many large cities, citizens, dissatisfied with city-wide averages which they considered inadequate evidence of the education of their children, demanded publication of school-by-school average grade scores on the standardized tests. The reporting of these school-by-school averages revealed that within any city, wide differences existed in the average performance of the students in the various schools. This was particularly evident in the case of the "inner city" schools where the average scores on standardized tests tend to be below the national average or "below the norm."

Although these efforts led to the reporting of more complete achievement information, there was, at that time, little relating of achievement to expenditures. Increasing expenditures for education, however, soon resulted in demands for some tangible evidence of what these expenditures were accomplishing. The lack of success that attended many efforts to improve the level of achievement of disadvantaged pupils, together with dissatisfaction on the part of many citizens regarding the results of public education, contributed to a growing feeling that educators should be held responsible for pupil performance; performance satisfactory in relation to the resources invested in its attainment.

An additional factor promoting the attaining of educational results or pupil achievement commensurate with expenditures came from government sources, in particular the Elementary and Secondary Education Act (ESEA) of 1965. In order to determine whether the expenditure of funds granted under this act resulted in meeting the objectives of a particular program, it was necessary to provide for a systematic evaluation of any program supported by these federal grants. ESEA Title I, for the improvement of academic achievement of children from low socioeconomic level homes, Title VII for bilingual education projects, and Title VIII for programs designed to decrease the number of school dropouts, all contain provisions requiring systematic evaluation of their programs in terms of educational outcomes, together with evidence as to the cost-effectiveness of the program.

In 1968 the United States Office of Education initiated educational audits. These audits are designed to examine and verify the measurement of educational outcomes under Titles VII and VIII. The auditor monitors the measurement of educational outcomes and is independent of any involvement in the operation of the educational program. The auditor examines the evaluation design, assesses the appropriateness of the measurement procedures used, and verifies the results. The purpose of the audit is not to provide additional evidence of the outcomes of an educational program, but rather, to ensure that the reported outcomes were, in fact, achieved, and that these outcomes were properly related to the various input measures.

There has, then, been a steady and ever increasing demand for better evidence concerning the outcomes of educational programs. In the 1920s the demand was for system-wide results. This later became a demand for school-by-school results and finally a demand for the results of a particular program which might involve only pupils in a particular school, or specified pupils in several schools. In all cases, the goal was to discover the extent to which an educational program was meeting its objectives. As was stated previously, the present innovative element goes a step further. No longer is it deemed sufficient to determine only the extent of improvement in pupil performance. Now evidence is sought to determine whether that improvement is satisfactory in relation to the expenditures entailed in achieving it.

Who Is Accountable and for What

If the concept of accountability is to be implemented, certain questions must be answered. Before the "who" can be identified, a determination must be made regarding "for what" the schools are to be held accountable. Since most persons agree that the schools are accountable for both the academic and the personal-social development of the pupils, this means that educational outcomes must be clearly stated in terms of observable and measurable changes in student behavior in these areas. Once the educational goals are established, a determination can be made as to "who" is accountable for attaining them.

Theoretically, only persons can be held accountable, not school systems as a whole. Therefore, it is reasoned that individuals (school personnel) are accountable for the desired changes in pupil behavior. Each person in the school system is responsible for those educational outcomes which he influences. This means that responsibility must be assigned to specific individuals throughout the school system from paraprofessional, teacher, supervisor, and administrator to the Board of Education.

But, if the principle of accountability is to be applied to persons within a school system, certain major difficulties must be recognized. The greatest problem is that of relating pupil achievement and development to the various influences on that achievement and development. These influences include factors both within and outside of the school. The entire school staff—teachers, principals, specialists, paraprofessionals—together with the Board of Education have impacts upon pupil learning that are virtually impossible to disentangle. The Board of Education is responsible for providing the means and the technical assistance which the staff uses to attain certain clearly defined and agreed-upon pupil-performance objectives. The various members of the staff then interact in the attaining of these desired changes in pupil behavior.

Equally difficult is the task of separating school achievement from the influence of home and neighborhood. With respect to factors outside the school which affect pupil performance, research has found that pupils from low socioeconomic neighborhoods, on the average, achieve at a lower level than do pupils from higher socioeconomic neighborhoods. Another finding has been that the level of education completed by parents has a close relationship to a pupil's academic achievement. This seems to mean that the socioeconomic level of a pupil's neighborhood together with his home environment affect his achievement in school. The influence of home, neighborhood, and other factors on pupil personal-social development must, then also be recognized. The identification and measurement of these within- and without-school interactive effects, is an overwhelmingly complicated undertaking. It may then be that assignment of responsibility to the specific individuals who contribute to pupil achievement will never be feasible and that responsibility may have to be allocated to a more comprehensive unit.

The Performance Contract

There are various ways in which the concept of accountability can be implemented. The method that has traditionally been used is one in which the school system itself institutes a program, undertakes its evaluation, and accepts the responsibility for the results of that program. Whether a systems or segmented approach is used, the tasks involved are the same: defining objectives, instituting programs designed to lead to the attainment of these objectives, measuring success in meeting the objectives, and evaluating and interpreting the results to the community.

All of these components of accountability have been performed by educators for years. A new method of implementing accountability, however, has recently emerged, namely, performance contracting. Instead of undertaking the entire educational program itself, a school system contracts with an agency (usually, but not necessarily, a private commercial company) to undertake one or more of the tasks ordinarily performed by the school system. The agency or contractor then accepts responsibility for changes in pupil behavior as specified in the terms of the contract and can be held accountable for resulting change in the defined areas of pupil behavior.

Essentially, a performance contract is a contractual agreement between two parties for specified performance by each. There are two basic types of performance contracts: general and guaranteed. In the general contract, an agreement is reached specifying what each party shall provide but no guarantees are offered regarding the results or outcomes of the agreed-upon performances. In the guaranteed performance contract, however, specific results from the agreed-upon performance are guaranteed. These guarantees generally provide for a straight or sliding-scale bonus when these results are met and sometimes provide, in addition, for a penalty when they are not met.

To the present time, performance contracts of either type typically have been instituted on a pilot basis and have provided for use of new instructional materials and techniques with students in disadvantaged areas; most often it has been those who have disabilities in certain subjects, especially reading and mathematics. Usually the agreement is such that the contractor provides an instructional or learning "package." This package may contain an all-inclusive systems approach in which all phases of an educational program are planned and carried out as a whole, or may be limited to one or more specific tasks ordinarily performed by the school system itself. The contract can provide for an instructional program which may include traditional and/or innovative classroom material, various types of technological equipment, and incentives to pupils and/or teachers. It also may include certain conditions, such as specified hours of pupil exposure to the program, or specified time limits in which objectives are to be met, as well as a carefully defined group of pupils who are to participate in the program. Provisions for teacher training and certain special facilities may be included. The contract will invariably provide for the measurement of the results of the learning package, and will usually provide, at the conclusion of a designated time interval, for the turning over of the program to the school system for subsequent implementation and management. This final step is referred to as the "turnkey" phase of a contract.

Under the conditions described above, a reasonable example of a guaranteed performance contract would be one in which a contractor guarantees that, after 180 hours of exposure to the instructional package, the reading achievement for an identified group of pupils will be raised by a specified amount such as one grade level. For every pupil who achieves the specified amount of gain (e.g., one grade level) the guarantor is to be paid a straight bonus on a sliding scale, depending on the amount of achievement gain attained above the guaranteed one grade level. He is also to pay a penalty for each pupil who fails to achieve the guaranteed gain. It should be noted that such payments could be made on the basis of average performance for the group as a whole or on the performance of each individual pupil. In contrast, a general performance contract would stipulate equally clearly the conditions of the learning package, target group, hours of exposure, etc., but would include no agreement as to the increase in achievement to be attained by the participating pupils.

It is well to point out once more that there is nothing particularly innovative in the concept of an instructional or learning package. School systems in establishing curricula essentially have set up such programs. What is new is the turning over of responsibility for a learning program to another agency, usually to private industry, in which the outside agency designs, institutes, implements and evaluates the package with varying degrees of independence from the school system. New also is the role of the independent auditor: "independent" meaning free of influence from both the school and the contractor.

Once the contract is awarded, the contractor may begin to initiate his program in the school system. He provides the instructional program in accordance with the terms of the contract and institutes procedures for measurement of the outcomes of the program. The independent auditor becomes involved at this point as he must monitor and verify the measurment procedures of the contractor, as well as the results of that measurement. Usually, the auditor will conduct a separate measurement as a check on the findings of the instructional contractor to make sure that the contractor has performed in accordance with his agreement. Based upon his findings, the auditor certifies the basis of payments to be made to the contractor.

At the conclusion of the contract, the contractor and the school system together undertake the "turnkey" phase, in which the contractor turns the program over to the school system for its independent operation. In order that the transition be made as smoothly as possible, the contractor may be asked to provide the school system with equipment, materials, training sessions and/or consulting services. The contractor is, of course, reimbursed for these transition activities and expenditures.

Role of Measurement and Evaluation in Accountability

Whatever method is used to implement accountability, evaluation is a necessary component and accurate measurement is prerequisite to evaluation. Without accurate measurement there can be no valid evidence of the extent to which a program has achieved its objectives or the relationship of that achievement to the resources invested in it. Unless results in terms of performance are known, there can be no evaluation of the merit of the program. Without evaluation, no one can be held accountable for his performance nor will there be any basis on which to make possible program revisions.

The evaluation of an educational program necessarily involves measurement of pupil achievement. This may entail the use of standardized or non-standardized tests, scales, inventories, and/or questionnaires. Although there has been some use of criterion-referenced tests as short-term interim measures of pupil progress in an educational program, most evaluation of educational programs has involved the use of nationally standardized achievement tests. In some cases these tests have been used to assess only the present status of individual pupils or groups of pupils. Increasingly, however, these instruments have been used, especially in accountability situations, to measure "growth," or the extent to which a pupil's performance has been changed by exposure to a particular instructional program. This is particularly true in the case of performance contracts. Growth or change in level of achievement, as measured by the test, is then used as evidence of the relative success or failure of the instructional program. The use of standardized achievement tests as a measure of growth has been largely the result of the availability of grade scores for these instruments. In fact, almost all performance contracts to date have included provisions requiring that change in pupil achievement be measured in terms of such a scale.

Too little attention, however, has been paid to investigating the appropriateness of a particular standardized test as a measure of pupil status, let alone pupil growth, in the particular educational program in which it is used. Standardized achievement tests are designed to measure objectives that are broader in scope than those sought in most performance contracts. This means that such tests may not measure with sufficient precision the objectives of a specific educational program. Part of the change, or lack of it, in pupil achievement as measured by any test, may be unrelated to the learning program. The learning program is designed to achieve certain objectives. However, it is only to the extent that these objectives coincide with those of the measuring instrument that the instrument is a valid means of measuring how well the learning program has succeeded. If the test fails to measure certain objectives included in the learning program, and/or measures other objectives not part of that program, to that extent the test is not a valid measure of success in the program.

Norm-Referenced and Criterion-Referenced Tests in Accountability

There has been much discussion recently as to the relative merits of *criterion-referenced* and nationally standardized *norm-referenced* tests for the measurement of the outcomes of an educational program. Both norm-referenced and criterion-referenced tests for a given area must draw from the same universe of items to assess performance in that area. Criterion-referenced tests, however, are likely to deal with a smaller content area than are norm-referenced tests, and to have more items measuring that limited area. Norm-referenced tests sample from a broader, more comprehensive area of content, and contain fewer items measuring each of the various components included. This difference in content, or content mix, between criterion- and norm-referenced tests reflects the differing purpose of the two types of test. Each is designed to be conducive to the drawing of particular inferences regarding pupil behavior through different kinds of interpretation of test results. It is in this interpretation of test results that the basic difference between criterion- and norm-referenced tests is to be found.

In the case of a norm-referenced test, the score of an individual or group is interpreted in relation to scores attained by the members of the group on which the test was normed; for example, a particular pupil performed better than did 50% of that group and/or achieved a grade equivalent score of 5.0. In the case of a criterion-referenced test, the score of an individual or group is interpreted in relation to performance with respect to the test criterion. A test criterion is an arbitrarily determined level of proficiency on that test. Interpretation of a pupil's score on a particular criterion-referenced test might, then, be in terms of the proportion of items correct or in terms of expected behavior in the particular area being measured. Because of the typical content of a criterion-referenced test, namely, many items measuring a limited area, the criterion-referenced test offers the possibility of being more conducive to the diagnosis of pupil strengths and weaknesses in that limited area than does the norm-referenced test. Each method of interpretation, therefore, answers a different question with respect to pupil performance. Norms need not always be national norms. If local norms are derived from scores obtained on a criterion-referenced test, then the two types of interpretation can be applied to the same sets of scores and the answers obtained to both kinds of questions regarding pupil performance. However, when nationally standardized norm-referenced tests, as they are presently constructed, are used, it may be preferable to supplement these tests with criterion-referenced measures if both types of score interpretation are sought. Both kinds of information, how well a pupil performs relative to others and how well he performs relative to a behavioral criterion, are desirable in order to assess more completely pupil performance in an educational program.

The proponents of criterion-referenced tests hold that such tests are more valid measures of the outcomes of a particular program than are nationally standardized norm-referenced tests. When a criterion-referenced test is specifically designed to assess particular outcomes, then this claim may be justified, especially in view of the more general content of the usual nationally standardized norm-referenced test. Implicit in this argument, however, is the assumption that the quality of the criterion-referenced test (item construction, reliability, etc.) is equal to that of the better nationally standardized norm-referenced tests. In the case where a particular criterion-referenced test is a more valid measure of the outcomes of a particular educational program than is any available norm-referenced test, the very real problem of measuring academic growth or gain in achievement by means of a series of criterion-referenced tests must still be resolved.

Standardized or norm-referenced tests have been and are currently the most widely used means of measuring growth or gain in achievement. Although most of the better series of standardized tests measure achievement in the various subject areas quite satisfactorily, these tests differ among themselves as to the content covered and as to the emphasis placed on various aspects of that content. For this reason one test may be a more valid measure than are others of what is taught in a certain program, but only careful examination of the content of both test and program can reveal this. The importance of program and test content examination cannot be overemphasized. Even when the issue of matching program and test content is resolved, there remains the special challenge of the measurement of growth or gain. In the next section, some of these problems and their possible solutions will be discussed.

MEASUREMENT PROBLEMS ASSOCIATED WITH ACCOUNTABILITY IN EDUCATION

The use of tests to measure gain should be contrasted with use of tests to measure present status. Identification of the latter involves answering such questions as: "At what level is this pupil or group of pupils performing now?" "How much does this pupil or group of pupils know now?" Knowing that a pupil ranks at the 72nd percentile in reading achievement for Grade 4 pupils or knowing that a pupil obtained a grade equivalent of 6.4 in arithmetic computation is knowing something about that pupil's present status. Traditionally, the most typical use of standardized achievement tests has been for this purpose. Indeed, most of our theories about constructing and interpreting tests, as well as most of the statistical data reported about the tests, assume that the tests will be used to identify present status.

Standardized achievement tests, however, have also been used to measure academic growth. When they are so used, they are attended by all of the problems associated with the use of these tests to measure present status. Selecting a test with high content validity, assuring that the teachers follow directions, and having tests scored efficiently are all problems common to testing for any purpose. When tests are used to measure gain, however, several special problems arise that are not encountered in the measurement of present status. These problems are rarely discussed, indeed some only by those people who are intimately concerned with the statistical concepts of test development. Nonetheless, these problems are very real, very practical, and have important consequences for the educational researcher who attempts to measure academic gain.

The purpose of this section is to identify special problems pertaining to measurement of gain and to suggest possible solutions. There has been no attempt to include all such problems; only those which seem most important and relevant to the implementation of accountability are raised. That problems related to measurement devices other than standardized tests are not included should not be construed as a minimization of the importance of other types of measuring instruments, but merely reflects the fact that these other measures are not typically used to measure academic growth.

Some consideration must be given here to the term "growth" itself. In this discussion, growth refers to academic progress or gain and was selected because it is the term used most frequently by educators. The word, growth, however, may give rise to certain possible misconceptions. Growth in a particular area implies that one is dealing with a single dimension. To determine growth two measurements must be obtained. To say that something has grown implies that these two measurements measure precisely the same thing. For example, a child's growth in height refers quite unambiguously to the difference between two measurements in terms of inches or some other standard linear units. Growth of a city's population clearly refers to two counts of the number of people living in the city. On the other hand the concept of academic growth, as measured by standardized tests, is an ambiguous one. Reading ability measured at the second grade level is not necessarily the same thing as reading ability measured at the sixth grade level. The skills measured by a computation test for the intermediate grades may not be just "more of the same kind of thing" that is measured by a computation test for the primary grades. At best, what is measured at successive levels by a test with the same subject-area title is only an approximation to a unidimensional scale. This should not, however, be a deterrent to an attack upon the problem of measuring academic growth. One way to circumvent the ambiguity in the concept, academic growth, is to define it operationally as the numerical difference between two test scores. Any difference may be reported in terms of raw scores, grade equivalents, or any other type of score units.

Some of the special problems involved in the measurement of academic growth or gain are discussed below. In each instance, the basic problem is identified, some examples are given, and possible solutions to the problem are suggested.

Problem 1. Definition of Normal Growth

In the typical educational growth study, two questions must be answered. The first is concerned with how much gain was shown; the second, with whether this amount of gain is more or less than expected. The first question deals only with the amount of gain obtained, whereas the second question concerns the size of the obtained gain in relation to some outside frame of reference or standard. Almost universally, when standardized achievement tests are used at the elementary level, expected or normal gain is defined in terms of grade equivalent (GE) units. At any particular grade level, normal gain, when all pupils in the norm group are considered together, is defined as one month of increase in grade equivalent scores for each month of instruction. The national norms are constructed so that there will be this 1.0 GE increment between consecutive grade levels for the norm group considered as a whole. For example, when pupils are measured at the beginning of Grade 3 and again at the beginning of Grade 4, the expected gain for the pupil whose achievement is at or near the average for the norm group is one year (1.0) of gain in GE units. Or, after six months of instruction, normal gain for the pupil whose achievement is at or near the average for the norm group is expected to be six months (0.6) of gain in GE units. This expected gain is true only for pupils whose achievement is at or near the level that is average for the norm group. It is not the expected gain for pupils who perform at other levels of achievement, particularly the extreme levels. This expectation of normal gain, 1.0 GE units for one school year of instruction, applies not only to the gain score of an individual whose achievement is at or near the average for the norm group but also to the average GE gain score for a group whose performance is at or near the average for the norm group. Because this definition of normal growth is not applicable to the entire range of GE scores, the question arises as to the legitimacy of defining normal growth in terms of GE units. It is, therefore, well to examine two alternative definitions.

Normal growth has also been defined in terms of the percentile rank scale that constitutes one type of the national norm for a test. If, over a period of time, a pupil maintains his position relative to the group of pupils on whom the norms are based, he may be considered to be showing the normal growth. This expectation of normal growth is true at all levels of achievement. A pupil who is at the 10th percentile in reading, both at the beginning of Grade 3 and at the beginning of Grade 4, can be considered to have shown normal growth. Similarly, a pupil who is at the 90th percentile at 3.1 and again at 4.1 grade placement, can be considered to have shown normal growth. But a pupil who scores at the 90th percentile at the beginning of Grade 3 and then at the 75th percentile at the beginning of Grade 4 is considered to have shown less than normal growth. On the other hand, a pupil who scores at the 10th percentile at Grade 3.1 and at the 25th percentile at Grade 4.1 is considered to have shown more than normal growth. (For purposes of these examples any effect of errors of measurement on gain score interpretation has been disregarded. This problem is discussed on subsequent pages.)

For purposes of comparison between GE and percentile interpretations of growth, the following example is presented. A pupil scoring at the 50th percentile in reading at the beginning of both Grade 3 and Grade 4 would have maintained his position relative to the group and, therefore, is considered to have shown normal growth. On the grade equivalent scale this constituted 10 months of gain or 1.0 GE units. It should be noted again that by definition of the GE scale, a pupil whose score was at the 50th percentile on both testings would have gained one year (10 school months) or 1.0 GE units. However, a pupil whose score, on this same test, was at the 10th percentile at the beginning of both Grade 3 and Grade 4 also would be considered to have shown normal growth in terms of percentile units. In this case, 5 months of gain would have been achieved or 0.5 GE units. Similarly, a pupil who, on this same test, scored at the 90th percentile at the beginning of both Grade 3 and Grade 4 also would be considered to have shown normal growth in terms of percentile units. In this case, however, 15 months of gain were achieved or 1.5 GE units. Therefore, when the percentile interpretation is used, normal growth for pupils tested at Grade 3.1 is to score at the same percentile again at Grade 4.1. In the examples above, however, anyone who scored at the 10th, 50th, or 90th percentile, at Grade 3.1 and again at 4.1 achieved a gain of 0.5, 1.0, 1.5 GE units respectively. In order to maintain a percentile position relative to the group, therefore, a superior pupil or group must gain more than 1.0 GE units whereas a low-achieving pupil or group need gain less than 1.0 GE units. This explains the fact that, when tested at successive grade levels, low-achieving pupils, while maintaining their percentile position relative to the norm, may fall further and further below the norm in terms of GE units. Below in Figure 1 is a graphic illustration of the above discussion. The example presented is typical and highlights the fact that the percentile definition of normal growth sets very different expectations from those set by the GE definition.

Another way of defining normal growth is in terms of a standard score scale. Reference is made here to the interval-type score scales derived by such methods as those of Thurstone, Flanagan, or Gardner. The units in these types of scales are theoretically equal at various points along the scale. One standard score unit at one point on the scale represents the same amount of whatever is being measured as does one standard score unit at any other

Figure 1 Illustration of Differential Rates of Growth in Terms of Grade Equivalent Units for Different Percentile Positions

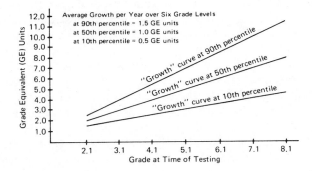

point on the scale. This equal-interval property is not possessed by grade equivalents or percentiles. In terms of a standard score scale, normal growth for an individual or group is defined as the difference between the mean standard scores obtained at any two testing times by the group whose scores formed the basis for the construction of the standard score scale. The definition of normal growth applies to all standard score scales.

The type of standard score scale derived for a particular test depends upon the purpose of that test and the way in which the test results are to be used. One type of scale is constructed so that the mean is held constant throughout the levels of a test. This is true of many mental ability tests. In this case there is no change in mean standard scores between any two levels. Therefore, normal growth is evidenced by obtaining the same standard score at successive testings. For example, when the standard score scale has a mean of 100 at each successive level of a test, there is no difference between the mean standard scores at any two levels. Therefore, the individual or group obtaining a score of 110 at any one level and 110 again at any higher level has shown no change and is considered to have shown normal growth. However, when the scale is constructed so that the mean increases throughout the levels of a test, as is true of many achievement tests, then a difference exists between mean standard scores at any two grades or levels and this difference constitutes normal growth.

An example is the case where a standard score scale has a mean of 60 at Grade 3.1 and a mean of 70 at Grade 4.1. As the difference between the two mean standard scores is 10 standard score units, normal growth from 3.1 to 4.1 is defined as 10 standard score units. This definition of normal growth applies at all levels of achievement on this test between these two grade levels. Two pupils were tested with this same test at 3.1 and again at 4.1. On the two successive testings, one obtained standard scores of 46 and 56; the other standard scores of 74 and 84. Each pupil, therefore, gained 10 standard score units. Because standard score units are equal-interval scores, the difference of 10 standard score units between 46 and 56 and between 74 and 84 represents equal amounts of gain or equal growth despite the fact that the levels of performance of these two pupils were quite different. Moreover, since for this test a gain of 10 standard score units between 3.1 and 4.1 represented normal growth, the two pupils may be said to have shown not only the same amount of growth but also normal growth even though they performed at different levels on the standard score scale. Any pupil who gained less than 10 standard score units between these two grade levels on this test may be considered to have shown less than normal growth while any pupil who gained more than 10 standard score units may be considered to have shown more than normal growth. (For purposes of this example, any effect of errors of measurement on gain score interpretation has been disregarded. This problem is discussed on subsequent pages.)

It is of interest to compare the standard score and percentile interpretations of normal growth. As mentioned above, in order to show normal growth in terms of standard scores, an individual must show the same amount of gain in standard score units as the difference between the standard score means obtained by the norm group at the two testings. To show normal growth in percentile units an individual must maintain his position relative to the norm group by obtaining the same percentile rank on the two testings. In any comparison between standard score and percentile interpretations of normal growth, mention should be made of the effect of changing variability of scores between any two testings. When the varability of scores is unchanged between two grades or levels of a test, as indicated by a constant standard deviation, or when a scale is so constructed that the standard deviation is held constant, then the individual or group showing normal growth in standard score units would be expected also to show normal growth in percentile units. This is true at all levels of achievement. For example, in the testing situation discussed in the above paragraph, 10 standard score units represented normal growth in terms of standard scores. A pupil who evidenced normal growth by achieving a gain of 10 standard score units between 3.1 and 4.1 would also show normal growth in percentile units by obtaining the same percentile rank at the two testings. The pupil who scored at the 50th percentile at 3.1 and again at 4.1 would show a gain of 10 standard score units or normal growth. Similarly, a pupil who scored at the 90th percentile or one who scored at the 10th percentile at both testings would show a gain of 10 standard score units or normal growth.

In the case of many educational measurements, including achievement tests, the variability of scores tends to increase with successive levels of whatever it is that is being measured. The increasing variability of scores is reflected in an increasing standard deviation. Because of the effect of increasing variability on the measurement of growth, it is desirable, in the case of achievement tests, to construct the standard score scale so that the increasing variability is reflected in the scale. As the variability, or standard deviation, changes from one grade or level to another, the gain for an individual or group in terms of standard score units will lead to a different interpretation of performance with respect to normal growth than will his gain in terms of percentile units. Normal growth as measured in standard score units will be accompanied by normal growth in terms of percentile units only for the individual or group whose scores are at or about the mean for the norm group. An individual or group whose performance is above or below the mean for the norm group and who shows normal growth in standard score units would not show normal growth in percentile units. The following example is based upon the same data as presented above, but assumes an increase in the standard deviation between 3.1 and 4.1. An individual whose standard scores at the two testings were 74 and 84, reflecting a gain of 10 standard score units or normal growth, would show a decrease in his percentile position from the 90th to perhaps the 86th percentile. On the other hand, an individual or group whose performance is below the mean for the norm group, who shows normal growth in standard score units, would show more than normal growth in percentile units. For example, an individual whose standard scores were 46 and 56, indicating normal growth in standard score units would show an increase in his percentile position from the 10th to perhaps the 14th percentile. Looking at these same data from the other point of view, the individual who, at two testings, maintains his position at the 90th percentile might show a gain of 12 standard score units, or more than normal growth, while the individual who maintains his position at the 10th percentile might show a gain of only 8 standard score units, or less than normal growth. It should be noted that the greater the change in the standard deviation between two grades or levels of a test the more divergent will be interpretations of an individual's or group's growth resulting from the use of the two different types of scales.

In order to illustrate how the different definitions of growth (grade equivalent, percentile, and standard score) result in quite different interpretations of pupil performance, the following data are presented. Regardless of the type of unit used to measure gain, the scores of Pupil B, whose performance was average, reflect normal growth. As the scores deviate from average performance, as do the scores of Pupil A and Pupil C, however, it becomes very apparent that different interpretations of pupil performance result from the different definitions of normal growth. It should be noted again that the raw scores obtained were based upon different forms of the same test given at 3.1 and 4.1 and that the data are the same as those used in the examples discussed above.

As measured in grade equivalent units, the three pupils showed different amounts of gain. Pupil B showed normal growth as indicated by the gain of

Grade 3.1

Pupil	Raw Score	Grade Equivalent	Percentile Rank	Standard Score[1]
A	32	5.2	90	74
B	19	3.1	50	60
C	10	1.8	10	46

Grade 4.1

Pupil	Raw Score	Grade Equivalent	Percentile Rank	Standard Score[2]
A	38	6.7	90	86
B	27	4.1	50	70
C	15	2.3	10	54

Gain

Pupil	Raw Score	Grade Equivalent	Percentile Rank	Standard Score[3]
A	6	1.5	0	12
B	8	1.0	0	10
C	5	0.5	0	8

[1] Standard deviation is 11 standard score units.
[2] Standard deviation is 13 standard score units.
[3] Increase in standard deviation from grade 3.1 to grade 4.1 is 2 standard score units.

1.0 grade equivalent units. Because the grade equivalent interpretation or normal growth is not legitimately applicable throughout the range of scores, no statement can be made as to whether or not the 1.5 gain of Pupil A and the 0.5 gain of Pupil C may be considered normal. All that can be said is that Pupil A showed a greater gain, and Pupil C a lesser gain, in grade equivalent than is normal for a pupil or group whose achievement is at the average for the norm group.

As measured in percentile rank units, there was no change obtained at the two testings by Pupils A, B, and C, indicating that each maintained his relative position. Each, therefore, experienced normal growth in terms of the percentile interpretation.

In terms of standard scores, normal growth amounted to 10 standard score units as determined by the difference between the means of the norm group on the two testings. As measured in standard score units, therefore, the three pupils showed unequal amounts of growth. Pupil B who gained 10 standard score units can be said to have shown normal growth with

Pupil A having shown more, and Pupil C less, than normal growth in terms of the standard score interpretation.

This example illustrates the very different expectations of normal growth set by grade equivalent, percentile, and standard score definitions and the very different interpretations of pupil performance that result from these several definitions. It should be re-emphasized that the different expectations of normal growth set by grade equivalent, percentile, and standard score definitions hold whether group average scores or individual scores are being considered.

POSSIBLE SOLUTIONS TO PROBLEM 1 The entire problem of what constitutes normal growth must be re-examined. Grade equivalents are used less frequently now for the measurement of present status than they were about 10 years ago. This is in general a healthy trend. However, grade equivalents are the units used almost universally to measure growth. The many problems inherent in grade equivalents suggest strongly that they are not the best type of score to use as a definition of growth. There is no single clearly most useful unit for the measurement of gains, but possibilities are the percentiles and standard scores discussed above. When an experimental program is being evaluated, another possible solution is to use a control group drawn from the same population as the group being evaluated and matched to that group on relevant characteristics. Because the control group is not exposed to the experimental program, the amount of gain it achieves can be used as the definition of normal or expected growth. The performance of the experimental group can then be compared with that baseline. It should be noted that if a control group is used, any type of score unit can legitimately serve to express the growth attained by the experimental group relative to the normal growth achieved by the control group.

Problem 2. Reliance on Interpolated Norms

Many growth studies in education require testing twice within a single academic year. This testing is often done in October and again in April or May. The amount of academic gain expected between the two testings is usually that reported in the norms. Norms for most standardized achievements tests, however, are empirically determined at only one testing time in the school year. Norms for other times in the year are obtained by interpolation between successive empirically determined points. These interpolated points may be considered as reasonably good estimates of the actual norm line if empirically determined points had been available for all times in the year. They are, however, almost certainly in error by some small amount in most cases and by a substantial amount in some cases.

Figure 2 serves as an illustration of the above situation. The Xs plotted in Figure 2 represent median (50th percentile) scores by grade obtained from the standardization program for a test standardized in October. Because of the October testing date, the points are plotted above 2.1, 3.1, etc., along the grade scale. (The school year is defined as the 10-month period from September through June. September of second grade would then be assigned a grade equivalent score of 2.0, October 2.1, June 2.9.) The grade norm line, from which the entire set of grade equivalent norms for this test is read, is the smooth curve drawn between successive Xs. This smooth curve permits the reading of grade equivalent scores for points other than 2.1, 3.1, etc. These grade equivalents that are not empirically determined are, therefore, interpolated.

The question may well be raised as to whether or not the learning curve actually increases throughout the school year in the manner suggested by the smooth curve drawn between the empirically determined points. In many cases, the answer is probably that it does not. Figure 3 shows an enlarged section of Figure 2. In addition, Figure 3 shows an empirically determined point for the eighth month of third grade, represented by the bold dot (•). Reading the empirically determined points on the chart reveals that at the first month of third grade (3.1), the median raw score on this test was 12.5 and at the eighth month of third grade (3.8) the median raw score was 18.5.

However, when the interpolated point on the grade norm line is read, the median score at 3.8 is 17.0. There exists, therefore, the seemingly contradictory case where normal growth (18.5 − 12.5 = 6.0) does not equal normal growth (17.0 − 12.5 = 4.5). The contradiction arises from the fact that although in both cases an empirically determined point was used for 3.1 (12.5),

Figure 2 Illustration of Grade Norm Line Based on Points Determined Empirically at Yearly Intervals

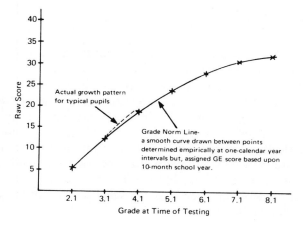

Figure 3 Enlarged Version of Section of Figure 2 Contrasting Growth Patterns from 3.1 to 3.8 and 3.1 to 4.1

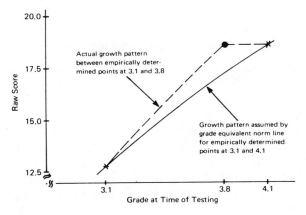

for 3.8, in one case an interpolated point (17.0) was used, whereas in the other case an empirically determined point (18.5) was used. As pointed out previously, the typical standardized achievement test has empirically determined points for only one time in the school year. Thus, whenever a school system tests twice within a school year, it usually must rely upon at least one set of interpolated norms.

POSSIBLE SOLUTIONS TO PROBLEM 2   There are three possible solutions to the problem of reliance on interpolated norms. First, twice-per-year testing can be avoided altogether. Testing in a school situation may be done once per year, at the same time each year, and preferably at the same time of year as the test standardization. For example, if a test was standardized in October, growth could be be measured from October of Grade 3 to October of Grade 4. Second, it is possible to use one of the tests that does have empirically determined norms for two times in the year. If this is done, it is obviously desirable to have the two testing periods coincide with the two times of year when the test was standardized. If the test was standardized in October and April, the school, too, should test in October and April. It is also important to take full advantage of the twice-per-year standardization by using the appropriate type of norm. Even for a test standardized at two different times during the school year, not all of the norms reported may reflect this twice-per-year standardization. Some of the norms may be based upon the only one of the empirically determined points with interpolated norms at all other points within the school year. Other types of norms, however, may be based upon the two empirically determined points within the school year. Third, a control group can be used to define normal growth from one time to another within the same academic year. The gain shown by the experimental group can then be compared with that shown by the control group over the same period.

Problem 3. Interlevel and Interform Equivalence

The typical standardized achievement test has several battery levels and two or more alternate or equivalent forms. Many growth studies require both the use of successive levels of the test as pupils progress from grade to grade and the use of more than one form as pupils are tested repeatedly. Comparison of the results from these different testings places special demands upon the equivalence of converted or derived scores for different levels and forms. If converted scores are not equivalent between levels and/or forms, the test scores obtained in the study can lead to invalid measurement of gains and consequently to possibly erroneous conclusions as to the merit of the program being studied.

As an example, suppose that a school used the Primary level of a reading test as a pre-test measure at the beginning of Grade 2 and the Elementary level of the same reading test as a post-test measure at the beginning of Grade 3. In Grade 2 the median grade equivalent score for the particular group was 2.3 and in Grade 3 was 3.4. However, if the Primary level had also been used as the post-test measure, the median grade equivalent score would have been 3.7. That the two levels of the test do not produce equivalent scores is evidenced by the different results: 3.4 and 3.7. This, of course, means different gain scores of 1.1 and 1.4, respectively. A similar example could be given for lack of equivalence of scores between forms of a test. Pupils should obtain the same converted score on a test regardless of what level or form is taken. A possible exception is when pupils perform at the very extreme upper or lower end of the scale for a particular level. Such extreme performances indicate that the level used was inappropriate and should not have been used with those pupils.

POSSIBLE SOLUTIONS TO PROBLEM 3   There are several possible approaches to the problem of interform and interlevel score equivalence. The most basic is to look for assurance that the determination of equivalence of levels and forms was well planned and well executed. Providing this evidence is the responsibility of the test developers and in general, the equivalence of levels and forms of the major achievement test series do seem to have been established in a responsible manner. However, in the occasional case where it appears that two successive levels or two alternate forms of a test are not yielding equivalent derived scores, the school should look to one of the solutions discussed below.

One possible solution applicable to any lack of equivalence between either levels or forms is to make use of a control group. Both experimental and control groups are given the same level and form of the test. Any lack of equivalence between levels and/or forms would have the same effect upon the scores of both groups. Performance of the experimental group can then be compared with that of the control group thereby providing a legitimate measure of gain. The gain score obtained would, of course, have to be based upon the average score for all pupils in each group, experimental and control.

The problem of lack of equivalence between alternate forms of a test can be solved by having the pre-test consist of giving one form to one-half of the pupils and another form to the remaining pupils. For the post-test administration, the forms given to each half of the group are switched. Again, in order to eliminate lack of equivalence, any gain score obtained would have to be based upon average scores for all pupils.

Problem 4. Reliability of Difference Scores

A discussion of the reliability of difference scores requires use of certain technical terms relating to test reliability. A brief review of these terms is presented here. More complete definitions can be found in almost any textbook on educational measurement. The terms reviewed are reliability, obtained score, true score, error score, and standard error of measurement.

Reliability refers to consistency of measurement and is usually expressed as a correlation coefficient. Although there are several different methods for obtaining reliability data for a test, only one will be described here. In this method one form of a test is administered to a group of pupils. This administration is followed immediately by the administration of a parallel or alternate form to the same group of pupils. The correlation between pupils' scores on the two tests is determined. It represents the test reliability, or the consistency with which the test rank-orders the pupils from high to low on the two testing occasions.

Obtained score refers to the score a pupil actually earns on a test. The obtained score may be thought of as being composed of the pupil's true score and his error score.

The *true score* is the score a pupil would have earned if the test were perfectly reliable. Or, the true score may be thought of as the average of all the obtained scores achieved by a pupil after an infinite number of testings. It is assumed that in an infinite number of testings, all of the errors of measurement due to test unreliability would cancel out.

The *error score* is the difference between the true score and obtained score. The error score results from lack of perfect reliability. It may be positive or negative, and is assumed to be positive as often as negative over a large number of cases. It is important to remember that for any individual on any test, the true score and error score are never really known. The obtained score is all that is available and only probability statements can be made about the true score and error score.

The *standard error of measurement* (*SEM*) refers to the reliability of a test with respect to an individual's test score and is expressed in score units. It indicates the size of an error score (difference between true and obtained scores) that can be expected for an individual's test score. The SEM permits making probability statements about the difference between true and obtained scores. For example in about two-thirds of the cases, the difference between an individual's true score and his obtained score will be no larger than the SEM for the test.

All studies of growth depend on difference scores. In the usual situation, the difference is obtained between pre-test score and post-test score for each individual. These difference scores usually are noticeably less reliable than either of the two obtained scores from which they were derived. This occurs because the errors of measurement in the pre-test score and the errors of measurement in the post-test score are both present in the difference score.

The reliability of difference scores, even as the reliability of a test, can be expressed as a correlation coefficient. Assume that in a Title I program reading is being evaluated. One form of a reading test was used for a pre-test and another form of the same instrument for a post-test. Based upon a reliability for the pre-test of .90, for the post-test of .90, and a correlation between pre-test and post-test scores of .75, the resulting reliability of the difference scores for the individuals in that Title I program is .60. Thus, even though two quite reliable tests were used, the resulting measure of academic gain based upon these tests is a relatively unreliable measure.

Reliability of a difference score can also be expressed in terms of the standard error of the difference score which is reported in score units. It refers to the size of the error score to be expected for an individual's gain score. (This is not to be confused with the standard error of measurement for a test which refers to a single test score for an individual.) When evaluating gain scores for individual pupils, it is particularly important to observe the magnitude of the standard error of the gain score relative to the expected gain.

The "expected" gain might be defined as the average gain achieved by the groups on which the test was normed. For example, the expected gain for pupils from Grade 7 to Grade 8 is the difference between the average score obtained by the norm group of 7th-grade pupils and the average score obtained by the norm group of 8th-grade pupils. As the standard error of the gain score increases in relation to the expected gain, it is less and less certain that an individual pupil really did or did not show the expected amount of gain or that growth in a subject actually did occur. For example, suppose that the gain made by pupils from Grade 7 to Grade 8 is being studied. Suppose that the norms show a 5-point difference between the average score of pupils in Grade 7 and the average score of pupils in Grade 8, and further suppose that the standard error of a gain score is also 5 points of score. In this case it can reasonably be expected that about one-third of the pupils whose gain in true score was 8 points would not show the required 5 points of gain in their obtained scores. About 15% of the pupils would show the expected gain in obtained scores with no gain in true score at all.

The problem of unreliability of difference scores is particularly acute when the average gain from pre-test to post-test is small. In many instances the average gain represented in the norms for a test, for example, for Grade 7 to Grade 8, is only a few points of raw score. This may occur no matter how carefully the test is constructed because the learning curves for such areas as reading, spelling, computation, etc., begin to level off in the upper grades.

POSSIBLE SOLUTIONS TO PROBLEM 4 One way of handling the problem of reliability of difference scores is to work with group averages rather than individual scores. Although the reliability of a difference score for an individual is often disturbingly low, this reliability need not be of concern when working with average scores for a group. The stability of the average gain for a group is a function of the size of the group, and not a function of the test reliability. This is true because of the assumption that for the entire group of pupils, the negative and positive errors of measurement "cancel out," or sum to zero. The average gain for a group may be determined by getting a difference score for each pupil, then averaging those difference scores, or by getting the average pre-test score for the group and subtracting it from the average post-test score for the group. The two procedures are mathematically equivalent.

In education many studies of growth do avoid the problems of unreliability of difference scores by depending on group average. For example, a typical Title I program may include several classes of pupils and evaluate the program on the basis of the average gain for the group as a whole. Even in a case such as this, however, there may be some confusion with respect to the interpretation of the gain. A typical comment is, "On the whole, the program was successful but quite a few pupils showed little gain or even some loss." The first part of this sentence refers to group scores and average gain, thereby avoiding the problem of unreliability of difference scores. The second part, however, refers to individual scores and individual gain with the attendant problem of low reliability of difference scores.

Even in situations similar to performance contracts, where payment is made to the contractor on the basis of individual—pupil gains, it would be preferable to work with group average rather than individual scores. In a situation of this type, the average can be expressed in terms of the percent of the group that exceeded the amount of gain specified in the agreement. For example, in a program involving 100 pupils the contract may call for a gain of 10 points in score. Suppose that 60 pupils show the required gain from pre-test to post-test, while 40 pupils cannot. For the group as a whole low reliability of the difference score does not invalidate or make questionable the gain score, since it may be assumed that the positive and negative errors of measurement have tended to balance out over the entire 100 pupils. It may be that 5 of the 60 pupils who did show the specified gain of at least 10 points in score had a true gain of less than 10 score points but obtained the 10 or more points of measured gain because of unreliability of measurement. At the same time, some of the 40 pupils who did not show the specified gain in score, may have had a true gain of more than 10 score points. Because of this balancing or canceling out effect, the result in terms of gain for the group as a whole should be an acceptable measure of the result of the program.

Another possible way of dealing with the problem of unreliability of difference scores is to increase the reliability of the tests used by increasing test length. One method is to combine two alternate forms of a test into the pre-test and two different alternate forms into the post-test. Another method is to use total scores, such as a total reading score derived from two or more reading subtests rather than simply using an individual subtest score. Because both of these procedures will increase test reliability, the result will be a decrease in the ratio of the standard error of the gain score to the gain score itself. It should be noted, however, that there is a practical limit to any increase in test length. If a test is too lengthy, errors due to fatigue, etc., may occur, thereby reducing reliability.

Problem 5. Regression toward the Mean

Many studies of academic gain are conducted using pupils who are particularly high or low in achievement. Such studies usually consist of four principal stages. Pupils to be included must be selected or identified. Selected pupils are pre-tested to provide a baseline for measurement of gain. The selected pupils then participate in the program designed to increase their achievement. At the conclusion of the program, the pupils are post-tested, and post-test scores are compared with pre-test scores. Frequently, the first step involves testing, as pupils are often identified for inclusion in the program on the basis of test scores. For example, in a study involving "poor readers," "poor readers" may be defined as those pupils who obtain less than a certain score on a particular reading test. If a test is used to select participants in the study, it may be desirable and efficient to combine the selection with the pre-test. When this is done, the test score, used as the basis of selection, can also serve as the pre-test score which will later be compared with the post-test score. Unfortunately, this apparent efficiency gives rise to serious problems relating to the phenomenon known as regression toward the mean.

The phenomenon of regression toward the mean is not well understood by many test users. Therefore, before describing why it is a problem in growth studies, it is advisable to review briefly what it is. Suppose a test is administered to a group of 100 pupils. The 25 pupils with the lowest scores are selected and immediately retested. It will be found that the average score for these 25 pupils will be somewhat higher on the second test than on the first test. This increase in average test score cannot represent a real gain in achievement as the second test was administered immediately after the first. Although part of the increase in score from first to second testing for these 25 pupils may result from practice effect, part of the increase is a statistical artifact caused by lack of perfect reliability of the test used, and by the fact that the 25 pupils selected were those pupils with the lowest scores on the basis of the first set of test scores. One reason why these particular 25 pupils had the lowest scores was that their true scores probably were quite low. Another reason was that on the average there were more negative than positive errors of measurement included in their obtained scores. Previously it was mentioned that positive and negative errors of measurement are assumed to be equally balanced. This assumption seems to contradict the statement that the errors of measurement were more often negative than positive for these 25 pupils. However, the assumption regarding balancing of errors applies only to a total "unselected" group, not to a subgroup specifically selected on the basis of its test scores. For example, it would be assumed that errors of measurement would balance out if the entire group of 100 pupils is being considered, but this could not be assumed to occur if the subgroup of 25 lowest-scoring or 25 highest-scoring pupils is considered separately.

Because on the average, the scores of the lowest-scoring pupils on the first test will be somewhat higher on an immediate retest, it can be said that their scores on the second test "regress toward the mean." The "mean" refers to the mean or average score of the total, unselected group. If the subgroup of 25 highest-scoring pupils on the first test was selected, then immediately retested, their scores also would regress toward the unselected group mean on the retest. Of course, the scores of these high-scoring pupils would regress downward. That is, on the average these high-scoring pupils would obtain somewhat lower scores on the second test.

Suppose that the same test scores have been used both to select those pupils to be included in a program, as well as to serve as the pre-test scores that later will be compared with post-test scores. Any resulting gain scores (post-test score minus pre-test score) will, then, include both the real gain achieved by pupils as a result of exposure to the program as well as whatever regression effect has taken place. This regression effect is a statistical artifact, a contamination of the data, and something that is clearly not part of the real gain.

The extent of regression toward the mean that would be expected to occur for either high-or-low-scoring pupils has deliberately not been specified. The extent of regression depends on such factors as the reliability of the test, or errors of measurement in the particular test used, as well as on how extreme were the scores of the selected group on the test. In general, it can be said that the more unreliable the test and the more extreme the performance of the selected pupils, the greater will be the expected regression effect. It is not necessary to pursue this in greater detail to make clear the point that regression toward the mean is a phenomenon which must be reckoned with in attempting to measure gain.

POSSIBLE SOLUTIONS TO PROBLEM 5   There are two possible solutions to the problem of regression toward the mean. The first solution is to keep separate the step of identifying pupils to be included in the program from the step of obtaining for these pupils pre-test scores to be compared later with the post-test scores. One test should be given to identify pupils for the program. Another test, either an alternate form of the identifying test, or a different test, should be given as the pre-test, the scores of which will serve as the baseline measure for determining gain. In this solution, whatever regression there may be will affect the relationship between identification test scores and pre-test scores, and not the relationship between pre-test scores and post-test scores.

The second possibility is to employ certain statistical techniques which, in effect, separate real gains from gains due to regression. If the appropriate statistical techniques are used, the same test can be given both for selection purposes and for a pre-test measure. Exercise of these techniques, however, requires statistical resources not usually available to most school personnel. They should be mentioned, however, as these methods are both efficient and time-saving.

CONCLUSION

Standardized achievement tests have been widely used to assess pupil growth in academic areas. The use of these tests for this purpose presents some special problems. It is extremely important that the test user or program evaluator be alert to these measurement problems and to possible ways in which the problems may be resolved. Appropriate measurement procedures are essential to evaluation. Inaccurate measurement of an educational program may lead to indeterminate or even misleading results in terms of pupil performance. The evaluation of a program based upon questionable evidence may then result in invalid conclusions as to the merit of the program. Without appropriate measurement procedures, therefore, it is impossible to evaluate the effect of a particular educational program. Evaluation, not only is essential to any implementation of the accountability concept in a particular educational situation but also is essential to any assessment of the usefulness of the accountability approach in general.

A persistent controversy in psychology is the heredity-environment debate. Many nonpsychologists, and indeed some psychologists, have not always understood the issues raised by the debaters. In the following article Anastasi clears up some of the common fallacies regarding the issue.

One fallacy is that heritability ratios can be applied to individuals. This is not so. A heritability ratio represents the proportion of the total variance of a trait that is attributable to heredity in a population. Such a ratio tells us nothing about what proportion of a single individual's trait is due to heredity, nor can that be determined. Jensen (1969), for example, states this clearly yet many of his readers misunderstand him and some take him to task for an incorrect position to which he does not ascribe.

Anastasi has long been a recognized expert on this topic. She takes a position somewhat more supportive of the environmentalists than hereditarians. But one can infer from the last sentence of her article that she would support further investigation of the issue. "It is only through a clear understanding of the operation of hereditary and environmental factors in behavior development that we can contribute toward effective decisions for the individual and for society."

Common Fallacies about Heredity, Environment, and Human Behavior

ANNE ANASTASI

Author's abstract   Misconceptions about the role of heredity and environment in human behavior can lead to inappropriate decisions for social action and public policy. Several of these common fallacies are examined and proper interpretations of the relations of heredity and environment are discussed. In particular, the

From *ACT Research Report No. 58*, May 1973. Reprinted by permission of the American College Testing Program.

limited meaning of the heritability ratio is described along with misinterpretations stemming from the work of Jensen. Finally, attention is directed to the potentially more useful considerations of how specific hereditary and environmental conditions lead to particular behavioral outcomes. It is argued that only through a clear understanding of the operation of hereditary and environmental factors in behavior development can effective decisions be made for the individual and for society.

Much of our thinking about contemporary social problems reflects tacit presuppositions regarding the operation of heredity and environment in human behavior. Here is a mixed bag of statements illustrating opinions expressed by persons in responsible positions:

> The use of Test X is discriminatory because members of a minority group score lower on it than do members of the majority culture.

> If an intellectual or emotional difficulty can be attributed to environmental handicaps in the individual's background, it should be discounted and overlooked because it is not part of his real nature.

> Specially developed culture-fair tests are needed to rule out the effects of prior cultural deprivation in assessing a child's educational readiness or an applicant's job qualifications.

And from a somewhat different angle:

> Congenital defects are hereditary.

> If such traits as mathematical talent, an irascible disposition, or a fear of snakes run in families, they are of genetic origin.

> This child's mental retardation cannot be attributed to cultural conditions because it results from an organic brain deficiency.

> Because the heritability index of intelligence is high, compensatory education programs cannot accomplish very much.

Each of these statements exemplifies a common fallacy, but the list is far from complete. Many other examples could undoubtedly be found. The beliefs these statements represent have important implications for practical decisions. The range of their influence extends from the formulation of public policy and the design of programs for social improvement to the treatment of an individual school child and the interpersonal relations of two co-workers from diverse cultural backgrounds. Advances in genetics, psychology, anthropology, and other disciplines have contributed much to a clarification of the operation of hereditary and environmental factors in human development. These contributions, however, have not yet been adequately incorporated into the tacit assumptions that underlie the day-by-day solution of practical problems. Thus it behooves us to bring the presuppositions into the open and reexamine them periodically in the light of pertinent research findings.

SOME QUESTIONS OF TERMINOLOGY

Some of the statements cited may reflect little more than a loose use of words. In fact, the survival of certain terms in the English language adds to the difficulty of clear communication in discussions of heredity and environment. The terms "innate," "inborn," "inbred," and "congenital," for example, refer to that which is present from birth. But to a greater or lesser extent all are employed as synonyms for "hereditary." This semantic confusion dates from a time when the effects of prenatal environment were largely unrecognized and it was generally assumed that whatever existed at birth could be attributed to heredity.

Another prevalent confusion is that between organic and hereditary etiology of behavioral characteristics. A behavioral defect or other psychological characteristic may have an organic or a purely experiential basis. The latter is traceable to some features of the individual's prior environment, such as parental attitudes or quality of available schooling. Organic etiology, on the other hand, may involve either hereditary or environmental factors, or some combination of both. It follows that to demonstrate an organic basis for a given psychological condition, such as mental retardation, does not necessarily imply that the condition is hereditary.

INTERRELATION OF HEREDITY AND ENVIRONMENT

Let us now inquire more directly into the operation of heredity and environment in behavior development. To ask whether a specific psychological trait results from heredity or environment is a meaningless question, since both enter into all behavior. The reacting organism is a product of its genes and its past environment; and the individual's present environment provides the immediate stimuli for current behavior. Nor can we arrive at a generalized estimate of the proportional contribution of heredity and environment to individual differences in any given psychological trait. To be sure, heritability ratios, representing the proportion of the total variance of a trait attributable to heredity, have been computed in many studies. It should be borne in mind, however, that such heritability ratios apply to populations, not to individuals. Moreover, they are descriptive of a particular population under existing conditions at a given time. When conditions are altered, the heritability ratio will change. If environmental conditions become more uniform in a given population, the heritability ratio rises; if genetic similarity increases by inbreeding, the heritability ratio drops.

Heritability ratios thus depend upon the range of individual differences in both heredity and environment in the population under consideration. To take an extreme example, susceptibility to diphtheria has been shown to depend upon a recessive hereditary factor, and immunity upon a corresponding dominant factor. This disease will not be contracted, however, without infection by the diphtheria bacillus. Thus in a population all of whom have inherited susceptibility, individual differences in the development of the disease can be attributed entirely to environmental factors, that is, exposure to infection. On the other hand, in a population in which all are equally exposed to the bacillus, any individual differences would be attributable to differences in heredity, namely, whether the dominant gene for immunity was present. To the question, "What proportion of the variance in the development of diphtheria is attributable to heredity?" opposite answers would be obtained in these two populations. And a whole range of intermediate answers would be reached in other populations, depending upon the relative frequency of exposure and the relative frequency of persons with the dominant gene for immunity in each population.

The relation between heredity and environment is further complicated by what is technically known as interaction. In this sense, interaction means that the effect of any one variable will itself vary as a function of another variable. When this concept is applied to heredity and environment, it means that any given environmental factor will exert a different influence depending upon the specific hereditary material or genotype upon which it operates. Similarly, any hereditary factor will be differently manifested under different environmental conditions.

Such interaction can be illustrated by the familiar experience of persons who try to control their weight by dieting. Under the same conditions of food intake and activity level, individuals will lose or gain weight at different rates because of genetic differences in metabolism. To take a more psychological example, the availability of symphonic recordings in the home is likely to affect the musical development of a normal child but will have little influence on a deaf child. Similarly, growing up in a culturally disadvantaged or in an intellectually stimulating home would make little difference to a child with a severe hereditary brain deficiency, but it would probably make considerable difference in the abilities manifested at school entrance by a normal child.

It has been argued that the proportional contribution of interaction to the total population variance in human intelligence is slight. Apart from the fact that the empirical evidence for this conclusion is meager and questionable, the implications of such an argument are quite limited. Even if interaction of hereditary and environmental factors accounts for a very small part of the total trait variance in a given population, such interaction may still be highly important for an understanding of individual development and for the planning and implementation of treatment programs.

Many different questions can be asked about the operation of heredity and environment in human development. Those who discuss heritability ratios and proportional contribution of different factors to population variance are answering one type of question. Those who are interested in assessing the effect of environmental change upon the development of individuals and subgroups of the population are asking a different set of questions. Heritability ratios (and similar measures based on population variance) do not provide appropriate answers to the second type of question. Much controversy and confusion have arisen from the failure to recognize the differences among such questions. One prominent example is the article by Arthur Jensen published in 1969 in the *Harvard Educational Review* which has engendered great furor and led to many heated arguments. Although there are many aspects to this controversy and the issues are complex, it is my contention that one element in the controversy is the failure to differentiate among the questions asked by different participants. When each assumes that the other is trying to answer *his* question, the answers do not fit and each side feels that the other is talking nonsense.

An extreme example may serve to highlight my point. Even if the heritability ratio for a trait in a given population is 100%, it does not follow that the contribution of environment to that trait is unimportant. Let us consider a hypothetical community of adults in which everyone has the identical diet. All are given the same food in identical quantities. In this population, the contribution of food to the total variance of health and physical condition would be zero, since food variance accounts for none of the individual differences in health and physique. Nevertheless, if the food supply were suddenly cut off, the entire community would die of starvation. Conversely, improving the quality of the diet could well result in a general rise in the health of the community.

Failure to understand what a heritability ratio can—and what it cannot —tell us may lead to highly fallacious conclusions, as illustrated by some of the popular misinterpretations of the Jensen article. A high heritability ratio does not, for example, imply that the trait is fixed and immutable. Any modification of environmental conditions may change the population variance and thereby alter the heritability ratio itself. Environmental change may also raise or lower the level of the trait in the population. Finally, environmental manipulations may shift the relative position of an individual or subgroup within the population, since the effect of such manipulations may vary among persons with different characteristics.

To summarize, heritability ratios are applicable to populations, not individuals; they are descriptive of existing conditions in a specified population and cannot be generalized to other populations or to the same population under different conditions; and they do not indicate the degree of modifiability of a trait.

HOW CAN HEREDITY AFFECT BEHAVIOR?

We have seen that traits cannot be classified into those that are inherited and those that are acquired. We have likewise found that to the question "How much does heredity contribute and how much does environment contribute to a given trait?" no meaningful answer can be given for individuals. And with regard to population variance, no single, generalizable, or stable answer is possible. From both a theoretical and practical point of view, a more fruitful question pertains to the modus operandi of heredity and environment in individual development. How do specific hereditary and environmental conditions lead to particular behavioral outcomes? What are the actual chains of events through which any given hereditary or environmental factor may ultimately influence the individual's intellectual or personality traits?

First consider the operation of heredity. It should be noted at the outset that the influence of heredity upon behavior is necessarily *indirect*. No psychological trait is inherited as such. Through its control of the development of physical structures such as eyes, hands, or nervous system, heredity sets limits for behavior development. If some essential chemical is lacking in one of the genes, or if there is an imbalance in the proportion of different substances, a seriously defective organism may result, with stunted body and severely retarded intelligence. In such individuals, some of the minimum physical prerequisites for normal intellectual growth are lacking. Except in the case of such pathological deviants, however, heredity sets very broad limits for behavior development. Within these limits, what the individual actually becomes depends upon his environment. In man, as contrasted with lower organisms, heredity permits greater flexibility of behavioral development, thus providing for more effective adaptation to environment.

If, now, we examine some of the specific mechanisms through which hereditary factors may influence behavior, we cannot fail but be impressed by their wide diversity. At one extreme, we find certain rare forms of mental retardation associated with hereditary metabolic disorders, such as Tay-Sachs disease and phenylketonuria (PKU). In these cases, considerable progress has been made in tracing the causal steps from defective gene, through metabolic disorder and consequent cerebral malfunctioning, to mental retardation and other overt symptoms. Unless the physical deficiency can be corrected early in life—as in the dietary treatment for PKU—such individuals will be mentally retarded, regardless of their training or experience.

A somewhat different situation is illustrated by hereditary deafness, which may lead to intellectual retardation by interfering with normal social interaction, with language development, and with schooling. In such a case, however, the hereditary handicap can be offset by appropriate adaptations of training procedures. It has been said, in fact, that the degree of intellectual backwardness of the deaf population is an index of the state of development of special instructional facilities. As available training procedures improve, the intellectual retardation arising from deafness is correspondingly reduced.

For a third example, let us turn away from pathology and consider sex differences. A major hereditary difference between males and females is to be found in the developmental acceleration of the female. Girls not only reach physical maturity earlier, but throughout childhood they are also farther advanced toward their adult status. Investigations by both cross-sectional and longitudinal methods have shown that, at each age, girls have attained a higher percentage of their adult height and weight than have boys. A similar acceleration is found in other aspects of physical development. It is well known that girls reach puberty earlier than boys, the difference averaging from 12 to 20 months in various populations. In skeletal development, as measured by the ossification or hardening of the bones, girls are also ahead of boys at every age. A similar difference occurs in dentition, girls shedding their deciduous teeth and acquiring their permanent teeth at an earlier age than boys. In the case of certain teeth, these differences amount to as much as a year or more. It is noteworthy that the general developmental acceleration of the female begins before birth. On the average, girls are more mature than boys at birth and there is some evidence that they tend to be born after a shorter gestation term than boys.

The indirect, psychological effects of sex differences in developmental rate probably vary widely from trait to trait. For example, the developmental acceleration of girls in infancy may be an important factor in their more rapid progress in the acquisition of language and may give them a headstart in verbal development as a whole. Because boys and girls enter school at the same chronological age, it has been suggested that the sex difference in linguistic readiness may account in part for the greater frequency of speech disorders and reading disabilities found among boys. Even more broadly, girls' developmental acceleration at school entrance may contribute to their better adjustment to the school situation and their tendency to earn higher grades than boys in elementary school.

Still another possible implication of the developmental acceleration of the female is a social one. Because of their physical acceleration, adolescent girls tend to associate with boys older than themselves. The same condition probably accounts also for the usual age discrepancy in marriage. Since the girl is generally younger than the boys with whom she associates—and younger than the man she marries—she is likely to be surpassed by most of her male associates in education and general information. This situation may well be at the root of many social attitudes toward the sexes. A younger person is likely to have less knowledge, wisdom, and sense of responsibility than an older one, and such an age difference may have been traditionally interpreted and fostered as a sex difference.

As a final illustration, consider how heredity may influence psychological development through the mechanism of social stereotypes. A wide variety of inherited physical characteristics has served as visible cues for identifying such stereotypes. These cues lead to behavioral restrictions or opportunities and—at a more subtle level—to social attitudes and expectancies. The individual's own self-concept tends gradually to reflect such expectancies. All of these influences eventually leave their mark upon his abilities and inabilities, his emotional reactions, goals, ambitions, and outlook on life.

Many social stereotypes tend to be perpetuated through this mechanism. If an athletic physique is associated with the stereotype of a leader, persons with such a body build will tend more often than others to be perceived as leaders, treated and accepted as leaders, and given an opportunity to serve in leadership positions. The experience thus gained in childhood and adolescence makes the individual better qualified for successful leadership in later life. In addition, his or her own self-concept may be affected, so that he or she comes to regard himself or herself as having leadership abilities and to approach leadership situations with confidence. This mechanism has been aptly described as the self-fulfilling prophecy. The mere fact that a behavioral outcome is predicted increases the probability of its occurrence. This self-fulfilling prophecy is likely to operate in the case of any group about which social stereotypes exist, such as persons with high foreheads, red hair, or brown skins. In another culture, of course, the behavioral correlates of such hereditary physical traits may be quite different. A specific physical cue may be completely unrelated to individual differences in psychological traits in one culture while closely correlated with them in another. Or it may be associated with totally dissimilar behavior characteristics in two different cultures.

The four examples cited to illustrate the operation of heredity fall along a *continuum of indirectness*. Along this continuum are found varying degrees of remoteness of causal links, from the relatively direct and immediate behavioral effects of hereditary metabolic disorders to the more indirect and subtle influence of physical cues that evoke social stereotypes. It should also be noted that, the more indirect the hereditary influence, the greater will be the range of possible behavioral outcomes. This follows from the fact that at each step in the causal chain there is fresh opportunity for other concomitant circumstances to alter the course of development. Thus the more indirect the role of heredity, the greater the feasibility of behavioral modification through environmental manipulation.

HOW CAN ENVIRONMENT AFFECT BEHAVIOR?

Turning now to the operation of environment, we must recognize at the outset that man's environment covers a vast multiplicity of factors, ranging from air and food to Grand Opera and TV commercials. An important part of our environment consists of the people with whom we interact—family, teachers, friends, co-workers. Environment comprises not only physical but also psychological surroundings. It includes the social and emotional climate of home, school, and community, as well as the beliefs, preferences, and attitudes of our associates.

For modern man, environment is virtually coextensive with culture. From the viewpoint of the developing individual, the culture in which he is reared comprises all man-made features of his environment. There is, in fact, little in his surroundings that has not been influenced by the actions of his predecessors. Perhaps the most obvious examples of culture are provided by such institutionalized activities as initiation ceremonies, marriage and burial customs, and college graduations. But there is much more to culture. Language is an extremely important aspect of the individual's cultural heritage. It not only serves as the most powerful medium for interpersonal communication and for the transmission of prior human achievement, but it also provides a major tool for abstract thought and thereby helps to shape our concepts and ideas. Our physical surroundings too reflect influences at every turn—in the food we eat, the type of buildings in which we live and work, the clothing we wear. Today, we should certainly add to this list the characteristics of the water we drink and the air we breathe! It is thus apparent that, when we speak of environment in relation to human behavior, the term "culture" could be substituted for "environment" in much of what we say.

Another point to note is that environment, as well as heredity, may account for family resemblances and differences. The family is not only a biological but also an environmental unit. Moreover, the closer the hereditary relationship between two persons, the greater the likelihood of environmental proximity between them. We can identify at least three ways in which environment may produce similarities between siblings, between parents and children, and—to a lesser degree—among more remote relatives. *First*, members of the same family share many features of their environment, such as socioeconomic level of the home and geographical and cultural milieu of the community. For siblings, such common environmental elements extend even to characteristics of the prenatal environment. *Second*, family contacts provide opportunities for mutual influence. Close relatives thus constitute a part of each other's environment. A *third* important psychological factor contributing to family resemblances is social expectancy. The child is often reminded of the special talents and defects of his forebears; and any chance manifestation of similar behavior on his part may be accentuated by such references. Furthermore, the fact that people expect him to have inherited his father's administrative ability or his mother's musical talent will tend to influence his own self-concept—which in turn is likely to affect his subsequent development.

It should be added that family environment, like heredity, can also account for some of the observed *differences* among family members. Although alike in many fundamental respects, the environments of two brothers reared in the same home, for example, are not psychologically identical. For one thing, the environment of one includes an older brother, that of the other contains a younger brother—no small difference in itself! Then, too, parental attitudes and child-rearing practices may differ for the two siblings as a result of the parents' intervening experiences. Similarly, any common occurrence in the home, such as moving from a rural to an urban area, will occur at different stages in the development of the two brothers and hence may have a very different significance in their development. These and many other environmental conditions may explain why two siblings exhibit characteristic differences in aptitudes or personality, just as other aspects of family environment may help us to understand their similarities.

Because of the inevitable mixture of hereditary and environmental factors in family relationships, the mere establishment of family resemblance cannot indicate the reasons for the resemblance. Hence a large amount of the available data on familial likenesses is at best descriptive and limited to existing conditions. This is true of the previously cited heritability ratios, which have usually been computed from the relative degree of trait similarity found between different degrees of kinship.

Let us now consider some specific examples of mechanisms whereby environment may affect behavior development, as we did for heredity. Psychologically, the individual's environment comprises the sum total of the stimulation he receives from conception to death. It is now well established that environment begins to operate before birth. Many conditions of the prenatal environment exert a pronounced influence upon behavioral as well as structural properties of the organism. Both animal experiments and clinical observations of human cases have demonstrated the part played by prenatal physical and chemical conditions in the development of bodily anomalies and of many well-known varieties of mental retardation.

Of special interest is the finding that inadequacies of maternal diet during pregnancy may have deleterious effects upon the child's intellectual development. Several studies have likewise established a relation between various complications of pregnancy and parturition, on the one hand, and intellectual deficiency in the offspring, on the other.

It is also noteworthy that such irregularities in the process of child-bearing and birth occur more frequently in lower than in high socioeconomic levels, probably because of differences in nutrition, medical care, and the like. Such findings suggest one possible environmental mechanism whereby social class and minority group status may produce mental retardation and other psychological disorders. In this connection, let me reiterate two points. The fact that a condition is present at birth is no indication that it is hereditary. Nor does the identification of an organic basis for a psychological deficiency imply hereditary origin. Adverse conditions in the prenatal environment can and do produce severe brain injury, glandular dysfunctions, and organic damage, which may in turn cause mental retardation or other psychological disturbances.

Insofar as environmental factors may cause organic disorders which then influence behavior development, they too, like heredity, can be ordered along a continuum of indirectness. This continuum closely parallels that of hereditary mechanisms. One end is typified by such conditions as mental retardation resulting from prenatal nutritional inadequacies or from cerebral birth injury. A somewhat more indirect etiological mechanism is illustrated by severe motor disorders, as in certain cases of cerebral palsy, *without* accompanying injury to higher brain centers. In such instances, intellectual retardation may occur as an indirect consequence of the motor handicap through the curtailment of educational and social activities. Obviously this causal mechanism corresponds closely to that of deafness cited earlier in the discussion of heredity.

Unlike heredity, environmental factors can also influence behavior directly. In such cases, the immediate effects of the environmental condition is a behavioral change. To be sure, some of the initial behavioral effects may themselves indirectly affect the individual's later behavior. But perhaps this relationship can be best conceptualized in terms of breadth and permanence of effects. Thus we might say that we are now dealing, not with a continuum of indirectness, as in the case of hereditary and organic-environmental factors, but rather with a continuum of breadth.

Many examples of direct behavioral effects of environment are provided by *child-rearing practices*. One factor that may play a significant part in early intellectual development is the way in which parents handle children's questions. What, for example, happens when the child asks "Why?" Is he rewarded or punished? Is he answered or ignored? If answered, is the explanation in terms of facts and logic or in terms of tradition and custom? Is the child encouraged to think about the answer himself, or is he actively discouraged from so doing? A related point pertains to parents' attitudes toward exploratory behavior in general. To what extent is the child given opportunities for first-hand contact with objects and situations through which he may arrive at his own answers? It is reasonable to expect that the habits built up through such childhood experiences would appreciably affect the child's later problem-solving behavior—in school, on intelligence and aptitude tests, and in other life situations.

In recent years there has been an increasing interest in the detailed comparison of lower-class and middle-class language patterns and their relation to perceptual and conceptual development. Data have been gathered through direct observations of parent-child interactions in the home and the laboratory. Such research has revealed a number of differences between the linguistic experiences of children from middle-class and those from lower-class or culturally disadvantaged homes. Middle-class parents not only use spoken language more extensively as a means of communication, but they also provide speech models that are more elaborate and more often grammatically correct. In addition, they encourage the child's own use of language, correct his errors, and reward proper word usage. In lower-class homes, on the other hand, language is employed more sparingly. Much communication occurs through gestures, facial expression, tone of voice, and other nonverbal means.

One investigator proposed two linguistic codes to characterize the differences between lower-class and middle-class language. Lower-class adults, he found, utilize a "restricted" code, in which few different grammatical forms are employed, verbal communication is terse and simple, and much meaning is assumed or implicit. In contrast, the middle-class adult is more likely to use an "elaborated" code that is grammatically more complex; allows for the development of meanings, feelings, and individual interpretations; and provides a conceptual hierarchy for organizing experience.

Somewhat related is the research on the development of perceptual responses in early childhood. An important environmental feature in this regard is the availability in the home of a variety of objects among which the child may observe differences in shape, size, color, texture, and other attributes. Attaching names to these obects and to their attributes, and calling attention to similarities and differences among them, will of course facilitate perceptual learning. Thus the importance of language and of active adult participation is again illustrated.

The examples of early experience and childrearing practices we have considered thus far illustrate direct effects of environment upon the development of aptitudes. Environmental conditions, of course, may also exert a profound influence upon motivations, attitudes, and other personality variables. Moreover, there is a growing body of research indicating that such personality differences may in turn account for individual and group differences in the development of certain abilities. These findings suggest another, more indirect or subtle mechanism whereby environmental influences may be manifested in behavior.

For example, on tests of mathematical reasoning, boys obtain consistently higher mean scores than girls—although, as in all group comparisons, there is extensive overlapping of the distributions and hence the relative performance of the two sexes may be reversed in individual cases. A similar sex difference in mean performance has been found in other problem-solving tests. Furthermore. the difference tends to be greater on tasks that require a re-restructuring of the situation, that is, reorganizing given facts in new ways and trying out different solutions. Of particular interest is the finding that performance in such problem-solving tasks is related to sex differences in attitudes toward problem solving and to degree of sex-role identification. Thus within each sex, closer identification with the masculine sex role, as indicated on a personality inventory, is associated with superior problem-solving skill.

Other studies provide evidence that individuals exhibiting more dependency and social conformity tend to be less successful in breaking a set or restructuring elements in problem solving. Hence, insofar as traditional female experiences and role models in our culture may have encouraged greater dependency and social conformity among girls than among boys, these personality differences could account for the observed sex differences on certain types of problem-solving. A similar mechanism could help to explain girls' superiority in such tasks as spelling and grammar, in which social conformity and dependence upon external, interpersonal cues provided by the teacher would represent assets.

The last example of the operation of environment in behavior development concerns the role of social expectancy. What is expected of an individual tends to affect what he does. When such expectation carries the force of social tradition behind it and is repeatedly corroborated in nearly all contacts with associates, it is difficult to resist. Consequently, the individual often becomes convinced that he is intellectually inferior or superior, or that he possesses this or that talent or defect according to the dictates of his particular culture. In his daily contacts with family, teachers, and playmates, the developing child finds constant reminders of what is expected of him. Gradually these expectations become a part of his own self-concept, which in turn may affect his motivation and achievement. By such a mechanism, social expectancy tends to influence what a person eventually becomes. It thus serves to perpetuate social stereotypes with regard to sex, race, nationality, and other culturally perceived categories.

This mechanism will be recognized as the same self-fulfilling prophecy cited earlier as an example of the operation of heredity. In that connection, we considered the association of a certain type of body build with the cultural stereotype of a leader. Now we have come full circle and are considering the same mechanism to illustrate the operation of environment.

There is no inconsistency here. The fact is, of course, that heredity and environment operate jointly in all the examples described. For purposes of analysis, we have drawn them apart; but they can more properly be regarded as two aspects of a single process. In most situations, the appropriate question is not whether heredity or environment operated, nor the proportional contribution of each—both are meaningless questions form the standpoint of the individual. Rather what we need to identify is the specific etiological mechanism or causal chain that led to a given condition. It is these mechanisms that have been illustrated.

CONCLUSION

This paper began with examples of popular misconceptions about heredity and environment. What are some relevant points that emerge from the intervening discussion?

A major point pertains to modifiability. The fact that a characteristic is hereditary does not imply it is fixed and immutable; it *can* be altered by environmental interventions, which may range from diet or medical treatment to remedial training programs or psychotherapy. Conversely, environmentally produced characteristics may be quite resistant to change, as illustrated by the behavioral effects of severe prenatal damage. To find that a behavioral difference between individuals or groups has an environmental or cultural origin does not imply that it is evanescent, superficial, or "unreal." The degree of modifiability of a characteristic cannot be judged by identifying its etiology as hereditary or environmental.

The long-standing, cumulative effects of prior environment cannot be willed away by the magic device of pointing to their cultural origins. Some environmental conditions have persisting and broad effects on behavior. A psychological test may—and frequently does—serve as an indicator of such environmental effects, which extend beyond performance on the test itself. The relevance of any given test to a particular situation needs to be empirically investigated in terms of the specific behavior to be predicted. To ignore the test score or abolish the test because it reflects cultural deficit merely retards efforts to overcome such deficits and to ameliorate cultural conditions. It is only through a clear understanding of the operation of hereditary and environmental factors in behavior development that we can contribute toward effective decisions for the individual and for society.

Flaugher presents a very good nontechnical discussion of the
issue of test fairness to minority groups in selection decisions.
He briefly discusses the four commonly recognized models of test
fairness: the Cleary, Thorndike, Cole, and Darlington models.

The Cleary model was the first of these four to be used
regularly. Considerable evidence suggests that her model shows
tests to be unfair to the majority ethnic group since the
performance of minority group members on the criterion is
overpredicted by the use of a single prediction system.

One limitation of both the Thorndike and Cole models is that
they do not consider the degree of success. The models assume
that all persons who can succeed on the job, or in school, are
equally good choices for selection. This is often not true.

The Darlington model holds considerable apeal to many
people but others suggest that it violates the Supreme Court
ruling which opposes an ethnic criterion in selection decisions.

Since ethical, logical, and psychometric arguments can be
made for and against each model, the issue of test fairness in
selection is far from resolved. Interested readers may want to
pursue the issue in more depth. A good starting point for such
pursuit would be the references at the end of Flaugher's article.

The New Definitions
of Test Fairness in Selection:
Developments and Implications

RONALD L. FLAUGHER

Until recent years the topic of test fairness in selection was not a controversial one for those familiar with the psychometric theory underlying it.
There was criticism of the use of tests as selection devices, but almost exclusively from a nontechnical standpoint, offering no effective challenge to the
supposedly immutable scientific understanding of the problem of fairness.

In the summer of 1971, the complacency of the theorists was shaken
with the publication of two articles, one by Thorndike and one by Darlington. In these articles the traditional model of test fairness was seen as a great
deal less immutable than had been supposed, and new models of fairness

From *Educational Researcher*, Vol. 3, No. 9, pp. 13–16. Copyright 1974, American Educational Research Association, Washington, D.C. Reprinted with permission of the
publisher and author.

were presented that not only competed with but were essentially incompatible with the traditional model and with each other.

The theory of test fairness was thus shown to be a complex issue, a discovery that had immediate real-life implication in a time of increased attention to the fair treatment of minority groups and concern with their selection for employment and education. In the remainder of this paper, an attempt will be made to describe the complexities of test fairness in non-technical language and to discuss implications for the selection procedures practiced in our society.

It is essential to the discussion to recognize the distinction between the *use* of tests in a manner which is "fair," and the concept of "test bias," which most frequently refers to the *content* of the items of the test, regardless of any particular use to which the test is being put. It is possible to conceive of a test which is biased in this sense being used in a manner that is fair (by awarding bonus points, for example), and also possible to imagine an unbiased test being used unfairly (by using a test that is unrelated to the task being predicted). The present discussion concerns the use, rather than the content, of tests.

For present purposes, there are just four clearly distinguishable models of fair selection, which can be named: the Cleary, or traditional, model, the Thorndike model, the Cole model, and the Darlington model. The Cleary model, so named because of its use by Cleary (1968) in one of the first formal investigations of the fairness of tests in selection, is that model which was most widely accepted until the recent developments. Simply, it states that *a test is fair for both of two subgroups of a population (for example, an ethnic minority and majority group) if the prediction equation that is used neither systematically overpredicts nor underpredicts the level of performance for either group.* This seems intuitively fair, in that underprediction is the frequent charge made against tests when used in the selection of minority group members; the accusation is that the test gives an artificially depressed estimation of the minority person's capacity to perform on the job, and if permitted to attempt the job, many would succeed who were predicted to fail. A fair test, on the other hand, is viewed as one which does *not* give this inaccurate picture of minority group members.

With the appearance of the Thorndike and Darlington articles, this definition was seen to have a flaw that resulted in a situation which most people would agree was obviously unfair when applied to certain frequently occurring real-life situations, even though remaining fair by the previous standards. The reasons for this paradox can be stated briefly in this way: The average test score for a minority group is often lower than that for the majority group; further, on a criterion such as rated performance on the job, there is frequently a difference in the same direction, but the difference is less.* Thorndike pointed out in his article that under this very common circumstance, and even when the procedure meets the Cleary definition of fairness, a distinctly smaller percentage of minority applicants will be selected than would have succeeded on the job. Another way of saying this is that if all minority applicants, had been hired, then, for example, a *third* of them would have succeeded on the job. However, under such circumstances it is entirely possible that one-half of the majority, *but none of the minority group*, would actually be selected by the traditional procedures. Thorndike very reasonably suggested that the traditional or Cleary definition of fairness is therefore unacceptable.

The alternative model Thorndike suggested is directed specifically to that inequity of selection-versus-success for two subgroups of a population. He suggested that the *base-rate of success for the various groups be determined empirically, then that percentage of the applicant group be selected, whether or not the same cut-off score on the test is used for each of the groups*. For example, if one-third of the minority group is found to be likely to succeed on the job, then the cut-off score for selection should be adjusted to hire one-third of that applicant group (or whatever proportion, relative to the other group, is permitted by the number of openings). The traditional method may be fair for the individual, claims Thorndike, but for the method to be fair for the group, his method must be used.

The impact of Thorndike's article on those concerned with test fairness was great indeed, although in terms of specific actions little of any consequence occurred for about one year. Evidently this constituted a period of absorbing the meaning of the new perspective, and considering its practical consequences.

Things became even more confused when Nancy Cole of the American College Testing Program presented a paper offering yet another model of fairness (1972). To Cole, a better definition of fairness would be stated in the following form: Applicants from different ethnic groups *who would be successful if they were selected should have the same probability of being selected*. If they do, then the selection process is fair; if they do not, for example in the case where a potentially successful black candidate has a one-third chance of being selected, while a potentially successful white candidate has a one-half chance of being selected, then the procedure is unfair.

Cole's model used the same assumptions and circumstances Thorndike had used, and both are concerned with relative proportions of the two applicant groups. They differ in that Thorndike concentrates on that proportion of each group selected by the test, advocating that it should equal the proportion of the group who would succeed on the job. Cole, on the other hand, looks first at the part of the group that succeeds on the job, then advocates the probability of selection for that group be the same for both minority and majority groups. Both the Thorndike and Cole models find the traditional model to be specifically unfair to minority groups, because a smaller percentage of minorities would typically be selected by that procedure than either of theirs. Thorndike's model deviates moderately, and Cole's more so, from the traditional one.

All three models appears intuitively reasonable and worthy of implementation. The trouble is, all three cannot be followed simultaneously, and in the absence of a perfectly valid test what is fair for one model is necessarily unfair according to each of the other models. It becomes clear that so long as the two selection groups in question differ on the criterion measure, *there can be no single objective standard for test fairness.* The traditional model is indisputably lacking in desirable characteristics, but so are the two alternatives that have been suggested, to the extent that they conflict with the traditional model and each other.

Darlington's 1971 contribution to the field may be considered the most definitive, in that his presentation incorporated all three of the competing models described above. Moreover he suggests a specific means of dealing with real-life situations.

Since there can be no single objective definition of test fairness, reasoned Darlington, then the only solution is to acknowledge this fact and openly decide upon some set of values that can then be invoked by means of the selection of the appropriate numerical quantities. Specifically, Darlington offers the "corrected criterion" model as the basic format, in which *the value system of the selector is used to determine the amount of correction to apply to the criterion scores for the lower-scoring group* of applicants. The correction can range from large to zero, but this determination must necessarily be rationalized on non-psychometric grounds. In effect, the Darlington model makes explicit what is only implicit in the Thorndike and Cole models, which involved adopting particular new definitions of the meaning of fairness. The Darlington method of correction permits an infinite range of explicit definitions of fairness that are open to examination and possible adjustment in response to changing conditions.

Darlington has labeled his model the "corrected criterion" because one way of implementing it is to decide on a specific increment to add to the criterion scores of the minority group. One practical means of arriving at the same effect is for the psychometrician to simply generate his estimates of the probability of success for each candidate in either group. The job of those doing the selecting then becomes one of deciding *how much more risk of failure one is willing to take, if any,* to include among those who are selected a number of the lower-scoring group who will be successful. A specific example might be that corresponding to the case described earlier, in which those members of the majority group are selected who have probabilities of one-half of succeeding on the job, while those of the minority group are selected who have probabilities of one-third. Is this an accurate reflection of the values the selecting institution wishes to invoke? If not, how should those proportions, those risk factors, be altered to do so? The traditional method would invoke no differential consideration, selecting the individual candidates with the highest probability of success regardless of group membership. The other endpoint of the range would treat group membership as the only consideration, selecting only the highest scoring individuals from the lower-scoring group; the "corrected criterion" would be based totally on group membership. Any point between these extremes is possible, depending upon the consciously chosen values of those doing the selection.

The Darlington model, then, seems to be the one most capable of accurately encompassing the intricacies of the problem, even though it necessarily offers no firmly anchored definition of fairness to which those doing the selecting can have recourse. In one sense, it amounts to an avoidance of the issue for the psychometrician, in that it removes him from the focus of attention and turns the problem over to others for solution. In another sense it represents a considerable advance in our understanding of the nature of the problem, and in addition, points up the necessity for an open and conscious examination of the value systems operating in any given selection setting. This is an important contribution in itself.

The "corrected criterion" approach was commonly used in actual situations, prior to its labeling and formalization by Darlington. The familiar veteran's preference in civil service selection, usually consisting of rewarding bonus points to those who served in the armed forces, is just that sort of system. Further, colleges have often "corrected the criterion" in attempting to control the available talent for the student orchestra, or to select a winning athletic team, and the sons and daughters of heavy contributors to the endowment of a college are likely to be given more careful consideration when they apply. Although the suggestion that special consideration be given to ethnic minorities is met in some circles with a great deal of resistance, in other circles it would be agreed that, given one white and one black candidate with precisely the same qualifications, it is a greater error to turn away the black student. If that is agreed, then it follows that some increment of correction to the criterion, however small, is acceptable. The question then becomes one of determining the size of the increment, rather than any setting of an ominous precedent.

THE CRITERION PROBLEM

Ultimately, one realizes the problem amounts to a rather special case of a phenomenon that has plagued psychometrics eternally, that known as the "criterion problem." No one can be found who will seriously defend the freshman year grade-point average as an important gauge of anything very important in life's list of desirable values, and in fact a case is often made for its perversity. Yet, primarily because it is so easily obtained, it is the most frequent criterion variable in use for validating college selection procedures. Other things are universally agreed to be more important, which is another way of saying that the criterion is in need of being corrected, in much the same way that Darlington's model has helped elucidate. A similar correction is called for in the employment setting, where it is agreed that supervisory ratings, or even most on-the-job evaluations, leave something to be desired as criteria of success, hence are in need of some correction toward a more desirable judgment. But other, more long-range criteria (income? contributions to humanity?) are enormously difficult to measure and subject to at least as much disagreement about the need for "correction."

Added to this increased appreciation of the ethereal qualities of what we are attempting to predict is the very practical realization that in a great number of selection settings, the total size of the operation is simply too small to apply even these imprecise and ultimately subjective methods to the process. However, rather than conclude from these travails that we have engaged in a useless exercise, let it be pointed out that the ultimate solutions are the same, both in large samples and small, and rest with the values of the selector. In fact, it is comforting to realize that the current legal inducements to the hiring of minorities are pointed in essentially the same direction that our very elaborate psychometric acrobatics, just described, would have us go. We have made advances, specifically in that we no longer adhere to a traditional model which was thought to be the ultimate definition of fairness, but in fact was not so fixed and unquestionable after all. The battle for fairness is by no means over as a result, but at least the lines have now been more clearly drawn.

Given this present understanding, and by way of review, what does the selector, either the admissions officer or the employment director, do in the real-life decisions that he must make? From a psychometric point of view, the procedure is quite straightforward and not greatly different from existing procedures. The probability of success of each applicant is obtained from the psychometrician, based on the performance of similar-scoring candidates of previous years, and on ethnic identity. The selector then chooses his group of "admits" basing his decisions on this information and the value he places upon the selection of a particular number of minority applicants. In any given circumstance, he may be required to use two different estimated probabilities of success to invoke these values, frequently taking a higher risk of failure with the minority group applicants.

There are additional points for consideration, to be sure, that may make the selector's task more difficult. If the number of minority applicants changes dramatically from one selection to the next, perhaps in response to increased recruitment activities, for example, then this is likely to alter the success rates and confuse the selection process, especially if it has been based upon some assumption about the success-rate in the applicant population (as is the case with the Thorndike or Darlington models). Further, the impact of the changing student body, or employee group, upon the manner in which the criterion behavior itself is performed (is a school changed by its students?), is likely to require constant updating of the success-rates as well as the contents of the selection test battery itself.

If these difficulties are overcome, then there may still be problems encountered by the selector as a result of the currently confused legal situation in this area. Although federal "affirmative action" programs would appear to conform rather completely to the psychometric conclusions described above, there is a characteristic of these procedures that makes them similar to the implementation of a "quota system." The apparent contradictions between "affirmative action" and "quota system" have yet to be legally resolved.

EEOC POLICY

Meanwhile, the Equal Employment Opportunity Commission has adopted a policy that conforms most closely with the traditional model and which, in particular, requires separate validation procedures for minority groups. This policy was intended to increase the incidence of minority employment. It was based on the early belief that the use of a single prediction equation for both minority and majority groups would be unfair to minorities. It is therefore surprising to encounter considerable empirical evidence suggesting that in the typical selection setting it is more often the case that the performance of minority group members on the criterion is *over*-predicted by the use of a single prediction system. The ultimate effect of the EEOC policy would be to eliminate this overprediction, thus ironically eliminating the small inadvertent bonus to minorities that had been inherent in the prevailing system. Some evidence (Linn, 1973) indicates that the degree of this overprediction is nearly but not quite sufficient to satisfy the Thorndike definition of fairness. At any rate, the elimination of that overprediction can hardly be considered a solution. Rather, its empirical effect of the selection of fewer minority group members should be acknowledged and dealt with.

Thus, the practical consequences of the developments described here are that the values held by those doing the selecting must ultimately be invoked in the selection process, as indeed they frequently have been in the past, but they now need to be described in objective terms. These objective terms, taking the form of particular levels of acceptable success likelihood for any subgroup, are the material from which a fair selection process must be built.

Also on the practical level, the modest size of a great many selection operations, especially in industry, is simply insufficient to permit the use of the statistical tools that provide such objectively precise forecasts of success. However, since it is now seen that subjective values must guide the decision anyway, perhaps there is less reason to attempt to approximate the large-sample models often invoked as the only means to fair selection. Abandoning the attempts to imitate such an inappropriate model might well result in fewer real selection errors.

Still another consideration in the attempts to effect the optimal selection system must be that of the consequences of those decisions, both those of rejection and those of acceptance, and this should interact with the invoked value system, if not made an integral part of it. The consequences of an error will vary from setting to setting. For example, the selection for employment in a high-cost or high-risk position, where a wrong selection decision might have very serious results, may be contrasted with a selection decision for an educational opportunity in which the consequences of a wrong decision might might not be so serious.

Two problems remain that may interfere with the practices just suggested. First, once selection is made differentially on the basis of ethnic identity, then other identifiable subgroups could reasonably request special treatment as well. The population is capable of infinite subdivision and cross-classifications that could be invoked, with sex and socioeconomic status being the most likely next divisions. It can be anticipated that disputes and difficult decisions will surround these topics in the future.

Second, the procedure suggested here could be interpreted as inconsistent with a Supreme Court ruling on the subject. In *Griggs vs. Duke Power*, as Campbell *et al.* (1973) have pointed out, the decision states that "Congress has made job qualifications the controlling factor so that race, religion, nationality, and sex become irrelevant." Making race irrelevant, of course, would specifically prohibit the suggested procedure. More recently, this precise question was brought before the Supreme Court on behalf of law student Marco De Funis Jr. It was claimed he was the victim of reverse discrimination because the university denied him admission while accepting minority applicants with lower traditional qualifications. By that time De Funis, who had been admitted by a lower court order, was on the verge of graduating, and the Court ruled the case moot. So the previous *Griggs* decision currently stands as their view of the matter.

Clearly all the problems are not yet solved, but it is now obvious that a final and fixed standard, derived from the psychometric characteristics of the problem are wishful at best and likely to have operational consequences inconsistent with the intent of "fairness."

NOTES

* This reduced difference on the criterion may be due to less reliability in its measurement: supervisor's ratings or academic grades which are typically less reliable than objective standardized tests, are frequently used as criterion measures.

REFERENCES

Campbell, J. T., Crooks, L. A., Mahoney, M. H., and Rock, D. A. An investigation of sources of bias in the prediction of job performance. PR 73–37. Princeton, N.J.: Educational Testing Service, 1973.

Cleary, T. A. Test bias: Prediction of grades of Negro and white students in integrated colleges. *Journal of Educational Measurement*, 1968, 5 115–124.

Cole, N. S. Bias in selection. ACT Research Report No. 51. Iowa City, Iowa: American College Testing Program, 1972.

Darlington, R. D. Another look at "culture fairness." *Journal of Educational Measurement*, 1971, *8*, 71–82.

Linn, R. L. Fair test use in selection. *Review of Education Research*, 1973, *43*, 139–161.

Thorndike, R. L. Concepts of culture fairness. *Journal of Educational Measurement*, 1971, *8*, 63–70.

RECOMMENDED READING FOR UNIT VI

Block, James H. "Criterion-Referenced Measurements: Potential." *School Review*, February 1971, 79, 2; 289–298.

Bowers, Norman E. "Public Reaction and Psychological Testing in the Schools." *Journal of School Psychology*, 1971, 9, 2; 114–119.

Cronbach, Lee J. "Five Decades of Public Controversy over Mental Testing." *American Psychologist*, 1975, 30, 1, 1–14.

Darlington, Richard B. "Another Look at 'Cultural Fairness.' " *Journal of Educational Measurement*, 1971, 8, 2; 71–82.

Dyer, Henry S. "Toward Objective Criteria of Professional Accountability in the Schools of New York City." *Phi Delta Kappan*, 1970, 52, 4: 206–211.

Ebel, Robert L. "Criterion-Referenced Measurements: Limitations." *School Review*, February 1971, 79, 2; 282–288.

Gage, N. L. "I.Q. Heritability, Rare Differences, and Educational Research." *Phi Delta Kappan*, January 1972, 53, 5; 308–312.

Jensen, Arthur R. "Social Class, Race and Genetics: Implications for Education." *American Educational Research Journal*, 1968, 5, 1–42.

Jensen, Arthur R. "How Much Can We Boost IQ and Scholastic Achievement?" *Harvard Educational Review*, 1969, 39, 1–123.

Jensen, Arthur R. "IQ's of Identical Twins Reared Apart." *Behavioral Genetics*, 1970, 2, 133–146.

Linn, Robert, L. "Fair Test Use in Selection." *Review of Educational Research*, 1973, 43: 2, 139–161.

Scarr-Salapatik, Sandra. "Unknowns in the IQ Equation: Book Reviews." *Science*, December 17, 1971, 174: 1223–1228.

Shockley, William. "Dysgenics, Geneticity, Raciology: A Challenge to the Intellectual Responsibility of Educators," *Phi Delta Kappan*, January 1972, 53, 5: 297–307.

Stake, Robert E. "Testing Hazards in Performance Contracting." *Phi Delta Kappan*, 1971, 52: 583–588.

Weiss, Carol H. "The Politicization of Evaluation Research." *Journal of Social Issues*, 1970, 26, 4: 57–68.

NAME INDEX

Abbott, M. M., 318
Adams, D. M., 312, 317
Airasian, P. W., 1, 9, 11, 20, 276, 277, 291
Alcorn, R., 243
Allport, G. W., 200, 214
Anastasi, A., 46, 48, 345, 369, 370
Armistead, E., 242
Astrup, C., 209, 217
Averch, H. A., 316

Backman, M. E., 217
Badal, A. W., 267
Baker, E. L., 291
Baker, R. L., 281, 284, 291
Baker, W. P., 251, 252, 277
Barro, S. M., 307, 316
Barron, F., 148, 155
Bechtoldt, H. P., 34, 70
Becker, H. S., 229, 230
Belinky, C., 124
Bennett, G. K., 145, 155
Berkley, C. S., 124
Black, H., 26
Blau, P., 301, 302
Block, J. H., 11, 367
Bloom, B. S., 10, 308, 316
Borden, E. S., 185
Borgatta, E. F., 119
Bormuth, J. P., 282, 292
Bowers, N. E., 367
Bracht, G. H., 11, 203, 214
Bramer, G. R., 230
Buros, O. K., 125, 127, 204, 214, 217
Burt, C. L., 153, 155
Burt, C., 160, 168
Butt, D. S., 201, 206, 214

Campbell, D. P., 126, 194, 195, 196
Campbell, D. T., 34, 70, 203, 217
Campbell, J. T., 366, 367
Carmichael, S. S., 317
Carrier, N. A., 119
Cashen, V. M., 124
Cattell, R. B., 153, 155, 204, 206, 214
Cawelti, G., 244, 258
Chalupsky, A. B., 300, 302
Chase, S., 128, 137

Chesire, L., 64
Christensen, P. R., 300, 302
Clark, B. R., 229
Clark, K. E., 171, 185
Claudy, J. C., 196
Cleary, T. A., 289, 292, 359, 360, 361, 367
Coffman, W. E., 71, 92, 99, 103
Cohen, D., 300, 302
Cole, N. S., 193, 196, 359, 360, 361, 362, 367
Coleman, J. C., 305, 316
Coop, Richard H., 124
Corsini, R. J., 119
Cowdery, K. M., 173, 185
Cox, R. C., 81, 92, 219, 265, 286, 292, 294
Criscuolo, N., 254, 256
Cromer, W., 229
Cronbach, L. J., 10, 34, 50, 70, 140, 155, 202, 203, 214, 285, 292, 367
Crooks, L. A., 367
Cureton, E. E., 47, 50

Dahl, D. A., 288, 292
Dailey, J. T., 150, 156
Damarin, F. A., 204, 214
Darlington, R. D., 359, 360, 362, 363, 364, 365, 367
Dashiell, J. F., 202, 214
Davis, F. B., 277, 289, 292
Dawes, R. M., 213, 214
Dicken, C., 206, 214
Diederich, P. B., 102, 103
Dion, R., 70
Dolliver, R. H., 185
Doppelt, J. E., 70
Drucker, P. F., 316
DuCette, J., 72, 104
Duncan, O., 301, 302
Dyer, H. S., 1, 32, 270, 303, 307, 308, 312, 316, 317, 367

Ebel, R. L., 70, 71, 72, 81, 92, 113, 119, 124, 218, 219, 220, 229, 263, 267, 268, 270, 289, 292, 294, 367
Edwards, A. L., 106, 111, 206, 214
Eibling, H. H., 246, 260
Eisner, E. W., 10, 81, 92

Eiss, A. F., 84, 92
Ellis, J., 246
Ellison, R., 147, 156
Endler, N. S., 202, 214
Englehart, M. D., 124

Fantini, M. D., 317
Feldmesser, R. H., 219, 220, 229
Findlayson, D. S., 94, 97, 103
Findley, W. G., 124
Fiske, D. W., 34, 70, 201, 206, 214
Flanagan, J. C., 196
Flaugher, R. L., 269, 359
Foot, R., 124
Forehand, G. A., 308, 316
Freyd, M., 173, 185

Gage, N. L., 230, 367
Geer, B., 229, 230
Getzel, J. W., 150, 155
Ghiselin, B., 156
Ghiselli, E. E., 146, 147, 155
Glaser, R., 277, 282, 287, 292
Godshalk, F. I., 99, 103
Gold, R. M., 230, 267
Goldberg, L. R., 126, 197, 200, 202, 203,
   204, 206, 207, 209, 210, 212, 213, 215
Goodenough, F. L., 48
Gough, H. G., 199, 200, 208, 215
Green, B. F., Jr., 212, 215
Greene, M. M., 206, 215
Grobman, H., 10, 317
Gronlund, N. E., 111, 293
Gross, M., 26
Guba, E. G., 302
Guilford, J. P., 96, 103, 126, 149, 155,
   157, 168, 268, 270

Hackman, J. R., 229
Hagen, E., 113, 120
Hamilton, C. V., 317
Hammond, K. R., 211, 212, 215
Hanson, G. R., 188, 193, 196
Harbeck, M. B., 84, 92
Harman, H. H., 168
Harmon, L. W., 126, 217
Harrell, T. H., 146, 155
Harris, C. W., 120, 277, 279, 290, 292
Harrison, R., 229
Hartog, P., 94, 103
Hase, H. D., 206, 215
Hastings, J. T., 10, 25
Hathaway, S. R., 206, 216, 217
Hawes, G. R., 219, 241, 270, 277
Hawkridge, D. G., 300, 302
Hawthorne, P., 316
Hayes, K. J., 153, 155

Hebb, D. O., 153, 155
Heer, F., 316
Hilton, T., 289, 292
Hirsch, E., 285, 293
Hively, W., 282, 285, 288, 292
Hoepfner, R., 168
Hoffman, P. J., 211, 212, 215
Hoffmann, B., 26, 92, 124
Hogan, T. P., 318
Holden, L. E., 251
Holland, J. L., 149, 155, 188, 189, 190, 194,
   196
Holt, J., 218, 267
Holtzman, W. H., 210, 215
Hornaday, J. A., 182, 185
Hughes, E. C., 229, 230
Hull, C. L., 57, 64
Hunt, J. McV., 153, 155, 202, 214
Hursch, C. J., 211, 212, 215
Husek, T. R., 266, 286, 289, 293

Jackson, D. N., 185, 206, 207, 215, 216
Jackson, P. W., 10, 150, 155
Jencks, C., 305, 316
Jennings, F. G., 314, 317
Jensen, A. R., 269, 345, 349, 367
Jewell, D. O., 119

Kaplan, M., 229
Karlins, M., 229
Keller, C. M., 277, 292
Kelley, T. L., 128, 137
Keys, H., 119
Kelin, S. P., 276, 281, 287, 289, 292, 293,
   309, 317
Kleinmuntz, B., 215
Koester, G. A., 113, 119
Kohen, E. S., 213, 217
Kosecoff, J. B., 276, 287, 292
Kriewall, T.E., 285, 293
Kuder, G. F., 126, 168, 182, 185, 186
Kuklenski, J. E., 243

Lacey, J. I., 168
Lange, A., 72, 120
Larsen, E. P., 267
Lee, H., 243
Lehmann, I. J., 72, 104, 120, 124
Lennon, R. T., 32, 44, 276, 310, 317
Lichtenstein, S., 211, 216
Link, F. R., 102, 103
Linn, R. L., 365, 367
Loevinger, J., 205, 216
Lorge, I., 186
Lundin, S., 292
Lunneborg, C. E., 210, 216
Lunneborg, P. W., 210, 216

MacDonald, J. B., 92
Mackie, R. R., 300, 302
MacKinnon, D. W., 148, 156
Madaus, G. F., 1, 9, 10, 277, 291
Magat, R., 317
Mager, R. F., 82, 83, 90, 92, 281, 293
Mahoney, M. H., 367
Mann, J., 300, 302
Marland, S. P., 304, 316
Marso, R. N., 72, 112
Mathews, C. O., 178, 185
Maxwell, G., 292
Mayeske, G. W., 316
McArthur, C., 211, 216
McAshan, H. H., 91, 92
McCloud, P. I., 245
McDonald, F. J., 307, 308, 316
McMahon, W. E., 219, 220, 230
McNemar, Q., 126, 137, 268, 270
Meehl, P. E., 34, 50, 70, 205, 206, 208, 209, 211, 216
Mehrens, W. A., 72, 104, 120, 124
Melby, E. O., 218, 267
Merriman, H. O., 246
Merwin, J. C., 32, 134
Messick, S., 185
Meyer, G., 94, 103, 106, 111
Miles, D. T., 81, 83, 92, 124
Miles, T. R., 138, 156
Millican, G. D., 94, 103
Millman, J., 218, 267, 290, 293
Mischel, W., 197, 202, 216
Moore, B. V., 173, 186
Morris, D., 146, 156
Morris, R. G., 179, 186
Moynihan, D. P., 316
Murphy, R. J., 179, 186
Murray, C. K., 124
Murray, H. A., 216

Nachman, M., 120
Naylor, J. C., 212, 216
Neyman, C. A., 150, 156
Nitko, A., 277, 282, 292, 293
Nixon, R. M., 305
Norman, W. T., 199, 200, 216
Noyes, E. S., 94, 103

Odbert, H. S., 200, 214
Opachinsky, S., 120
Ornstein, A. C., 269, 294, 303, 318
Orr, D. B., 150, 156
Ottinger, A. G., 300, 302
Ozenne, D. O., 287, 293

Palmer, O., 92, 124
Parker, C. A., 211, 216

Pearson, K., 64
Pearson, R., 94, 103
Pollie, D., 119
Popham, W. J., 81, 85, 92, 266, 281, 282, 286, 287, 289, 293
Pophen, I. W., 120
Prediger, D. J., 192, 196

Quie, A., 278

Rabehl, G., 292
Ramseyer, G. C., 124
Ream, M. J., 173, 186
Redfern, G. B., 316
Renzulli, J. S., 294
Rhodes, E. C., 94, 103
Richards, J. M., Jr., 196
Ricks, J. H., Jr., 267
Riles, W. C., 252
Robinson, D. W., 313, 317
Robinson, R. E., 81, 83, 92, 124
Rock, D. A., 367
Rorer, L. G., 186, 206, 215
Rosenstein, A. J., 202, 214
Ross, J., 185
Rossi, P. H., 300, 302
Roth, J. D., 193, 196
Roudabush, G. E., 282, 286, 287, 293
Ruch, G. M., 128, 137
Rundquist, E. A., 186
Runkel, M., 229
Runkel, P., 229
Russell, J. T., 34, 53

Saffir, M., 64
Sandhu, H., 200, 215
Sawyer, J., 208, 216
Scannel, D. P., 106, 111
Scarr-Salapatik, S., 368
Schlink, F. J., 128, 137
Schultze, C. L., 316
Schutz, R. E., 1, 2
Schwartz, R. D., 203, 217
Scriven, M., 10
Seashore, H. G., 64, 145
Sechrest, L. B., 203, 217
Sells, S. B., 210, 215
Sension, D., 292
Sgan, M. R., 229
Shaycroft, M. F., 150, 156, 196
Sherman, S. E., 150, 156
Shockley, W., 368
Siegel, L., 203, 216
Siegel, L. C., 203, 216
Simon, S. B., 229
Skager, R., 279, 284, 285, 293
Slovic, P., 211, 216

Smith, W. R., 147, 156
Snow, R. E., 203, 214
Soar, R. S., 310, 317
Spearman, C., 139, 158, 168
Speisman, J., 119
Spillane, R. R., 246, 258
Spranger, E., 217
Sproule, C. F., 124
Stake, R. E., 10, 303, 309, 310, 317, 368
Stallings, W. H., 267
Stalnaker, J. M., 111
Stanley, J. C., 96, 103
Statler, L. S., 120
Steinmetz, H. L., 181, 186
Sterrett, B. G., 219, 265, 294
Stilson, D. W., 209, 217
Stone, G. R., 120
Strong, E. K., 173, 180, 186
Stuart, W., 229
Summers, D. A., 211, 215
Swineford, F., 99, 103

Talmage, H., 269, 294, 303, 318
Taylor, C. W., 147, 156
Taylor, D. W., 148, 156
Taylor, H. C., 34, 53
Thelen, H., 11
Thorndike, E. L., 162, 168
Thorndike, R. L., 113, 120, 292, 359, 360, 361, 362, 365, 367
Thornton, C. F., 124
Thurstone, L. L., 58, 64, 139, 156, 158, 159, 168, 174, 186
Todd, F. J., 211, 215
Torbert, W. R., 229

Torrance, E. P., 152, 156
Travers, R. M. W., 230
Tumin, M. M., 229
Turnbull, W. W., 32
Tyler, R. W., 9, 309, 317

Vargus, J. C., 286, 292
Vernon, P. E., 94, 103, 160, 168

Wallen, N. E., 230
Warren, J. R., 229
Webb, E. J., 203, 217
Weiss, C. H., 368
Wesman, A. G., 33, 35, 145, 267
Wexley, K. N., 124
Wherry, R. J., Sr., 212, 216
White, K. P., 124
Whitney, D. R., 196
Wiggins, N., 213, 217
Wight, A. R., 71, 80
Wilson, H. A., 281, 285, 293
Wingo, M. G., 120
Wiseman, S., 105, 111
Wolfson, B. J., 92
Wolk, S., 72, 104
Wood, D. A., 113, 120, 283, 293
Wright, B. D., 176, 186
Wrightstone, J. W., 269, 294, 303, 318
Wrigley, J., 105, 111

Yamamoto, K., 155, 156

Zimmerman, W. S., 47
Zweig, R., 285, 293
Zwicky, F., 168

SUBJECT INDEX

Abilities, multiple, 159–168
Accountability, 303–345
  definition of, 304, 318
  demand for, 306, 320
  measurement problems of, 327–345
  models, 307–308
  NEA position on, 307
  role of measurement in, 325–327
Actuarial models, 209–210
Alienation coefficient, 53
Anxiety, function of, 227
  test, 112–120
Behavioral objectives, 80–92, 312
  an alternative to, 86–90
  problems with, 81–86
Bias, 289
Classification of data, 235
Coleman Report, 305
Collection of data, 234
Compensatory programs, 312
Competition, 226
Computer-assisted instruction, 7
Computer-assisted testing, 7
Computer-managed instruction, 7
Construct validity, 34
Content validity, 33, 45–52, 288
  assumptions underlying the use of, 49–52
  of criterion-referenced tests, 288
  a definition, 46
  justification for use of, 48
  measurement of, 47
Cooperative Accountability Project, 306
Creativity tests, 149
Criterion-referenced measurement, 21, 22, 266, 268, 269, 276–294, 311, 326
  in accountability, 326
  content validity of, 288
  item analysis in, 285–288
  item construction and selection, 282–285
  objectives chosen, 281–282
  purpose and defining characteristics of, 278–280
Criterion-related validity, 33
Curricular validity, 46, 47
Derived scores, 65–70

Deviation scores, 68
Diagnostic evaluation, 16
Difference scores, reliability of, 339–342
Differential Aptitudes Tests, 142–146
Dissemination, of test data, 219, 236–263
Empirical validity, 46
Enroute objectives, 88
Environment, 345–358
  effects on behavior, 352–358
  and heredity, 345–358
Equivalence, of tests, 338–339
Error score, 339
Essay examinations, 93–103
  arguments for, 93
  interrater variability, 94
  intrarater variability, 96
  reducing rating error, 100
  sampling error, 99
  sources of error, 94
Evaluating teachers, using standardized tests, 263–264
Evaluation, 9–26, 268–368
  issues in, 268–368
  politics of, 295–297
  program, 294–302
  and research, 299–301
  role of testing, 301–302
  trends in, 268–368
  types of, 9–26
Face validity, 47
Factor analysis, 139
Fairness of Tests in Selection, 359–367
  criterion problem, 363–365
  EEOC policy, 365–367
  models of, 360–363
Family Educational Rights and Privacy Act, 238–241
Feedback, 112, 114
Formative evaluation, 3, 4, 11
Frequency of exams, 112, 114
Grade point average, 221
Grades, 220–233
  positive function of, 220–230
  vs. success, 225
Growth, definition of, 329
Heredity, 345–358
  common fallacies about, 345–358

Heredity (*cont.*)
    effects on behavior, 350–352
    and environment, 345–358
    interrelation of, 347–349
Heritability ratios, 347–349
Hull's measure of efficiency, 53
Intelligence, general, 126, 137–156
    structure of, 160–168
    three facets, 157–168
Intelligence tests, 126
Interest measurement, 168–196
    principles of, 168–186
    purpose of, 169
    sex bias, 186–196
Interpolated norms, 335–338
Intrinsic validity, 47
IQ, 31, 272
Item analysis, 120–124
    in criterion-referenced tests, 285–288
Item difficulty, 78
Item discrimination, 78
Item revision, 120
Job element approach, 141
Logical validity, 46
Maintenance of data, 235
Marks (*See* Grades)
Mastery, 290
Measurement and evaluation, 1–80
    basic principles of, 33–70
    role of, 1–32
    and the teacher, 72–80
Mental Measurements Yearbooks, 127–137
Multiple aptitude batteries, 141–146
Multiple-factor theory, 158
Norm-referenced measurement, 21, 268, 269, 311, 326
Normal curve, 65
Norms, 335–338
Objectives, 80–92
    behavioral, 80–92
    enroute, 88
Odell's *g*, 53
Optional questions, use of, 104–111
Pearson *r*, 53
Percentile, 67
Performance Contract, 322–325
Personality assessment, 126, 197–217
Placement evaluation, 10
Principle of Psychological Progress, 139
Principle of Psychological Regress, 140
Principles of Measurement, 33–70
Program evaluation, 294–302
Records, management of, 233–238

Regression, toward the mean, 309, 342–345
Releasing test scores, 241–263
    methods for, 252–258
    possible dangers, 242
    rationale for, 243
Reliability, 22, 33, 35–44, 77, 339–342
    of difference scores, 339–342
    part vs. total, 41
    of speed tests, 40
    test vs. scorer, 43
    for what group, 42
Reliability coefficients, 35–44
    factors affecting, 37–40
    purposes of, 36   –
Reporting results, 218–263
Responses bias, 178
Scale construction, strategies of, 204–208
Scores, methods of expressing, 65–70
Scoring and reporting, 21
Selection ratio, 54
Sex bias in interest inventories, 186–196
Sex-restrictiveness in interest inventories, 186–196
Standard error of measurement, 340
Standard scores, 65–70
Standardized evaluation procedures, 125–217
Standardized tests, 263–266
    increase meaning of scores, 265, 266
    use in evaluating teachers, 263–264
Stanines, 68
Statistical validity, 46
Structure of Intellect Model, 160–164
Stull Act, 306
Summative evaluation, 8, 11, 221
T-scores, 68
Test anxiety and achievement, 112–120
Test bias, 360
Testing, 26–32, 270–275
    the menace of, 26–32
    social consequences of, 270–275
True score, 339
Unintended outcomes, 17
Unobtrusive measures, 203
Validity, 23, 33, 34, 45–52, 53–65
    construct, 34
    content, 33
    criterion-related, 33
    by definition, 47
    and effectiveness of tests in selection, 53–65
    kinds of, 45–46
z-scores, 68